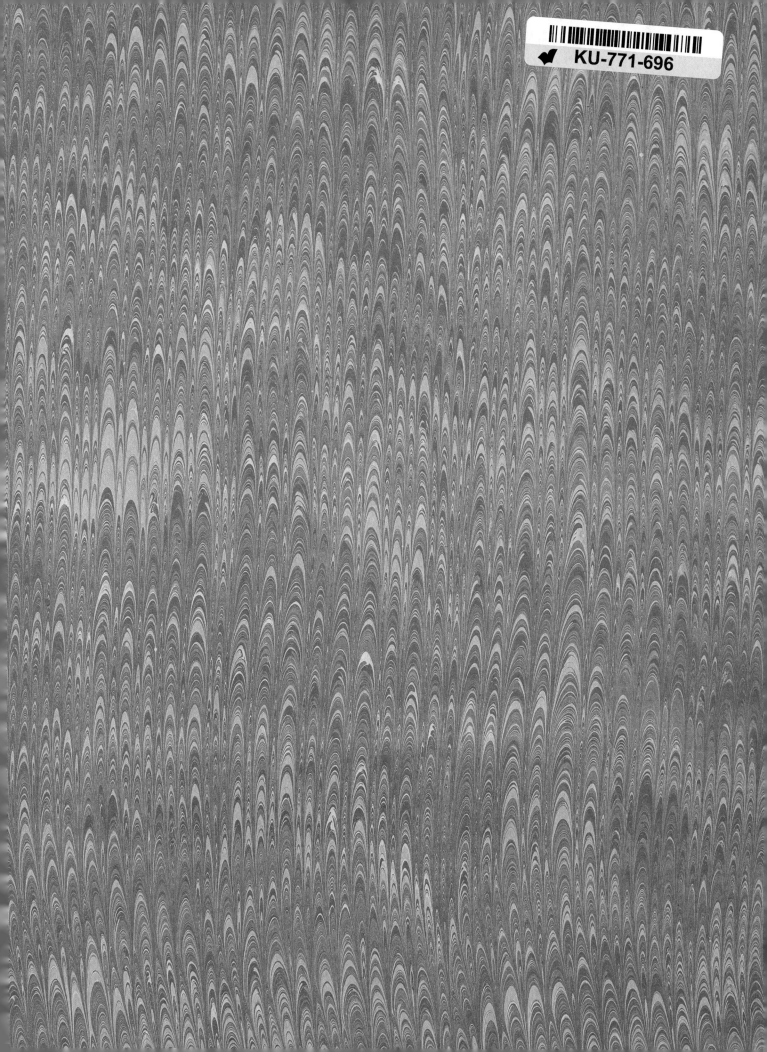

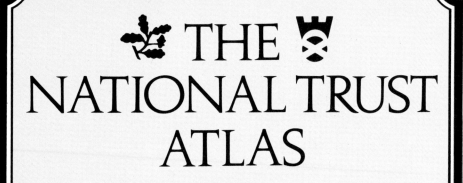

THE NATIONAL TRUST ATLAS

♦

The National Trust and The National Trust for Scotland

Foreword by Nigel Nicolson

Book Club Associates, London

Illustrations

Half-title Detail of an early eighteenth-century view of Uppark, West Sussex, by Pieter Tillemans (1684–1734); *title page* Polesden Lacey, Surrey, from a watercolour (*c.*1825) by John Varley (1778–1842); *foreword* Hanbury Hall, Hereford and Worcester, in an engraving from Nash's *Worcestershire*, 1781; *contents page* Lindisfarne Castle in an oil painting by John Varley.

Acknowledgments

The watercolours at the beginning of each chapter (pp. 10, 20, 44, 62, 70, 78, 98, 104, 118, 153) are by Dorothy Tucker. All other illustrations of properties in England, Wales and Northern Ireland are the copyright of and have been supplied by The National Trust, with the exception of those of the Dunstable Downs and the Ashridge Estate on p. 62 which have been supplied by John Bethell. All other illustrations of properties in Scotland are the copyright of and have been supplied by The National Trust for Scotland. The marbled end paper was designed by Mitchell & Malik Ltd, © 1981.

Editor Lydia Greeves
Art Editor Frank Phillips

Maps and map index edited by R. W. Lidbetter, with research by H. Snape, and prepared by the cartographic staff of George Philip Cartographic Services Ltd under the direction of Alan Poynter MA, Director of Cartography.
Printed in Great Britain.
The representation in this atlas of a road or track is not evidence of the existence of a right of way.
The maps in this atlas are based upon the Ordnance Survey Map with the sanction of the Controller of Her Majesty's Stationery Office, Crown Copyright Reserved.
This edition published 1981 by Book Club Associates by arrangement with George Philip & Son Ltd.

FOREWORD

This book can be read in three ways: it dangles before you a string of succulent baits enticing you to get into your car and go and see them; it is a useful and informative guidebook when you are on the spot; and it is an excellent gazetteer of many of the most pleasant places in the United Kingdom, all of them properties of the two National Trusts.

No other country possesses a richer variety of historic buildings, and none has taken more trouble to preserve the best. The best does not simply mean the biggest or most famous but includes, too, relatively obscure houses and gardens that are perfect of their type, prehistoric sites and medieval castles, and functional buildings such as chapels, windmills and market-halls. Together they provide the visual equivalent of our literature. The Trusts do not merely protect these buildings against decay. Most of them are not only in better condition than they ever were but are still inhabited and used. To have saved this legacy of our past is to hand over an irreplacable legacy to the future.

The two Trusts have also acquired land, for what are buildings divorced from their context? Throughout the United Kingdom they own large slices of wild and lonely places, Lakeland shores and Derbyshire moorland, rocky capes along the Cornish coast and the remote islands of Lundy and St Kilda.

The Trusts also own important examples of the gentler landscapes of the British Isles, such as the meadows at Runnymede and East Anglian fen country. Wherever you live or travel, you will rarely be more than ten miles from a Trust property of some sort. This book will lead you to them, and compensate by its text and illustrations for those which the most ardent traveller will inevitably miss.

NIGEL NICOLSON

CONTENTS

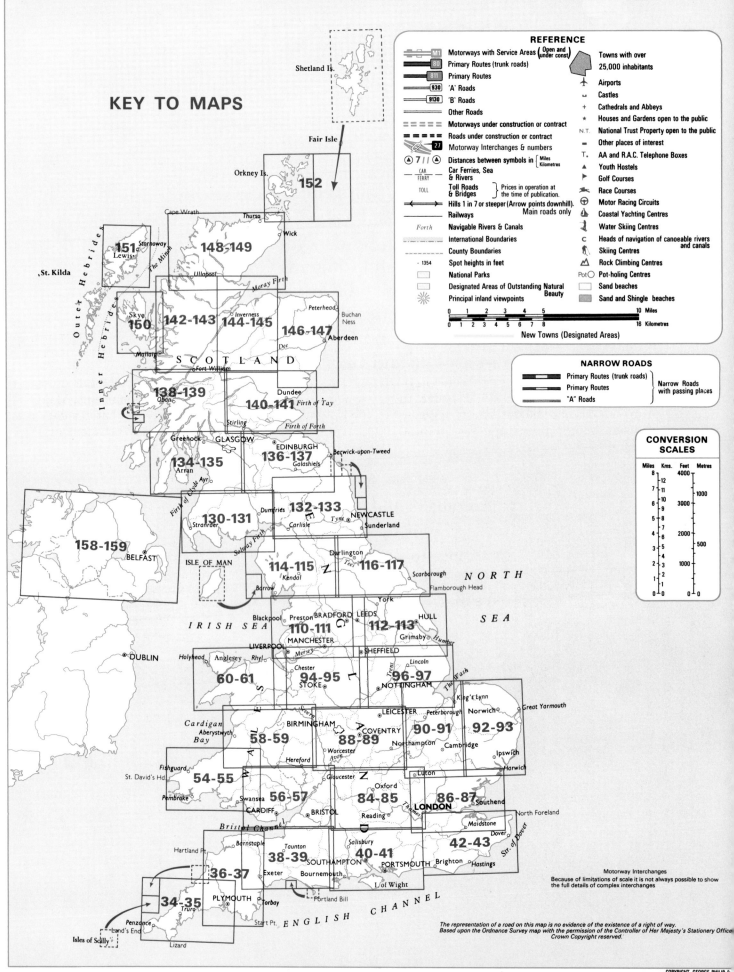

KEY TO MAPS

REFERENCE

M1	Motorways with Service Areas (Open and under const)
80	Primary Routes (trunk roads)
811	Primary Routes
930	'A' Roads
9130	'B' Roads
—	Other Roads
=====	Motorways under construction or contract
-----	Roads under construction or contract
27	Motorway Interchanges & numbers
▲ 7 ‖ ▲	Distances between symbols in [Miles / Kilometres]
CAR FERRY	Car Ferries, Sea & Rivers
TOLL	Toll Roads & Bridges } Prices in operation at the time of publication.
←→	Hills 1 in 7 or steeper (Arrow points downhill). Main roads only
	Railways
Forth	Navigable Rivers & Canals
	International Boundaries
	County Boundaries
· 1354	Spot heights in feet
☐	National Parks
☐	Designated Areas of Outstanding Natural Beauty
❋	Principal inland viewpoints

Towns with over 25,000 inhabitants

✈	Airports
⌂	Castles
+	Cathedrals and Abbeys
✳	Houses and Gardens open to the public
N.T.	National Trust Property open to the public
▬	Other places of interest
T.	AA and R.A.C. Telephone Boxes
▲	Youth Hostels
►	Golf Courses
	Race Courses
⊗	Motor Racing Circuits
⚓	Coastal Yachting Centres
	Water Skiing Centres
C	Heads of navigation of canoeable rivers and canals
🎿	Skiing Centres
⛰	Rock Climbing Centres
Pot◯	Pot-holing Centres
☐	Sand beaches
☐	Sand and Shingle beaches

0 1 2 3 4 5 10 Miles
0 1 2 3 4 5 6 7 8 16 Kilometres

New Towns (Designated Areas)

NARROW ROADS

	Primary Routes (trunk roads)
	Primary Routes } Narrow Roads with passing places
	"A" Roads

CONVERSION SCALES

Miles	Kms.	Feet	Metres
8	12	4000	
7	11		
	10		1000
6	9	3000	
5	8		
	7	2000	
4	6		500
3	5		
	4	1000	
2	3		
	2		
1	1		
0	0	0	0

Shetland Is.

Fair Isle

Orkney Is. **152**

Cape Wrath Thurso Wick

151 Stornoway Lewis

St. Kilda

Outer Hebrides

The Minch

148-149

Ullapool

Inner Hebrides

Skye **150** **142-143** Inverness **144-145** Peterhead **146-147** Buchan Ness

Mallaig Dee Aberdeen

SCOTLAND

Fort William

138-139 Oban **140-141** Dundee Firth of Tay

Stirling

Firth of Forth

Greenock GLASGOW EDINBURGH **136-137** Berwick-upon-Tweed

134-135 Galashiels

Arran Ayr

Firth of Clyde

130-131 Dumfries **132-133** NEWCASTLE

Stranraer Carlisle Tyne Sunderland

Solway Firth

158-159 BELFAST

Darlington Tees

ISLE OF MAN **114-115** **116-117** Scarborough

Kendal Flamborough Head

Barrow York NORTH

Blackpool Preston BRADFORD LEEDS HULL SEA

IRISH SEA **110-111** **112-113** Grimsby Humber

Liverpool MANCHESTER SHEFFIELD

DUBLIN Holyhead Anglesey Rhyl Chester Lincoln

60-61 **94-95** **96-97** The Wash

STOKE NOTTINGHAM

Cardigan Trent King's Lynn Great Yarmouth

Aberystwyth Bay BIRMINGHAM LEICESTER Peterborough Norwich

58-59 **88-89** **90-91** **92-93**

WALES COVENTRY Northampton Cambridge Ipswich

Hereford Worcester Avon Harwich

54-55 Fishguard Gloucester **84-85** Oxford **86-87** Luton

St. David's Hd. Pembroke Swansea **56-57** Oxford Southend

CARDIFF BRISTOL Reading LONDON

Bristol Channel Thames Maidstone North Foreland

42-43 Dover

Hartland Pt. Barnstaple Taunton Salisbury PORTSMOUTH Brighton Hastings

38-39 SOUTHAMPTON **40-41** Str. of Dover

36-37 Exeter Bournemouth I. of Wight

34-35 PLYMOUTH Torbay Portland Bill Start Pt. ENGLISH CHANNEL

Penzance Truro

Land's End Lizard

Isles of Scilly

Motorway Interchanges
Because of limitations of scale it is not always possible to show the full details of complex interchanges

The representation of a road on this map is no evidence of the existence of a right of way.
Based upon the Ordnance Survey map with the permission of the Controller of Her Majesty's Stationery Office Crown Copyright reserved.

INTRODUCTION

The properties in the care of The National Trust for Places of Historic Interest or Natural Beauty and The National Trust for Scotland are a priceless and unique heritage visited annually by millions of people. They include several hundred miles of unspoilt coastline, vast tracts of countryside, country houses on a majestic scale, and also many minor properties of architectural and historical importance.

This *Atlas* is a guide to properties of the Trusts throughout the United Kingdom, including Scotland and Northern Ireland as well as England and Wales. In each of the ten regional chapters, properties have been grouped in four sections. The first, *Coast and Countryside*, describes the open spaces in the Trusts' care and includes wildfowl refuges and nature reserves. The National Trust and The National Trust for Scotland are both major landowners and it has not been possible to describe every holding in detail. Sites of particular interest or beauty are covered individually in the text, general reference is made to many more and all are marked on the accompanying road maps.

The following three sections – *Houses, Gardens and Parks*; *Castles, Abbeys and other Buildings*; *Archaeological and Industrial Sites* – are alphabetical listings of all properties open to the public. Covenanted properties are excluded but important properties owned by the Trusts and managed by other bodies are included, and so are significant properties that can be viewed from the outside, such as Sailor's Walk (Fife) and Blaise Hamlet (Avon), but whose dwellings are privately tenanted. The majority of properties appear under *Houses, Gardens and Parks*. This section includes the many great houses in the Trusts' care, such as Petworth (West Sussex) and Saltram (Devon), and also buildings that have their origin in medieval castles but which have been much altered and improved over the centuries, such as Croft Castle (Hereford and Worcester). Lesser properties attached to great houses – churches, dovecotes, barns and villages – are also included.

Castles, Abbeys and other Buildings includes churches, chapels, villages, barns, follies, monuments, gatehouses, guildhalls and theatres. *Archaeological and Industrial Sites* includes prehistoric remains, Roman antiquities, windmills, water-mills and industrial monuments. Major prehistoric sites are described individually but in some parts of the country, such as the South-West, many of the open spaces in the Trust's care contain minor remains and not all these are listed. In the chapter on Scotland, this final section has been expanded to include historic sites, notably battlefields and their visitor centres.

Each property described in the text has been given a map reference. For example, the reference 35 G6 indicates that the site concerned is located on map page 35, in the square formed by the grid references G and 6. All properties are denoted on the maps by the symbols NT and the majority of the properties open to the public are also named. Anyone looking for properties to visit within a particular area should also consult the county index. Cross references to other properties within the text are italicized.

No information has been given on admission prices, availability of refreshments or facilities for the disabled. There is also no information on opening times, but where houses can only be viewed by appointment this is clearly stated. A complete register of the National Trust's holdings is given in *Properties of The National Trust**, reissued every five years. Both The National Trust and The National Trust for Scotland publish annual booklets on properties open to the public. These booklets give information on opening times, admission fees, shops, restaurants, facilities for the disabled, car parking, picnicking and new properties acquired.

Any enquiries about properties, publications or membership should be addressed to The National Trust, 42 Queen Anne's Gate, London SW1H 9AS, or to The National Trust for Scotland, 5 Charlotte Square, Edinburgh EH2 4DU.

*i.e. properties in England, Wales and Northern Ireland

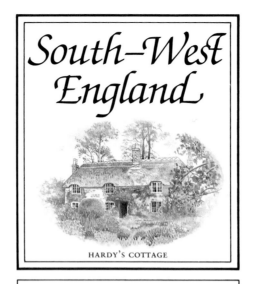

South-West England

HARDY'S COTTAGE

T he south-west of England has a special character which sets it apart from the rest of the country. This is partly because of its geographical isolation, partly because of its Celtic affiliations, seen so clearly in the distinctive place names of Cornwall, and partly because of its associations with so many legends and tales of romance and adventure, from King Arthur and the knights of the Round Table to Daphne du Maurier's *Frenchman's Creek*. The south-west is also exceptionally beautiful, and despite the annual influx of tourists there are still many unspoilt stretches of coast and many wild and lonely places on the moors that fill the heart of the peninsula.

The National Trust plays a prominent part in helping to retain the area's uniquely unspoilt atmosphere. It cares for some of Britain's loveliest and most dramatic stretches of coastline from the craggy cliffs of the north Devon and Cornish coasts to the gentler chalk landscapes of the Dorset coastline. The Trust also controls key land along the shores of the characteristic 'drowned' valleys (rias) that are so much a feature of Devon and Cornwall.

The Trust's great houses in this part of the country range from Cotehele, centre of a self-contained community in Tudor times, through Saltram, a superb example of eighteenth-century gracious living, to Castle Drogo, probably one of the last houses to be built on the grand scale in this country. The many lesser properties include several with particular historical or literary connections, from T. E. Lawrence's Clouds Hill to the Wellington Monument in the Blackdown Hills which recalls the glories of Waterloo.

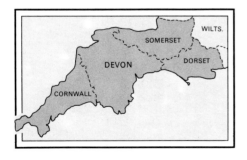

Coast & Countryside

In the gap between Somerset's Mendip Hills and the North and South Dorset Downs, all the roads lead to the West Country. Yet Nature has still erected barriers along the way, as if to deter the traveller determined to reach the farthest south-western corner of England: the massive, granite bulk of Dartmoor, for example; or the rushing rivers of Exmoor; or even lonely Bodmin Moor, straddling the centre of Cornwall.

Yet it is on these inhospitable uplands that prehistoric man made his home and left behind many a reminder of his occupation. This corner of England is rich in Neolithic and Iron Age sites such as *Lanyon Quoit* (34 F1), north-west of Penzance. This massive granite slab balanced on three equally massive uprights is the remains of the tomb chamber of a Neolithic long barrow. Perhaps because of these visible remains of prehistoric man, the south-west has a feeling of mystery and timelessness, a primeval quality. The landscape – particularly between St Ives and Land's End – still has an oddly haunted atmosphere which is not wholly attributable to the unexpectedly wild scenery.

It is easy to believe the fairy stories in this part of the world: the stories of the 'little people' or Cornish 'piskies', and the tales of legendary giants. At **Bedruthan Steps** (34 C5), on the north Cornish coast near Padstow, the giant Bedruthan is said to have clambered from the sea by way of a 'staircase' of rocky islets just offshore – and the islets really do look like a giant's stepping stones. Although the Steps themselves do not belong to the Trust, the clifftop above Bedruthan Beach does, and the unspoilt view – north to Trevose Head and south towards Newquay – is rightly acclaimed as one of the most beautiful in Britain.

Besides fairy stories, there are legends such as the one attached to **Bodrugan's Leap** (35 E7), just south of Mevagissey on the coast of southern Cornwall. Sir Henry Trenowth is said to have leapt from this headland into the sea in a successful attempt to escape from Sir Richard Edgcumbe whose home, *Cotehele*, is one of the

Trust's prime properties in this part of the country. Realism returns with a look at some of the other magnificent scenery which is in the Trust's care. A big stretch of the **West Penwith** – or Land's End – peninsula (34 F1/2) belongs to the Trust and includes both cliff and inland scenery around Zennor, Porthmeor, Morvah and Pendeen. **Mayon and Trevescan Cliffs**, between Land's End and Sennen (34 G1), are a popular tourist attraction, while less well known are **St Levan Cliffs** (34 G1), on the southern side of the peninsula.

In Mount's Bay, separating the Land's End peninsula from the Lizard, and dominated by another Trust property, *St Michael's Mount*, the heather-covered **Rinsey Cliff** (34 G3) is noted for the dramatic ruins of *Wheal Prosper*, an abandoned tin and copper mine. On the **Lizard Peninsula** itself (34 H4/5), much of the coastline comes under the Trust's protection – from the odd but very attractive freshwater lake known as **The Loe**, two miles south of Helston, round to such famous beauty spots as **Mullion Cove and Island**; the cliffland above **Polurrian Cove**, one mile south-west of Mullion; **Kynance Cove**, with its richly-coloured serpentine cliffs and fantastic rock formations; and **Bass Point**, one mile east of Lizard Point. Prehistoric remains can be seen on the heath-covered **Lower Predannack Downs** (34 H4).

East of the Lizard, there are the great, flooded valleys of the Helford and Fal rivers. Much of the **Helford River** (34 G4/5) is owned by the Trust, including **Frenchman's Creek** on the south side, the peaceful, wooded creek from which Daphne du Maurier's novel took its name. In the larger Fal estuary the Trust owns **Turnaway Point** at the head of the Carrick Roads on the east bank of the Fal (34 F5) as well as cliffland near **St Mawes**, **St Anthony Head** at the eastern entrance to Falmouth Harbour (fortified in 1895, now much cleaned-up and restored), and a large stretch of coastal farmland and foreshore at **St Anthony-in-Roseland** and **St Just-in-Roseland**, south-east and north of St Mawes respectively. There are extensive holdings, too, on the coast north-east of the Fal: among them the land overlooking sandy **Pendower Beach** on Gerrans

below The inlet of Crackington Haven, north of Boscastle, lies below some of the finest cliff-walking in England.

above Looking out to sea from Mullion Harbour. The quays are often damaged in stormy weather and need frequent repairs.

West Pentire Head on the River Gannel, but it is worth noting that much of the south bank of the **Gannel Estuary** (34 D5) is protected from the encroachment of hotels and amusement arcades – and provides a haven for walkers and wildlife despite its proximity to the town.

The stretch of coastline to the north of Newquay, around Bedruthan Steps, has already been described. Farther north Padstow, on the south bank of the River Camel and nestling behind the protective arms of Trevose Head and Pentire Point, is a growing resort, but much of the farmland and coast around **Pentire Point** (34 A6), north of Padstow Bay, is Trust land. On Pentire Point itself there are the remains of an Iron Age Cornish cliff castle and there are also prehistoric remains on the beautiful headland known as the Rumps to the north. The same applies to the coastline round **Tintagel** (35 A7), reputedly the site of King Arthur's Castle. The Trust owns some dramatic cliffland here, with fine views. At neighbouring **Boscastle** (35 A8) the Trust owns the entire harbour as well as much of the nearby **Valency Valley**. The harbour, almost hidden behind a protective wall of cliffs, is one of the Trust's major success stories. Built partly by the famous mariner Sir Richard Grenville in the sixteenth century, and once used mainly for the shipping of slate, it fell into disuse after the outer jetty was blown up by a drifting mine in 1941. The Trust rebuilt the harbour in 1962, and has since acquired several harbourside buildings. It is now a pretty, as well as an historic, spot. Beyond Bude, where Cornwall gives way to Devon, there are more stretches of dramatic coastline on the west coast of the vast headland of **Hartland Point** (36 D/E1).

The splendours of the Cornish coast are most widely known but the Trust also owns many notable areas of countryside. These include the heath-covered moorland at **Chapel Porth** above St Agnes (34 E4), where a wild valley leads down to a tiny cove; and the typical moorland scenery of **Rough Tor** (35 B8), on Bodmin Moor. At 1,311 feet, Rough Tor is the second-highest point in Cornwall and contains a Bronze Age settlement as well as being at the heart of excellent walking country. Another noteworthy viewpoint is gorse-covered **Trencrom Hill** (34 F2), between St Ives and Penzance, where an Iron Age hill-fort overlooks stunning countryside and coastal scenery and at the same time acts as a memorial to the Cornishmen who died in the two World Wars. At the other end of the scenic scale, the Trust owns **Trelissick** (34 F5), just south of Truro, where parkland, farmland and woods, including the famous *Trelissick Garden*, overlook the Fal Estuary.

The Trust's holdings in Devon serve to emphasize the variety of the scenery. The accent is on the coast, particularly in the less well-known north, but properties also include land on Dartmoor and Exmoor, the two upland areas that provide a welcome contrast to the pastoral scenery of so much of Devon.

North of Bude is the promontory of Hartland Point, beyond which the coastline falls away to the east around Barnstaple – or

Bay (34 F6), and land around **Dodman Point** (35 F7) and **Gorran Haven** (35 F7). Dodman Point is the *Dead Man's Rock* of Sir Arthur Quiller Couch's novel.

East of the china clay country behind St Austell, **Fowey** (35 E8) stands at the entrance to another of the drowned valleys and there is plenty of good walking on the unspoiled cliffs and countryside around the estuary and in the river valley itself, with **Hall Walk**, **Lanteglos**, opposite Fowey, and **St Catherine's Point** around Fowey Castle particularly noteworthy.

Then there are the famous ports and beauty spots of **Polperro** (35 E9) and **Looe** (35 E9/10). Besides cliffland on either side of Polperro harbour (Chapel Cliff, on the west of the village, is particularly good for walking), the Trust owns land close to East and West Looe.

Although Cornwall is only about twenty miles across in places, those twenty miles separate scenery that is worlds apart. The wooded river valleys and tiny, picturesque ports of the south give way to soaring cliffs and vast, sandy, dune-backed beaches in the north. They stretch from St Ives to Bude and beyond and include such beauty spots as the six-mile stretch of cliff and farmland from **Godrevy** to **Portreath** (34 E3/4), along which (from east to west) a footpath affords glimpses of Portreath harbour, the precipitous Ralph's Cupboard, the evocatively-named Hell's Mouth, Navax Point, the Godrevy peninsula, and coves and beaches where the only sign of life may be sea-birds or the inquisitive Atlantic seal.

North of Portreath, **St Agnes Beacon** (34 E4) soars to 628 feet to give views of no less than twenty-six miles of this coastline: a coastline which is often a wild, sandy wasteland pounded by the Atlantic rollers. Immediately to the north-east the Trust has holdings of cliffs, farmland, common land and dunes around **Cubert** (34 D5), including Cubert Common, one of the few enclosed commons in England, as well as Kelsey Head, Holywell Beach and West Pentire Head. Newquay, Cornwall's most famous holiday resort, shelters below

Bideford – Bay. Between **Hartland Point** (36 C1) and the very attractive hillside fishing village of **Clovelly** (36 C2), with its famous steep cobbled main street dropping precipitously down to the sea, much of the beautiful cliff scenery is protected by the Trust, and from the car park at Brownsham west of the village walkers can join the recently reopened coastal footpath. A good viewpoint over Bideford Bay is **Mount Pleasant**, just above Clovelly.

Offshore can be seen the granite cliffs of **Lundy Island**, eleven miles north of Hartland Point in the Bristol Channel. Bought by the Trust a decade ago, in conjunction with the Landmark Trust which administers the island, Lundy is, at 1,116 acres, far larger than it appears from the coast, and is now principally a bird sanctuary which can be visited from the ports of Bideford and Ilfracombe. Most of the buildings on the island, among them the ruins of the thirteenth-century Marisco Castle, and the late-Victorian church of St Helena, are now abandoned, but there are some interesting Neolithic and Bronze Age sites.

Farther along the mainland coast, at **Westward Ho!** (36 C3), Kipling Tors, eighteen acres of gorse-covered hillside to the west of the town, is famous as the setting for much of Rudyard Kipling's novel *Stalky & Co.* Farther east still, one comes to one of the Trust's finest stretches of coastline, running from **Croyde** (36 B3) up to **Woolacombe** (36 B3) and then in an uninterrupted five-mile expanse to the rocky bay below **Lee** (36 A3). The cliffland to the west of **Ilfracombe** (36 A4) also includes many stretches belonging to the Trust, and taken as a whole this is a spectacular and totally unspoiled piece of coast which includes many fine walks along well-defined footpaths and views of Lundy.

There is more fine coastal scenery to the east of Ilfracombe, where Exmoor reaches the sea. Trust holdings here are fragmented, but of note are cliffland at **Holdstone Down** (36 A5), between Coombe Martin and Heddon's Mouth, near Trentishoe; the **Heddon Valley** (36 A5), a large area of woodland and moorland leading down from Trentishoe Common to Heddon's Mouth, with good views of the Bristol Channel en route; and in particular the steep wooded valleys of the East Lyn above **Lynmouth** (36 A6)

The view towards Ilfracombe from Bull Point encompasses a typically dramatic stretch of the north Cornish coast.

and at **Watersmeet**, between Lynmouth and Brendon, as well as land around **Foreland Point** – the eastern bastion of Lynmouth Bay – and **Countisbury Hill**. This very attractive area is again fine walking country (motorists can park at Barna Barrow, above Countisbury village), and there are many miles of signposted footpaths.

Like Cornwall, Devon's coasts present a contrast. From the cliffs in the north of the county it is a sharp change to the South Hams: farming country of steep-sided lanes which hide the view so that one seems always to come suddenly, and surprisingly, across the deeply-wooded valleys of the Salcombe and Dart estuaries or the beaches of Bigbury Bay, Start Bay and Torbay.

The sheer size of this area means that a car is needed to explore it properly, but the countryside is particularly lovely and repays exploration. Favourite viewpoints include **Clematon Hill, Bigbury-on-Sea** (37 L5), where there are panoramas over the Avon and Bolt Tail and to Burgh Island; the six-mile stretch of cliff between **Bolt Head** and **Bolt Tail** (37 M5/6); **Prawle Point** (37 M6/7), the most southerly point in Devon; and **Beesands Cliff** (37 L7), at the north end of Beesands Beach, half a mile south of Torcross. The Trust also has extensive holdings around the Salcombe estuary and, to the east, around the Dart Estuary, including cliffs and farmland forming the western approach to Dartmouth harbour at **Little Dartmouth** (37 L8). The Dart estuary itself, especially in early summer, is very attractive, with woodland stretching right down to the water's edge. With the Dart and Start Bay appeal, the Trust hopes to protect more of this coast. Much farther east, five miles from Sidmouth, the Trust owns much of the **Branscombe valley** (including the peaceful and attractive village), as well as part of the cliffs towards Beer Head on the east and Weston on the west (38 G5).

The lofty granite mass of Dartmoor, vast and inhospitable, has its status as a National

Park, and its bleak character, to protect it. None the less, the Trust has representative holdings on the moor – among them a typical stretch of the south-west corner at **Goodameavy** (37 J4), which lies six miles north-east of Plymouth, near Clearbrook, and includes Dewerstone and Cadworthy Woods, the Dewerstone Rock (on which there are the remains of an Iron Age fort), and part of Wigford Down (on which there are Bronze Age hut circles); 3,333 acres of open moorland on the south-west flank of Dartmoor around **Hentor** and **Willings Walls Warrens** (37 J4), which rises to 1,550 feet and overlooks the head-waters of the River Plym; and **Holne Woods** (37 J6), an area of oak woodland on the upper reaches of the River Dart with fine views from the higher paths.

Also noteworthy in the Devon countryside are **Hembury** (37 J6), on the southern edge of Dartmoor, where there are woodland walks through the upper Dart Valley to a 500-foot summit with fine moorland views; **Lydford Gorge** (37 G4), on the far western side of Dartmoor between Okehampton and Tavistock, where the River Lyd has scooped out a deep ravine to form a series of potholes and is joined by a stream that falls over the dramatic 90-foot high White Lady Waterfall; and the **Plym Bridge Woods** (37 K4), a wooded river valley on the edge of the moor.

In Somerset, pride of place might be thought to go to the big Trust holdings on **Exmoor**. These include 12,500 acres between **Porlock** (36 A7/8) and Minehead, stretching from the coast to the south of Dunkery Beacon, and incorporate not only some very beautiful countryside but also the villages of Bossington, Luccombe and Selworthy; **South Hill, Dulverton** (36 C7); and the viewpoint of **Winsford Hill** just to the north (36 C7), between Exford and

In summer, the wooded lower reaches of Lydford Gorge are a patchwork of sunlight and shade.

Dulverton. But, in many visitors' minds, these landscapes cannot match the dramatic quality of the **Cheddar Gorge** (39 A8), where the Trust owns the north side of **Cheddar Cliffs**, including the Lion and Monkey Rocks. Sun Hole Cave, in the Gorge, is of great archaeological interest, and items dating back to the Palaeolithic Age have been found there. Mysterious **Glastonbury Tor** (39 B8), with its legends of Joseph of Arimathea and King Arthur and Queen Guinevere delving deep into England's religious and secular past, is another much-visited spot in the Trust's care.

In the Mendip Hills, north-west of Wells, the Trust owns **Ebbor Gorge** (39 B8), a wooded limestone gorge run by the Nature Conservancy as a nature reserve. Other beauty spots include the **Blackdown Hills** (38 E5), with their views across the Vale of Taunton and the Quantocks to the Bristol Channel and surmounted by the *Wellington Monument*; and the headland of **Brean Down** (56 H6) overlooking Weston-super-Mare from a 300-foot high vantage point. In the Quantocks the views from **Longstone Hill** should not be missed (38 B5); while on Sedgemoor there are good views from *Burrow Mump* (39 C7), a nine-acre hill just south of Othery near Burrow Bridge. At **Turn Hill** (39 C7), one mile west of High Ham, there is another good viewpoint, looking across the battlefield of Sedgemoor (the site of Monmouth's defeat in 1685) to the Quantocks; while in the Polden Hills, to the east of Sedgemoor, **Cock Hill** (39 C8) stands on the crest – again with good views – beside the course of a Roman road.

Dorset's countryside is perhaps best epito-mized by the **Golden Cap Estate** (39 G7/8), the National Trust's large holding of hills, cliffs, farmland and beach between Charmouth (just east of Lyme Regis) and Eypemouth – including five miles of the coast itself. This south Dorset downland is particularly attractive, and with fifteen miles of footpaths the estate lends itself to walking.

One of its attractions is that it is still not very well known, and thus remains uncrowded. This cannot be said of the county's most famous landmark, the **Cerne Giant** (39 F10), a 180-foot high Romano-British figure cut into the chalk of the 600-foot high Giant Hill, eight miles north of Dorchester.

Dorset is a county that tourists often forget – visitors either head for the New Forest, to the east, or else drive on through Dorset towards Devon and Cornwall. But the countryside is very attractive, and the coastline – and in particular the vast shingle beach of **Chesil Bank** (39 H9) – is often totally unspoilt. Lovers of coastal scenery may especially enjoy **Burton Cliff** (39 G8), a high bluff running west from Burton Bradstock which rises to 100 feet sheer above the sea before dropping down to Freshwater Bay, and provides both riverside and cliff walks, and **Ballard Down** (40 H2), south-east of Studland, on the Isle of Purbeck. Inland, there is **Lambert's Castle Hill** (39 F7), near Marshwood, an 842-foot high wooded hilltop and escarpment with views across to

Chesil Bank in the east and Dartmoor in the west; while three counties – Devon, Dorset and Somerset – can be seen from the top of **Lewesdon Hill** (39 F7/8), three miles west of Beaminster.

Finally, **Brownsea Island** (40 G2), in Poole Harbour. Famous as the site of Lord Baden-Powell's first Scout camp in 1907, the 500-acre island of heath and woodland, with magnificent views across Poole Harbour, was inaccessible for many years. It was transferred to the Trust in 1962, and although part of the island is a nature reserve its woodland walks and beach are now accessible to everyone. There is a famous heronry on the island, but wildfowl and holidaymakers both find room here, in tranquil and beautiful surroundings.

above **The heavily-wooded acres of Brownsea Island are a paradise for a rich variety of wildlife and are one of the last haunts of the red squirrel.**

below **Selworthy is contained within the Trust's holdings on Exmoor and lies at the heart of some exceptional countryside.**

Antony House overlooks a crossing-point of the River Tamar and must always have been of strategic importance.

Houses, Gardens & Parks

Antony House, Cornwall This fine, solid, rectangular house of silvery-grey Pentewan stone, with red-brick wings attached to it by colonnades, was built by an unknown architect for Sir William Carew in the early part of the eighteenth century. The Carew family – among them the seventeenth-century historian Richard Carew, author of *The Survey of Cornwall* – had lived on the site for nearly 300 years before the completion of Antony House in 1721, but the stable block and early seventeenth-century building beside it replace an earlier house on this site.

Most of the rooms in the house are panelled, and contain contemporary furniture and portraits of the Carew and Pole families, whose descendants have always lived there. The brilliantly-coloured tapestry coverings on the chairs outside the dining room, the Queen Anne pier-glass between the dining room windows, the three Reynolds in the saloon, and the Soho tapestries in the tapestry room are all worth noting. The library contains a copy of the original edition of Richard Carew's *Survey*, published in 1602. The cannon balls outside the house date from Charles I's unsuccessful siege of Plymouth in the seventeenth century.

The beautifully laid out gardens, much influenced by Repton, run down to the River Lynher. A splendid terrace, complementing the house, overlooks the lawns on the north front. Of special interest are the stone carvings and temple bell, brought back to Cornwall by Sir Reginald Pole-Carew after military expeditions in India and Burma, and the gingko – or maidenhair tree – in the yew alley leading to the terrace: one of the oldest and largest trees of its kind in Britain.

2M N of Torpoint, N of A374   (37 K3)

Arlington Court, Devon Designed for Colonel John Palmer Chichester by Thomas Lee of Barnstaple in 1820, Arlington Court contains a collection of model ships, shells, pewter, snuff boxes and small *objets d'art*. There is a good collection of horse-drawn vehicles in the stables. The grounds, with their wide lawns and clumps of rhododendrons, merge into the surrounding woods, where buzzards and ravens nest. The lake below the house is a wildfowl sanctuary, and the surrounding parkland contains flocks of Jacob sheep and a herd of Shetland ponies.

7M NE of Barnstaple, on E side of A39   (36 B5)

The south front of Barrington Court, crowned with finials and chimneystacks, with the red-brick stable block on the left.

Barrington Court, Somerset An imposing mid sixteenth-century house probably built by William Clifton, a Norfolk merchant, Barrington Court has changed little externally. The windows are late Gothic, and the red-brick stable block dates from 1670. The interior was restored this century. The garden is one of the best preserved of Gertrude Jekyll's schemes.

3M NE of Ilminster, at E end of Barrington, entrance on B3168   (39 D7)

Bradley Manor, Devon The Perpendicular chapel is the principal item of architectural interest at Bradley Manor, a small, roughcast, fifteenth-century manor house in the steep valley of the River Lemon.

On W edge of Newton Abbot, entrance on A381   (37 J7)

Buckland Abbey, Devon Associations with the Grenville and Drake families, of seafaring fame, have made this thirteenth-century Cistercian abbey one of Britain's best-known country houses. Sir Richard Grenville, captain of the *Revenge*, whose grandfather and namesake had been given the building by King Henry VIII in 1541, re-modelled the abbey and added the plaster ceiling in the hall. Sir Francis Drake bought the house from the Grenvilles in 1581, after completing his voyage around the world, and his arms are on the chimneypiece in the top storey. The house's contents include Grenville and Drake relics, and a naval and county folk museum, which among many exhibits contains Drake's Drum. There is a large medieval tithe barn in the grounds.

6M S of Tavistock, off A386   (37 J4)

above **Buckland Abbey is centred on the tower of the abbey church.**

right **The medieval dovecote and pond in the valley garden at Cotehele.**

Castle Drogo, Devon A romantically eccentric building, Castle Drogo is a cross between a medieval castle and an eighteenth-century country house. It is in fact entirely twentieth-century in origin, having been built between 1910 and 1930 by Sir Edwin Lutyens for Julian Drewe, the founder of a grocery chain. Constructed entirely of granite, Castle Drogo has a superb setting: it stands on a rocky outcrop 900 feet above the wooded gorge of the upper reaches of the River Teign. Below the castle windows on the far side of the river rise the steep slopes of Whiddon Deer Park, which dates from Elizabethan times and still has its original walls. The castle garden itself is formally terraced, and has an immense circular lawn hedged with yews.

The building's grey exterior is a profusion of castellations, turrets and mullioned windows – a mixture of architectural styles that is the result not of additions over the centuries but of frequent changes of plan during the actual building of Castle Drogo. The interior is equally haphazard: a jumble of styles and ideas that paid little heed to practicality. The kitchens, for example, are fifty yards from the dining room. With the notable exception of the drawing room, the interior is also stark and austere. With bare granite walls and timber, it is reminiscent of a medieval castle, an effect that is heightened by the tapestries that hang in the library and hall.

Already recognized as unique, Castle Drogo could find itself with a double place in English architectural history: as the last large building to be constructed of granite and as one of the last private houses to be built in Britain on the grand scale.

At Drewsteignton, off A382   (37 G6)

Compton Castle, Devon The two portcullised entrances, handsome battlements and angular towers on the north front give Compton Castle an almost fairytale appearance. It is, in fact, one of the finest fortified manor houses in Britain, and is famous as the home of Sir Humphrey Gilbert, Sir Walter Raleigh's half-brother, who colonized Newfoundland. It was built in three distinct periods (the early four-teenth, fifteenth, and sixteenth centuries) and remained in the Gilbert family until 1800. The house is surrounded by a massive 24-foot high wall, and the towers have interior shafts which provided an early, if rudimentary, form of sanitation. The reconstructed hall is full of Gilbert mementoes and the old kitchen, prob-ably built in about 1520, has an open fireplace which extends for its full width.

The house stands in 346 acres of land, and there is a beautifully built, eighteenth-century barn of limestone and thatch beside the house.

4M NW of Torquay (37 J7)

Cotehele, Cornwall This remarkable early Tudor manor house overlooking the Tamar, and fronted by a bright display of daffodils every spring, has hardly changed in the past 300 years. Built between 1485 and 1627 round three courts, on the foundations of an earlier house, it is a microcosm of an era – and a fine example of a self-contained community, with everything coming up by river from Plymouth to the

left **Castle Drogo is architecturally one of the Trust's most remarkable houses.**

picturesque Cotehele Quay, on a bend in the Tamar. It contains Cromwellian armour, and fine furniture and tapestries, which have always been there. Charles I is said to have slept in the Jacobean Tower in the north-west corner of the building; and in the South Room, one of the bedrooms, are peeps which enabled the occupants to see what was happening in the hall and chapel below. The medieval hall, 40 feet long, is one of the most impressive in the West Country. Another notable feature is the simple chapel, which has a barrel-vaulted ceiling with oak ribbing and a fine carved oak screen. The chapel contains a fifteenth-century clock which is one of the three oldest unaltered pre-pendulum clocks in Britain.

In the grounds there is a medieval barn and, alongside the path leading to Cotehele Quay, an old dovecote shaped like a giant beehive – both reminders of the house's ability to be self-supporting. The gardens have Victorian ter-races, and there are several attractive eighteenth-century and nineteenth-century buildings, and a small shipping museum, at Cotehele Quay. Cotehele Mill, the manorial water-mill, lies on the Tamar half a mile up the valley from Cotehele Quay.

9M SW of Tavistock, near Calstock (37 J3)

Dunster Castle, Somerset The 600-year-old fortified home of the Luttrell family rises impressively above the village of Dunster, between the wooded hills of Exmoor and the sea. The castle – in fact a mansion, despite its name – was remodelled by Anthony Salvin in the nineteenth century, although the seventeenth-century staircase and plasterwork

A Grecian urn in the terrace garden at Killerton.

were retained. The stables date from Crom-wellian times, and the castle stands in forty-nine acres of parkland which are sufficiently well protected from the elements for semi-tropical shrubs to flourish on the terraced walks.

3M SE of Minehead, entrance on A39 (38 B3)

Glendurgan, Cornwall The wooded valley garden of Glendurgan, running down to the estuary of the Helford River, contains many fine trees and shrubs, a walled garden, a water garden, and a maze.

½M S of Mawnan Smith, on road to Helford Passage (34 G5)

Killerton, Devon This fine eighteenth-century house was built to the design of John Johnson, and stands in a hillside garden with large, open lawns and a notable collection of rare trees and shrubs. Two nineteenth-century chapels, one with immense tulip trees outside, and an arboretum, are particularly worth seeing. One of the chapels stands beside the ruins of the Aclands' house at Culm John, which was destroyed during the Civil War. The house contains the Paulise de Bush collection of costumes, which is shown in a series of rooms furnished to 'match' the costumes in different periods. Killerton Park is 300 acres of park and woodland surrounding the isolated Dolbury Hill while the estate as a whole is over 6,300 acres of agricultural land and woodland.

7M NE of Exeter, entrance off B3185 (38 F3)

Knightshayes Court, Devon A sandstone house, built in idiosyncratic Gothic style by William Burges between 1869–74 and possessing a fine collection of pictures, Knightshayes Court is best-known for its garden. This was created by Sir John and Lady Heathcoat-Amory after World War II, and includes specimen trees,

formal terraces, rare shrubs, a collection of willows, and a fine display of spring bulbs. But not everything is new: the group of massive Douglas firs is over 100 years old.

2M N of Tiverton, off B396   (38 E3)

Lanhydrock, Cornwall One of the most beautiful houses in Cornwall, Lanhydrock is a seventeenth-century building which was severely damaged by fire and rebuilt in 1881, and it thus includes a variety of architectural styles. The gatehouse, and the north wing, are all that remain of the original building, completed in 1651, but the interior of the present house – which is on a larger scale than the original and epitomizes late Victorian splendour – is particularly interesting. Of special note are the English and Flemish tapestries on the walls of the morning room, and the panelled picture gallery with its 116-foot-long plaster barrel ceiling – a survivor of the fire – containing twenty-four panels depicting stories from the Old Testament starting with the Creation and ending with the burial of Isaac.

The 741 acres of park and woodland, falling away into the valley of the River Fowey, are particularly beautiful.

2½M S of Bodmin, entrance on B3269   (35 C8)

Lytes Cary, Somerset A typical Somerset manor house, and the home of the Lyte family for 500 years. It has been added to over the centuries, but the chapel, the oldest part of the present building, is fourteenth-century and the great hall fifteenth-century. The 365-acre grounds contain an ancient dovecote.

2½M NE of Ilchester, on road to Charlton Adam off A372   (39 D8/9)

Montacute, Somerset Built of Ham Hill stone from nearby Ham Hill to an H-shaped ground plan, Montacute is a magnificent Elizabethan mansion, glittering with glass and elaborate honey-coloured stonework. Inside there is some excellent heraldic glass, plasterwork, panelling and tapestries. There is an exhibition of sixteenth-century portraits, belonging to the National Portrait Gallery, in the Long Gallery. At 172 feet, this is the longest surviving sixteenth-century gallery. The house was completed in about 1600, and stands in contemporary gardens in which the two pavilions, which once flanked the entrance, are a feature.

4M W of Yeovil, entrance off A3088   (39 E8)

St Michael's Mount, Cornwall The magnificent, conical-shaped offshore island of St Michael's Mount rises 200 feet from the sea opposite Marazion, east of Penzance in Mount's Bay. It is crowned by a fourteenth-century castle. The island is reached by a causeway from Marazion at low tide, and by boat when the causeway is impassable.

The history of St Michael's Mount, which resembles the larger Mont St Michel in Brittany, goes back to Roman times, and it has been associated with Christianity since the fifth century. Edward the Confessor built a chapel on the Mount in 1047, then presented it to the Benedictine monks from the abbey on Mont St Michel. It later developed into a military stronghold, but in 1657 it became the property of the St Aubyn family and was converted into a private home.

There are remarkable views of Mount's Bay, and towards Land's End and the Lizard, from the terraces, and in the castle itself the drawing room (formed from the Lady Chapel), the refectory, the fifteenth-century chapel, and the armoury are all outstanding.

½M S of Marazion, off A394   (34 G2)

Every detail in the saloon at Saltram, including the gilt-brass door handles, was planned to contribute to the overall effect.

Saltram, Devon Standing in a landscaped park looking towards Plymouth Sound, Saltram was described by the eighteenth-century historian Polwhele as 'one of the most beautiful seats in the West of England' – a title to which it can still lay claim. The classical façade, built

above **The east front of Montacute seen across the late nineteenth-century balustraded pond.**

in the mid eighteenth century, masks the remains of a large Tudor house, and the house's history may go back even further than that, for there are references to a homestead on the site as long ago as 1218, when it may have been associated with the production of salt from the tidal estuary.

Today, the house is noteworthy as the finest complete and unspoiled example of the work of interior designer Robert Adam in the south-west – with the saloon and the dining room, completed in 1768, seen as his outstanding creations. Among the contents are fourteen portraits by Sir Joshua Reynolds, who lived nearby and had a lifelong association with Saltram, as well as fine period furniture and china. The great kitchen – which was still in use until 1962 – is of historic and social interest, and includes a Victorian range as well as a display of cooking utensils needed for catering on the grand scale.

The grounds include magnificent belts of timber on the higher points of the undulating parkland, which give Saltram a setting of considerable grandeur. There is also an orangery by the wood carver Henry Stockman, completed in 1775 and rebuilt by the Trust after a disastrous fire in 1932; the classical garden house or temple known as 'Fanny's Bower'; a chapel adjacent to the house which is thought to be a conversion of a medieval barn; and a pleasant little building known as The Castle, in the design of which Adam is thought to have had a hand.

3½M E of Plymouth city centre, between A38 and A379 (37 K4)

Sharpitor, Devon The six-acre garden of this early twentieth-century house affords beautiful views over Salcombe Bay and the entrance to Salcombe harbour to the east. The house contains a museum of local interest, with special appeal to children.

1½M SW of Salcombe (37 M6)

Tintinhull House, Somerset This is a fine seventeenth-century farmhouse with a classical façade. It is noted for its modern formal garden.

5M NW of Yeovil, in Tintinhull village, ½M S of A303 (39 D8)

Trelissick, Cornwall The grounds of Trelissick House, overlooking the Fal estuary and Fal-mouth harbour, include a very good collection of shrubs, and are interesting and attractive at all times of the year. In all, there are 376 acres of gardens and parkland, including farmland and some woodland, above the Fal estuary. There is a well-preserved Iron Age promontory fort at Round Wood, at the entrance to Cowlands Creek on the estate.

4M S of Truro, entrance on B3289 (34 F5)

Trengwainton, Cornwall The gardens of Trengwainton House contain a magnificent collection of shrubs, mainly magnolias and rhododendrons, including many half-hardy species. The theme of a place in which the climate permits the growth of many species not normally seen in England is continued in the walled garden, where there are many tender plants. The gardens and surrounding park total 98 acres.

2M W of Penzance (34 G2)

Trerice, Cornwall A fine Elizabethan manor house, Trerice contains notable plaster ceilings and fireplaces, oak and walnut furniture, portraits and tapestries. On the south side is a fine sixteenth-century two-storeyed bay, whose windows on the first floor light the solar (now the drawing room). The E-shaped east-facing frontage, with its splendid scrolled Dutch gables, betrays the house's Tudor origins – it was rebuilt in 1571. There are fourteen acres of delightful gardens.

3M SE of Newquay (34 D5)

Castles, Abbeys & other Buildings

Bruton Dovecote, Somerset This is a sixteenth-century, roofless tower used latterly as a dovecote, standing alone in the deer park of the abbey which once stood on the south side of the town.

½M S of Bruton, across railway, ½M W of B3081 (39 C10)

Burrow Mump, Somerset On the summit of isolated Burrow Mump, on Sedgemoor, is an unfinished late eighteenth-century chapel, built over the foundations of an earlier one. There was previously a small Norman castle on this site. Burrow Mump also serves as a World War II memorial.

2½M SW of Othery, just S of A361 (39 C7)

Grange Arch, looking north over an unspoilt stretch of Dorset countryside. The sea can be seen in the view south.

Clouds Hill, Dorset T. E. Lawrence – Lawrence of Arabia – retired to this cottage when he was discharged from the RAF. It contains some of Lawrence's furnishings.

9M E of Dorchester (39 G11)

Coleridge Cottage, Somerset The poet Samuel Taylor Coleridge lived in this cottage, at the west end of Nether Stowey, between 1797 and 1800, while he was writing *The Ancient Mariner* and the first part of *Christabel*. The parlour only is shown.

Nether Stowey, 8M W of Bridgwater, S side of A39 (38 B5)

Grange Arch, Creech, Dorset Commonly known as Bond's Folly, Grange Arch was built early in the eighteenth century by Denis Bond, of Creech Grange. It stands silhouetted against the sky to the south of Creech Grange, in the Purbeck Hills.

3M W of Corfe Castle (39 H12)

Hardy Monument, Dorset Erected in 1846, the monument commemorates Vice-Admiral Sir Thomas Masterman Hardy, flag-captain of the *Victory* at the Battle of Trafalgar (1805). The monument's site offers good views over Weymouth Bay.

6M SW of Dorchester (39 G9)

Hardy's Cottage, Dorset This small thatched house at Higher Bockhampton was the birth-place of Thomas Hardy in 1840 and was where he wrote *Under the Greenwood Tree* and *Far from the Madding Crowd*. It contains a small museum of items of Hardy memorabilia.

3M NE of Dorchester, S of A35 (39 G10)

King John's Hunting Lodge, Somerset Standing on a corner of the square in the centre of the ancient town of Axbridge, where Tudor-fronted houses line the High Street, King John's Hunting Lodge dates from about 1500 and is illustrative of the new prosperity enjoyed by the merchant class at that time. It contains a small museum.

Axbridge, at junction of A38 and A371 (39 A7)

Loughwood Meeting House is made of local sandstone and stands within a small burial ground.

Lawrence House, Cornwall This country town house, built in 1753, typifies the character of Castle Street, the attractive street in which it is situated. It contains a local museum.

Castle Street, Launceston (37 G2)

Loughwood Meeting House, Devon Built in the mid seventeenth century by Baptists from Kilmington, the Loughwood Meeting House stands in remote wooded countryside and is an unusual survival of an early Nonconformist chapel. The interior, which has a plastered barrel ceiling, contains simple, original eighteenth-century fittings.

1M S of Dalwood (38 F6)

Martock: The Treasurer's House, Somerset A small thirteenth- and fourteenth-century house, containing an interesting medieval hall and kitchen and a fine collar-braced timber roof. It was once the home of the Treasurer of Wells Cathedral. (Open by written appointment.)

1M NW of A303 between Ilminster and Ilchester, opposite Martock church (39 D8)

Muchelney Priest's House, Somerset This late medieval house with its large Gothic hall window was originally the residence of the secular priests serving the parish church. (Open by written appointment with the tenant.)

1½M S of Langport (39 D7/8)

Old Blundell's School, Devon This is the famous grammar school in Tiverton, Devon, which was built by a local clothier, Peter Blundell, in 1604. When a new school was built in 1882, the old building was converted into dwelling houses. Old Blundell's School is the setting for a dramatic fight in R. D. Blackmore's classic novel *Lorna Doone*.

Station Road, Tiverton (38 E3)

Old Post Office, Tintagel, Cornwall Used as Tintagel's Post Office (for incoming mail only) between 1844 and 1892, the Old Post Office is a very small, fourteenth-century stone manor house, with an ancient roof of uneven slates. The large hall is open to the roof.

In village centre, off B3263 (34 B/C1)

Shute Barton, Devon The remains of a fourteenth- to sixteenth-century manor house, whose battlemented tower and late Gothic windows still look attractive from the outside. Inside, a newel stair, a large open fireplace, a collar-beam hall roof and a late seventeenth-century panelled room survive. The detached gatehouse dates from the 1570s, but has nineteenth-century alterations.

3M SW of Axminster, entrance on B3161 (38 G6)

Stoke-sub-Hamdon Priory, Somerset Built of Ham Hill stone in the fourteenth and fifteenth centuries, Stoke-sub-Hamdon Priory formerly housed the priests of the chantry of St Nicholas in a nearby manor house, Beauchamp, which no longer exists. The great hall and screens passage of the chantry house remain, although only the former and the ruins are open.

2M W of Montacute, just N of A3088 (39 D/E8)

Watersmeet Cottage, Devon This nineteenth-century fishing lodge near Lynmouth serves as a National Trust Information Centre.

E of Lynmouth, close to A39 (36 A6)

Wellington Monument, Somerset A 175-foot-high obelisk designed by Thomas Lee (the architect of *Arlington Court*) and built 1817–18 to commemorate the military achievements of the Duke of Wellington. There are breathtaking views from the top.

2M S Wellington (38 E5)

West Pennard Court Barn, Somerset A fifteenth-century barn with five bays and an interesting roof. (Open on application.)

3M E of Glastonbury, S of West Pennard (39 C8/9)

Widecombe-in-the-Moor: Church House, Devon This fifteenth-century granite building near Widecombe-in-the-Moor church is used partly as a cottage with a National Trust Information Centre and shop, and partly as a village hall.

6M NW of Ashburton (37 H6)

Archaeological & Industrial Sites

Bolt Tail, Devon Bolt Tail Camp is an Iron Age promontory fort west of Salcombe, above the lovely beach of Hope Cove.

2½M W of Salcombe (37 L5/6)

Brean Down, Somerset There is a small Iron Age promontory fort on this 300-foot high headland, as well as field systems and evidence of occupation from Beaker times onwards.

2M SW of Weston-super-Mare (56 H6)

Cadsonbury, Cornwall This is an important hill-fort crowning a steep, isolated hill in the valley of the River Lynher. As yet unexcavated, it probably dates from the early Iron Age in the third to fifth centuries BC.

2M SW of Callington (35 C10)

Cerne Giant, Dorset Thought to date from Roman times, this 180-foot high figure is cut into the chalk of the hillside above the village of Cerne Abbas. The naked Giant brandishes a 120-foot-long club. He is thought to represent either a Celtic deity or the classical Hercules, but whichever, he must have been a local cult figure. (Best viewed from lay-by on A352.)

8M N of Dorchester (39 F10)

Chapel Carn Brea, Cornwall This 657-foot high hill, the most westerly on the British mainland, includes several Bronze Age barrows.

3M NE of Land's End (34 G1)

Coneys Castle, Dorset The defences on this hilltop belong to an Iron Age hill-fort.

6M E of Axminster, adjacent to Lambert's Castle Hill (39 F7)

Cornish Beam Engines, Cornwall Five Cornish beam engines, which were used to bring steam power to the Cornish mining industry, belong to the Trust, and are an interesting relic of the earliest stages of Britain's Industrial Revolution. The easiest to see are at **Holman's Museum,** Camborne (34 F3/4), and at the **East Pool and Agar Mine,** Camborne (34 F3/4), reached from an entrance on the A3047. The other engines are at the **Levant Mine,** St Just, which can be visited by arrangement (34 F1), and at the **South**

Crofty Mine, Camborne, which is not a working mine and therefore not open at present (34 F3/4). The tin mine pithead at Redruth (34 F4) is also open to the public. **Trevithick's Cottage**, the birthplace of the engineer Richard Trevithick (1771–1833), at Lower Penponds, Camborne, also belongs to the Trust and may be visited on application (34 F3/4).

The Dodman, Cornwall There are a well-preserved Iron Age promontory fort and the remains of a medieval field system on Dodman Point.

4M S of Mevagissey *(35 F7)*

Exmoor, Somerset Exmoor includes several interesting prehistoric sites: the Bronze Age barrow group known as the **Wambarrows**, and the **Caratacus Stone**, are on Winsford Hill, between Exford and Dulverton (38 C2); and the hill-fort of **Bury Castle** is on the Holnicote Estate, east and south of Porlock (38 B2). The Holnicote Estate also includes several groups of round barrows and a stone circle.

Goodameavy, Devon This south-west corner of Dartmoor is rich in prehistoric sites: the remains of an Iron Age promontory fort on the **Dewerstone Rock**, and Early to Middle Bronze Age hut circles on **Wigford Down**. An unusual pottery cup, probably dating from the Middle Bronze Age, was found at Dewerstone in 1960, and is now in Plymouth City Museum.

6M NE of Plymouth, near Clearbrook *(37 J4)*

Hembury, Devon Hembury Castle, on the 500-foot summit of Hembury, is an Iron Age hill-fort.

2M N of Buckfastleigh *(37 J6)*

Hentor, Devon The Trust's holdings at Hentor, Willings Walls and Trowlesworthy Warrens (see also entry under *Coast and Countryside*) were well populated in prehistoric times, and include a large number of ruined cists with partial covering cairns, more than a hundred hut circles, many enclosure walls, a standing stone, and possibly a stone circle, all of the Bronze Age.

On SW flank of Dartmoor *(37 J4/5)*

High Ham Mill, Somerset This is a thatched windmill, dating from 1820, which was in regular use until 1910. (Open by appointment.)

2M N of Langport, ½M E High Ham *(39 C7/8)*

Lambert's Castle Hill, Dorset This Iron Age hill-fort has more recently been the site of an annual pony fair. Wide views east and west.

5½M E of Axminster *(39 F7)*

Lanyon Quoit, Cornwall This huge granite capstone, on three upright stones, re-erected in 1824, is the remains of a megalithic chambered long barrow dating from 2000–1600 BC, and is one of the south-west's most famous prehistoric sites.

4M NW of Penzance *(34 F1/2)*

Maen Castle, Cornwall An Iron Age cliff castle on the Mayon and Trevescan cliffs between Sennen Cove and Land's End. *(34 G1)*

Old Mill, Wembury, Devon This medieval mill house stands on the shoreline of Wembury Bay, and is run as a shop.

5–6M E of Plymouth *(35 E12)*

Rough Tor, Cornwall There is a Bronze Age settlement site, preserving hut circles and enclosed fields, some with lynchets, on Rough Tor, the bleak moorland peak on Bodmin Moor.

3M SE of Camelford *(35 B8)*

Tolpuddle Martyrs' Monument, Dorset A seat commemorates the six Dorset farm labourers sentenced to transportation in 1834 for trying to form a trade union.

7M NE of Dorchester, on S side of A35 *(39 G11)*

Trencrom Hill, Cornwall A well-preserved Iron Age B hill-fort, stone-walled and enclosing hut circles, can be seen on this gorse-covered hill overlooking a wide panorama of countryside and the sea.

3M S of St Ives *(34 F2)*

Treryn Dinas (Treen Castle), Cornwall This is an Iron Age cliff castle of uncertain date consisting of a series of banks and ditches. Close by there is the famous, rocking Logan rock, a natural wonder.

4M SE of Land's End *(34 G1)*

Wind Hill, Lynmouth, Devon Countisbury Camp, an early Iron Age linear earthwork, is on Wind Hill, between Countisbury and the sea, while there are also two defensive earthworks on the spur of Myrtlebury Cleave.

E of Lynmouth, beside A39 *(38 A1)*

Wheal Betsy, Devon This is the roofless engine house and stack of an abandoned lead mine on Black Down, on the edge of Dartmoor. A romantic and picturesque industrial relic.

5M N of Tavistock, just E of A386 *(37 H4)*

Wheal Coates, Cornwall The ruined buildings and engine houses of the disused tin and copper mines of Wheal Coates, Towanwroath, Wheal Charlotte and Charlotte United stand on the cliff and heath-covered moorland of the Trust's holding at Chapel Porth, and can be reached on foot.

1½M SW of St Agnes *(34 E4)*

Wheal Prosper, Cornwall The dramatic ruin of the engine house and stack of the Wheal Prosper tin and copper mine, which was abandoned in about 1860, dominates Rinsey Cliff above sandy Porthcew Cove.

1½M SW of Ashton *(34 G3)*

The 1892 Harvey water pumping engine at Taylor's Shaft, East Pool mine.

The romantic ruin of Wheal Betsy stands on the western edge of Dartmoor.

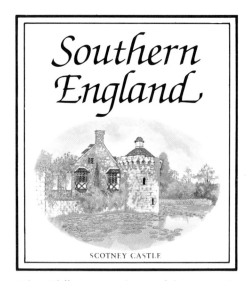

Southern England

SCOTNEY CASTLE

The long, narrow strip that makes up this region – about 160 miles east to west but only forty miles north to south – is unified by the fact that chalk underlies most of it. The well-drained chalk lands gave early man access to the interior of the country, along downland routes like the Ridgeway and the Pilgrims' Way, and these prehistoric links are reflected in National Trust properties such as Cissbury Ring on the South Downs, the Coldrum Long Barrow on the North Downs, and above all in Avebury stone circle to the west.

This ancient region also contains the seed from which the whole wide-branching tree of the National Trust grew – the little Clergy House at Alfriston, on the South Downs behind Eastbourne, which was the first building ever bought by the Trust. Compared with the great mansions acquired since – Knole, Ham, The Vyne or Petworth – it is a pygmy among a group of giants; but it is linked to them by a host of intermediate-sized buildings, from small manor houses to water-mills, which cover the whole range of our ancestors' homes and places of work.

Leaving aside the Iron Age forts and the stronghold of Bodiam Castle, it is a region of peace rather than war; and the Trust's properties reflect this, in their emphasis on fine collections of paintings and furniture, in their gardens and arboreta, and in the domestication of their settings, which are lacking in any wildness or harshness.

Coast & Countryside

All the south coast resorts, from Ramsgate round almost to Bournemouth, come into this region; and the towns' insatiable appetite for building land has meant that the Trust's acquisitions have been of the greatest importance. The Trust has no properties at all on the north Kent coast. They begin south of the Kentish Stour, at **Sandwich Bay** (43 B12). Nearly 200 acres of estuary land are run as a nature reserve here by the Kent Trust for Nature Conservation. Heading south to Dover and beyond, the Trust has farmland above the

White Cliffs to east and west of the port, with two-thirds of a mile of cliff-top walk above St **Margaret's Bay** (43 D12), and one mile or so westward from **Shakespeare Cliff**, above the old Channel Tunnel workings just west of Dover harbour (43 D11).

West of Romney Marsh towards Hastings there are two more fair-sized areas of farmland – nearly 400 acres in and around **Winchelsea** (43 F8), including the meadows that provide the background to Millais' painting of the *Blind Girl* (in the Birmingham Art Gallery); and more than 200 acres, including cliffland, at **Fairlight** (43 G7). Between Beachy Head and Seaford the Trust has a large holding of cliffland (42 H4). Central to this stretch are the spectacular **Seven Sisters**; the Trust has over 600 acres of farmland between the A259 and the cliffs, and further land on the Beachy Head side of Birling Gap. Along the rest of the South Downs coast its properties are mainly inland, like the lofty summits of **Ditchling Beacon** (42 G2) and **Cissbury Ring** (41 E12), and the 3,500 acres of the **Slindon Estate** (41 E11), inland from Bognor.

West of Chichester the Trust has fifty or so acres of dune and saltings at **East Head** (41 F9), which guards the entrance to Chichester Harbour opposite Hayling Island; while inside that sailor's paradise of small creeks and marinas it maintains **Quay Meadow** at Bosham (41 F9) – an acre of grass between the church and the water of the creek.

In contrast to the Trust's precarious grip on the south coast, it has so much property on the Isle of Wight – about 5,000 acres – that the island might almost be regarded as the Trust's private domain. The two main promontories, **St Catherine's Point** to the south (40 H6) and the **Needles Headland** at the westernmost

The Trust's meadow at Bosham. It may have been here that King Canute attempted to turn back the tide.

Box Hill rises to nearly 700 feet and is one of the best-known beauty-spots in south-east England.

extremity (40 G/H4/5), belong to the Trust, as does **Tennyson Down**, near Easton (40 G/H5), where the poet used to ramble when he lived at Farringford near by. The Needles Headland is a Site of Special Scientific Interest; rising to nearly 500 feet, it is a sanctuary for sea-birds. Apart from the downland areas, both on the coast and inland, the Trust owns the entire **Newtown River estuary** (40 G5/6) on the north side of the island, with footpaths giving views

over the Solent and plenty of sea-birds.

There is a cluster of important Trust properties in the Haslemere area on the border of West Sussex and Surrey: **Blackdown** (41 C10), 600 acres; **Woolbeding Common** (41 D10), more than 1,000 acres; **Frensham Common** (41 B9/10), 900 acres; and biggest of all **Hindhead Common** (41 C10), nearly 1,100 acres, with the great wooded valley of the Devil's Punch Bowl at its eastern edge.

Some twenty or so miles to the north-east another cluster of Trust-owned areas of countryside is dominated by the steep chalk bastion of **Box Hill** (42 C1). Like the Alfriston Clergy House, Box Hill was a key purchase for the Trust, as it was the first major piece of countryside it bought. The 230 acres of the Hill cost £16,000 in 1913, and now form the nucleus of the Trust's properties round Dorking, which total more than 6,500 acres. Box Hill is of major interest to naturalists, as it is one of the few areas on the North Downs without grazing animals or arable farming, and so the plant life grows unchecked, apart from the control exercised by forestry operations. The box trees from which it gets its name can still be found here and there; there are yew, ash and many other tree varieties; and the animals include roe and fallow deer, and colonies of badgers. Box Hill adjoins the bracken-covered expanses of **Headley Heath** (42 C1), on the summit of the Downs; while across on the west side of the valley of the River Mole (the route taken by the Dorking–Leatherhead road), **Ranmore** and **Bookham Commons** (41 A12) total up to a further 900 acres between them.

These naturalists' paradises would have delighted Gilbert White, the quiet eighteenth-century clergyman who lived at Selborne across the Hampshire border from Surrey. Here the Trust owns about 250 acres of **Selborne Hill** (41 C8/9), with its beech hangers and meadows, which White described meticulously in his *Natural History of Selborne*, jotting down his day-to-day observations in his ever-fresh *Naturalist's Journal*. Gilbert White fought against an enclosure scheme that threatened his beloved hangers. Had he lived a century longer, he might well have been a founder-member of the National Trust.

left **Gilbert White** recorded many observations in the beech woods behind Selborne in his *Natural History*.

above **Kipling's study at Bateman's.** The walnut writing chair is fitted with blocks to raise it to the right height.

right **Alfriston Clergy House** was built in about 1350 and designed for a small community of parish priests.

Houses, Gardens & Parks

Alfriston Clergy House, East Sussex One of the few pre-Reformation clergy houses remaining in England, it was the first building acquired by the National Trust, who bought it in 1896 for only £10. Built about 1350, it is a thatched and timbered building, with wattle and daub between the timbers, and a fine king-post roof in the hall. As late as the seventeenth century it was still lived in by the vicar, but it then became a farm labourer's cottage. By 1890 it was so dilapidated that it was proposed to pull it down. Fortunately it was saved by the combined protests of the vicar of the time and the Sussex Archaeological Society.

In Alfriston, 4M NE Seaford, E of B2108 (42 H4)

Bateman's, East Sussex Bateman's, where Rudyard Kipling lived from 1902 until his death in 1936, is a handsome stone-gabled building, with mullioned windows and brick chimneys. It was built by a local ironmaster about 1634, though parts of it are probably earlier; the stone comes from a quarry near by and has rusted in stripes where the iron ore runs through it. The rooms that are open form

a Kipling museum, with his upstairs study looking very much as he left it, the walls lined with novels, poetry and travel books, and the inkwell and pipe cleaners still lying on the desk.

Many of Kipling's best-known books were written at Bateman's, including *Puck of Pook's Hill* (1906), the hill of the title being visible from one of the bedrooms. *If*, the most famous of all his poems, was also written here.

The fine garden, largely planned by Kipling himself, leads down to the little River Dudwell. The water-mill that Kipling harnessed for electricity when he first came to Bateman's has been restored, and is now used for grinding flour sold in the Trust shop.

½M S Burwash, off A265 (42 F5)

Cedar House, Surrey Now an old people's home, this imposing red-brick house looks out across the River Mole. The river façade dates from the eighteenth century, but behind there is a far older building, basically of the fifteenth century, with a fine timbered dining-hall. This is lit by a large traceried Gothic window, which was removed from a Yorkshire church and

The design of Clandon Park betrays the origins of its Italian architect, Leoni.

An anonymous oil painting of Claremont (c.1740) showing Bridgeman's amphitheatre and Kent's lake with its island pavilion.

incorporated into Cedar House in the 1920s. The splendid wrought-iron gate comes from the house of the playwright Sheridan (*see also Polesden Lacey*) at Eltham, and incorporates his monogram. (House seen by appointment.)

On N side of A245, E side of old Cobham (85 H12)

Chartwell, Kent The home of Sir Winston Churchill from 1922 until his death in 1965, Chartwell evokes the spirit of one of the giants of the twentieth century. It stands in a south-facing combe with spectacular views across the Weald, and is basically a brick Victorian country house, remodelled by the architect Philip Tilden.

Chartwell embodies the private rather than the public face of Churchill, though there are plenty of mementoes of his long and active life, from the Boer War poster offering £25 for him 'dead or alive' to the assorted *objets d'art*, given to him by international statesmen and assembled in the Museum Room. There is a collection of his more exotic clothes, such as the full dress of Warden of the Cinque Ports, and a green velvet siren suit. The creative side of his nature is reflected both in the study where he wrote his *History of the English-Speaking Peoples* and other major works, and in his own paintings, which hang on the walls of Chartwell.

The garden reflects another side of Churchill's creativity, especially the famous wall round the kitchen garden, which he built as a hobby when he was in the political wilderness during the 1920s and 1930s. This part of the garden includes the 'Golden Rose Garden', planted in 1958 to mark the Churchills'

The study at Chartwell is as Churchill left it in 1964, with pictures and photographs of family and friends.

golden wedding with thirty-two yellow and gold species of rose.

(*Note:* Chartwell is liable to be extremely crowded, especially during the summer months. Visitors often have to wait a considerable time before entering the house, and there is a timed ticket system.)

2M S Westerham, off B2026   (42 C3)

Clandon Park, Surrey Designed by a Venetian architect, Giacomo Leoni, in the 1730s, Clandon is like an Italian villa set down in the Surrey countryside. It was built for Thomas Onslow (the 2nd Baron Onslow), whose family was unique in having provided three Speakers of the House of Commons.

Externally the house is remarkable for the contrast between the white stone of the central section and the red brick of the remainder. Internally the main feature is the Marble Hall, the first room the visitor enters, which runs the full height of both the ground and first floors. Painted white, it has superb plasterwork on the ceiling, representing subjects from classical mythology. The house is unusual in having one oak and one stone staircase of seemingly equal importance on either side of the hall.

The varied collection of furniture, porcelain and metalwork at Clandon came originally from Little Trent Park in Hertfordshire and was left to the National Trust by Mrs David Gubbay. Especially rare are the Chinese porce-

The entrance front of Ham House once had a pair of turrets and a central bay.

lain birds which stand on ledges and in niches round Clandon. In the basement is the restored old kitchen and the Museum of the Queen's Royal Surrey Regiment.

The main feature of the garden is a Maori house, brought home by the 4th Earl Onslow, who was Governor of New Zealand from 1888–92.

West Clandon, 3M E Guildford, on A247 (41 A11)

Robert Adam had his first recorded commission as a decorator at Hatchlands and probably designed the ceiling in this hall.

Great Chalfield Manor is today the centre of an agricultural estate, as it has been for 900 years.

Claremont Landscape Garden, Surrey Tucked away beside the old Portsmouth Road, Claremont is the epitome of the development of the eighteenth-century landscape garden, which became popular in reaction to the stiff formality of the seventeenth century. The greatest names in landscape design were associated with Claremont – Charles Bridgeman, who in about 1725 designed the huge grass amphitheatre, the only one of its kind to survive in Europe, setting off the round pond which forms the garden's main feature; William Kent, who in the 1730s enlarged the pond, altering its shape and giving it an island with a pavilion built on it; and Lancelot 'Capability' Brown, who planted trees on the amphitheatre, hiding it from view until it was cleared and restored by the Trust from 1975 to 1977.

Brown was working for Clive of India, who bought Claremont in 1768. One of his alterations was to move the Portsmouth Road a couple of hundred yards away from the lake – an improvement the visitor can appreciate today. Among other features of the garden are a long ha-ha, or sunken barrier, a grotto, a skittle alley and a bowling green.

1M S Esher, on A307 (formerly A3) (86 H1)

The Courts Garden, Wiltshire An interestingly varied garden, around a fine eighteenth-century stone house (house not open). The garden includes lawns with long herbaceous borders, a rectangular lily pond, and a small lake surrounded with gunnera and other water-loving plants.

3M N Trowbridge, S side of A3053 (57 H11)

Emmetts Garden, Kent A small, hilltop garden (4 acres) of fine trees and shrubs, with wide-ranging views south across the treetops towards the Bough Beech Reservoir. Some of the shrubs, which include pure white hydrangeas, were planted at the turn of the century. A good time to visit is May, when the bluebells and late daffodils are out.

½M N Ide Hill, near Sevenoaks, 2M S of A25 (42 C4)

Great Chalfield Manor, Wiltshire Great Chalfield was built by Thomas Tropnell, a successful politician and landowner, about 1470: the great hall, with first-floor solar on one side and dining room on the other, was built by Tropnell, though the wall beside the remains of the moat and the gatehouse is earlier, and there has been a good deal of reconstruction since. The house was originally much bigger, as is shown by the foundations that remain in the garden.

Though it is some way south of the Cotswolds, its gables, mullions and mellow stonework give it the look of a typical Cotswold manor. The gable ends are decorated with stone figures of soldiers in fifteenth-century armour, giving an almost playful appearance to the exterior. Inside there are fine beams and a reconstructed musicians' gallery in the main hall. The house's greatest curiosity is the three stone masks, of a bishop with mitre, a king with asses' ears, and a laughing face, which look down into the hall; the eyes are cut away so that the women of Tropnell's household could see what went on in the hall without being seen.

The house was restored in the early years of this century.

4M NE Bradford-on-Avon, off B3109 – there are two driveways, one NW of Broughton Gifford and one near Holt (57 H11)

Ham House, Surrey This grand and melancholy house looks north towards the Thames flowing by a couple of hundred yards away, and south beyond Ham Common to the Surrey hills. Little in it has changed since the period between about 1670 and 1730, when the main structural alterations were made, the furniture and pictures were collected, and the lawns and parterres were laid out.

It was built in 1610 in the reign of James I, but it owes its present appearance, both inside and out, to the Duke and Duchess of Lauderdale, two of the most ambitious and unpleasant characters of the late seventeenth century. A joint portrait of the Lauderdales by Lely hangs in the Round Gallery at Ham.

Externally, Ham is a sober red-brick house; the ground plan is in the form of a shallow U, with the projecting wings on the north or entrance front. Internally it is still largely as the Lauderdales left it, with much the same furniture and pictures. Their positions can be checked from the inventory of 1679 (in the Museum Room), and where the furniture is not original it has been possible to find near-equivalents. The layout of the rooms has the Duke and Duchess's living accommodation on the ground floor, with the state rooms, centring on the Queen's Bedchamber, on the first floor or *piano nobile*.

The most attractive rooms in Ham are not the great rooms so much as the little 'closets' leading off them, full of furniture and pictures, and with richly decorated walls. There are a good many portraits of the Dysart and Tollemache families, related to the Duchess, and some superb Elizabethan miniatures in the small room called the Cabinet of Miniatures.

The garden's formal lawns and parterres are at present being restored to their seventeenth-century appearance, following plans of the Lauderdales' time.

By the Thames, 1M SW Richmond, off the A307 (86 G2)

Hatchlands, Surrey Hatchlands is a foursquare red-brick Georgian country house, only a couple of miles from *Clandon Park*, with which it makes a good contrast. It was built in 1757 for Admiral Boscawen, known as 'Old Dreadnought', who paid for it with prize money won from his victories over the French. The chief feature of the interior (not much of which is shown) is the decoration and plasterwork by Robert Adam. The most notable modern addition is a fine music room, designed by Sir Reginald Blomfield and built about 1903.

Externally there is one strange feature: the main south front has only two storeys, whereas part of the west front has three. This arrangement is due to the internal layout of the house, and six windows on the west front are in fact sham.

Just E of East Clandon, N of A246 (41 A12)

Knole, Kent Set in a magnificent park where deer browse among ancient gnarled trees, Knole must be high on the list for the National Trust's grandest house. It is popularly said to be linked to the days, weeks and months of the year by having 365 rooms, 7 courtyards, 52 staircases and 12 entrances; and its sheer size, best grasped by looking round the exterior before going in, makes it more like a village – or at least a large Oxford or Cambridge college – than a private house. The name comes from the low hill, or knoll, on which it stands.

Knole owes much of its dignified medieval appearance to Thomas Bourchier, Archbishop of Canterbury, who bought it for £266 in 1456 and transformed it into a palace fit for an archbishop. It passed from the Church to the Crown in the 1530s, when Henry VIII hinted to Archbishop Cranmer that he would like it and Cranmer naturally complied; then from the Crown into private ownership in 1566, when Queen Elizabeth I gave it to her cousin Thomas Sackville, whose descendants live in the private quarters of Knole to this day.

The interior of Knole combines the history of the Sackville family with the history of English furniture and design. This historical sense is at its strongest in the Brown Gallery, where rows of portraits gaze down upon seventeenth-century chairs which still keep their original upholstery. Among the furniture are the original drop-end Knole sofa or settee, dating from the time of James I (in the Leicester Gallery), and the silver-mounted table, mirror and candle-stands in the King's Bedroom. The paintings include a series of portraits by Sir Joshua Reynolds (in the Reynolds Room).

The 1,000-acre park is open to the public; it has plenty of hills and valleys, and is an ideal place for a walk on a fine day.

On S side of Sevenoaks, E of A225 (42 C4)

Lacock Abbey, Wiltshire Lacock is the goal of photographers from all over the world, since it was here, in 1835, that William Henry Fox Talbot made what is generally acknowledged as the world's first photographic negative. This was of the latticed oriel window in the South Gallery, where a print from that first negative, hardly bigger than a postage stamp, hangs near the window.

The Abbey is also of great architectural interest. A medieval nunnery was founded among the Lacock watermeadows in 1232 by Ela, Countess of Salisbury, who became the first abbess. Though it was dissolved by Henry VIII in 1539, fortunately the monastic buildings largely survived. In the mid eighteenth century, Lacock Abbey was in the forefront of the Gothic Revival, when the lofty Great Hall was rebuilt in Gothick style by John Ivory

Talbot, Fox Talbot's great-grandfather. As it now stands, Lacock Abbey is a mixture of styles – medieval cloisters, Tudor stable court (shown in a number of Fox Talbot's early photographs), and the Gothick Hall.

A large barn outside the Abbey gates has been converted into an excellent small museum (the Fox Talbot Museum) tracing the history of photography.

Lacock village is now largely owned by the National Trust. It is a perfect, small, mainly stone-built village with a street plan in the form of a square, and with medieval timbered buildings here and there. There is a medieval packhorse bridge and a ford down a lane near the church.

3M S Chippenham, E of A350 (57 G12)

Lamb House, East Sussex A fine Georgian town house facing down a cobbled street in Rye, Lamb House is chiefly famous today for its connection with the American novelist Henry James, who lived in it from 1897 until shortly before his death in 1916. The house takes its name from James Lamb, the founder of a leading Rye family, who built it in 1723.

The small garden room where James wrote his novels was destroyed by a bomb in 1940. Mementoes of the author are kept in the Henry James Room.

West Street in the centre of Rye (43 F8)

Mompesson House, Wiltshire With its elegant stone façade looking across Choristers' Green to the soaring spire of Salisbury Cathedral, Mompesson House is the epitome of the Queen Anne town house. It was built about 1701 for Charles Mompesson, a Salisbury lawyer, and is chiefly remarkable for its superb interior

The famous silver furniture in the King's Bedroom at Knole, dating from the seventeenth century, is a rare survival.

The fine urban architecture of Mompesson House is shown here in a watercolour by George Henton (dated 1888).

moulded plasterwork, especially in the staircase hall, which dates from the 1740s, and includes flowers, fruit and even the head of King Midas with asses' ears. The comprehensive collection of over 370 English glasses assembled by Mr O. G. N. Turnbull is kept at Mompesson, and there are a number of pictures from *Stourhead*.

The brick-built back of the house is much less grand than the front, and looks out over a neat town garden.

In Salisbury Cathedral Close (40 C3)

Monks House, East Sussex A small weatherboarded house, down the lane in the centre of Rodmell village. Virginia Woolf lived here with her husband Leonard, from 1919 until her death in 1941. (Due to be opened in 1982.)

Rodmell, 3M S Lewes, on the A275 (42 G3)

Mottisfont Abbey, Hampshire Mottisfont is remarkable for the beauty of its setting, among lawns shadowed by vast cedar trees and a giant London plane, and with the Test flowing crystal-clear along the east side of the garden (since 1972 enhanced by an old-fashioned rose collection). It is also an extraordinary architectural blend of medieval, Tudor and Georgian elements. The original priory of Augustinian Canons was founded here in 1201. Dissolved at the Reformation in 1536, it was given by Henry VIII to his Lord Chamberlain, William Lord Sandys, whose main house was *The Vyne*. Instead of adapting the monk's living quarters, Sandys set about turning the priory church into a house, knocking down the north transept and choir, and keeping the nave, the base of the tower and the south transept, which he converted into a U-shaped Tudor mansion. The

Mottisfont's elegant south front was the final stage in the transformation of the abbey into a country house.

final adaptation came in the 1740s, when Sir Richard Mill turned it all into a Georgian country gentleman's home, reducing the projecting Tudor wings in size and building the elegant, red-brick south front, with its sash windows and pediment.

Internally, the outstanding feature of the house is the Whistler Room, which takes its name from the wall and ceiling decoration by Rex Whistler, painted in 1938–9. The *trompe l'oeil* painting, done with amazing lightness and delicacy, gives the effect of moulded plasterwork, though it is all painted on the flat.

4M NW Romsey, W of A3057 (40 C5)

Nymans Garden, West Sussex Nymans, conceived in 1885 by Ludwig Messel, is a garden that has something for all garden-lovers – huge red and white rhododendrons bursting into bloom in May, a heather garden with heather shoulder-high, formal topiary and carefully tended herbaceous borders, a gazebo crowned by a dovecote full of white doves. There is even a romantic ruin, in the form of the stone shell of the great house, much of which was gutted by fire in 1947 and now forms the background to the lawns and flowering shrubs. The sections of the garden form an attractive series of outdoor 'rooms', such as the Sunk Garden, which has a white Byzantine urn as its centrepiece.

4½M S Crawley, off M23/A23 (42 E2)

Old Soar Manor, Kent Originally a complete medieval manor stood on the site, but in the eighteenth century the main hall block was demolished and the present Georgian farmhouse built in its place. However, the original solar block remains; this was the lord of the

manor's private quarters, and the solar, on the first floor, would have had a small viewing window through into the hall, as at *Great Chalfield*. Two small rooms lead out of the solar, a chapel in one corner and a *garderobe* or lavatory in the other. The ground floor consists of a vaulted undercroft and a *garderobe* pit that could be cleaned out.

1M E Plaxtol, off A227 (42 C5)

Owletts, Kent A handsome brick house of Charles II's time, built for a prosperous Kentish farmer, Bonham Hayes. Above the staircase well is a fine moulded plaster ceiling, dated 1684. Sir Herbert Baker, architect of the Bank of England and Lutyens' partner in New Delhi, was born and lived at Owletts until his death in 1946.

In Cobham village, off A2 (42 A5)

Petworth House and Park, West Sussex With its great main front, some 300 feet long, Petworth looks westwards across superb parkland, immortalized by Turner in a number of his finest landscapes. In many respects Petworth is as much an art gallery as it is a country house, since the ground-floor rooms are given over to paintings, from Italian primitives to the canvases of Turner himself. The present house is a virtually complete unity, as it was built almost entirely between 1688 and 1696 by Charles Seymour, the 6th Duke of Somerset, known as the 'Proud Duke' from his arrogant nature. There was a medieval manor house on the site, which belonged to the Percy family (the Earls of Northumberland) from the twelfth to the seventeenth century, but all that survives of this ancient building is the chapel and parts of the basement, embedded in the Proud Duke's mansion. Some alterations were made to the south and east fronts in the mid nineteenth century.

Apart from the Turners (all brought together

The Italian fountain in the centre of the walled garden at Nymans is guarded by four old topiary pieces.

interest in the estate as in the house, planting no fewer than 20,000 trees which have grown into the fine specimens that now surround Polesden Lacey.

After various alterations and enlargements through the nineteenth century, the house was taken in hand in 1906 by the Hon. Mrs Greville. A leading society hostess in Edwardian times and later, she was also a great collector of paintings, porcelain and fine furniture. At her death in 1942, the house and its contents passed by bequest to the Trust. Her chief memorial is the sumptuously decorated drawing room, the walls glittering with mirrors and gilding, filled with the Louis XV and XVI furniture popular in the early years of this century.

The finest of the paintings are assembled in the corridor around the central courtyard; they include a delicate little Perugino, a number of sixteenth-century French court portraits, and some typical Dutch landscapes.

During the summer there is a short season of plays in the open-air theatre at the edge of a copse in the grounds.

3M NW Dorking, 1½M S Great Bookham, off the A246 (41 A12)

The delightful rococo decoration of the White and Gold Drawing Room at Petworth (*above*) was an eighteenth-century addition to the Proud Duke's house (*right*).

in the Turner Room), there are several portraits of the Northumberlands, including a sombre Van Dyck, some fine Dutch landscapes, and a whole room, somewhat flatteringly known as the 'Beauty Room', devoted to the ladies of Queen Anne's court. Turner's patron at Petworth, the 3rd Earl of Egremont, added the T-shaped North Gallery, which is filled with statues and busts and lined with pictures. The Proud Duke commissioned Grinling Gibbons to work at Petworth, and among Petworth's artistic triumphs are Gibbons' limewood carvings of dead game, fruit, flowers and musical instruments that riot over the wall surfaces of the Carved Room.

Petworth Park, visible to motorists over the wall as they approach Petworth along the A272, is still very much as Turner painted it, with deer browsing on the turf.

In Petworth, junction of A272/A283 (41 D11)

Philipps House, Dinton Park, Wiltshire An austere country house set in gently rolling parkland, Philipps House was built in 1814–17 for William Wyndham, whose family had lived in Dinton since the end of the seventeenth century. The architect was Jeffry Wyatt (later Sir Jeffry Wyatville), and the house has a neo-classical appearance, with an imposing south portico and symmetrical façade. It is built of Chilmark limestone, from a quarry whose stone had been used for Salisbury Cathedral 600 years previously. The main internal feature is

the grand staircase, lit from above by a circular lantern window. Ducted air heating was installed as early as the 1820s.

Philipps House is let to the YWCA as a conference centre and subject to limited viewing.

9M W Salisbury, on N side of B3089 (40 C2)

Polesden Lacey, Surrey Polesden Lacey has a comfortably opulent appearance. Tucked away in glorious countryside on the fringes of the North Downs, it is a low sprawling house, yellow-stuccoed and white-painted, set above sloping lawns and looking across to the woodlands of *Ranmore Common*. A succession of houses has stood on the site since the Middle Ages; Polesden's most famous owner was the playwright Richard Brinsley Sheridan, who lived there from 1797 to 1818. The present house is basically a Regency country villa, built in the 1820s for Joseph Bonsor to designs by Thomas Cubitt. Bonsor took as much

Quebec House, Kent Quebec House is a compact Tudor brick building, with a remarkable number of gables. It owes its fame to its connection with General Wolfe, the hero of the Heights of Abraham, who lived there for the first decade of his life (1727–38); Wolfe's statue is just up the hill, on the village green, as is that of Churchill, who lived at *Chartwell* nearby. The downstairs rooms are full of Wolfe possessions, such as his field canteen, and the dressing gown in which his body was brought back to England after he was killed at Quebec in 1759. A museum displays Wolfe relics.

At E end of Westerham, N side of A25 (42 C3)

St John's Jerusalem Garden, Kent The garden of St John's is an oasis of peace away from the main-road traffic and industry of Dartford. In the Middle Ages St John's was a 'commandery' (manor) of the Knights Hospitallers, a half-military, half-religious order. Henry VIII dissolved the Hospitallers in 1540, and their buildings were pulled down, apart from the former chapel which is open to the public. The brick house on the site was probably built about 1700 by Abraham Hill, who was one of the founders of the Royal Society and introduced cider-making from Devon to Kent; and from 1755 to 1776 Edward Hasted, the leading county historian of Kent, lived there. The moated garden has some splendid specimen trees, including the 'Napoleon willow', descended from the St Helena willows under which the Emperor was buried.

Sutton-at-Hone, 3M S Dartford, on E side of A225 (42 A4)

The white garden at Sissinghurst is perhaps the most original of the outdoor 'rooms'.

Sheffield Park is magnificent in the autumnal colouring of its trees and shrubs.

Polesden Lacey. The garden front on the left looks over a great lawn and is fronted by superb eighteenth-century urns.

Scotney Castle Garden, Kent A magnificently romantic landscape garden, Scotney is largely the creation of Edward Hussey, who from 1837 to 1843 built himself a new house (not open) designed by Anthony Salvin on top of the hill and turned old Scotney Castle into a picturesque centrepiece. The round stone tower of the medieval castle, reflected in the moat and backed by plantings of rhododendrons, azaleas and specimen trees, is a prospect that offers something new from all angles, and in all weathers and seasons. Apart from the tower, built about 1380, old Scotney is mainly seventeenth-century in date.

1½M S Lamberhurst, on the A21 (42 D/E5/6)

Sheffield Park Garden, East Sussex These famous gardens, covering some 100 acres and laid out round a series of lakes, were originally designed about 1775 by 'Capability' Brown for John Baker Holroyd, the 1st Earl of Sheffield. The five lakes stretch in the form of an inverted T below Holroyd's Gothic Revival house designed by James Wyatt in 1779 (not NT and not open). The gardens are a tree-lover's delight; many of the superb conifers were planted by the 3rd Earl towards the end of the nineteenth century, and have now reached full maturity, but the present appearance of the garden owes much to Arthur G. Soames, who acquired it in 1909.

The best time to see the gardens is in late October, when the leaves, especially those of the tupelo trees, are in their full autumn glory, but they are well worth a visit in late spring, when the rhododendrons and azaleas are in bloom.

5M NW Uckfield, E side of A275 (42 F3)

Sissinghurst Castle Garden, Kent All that survives of Sissinghurst Castle, a moated Tudor manor house built about 1550 by Sir John Baker, is a long low gatehouse, a tall red-brick tower and two isolated cottages beyond. These were the fragments round which Victoria Sackville-West and her husband Harold Nicolson built their famous garden, using the buildings and various brick walls to create a series of open-air 'rooms' – miniature gardens, each with a different theme, leading into one another.

When they came to Sissinghurst in 1930, the task must have seemed almost impossible; it took three years before the rubbish of generations of neglect had been cleared and they could embark on serious planting. Apart from individual beauties like the cottage garden where flowers of all sorts grow in jumbled profusion, the medieval-looking herb garden, and the white garden entirely planted with white or grey plants, Sissinghurst has an incomparably beautiful setting, in one of the lushest corners of Kent.

The tower rooms can be visited. The first floor was Victoria Sackville-West's writing room, and is as she left it; the second floor is a small museum devoted to the history of Sissinghurst; and the third floor houses an exhibition illustrating the work of the National Trust. The long library in the entrance block can also be seen.

2M NE Cranbrook, off the A262 (43 D7)

Smallhythe Place, Kent This timber-framed yeoman's house, built in the sixteenth century, was the home of the actress Ellen Terry from 1899 until her death in 1928, and now houses a theatrical museum illustrating her career as well as her interest in the theatre and its history. In the Middle Ages Smallhythe was the port of Tenterden for shipping coming up the Rother, and the house was built for the harbour-master; the rectangular pond below was once the repair dock.

Born in Coventry in 1847, Ellen Terry first appeared on the stage in 1856. Her last appearance was in 1926, only two years before her death. The exhibits at Smallhythe include costumes, many of them from her Shakespearean roles; portraits; and mementoes of some of the greatest names in acting.

2M S Tenterden, on the B2082 (43 E7)

Sprivers Garden, Kent A small garden, whose shrubs, herbaceous borders and spring and

27

The drawing room at Standen has a superb Morris carpet and original electric light brackets designed by Webb.

summer bedding form the background to a display of garden ornaments.

Horsmonden, 3M N Lamberhurst, on B2162 (42 D6)

Standen, West Sussex Standen was built in 1892–4 for James Beale, a prosperous solicitor, and his wife Margaret, by Philip Webb the friend and colleague of William Morris, and is the only one of Webb's major houses to remain intact. The interior was decorated with Morris and Co. textiles and wallpapers, and many of them survive. It stands on a terrace, half way down a steep hill with wide views southwards across Weir Wood Reservoir to the high ground of Ashdown Forest beyond.

Like Morris, Webb set great store by good materials and craftsmanship; and both can be found in abundance at Standen. The main front is on the garden side, facing the view, and is remarkable for its row of five weather-boarded gables. Webb cleverly linked the new house to the old farmyard at the back of the site; the stone he used comes from a quarry that now forms part of the garden.

1½M S East Grinstead (signposted from B2110) (42 D3)

Stoneacre, Kent A fine Kentish yeoman's house of about 1480, rescued from dereliction by Aymer Vallance in 1920 and restored and enlarged by the addition of two timber-framed houses from Faversham and Chiddingstone. Its most striking features are a twelve-light oriel window giving on to the great hall, an oak screen across the hall, and a rare king-post, made of four engaged shafts, supporting the roof.

Otham, 3M SE Maidstone, 1M N of A274 (43 C7)

Stourhead, Wiltshire The grounds of Stourhead are an idealized Italian landscape, like one of those painted by Claude, set down in the Wiltshire countryside. The dream was made reality by Henry Hoare II (a member of the famous banking family) from 1741, when he came to settle at Stourhead, until his death in 1785. All the elements of the dream landscape are there: the broad lake, reflecting the trees and shrubs that come down to the water's edge; the domed temples; the stone bridge that forms an attractive foreground to the picture; the grotto, complete with river god and nymph, built over the spring where the Stour rises.

The gardens are the part of Stourhead that most people visit, but it is well worth visiting the house as well; it lies on high ground above the lake, invisible both from the lakeside paths

An early nineteenth-century watercolour of Stourhead showing the lake, the Pantheon and the Temple of Apollo (*left*).

and from Stourton village. The Stourton estate was bought by Henry Hoare II's father, Henry Hoare I, in 1717. He commissioned Colen Campbell to build him a new villa in the Palladian style (the central block of Stourhead) – a severely classical stone building, with a grand porticoed entrance front on the east side. Henry II was more interested in the grounds than the house, and his excursions into architecture were limited to the temples and other buildings designed by Henry Flitcroft which are set round the lake. The main additions were made by Sir Richard Colt Hoare, 2nd Baronet, Henry II's grandson, in the 1790s; an antiquarian, scholar and amateur artist, he built the two projecting wings for his books and his

picture collection. The library is a splendid room, with a barrel-vaulted ceiling. Its furniture, including a fine flight of library steps, was made by Thomas Chippendale the Younger in the early 1800s.

The little village of Stourton, down by the lake, enjoys an idyllic setting. The medieval church has several monuments to the Stourton family and the Hoares.

3M NW Mere (A303), off B3092 (39 C11)

Tudor Yeoman's House, Kent A fourteenth-century hall house, bought and restored by Sir Herbert Baker (*see also Owletts*). The hall has a magnificent main beam and king-post. (Seen by appointment only.)

Sole Street, 1M SW Cobham, on B2009 (42 A5)

Uppark, West Sussex There can be few houses that owe their existence to a mechanical device, but Uppark is one of them. As its name suggests (it was originally split into Up Park), it stands very high up, on the summit of the South Downs; and it was not until Uppark's owner, Sir Edward Ford, invented a satisfactory water pump in about 1650 that it became possible to build a large house on the site. Uppark is a big square red-brick house, looking like a giant doll's house (suitably enough, as one of its prize exhibits is an eighteenth-century doll's house). It was built in the late 1680s for Sir Edward Ford's grandson, Lord Grey of Werke, later Lord Tankerville, a shady character who was one of the instigators of the Duke of Monmouth's rebellion of 1685, but got off by turning King's Evidence. The architect was William Talman, who gave his client a modern home in the latest Dutch style.

The rich interior of the house is mainly the work of Sir Matthew Fetherstonhaugh, who bought Uppark in 1747. Uppark's centrepiece is the magnificent saloon, decorated in greyish-white and gold and hung with large pictures such as the portraits of George III and Queen Charlotte by Nathaniel Dance. Sir Matthew

left Uppark to his son Sir Harry, a rakish friend of the Prince Regent, with whom he drank, raced and gambled. When he was seventy, Sir Harry turned respectable by marrying Mary Ann, his head dairymaid; her tiled dairy along the terrace, probably designed for Sir Harry by Humphry Repton, is one of the minor delights of Uppark.

The open ground to the south has been left unplanted, and on a clear day there is a view across rolling farmland to the Solent and as far as the Isle of Wight.

1½M S of South Harting, 5M SE Petersfield, on B2146 (41 D9)

The Vyne, Hampshire The name of The Vyne harks back to medieval wine-producing days, if not earlier, as there may even have been a Roman villa called *Vindomis* (House of Wine)

Uppark stands four-square on the crest of a steep hill looking southwards across the Sussex Downs to the Solent and the Isle of Wight.

on the site. It lies within half a mile of the Roman roads to Winchester and Chichester, in a hollow beside a stream, now dammed and enlarged into a lake. The present house dates almost entirely from 1500–20. A long low comfortable building, made of glowing red brickwork laid in a diaper pattern, it typifies early Tudor domestic luxury.

The builder was William Lord Sandys, Lord Chamberlain to Henry VIII. The ground plan is in the form of a shallow U, with projecting wings on the south or entrance front; visitors now enter the house via a gallery on the west side, which takes them through a long series of interconnected rooms to Sandys' sumptuous private chapel, still with its original stained glass made about 1520. After Sandys acquired *Mottisfont Abbey* at the Dissolution in 1536, he seems to have lost interest in The Vyne, and about 1650 his descendants sold it and moved to Mottisfont.

The Vyne's most unexpected external feature – the classical portico on the north front – was added by the next owner during the 1650s. This was Chaloner Chute, Speaker of the House of Commons, who died in 1659; the portico is reputedly the oldest such embellishment on any

English country house, and was probably designed by John Webb, pupil of Inigo Jones. The only other major alterations to the house were carried out by Chaloner's descendant John Chute about 1770. His main additions were the ingenious and graceful flight of stairs in the front hall, and the Tomb Chamber, with a splendid monument to Speaker Chute, opening off the chapel.

The Oak Gallery, which takes up the whole of the first floor of the west wing, has fine linenfold panelling covering the walls from floor to ceiling. Untouched since Tudor times, the panels are carved with the crests and devices of Lord Sandys and his contemporaries, together with purely imaginative decoration. Concerts are given in the gallery from time to time.

Before leaving The Vyne, it is well worth walking to the far side of the lake for the view of the house across the water.

4M N Basingstoke, just outside Sherborne St John, off A340 (41 A8)

Wakehurst Place Garden, West Sussex Conceived on an impressive scale, this garden is an offshoot of the Royal Botanic Gardens at Kew. The superb collection of trees and shrubs was largely built up during the first decades of this century by Gerald W. E. Loder, whose name lives on in the *loderi* group of rhododendrons. The garden is laid out in the form of a large horseshoe, and as there are several miles of pathway among the rocky outcrops and skirting the lake, it can take several hours to do justice to Wakehurst. Many of the trees are exotics, from places as far afield as Taiwan and Tibet; fortunately for the non-expert, they are all clearly labelled.

1½M NW Ardingly, on B2028 (42 E2)

Winkworth Arboretum, in one of the most beautiful parts of Surrey, was planted mainly for autumn colour. Bluebells and daffodils carpet the ground in spring.

West Green House, Hampshire A modest red-brick house, probably built about 1700, it was remodelled about 1750 by General Henry Hawley, nicknamed 'Hangman' Hawley because of his brutal treatment of the Scots after the Battle of Culloden in 1745. Unusually for a house of this size, a large panelled room (the saloon) takes up two storeys on the west front, filling almost a quarter of the entire house. There is a central staircase well, which is top-lit; the present stone staircase replaces the original oak one.

The attractive garden has been largely replanted. West Green has been let to a tenant who has introduced wildfowl and rare breeds of sheep and cattle.

1M W Hartley Wintney, off A30 (85 H8)

Westwood Manor, Wiltshire A small manor house in a fascinating amalgam of building styles. Now an L-shaped house, clearly showing the divisions of different phases of building, Westwood was originally U-shaped in plan, with a second wing across the courtyard corresponding to the existing west range. The great hall was probably built by Thomas Culverhouse, a prosperous Wiltshire farmer, about 1490. Some time early in the sixteenth century it was enlarged by Thomas Horton, one of the region's leading clothiers. It reached more or less its present appearance at the hands of John Farewell, early in the seventeenth century. He pulled down parts of the building, possibly the east wing, and decorated many of the rooms with fine moulded plasterwork and wooden panelling.

The topiary 'cottage' to the east of the house marks the end of the demolished east wing.

1½M SW Bradford-on-Avon, off Frome Road (B3109), beside Westwood Church (57 H11)

Winkworth Arboretum, Surrey Though it is small as arboreta go, Winkworth (started by Dr Wilfrid Fox in 1938) contains an amazing variety of trees and shrubs in a limited space. It is helped by its magnificent site, on a steep hillside falling away to two lakes in the valley, giving constantly changing vistas of landscape and foliage.

There are two useful leaflets, one for spring and one for autumn, for those exploring the arboretum.

3M S Godalming, on B2130 (41 B11)

Wool House, Kent A fifteenth-century timbered house, with very close-set vertical timbering. The stream that splashes down outside may well have been used for cleaning the wool that gave the house its name. Inside, the rooms (seen by appointment only) are long, low and heavily beamed.

Wells Street, Loose, 3M S Maidstone off A229 (42 C6)

Bodiam Castle, East Sussex Everyone's idea of the perfect medieval castle, Bodiam rises strong and sheer from a wide moat. It was built by Sir Edward Dalyngrygge in 1385, and formed part of the south coast defences against the French, guarding an important crossing of the River Rother, which in the Middle Ages was navigable right up to Bodiam. The castle was never attacked, and so the great gatehouse, round corner towers and curtain wall are still much as they would have been in Dalyngrygge's time. Inside, it is still possible to trace the medieval domestic arrangements, as a good deal of the inner walling still survives. The buildings – among them the great hall, ladies' bower, chapel and kitchen – were grouped round all four sides of a central courtyard; the castle's well can be seen in the south-west tower.

The castle was restored by Lord Curzon, who bought it in 1917 and left it to the Trust when he died nine years later.

A small museum in the curator's cottage contains relics found during the restoration, and also a fine model of the castle as it was in its prime.

3M S Hawkhurst, 1M E of A229 (42 F6)

Bramber Castle, West Sussex A tall stump of masonry is all that is left of what was one of the most powerful Norman castles in the south of England. It was built by William de Braose, who came over with the Conqueror, and it was probably complete by about 1090; it consisted of an outer and an inner bailey, each with a gatehouse or barbican, leading to the keep, of which the surviving stonework formed a part. The present parish church was originally the castle's chapel.

After surviving the Middle Ages largely unscathed, the Royalist castle was destroyed during the Civil War by the Parliamentarians.

In Bramber village, on A283 (42 G1)

Chiddingstone, Kent A perfectly preserved medieval and Tudor village. The oldest documentation of the houses goes back to 1453 (a deed of that year refers to what is now the village shop and post office); other houses carry the dates 1638 and 1645, though they are a good deal older.

The 'Chiding Stone', from which the village is said to get its name, lies behind the houses opposite the church. What kind of 'chiding' took place there has never been specified.

4M E Edenbridge, 1M S of B2027 (42 D4)

Eashing Bridges, Surrey The River Wey splits into two at Eashing, and so there are in effect two bridges, one across each arm of the river. The stonework of these picturesque medieval (probably thirteenth-century) bridges is built of local Bargate stone.

1½M W Godalming, off A3 (41 B10/11)

Joiners' Hall, Wiltshire A magnificent twin-gabled façade, dating from about 1550. Between the ground and first floors the ornate external beam is carved with dragon-like figures and roses, and the first-floor oriel windows are supported by carved corbels. (Let as an antique shop and not open.)

E end of St Ann's Street, Salisbury (40 C3)

Leith Hill Tower, Surrey A battlemented folly tower, built by Richard Hull in 1766, according to an inscription on it. Its top is 1,029 feet above sea-level. From the hilltop plateau there are magnificent views to the South and North Downs. The hill was the site of a battle in 851 between Danes and Saxons.

4M SW Dorking, reached from A25, A24 or A29 (41 B12)

Newtown, Isle of Wight Despite its name, Newtown is an ancient place, going back to the time of King Egbert in the ninth century. The borough got its present name in 1256, when

Bodiam Castle never had to withstand a serious siege and probably could not have done so as its defences are unimpressive for its time.

Aymer de Valance, Bishop of Winchester elect, founded a 'new town' there. The estuary of the Newtown River provides an excellent harbour, and Newtown was prosperous throughout the Middle Ages, in spite of periodic raids by the French. But by Queen Elizabeth's time it was in decline.

Newtown's past glories are recalled by the Town Hall, built in 1699, with Gothic Revival windows inserted in the eighteenth century. After 1832 this neat little building was first a house, then a school, and finally became derelict. In 1933 it was restored by an anonymous band of conservationists, who called themselves 'Ferguson's Gang' (*see Shalford Mill*), and presented to the Trust; it now houses documents relating to Newtown's history, has a royal coat-of-arms (originally at Ryde), and has been refurnished.

The Trust owns a good deal of other property in Newtown, including the eighteenth-century building known as Noah's Ark. It has also acquired fourteen miles of bank on either side of the river, and four miles of foreshore along the Solent. The Isle of Wight Natural History and Archaeological Society runs a 300-acre nature reserve round Newtown, much of it on National Trust land.

Between Newport and Yarmouth, 1M N of A3054 (40 G5/6)

With its half-timbered houses, Chiddingstone is one of the most attractive villages in Kent. It was built at a time when the Wealden iron industry was thriving.

The Pepperbox may have been a viewpoint to enable ladies to follow the hunt.

The Pepperbox, Wiltshire Also called Eyre's Folly, an octagonal tower of 1606, of unknown purpose, standing on Brickworth Down. Fine viewpoint.

5M SE Salisbury, N of A36 (40 D4)

above For some two hundred years Bembridge windmill ground flour and meal for the village and surrounding countryside.

Avebury is perhaps the most important early Bronze Age monument in Europe. Dating from about 2000 BC, it is roughly contemporary with parts of Stonehenge.

Sandham Memorial Chapel, Hampshire A small red-brick chapel, built in 1923–6, and filled with Stanley Spencer's visionary paintings inspired by his experiences in World War I. The greatest of them is the *Resurrection of the Soldiers*, which covers the entire east wall; there are eighteen smaller paintings on the north and south walls, based on Spencer's war service in Macedonia. The chapel is named after Lieutenant H. W. Sandham, who died in 1919 from an illness contracted in Macedonia. The paintings took Spencer nine years to complete, from 1923–32.

In Burghclere village, 4M S Newbury, off A34 (84 H5/6)

Witley Common Information Centre, Surrey Witley Common is a small area of heathland, with a wide variety of animal and plant life. It centres on its Countryside Interpretation Centre, a modern chalet-like building. The Centre sets out the whole story of the Common on display panels, which describe, for example, the early enclosures, the soil types and the plants. There is also an audio-visual display programme. The Centre has a choice of leaflets for visitors wanting to explore the Common, with different walks covering every aspect of wildlife and countryside management.

1M SW Milford, between A3 and A286 (41 B10)

Archaeological & Industrial Sites

Avebury, Wiltshire The largest prehistoric stone circle in Europe, Avebury lacks the stark grandeur of Stonehenge, as it has been domesticated by the houses of Avebury village which cluster round it. Yet in some ways it is even more impressive than Stonehenge, because of its area (nearly thirty acres), the immense height of its outer bank and ditch, the number and size of its standing stones, and the complexity of its layout. It originally consisted of an outer circle with four main entrances, and two smaller inner circles; most of the surviving stones are on the west side of the circle, and especially in the south-west quadrant. Avebury was probably constructed about 2000 BC. One and a half miles to the north-west is the early Neolithic causewayed camp of Windmill Hill.

Near Marlborough, 1M N of A4, on A361 (84 G2)

Bembridge Windmill, Isle of Wight This fine example of an eighteenth-century tower mill is the last remaining windmill on the Isle of Wight. Built about 1700, it is of the type known as a 'cap' mill – that is, its stone tower is surmounted by a revolving wooden cap carrying the wind shaft, driving wheels and four 'sweeps' or sails. The windmill last functioned

Spencer's murals in Sandham Memorial Chapel illustrate the life of the British soldier, here shown washing and moving kit-bags.

The meadows at Runnymede have been enshrined in British history as the site of the signing of Magna Carta.

in 1913; after falling derelict, it was restored first in the 1930s, and then again about thirty years later, after being used as a look-out tower in World War II. It is now fully restored, and visitors can follow the whole process of milling from grain to flour, and admire the massive craftsmanship of the wooden shafts, cogwheels and other working parts.

½M S Bembridge   (41 G8)

Cissbury Ring, West Sussex A magnificent Iron Age hill-fort, surrounded by a ditch and rampart, 600 feet above sea-level and covering about eighty acres. Hollows at the western end of the fort mark the positions of Neolithic flint mines, dug about 2000 BC.

Near Worthing, 1½M E Findon, off A24 (41 E12)

Coldrum Long Barrow, Kent Known also as Coldrum Stones, this Neolithic burial chamber consists of a chalk mound topped by a U-shaped group of standing stones and surrounded by a ditch. It stands beside the Pilgrims' Way, and was presumably the tomb of a local king or chieftain. There is a display cabinet with bones from Coldrum in Trottis-cliffe church.

1M W Trottscliffe, off A227 (42 B5)

Curbridge, Hampshire There are sites of Roman brick and tile kilns and other Roman buildings on the Curbridge Estate, beside a beautiful stretch of the Hamble.

On River Hamble, 1M S Botley via A3051 (40 E6)

Figsbury Ring, Wiltshire An impressive Iron Age hill-fort, covering about fifteen acres, with an outer ditch and rampart and a smaller inner ditch. There were probably gatehouses at the entrances to the fort.

4M NE Salisbury, just N of A30   (40 C3)

Highdown Hill, West Sussex A prehistoric site which combines an Iron Age hill-fort with a Bronze Age settlement. The Saxons later used it as a burial ground, and coins and spearheads have been found on the site.

Near Worthing, 1M N Ferring, S of A27 (41 F12)

Oldbury Hill, Kent A heavily wooded site, with a ditch and ramparts marking an Iron Age fort of about 100 BC.

Near Ightham, on N side of A25   (42 B/C4/5)

River Wey and Godalming Navigations, Surrey Twenty miles of waterway owned by the Trust, running from Godalming Wharf to the Thames at Weybridge. The Wey Navigation (15½ miles from Guildford to Weybridge) was made navigable for barge traffic in the reign of Charles II, while the remaining 4½ miles from Guildford upstream to Godalming was opened in 1760. In the early nineteenth century there were further canal links through to the south coast, but the coming of the railways killed this traffic. In the heyday of the Navigations timber and agricultural produce were taken by barge down to London, while corn and general merchandise was brought up to Guildford and Godalming. During the late nineteenth and twentieth centuries traffic dwindled, but with the rise in popularity of pleasure boating the Wey is crowded once again.

Good viewpoints are at Tilthams Bridge, Peasmarsh, half way between Guildford and Godalming; Guildford town bridges; and Pyrford Lock, upstream from Byfleet and not far from Wisley.

(41 B11, A11. 85 H11, G11)

Royal Military Canal, Kent The Royal Military Canal, which runs along the inner edge of Romney Marsh, linking the Rother near Rye with the sea at Hythe, was dug in 1804–07 as part of the defence system against invasion by Napoleon's forces. Now it is a tranquil water-way, lined in places by avenues of trees, and a delightful place for a peaceful stroll on a fine day.

3½M of canal, from Appledore (B2080) to Warehorne (43 E8)

Runnymede, Surrey It was in the Runnymede watermeadows – still surprisingly rural in spite of their nearness to London – that King John signed Magna Carta on 15 June 1215. The boundaries are marked by two pairs of pavilions, designed by Sir Edwin Lutyens, on either side of the road – tall-roofed bungalows at the upstream end, and small octagonal kiosks at the Egham end. On the south side of the A308 is a memorial to President Kennedy, erected in 1965.

On S side of Thames above Egham, off the A308 (85 G10/11)

Shalford Mill, Surrey A fine eighteenth-century water-mill on the Tillingbourne, a tributary of the Wey. Tile-hung and with a massive timber frame, it was still grinding corn until 1914. After World War I it fell into disrepair, and in 1932 it was given by its owner to the anonymous group of conservationists who called themselves 'Ferguson's Gang' (*see also Newtown, Isle of Wight*). They restored it and handed it over to the Trust. They held their secret meetings in the mill. The identity of 'Sister Agatha', the 'Bloody Bishop' and other members of the Gang, including Ferguson himself, has never been disclosed.

The mill still has much of the working machinery in place; one of the three sets of grinding-stones is complete. (Part open on application.)

1½M S Guildford, east side of A281   (41 A11)

Stonehenge Down, Wiltshire The monument is protected by the DOE, though Trust members have free entry to it; however, the Trust owns over 1,400 acres of farmland in the area, including some of the many Bronze Age barrows (burial mounds) that stand up above the fields.

2M W Amesbury, on A303   (40 B3)

Waggoners' Wells, Hampshire A string of three small lakes linked by sluices, they may have been the hammer ponds for an iron foundry known in the sixteenth century as Wakeners' Wells. Set in the valley below the 570-acre Ludshott Common (also National Trust), they are surrounded by beech trees, which make a magnificent sight in the autumn. The wishing well near by has links with Tennyson. The lakes are the starting-point for two nature trails.

1½M W Hindhead, S of B3002 (41 C10)

Winchester City Mill, Hampshire This attractive water-mill, brick below and tile-hung above, was built in 1743, on a site occupied by a succession of mills since Saxon times, and was working until 1928. It is powered by the fast-flowing Itchen, and the undershot water-wheels are still in place. Upstairs there are displays of milling and millwrighting. (Leased to the Youth Hostels Association.)

At foot of Winchester High Street (40 C6)

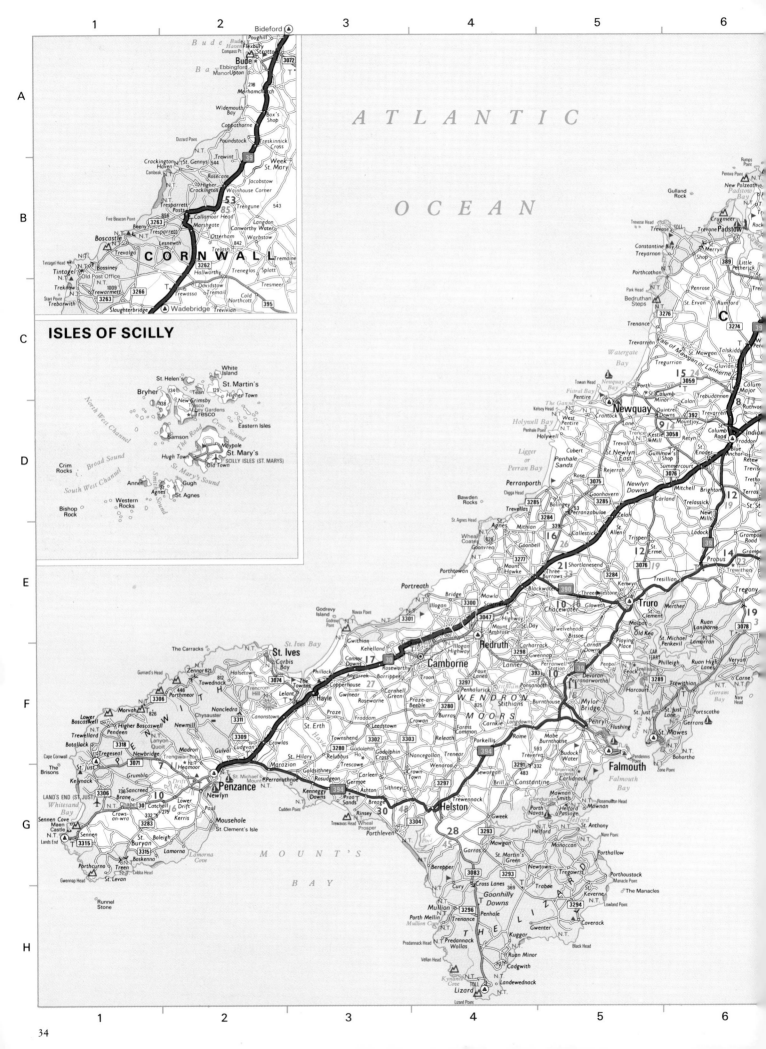

ISLES OF SCILLY

CORNWALL

ATLANTIC

OCEAN

MOUNT'S BAY

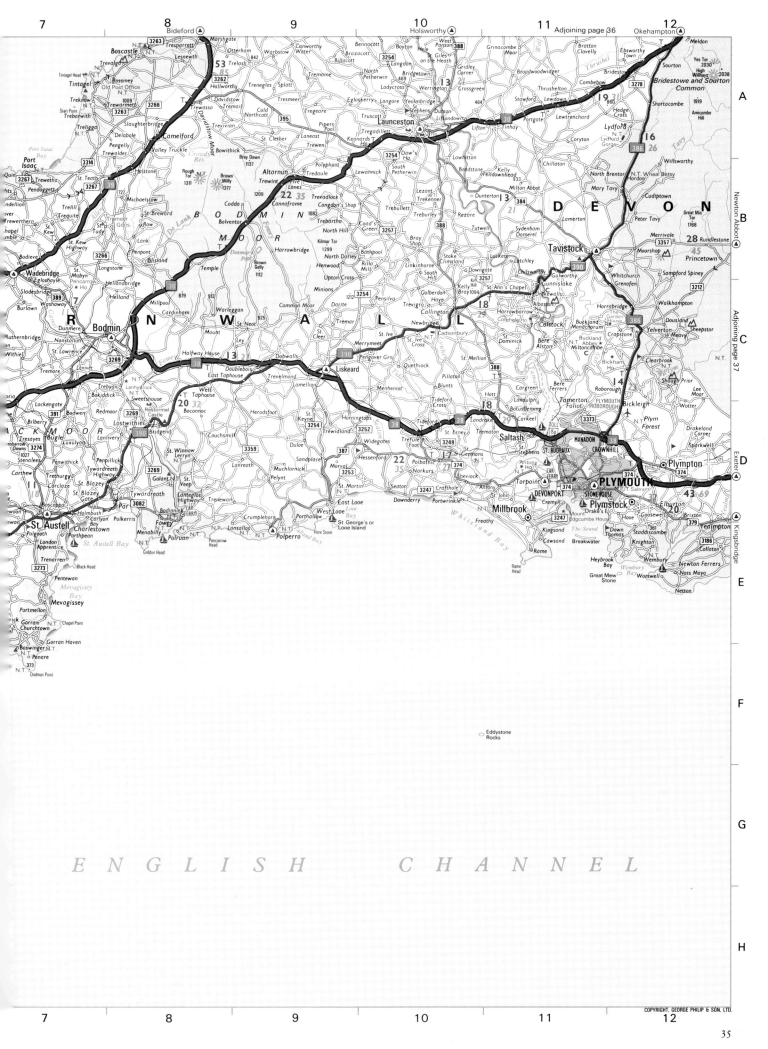

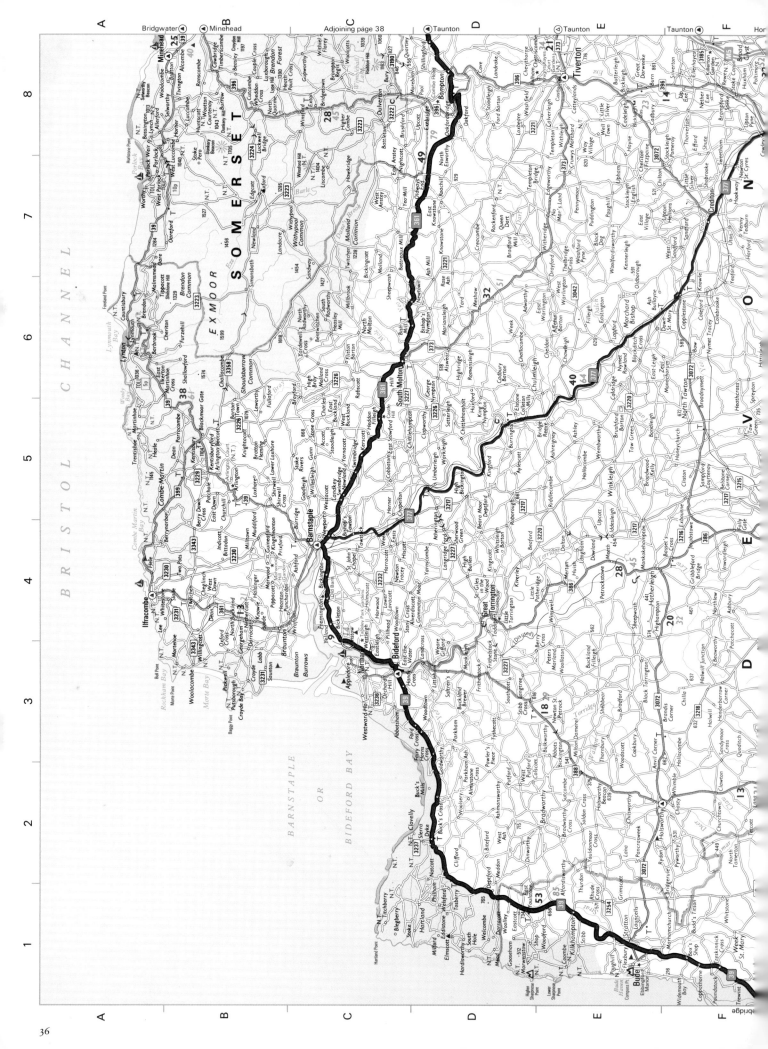

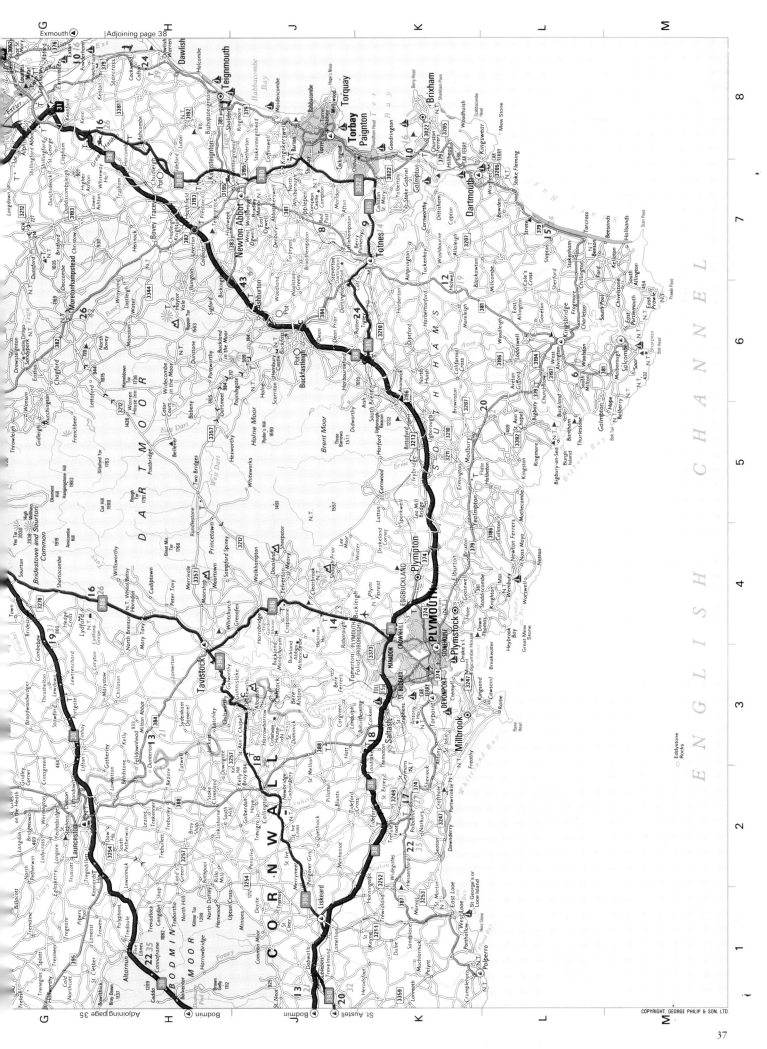

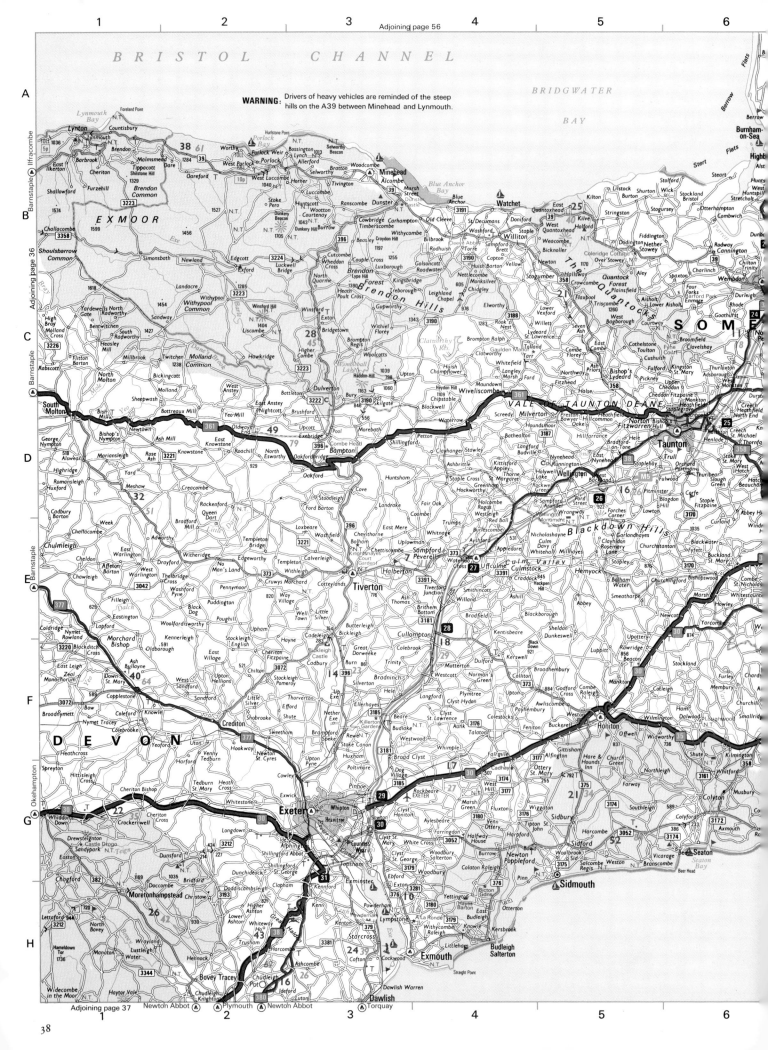

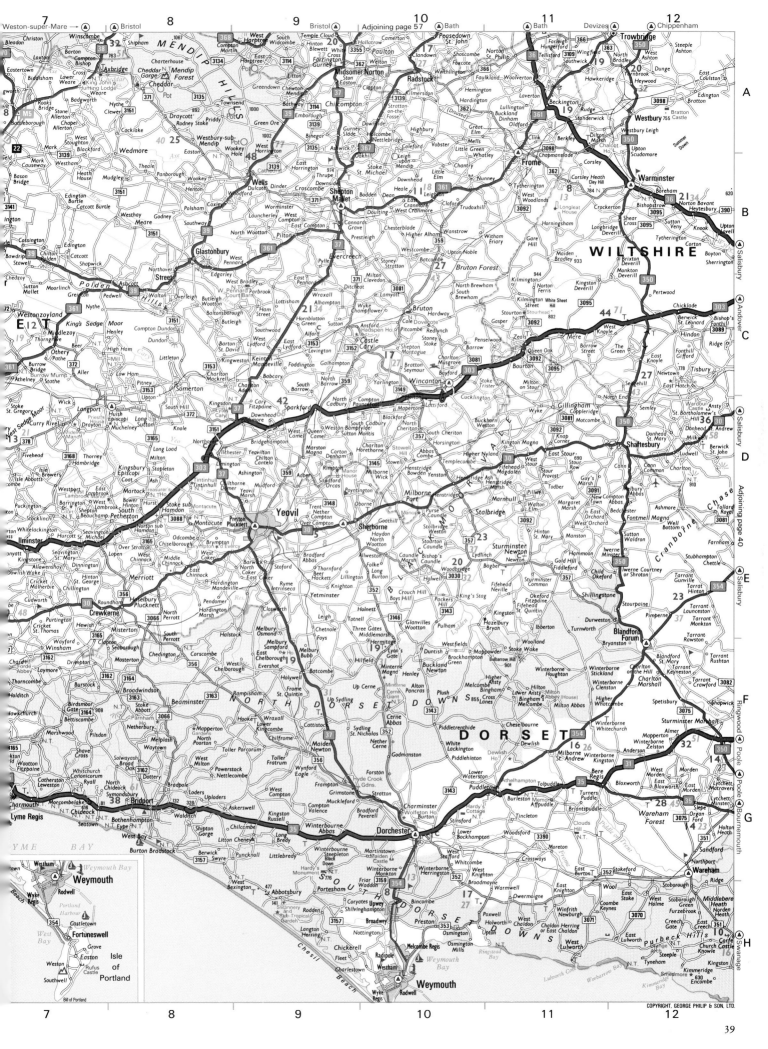

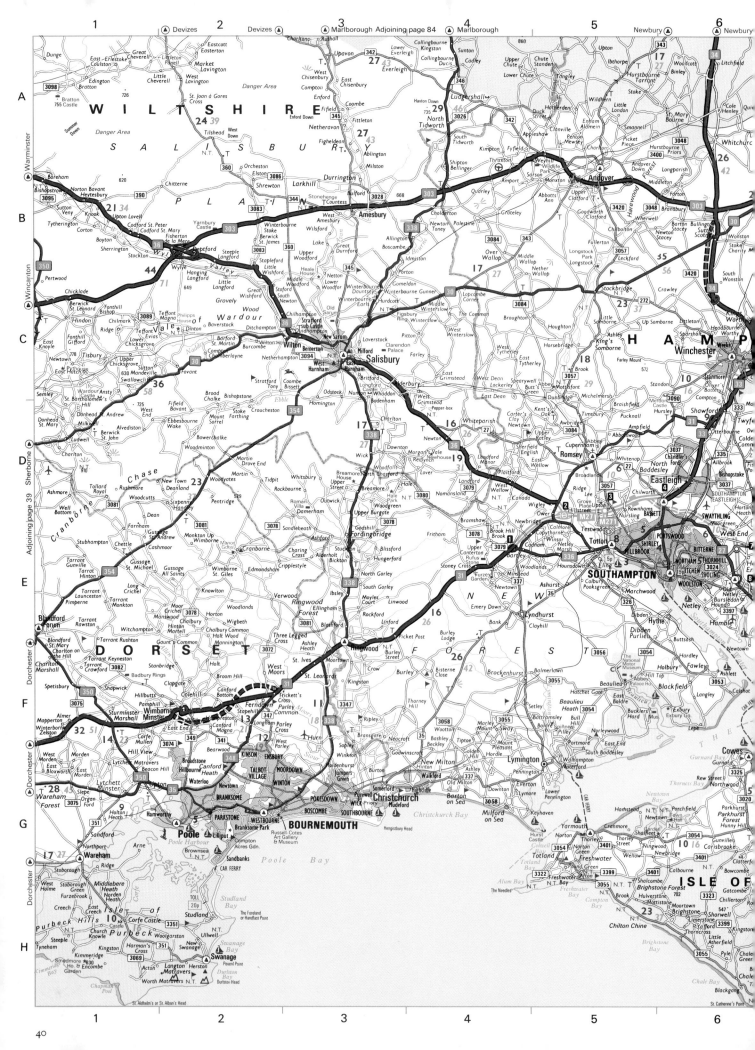

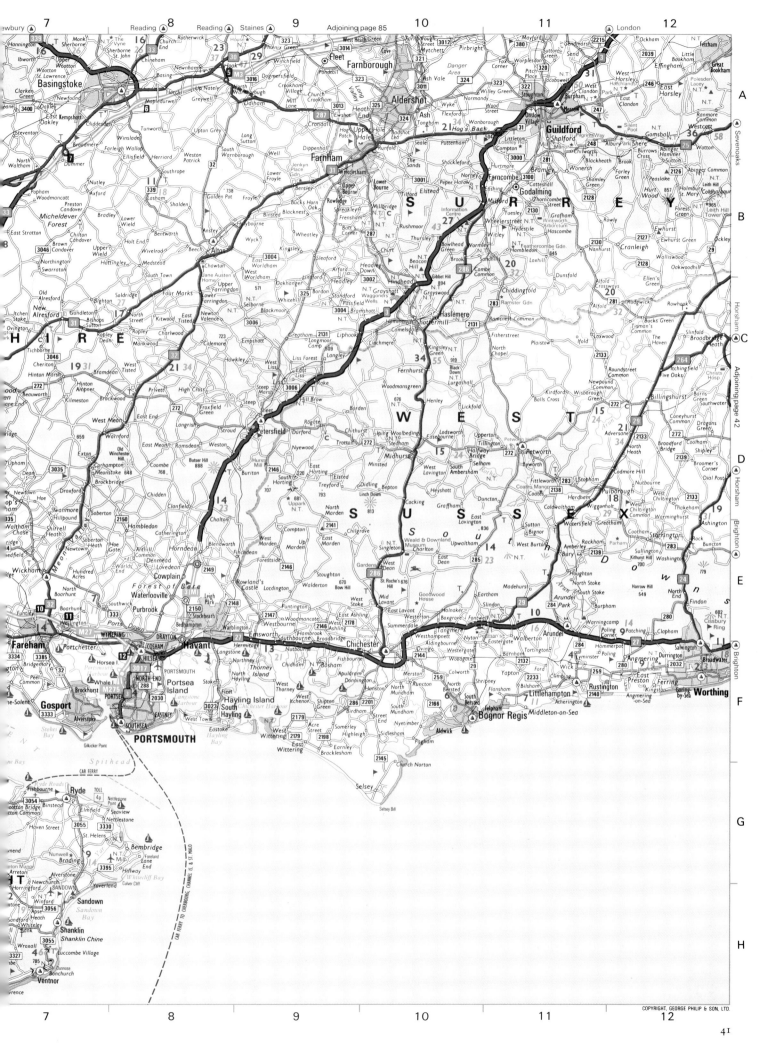

A

B

C

D

E

F

G

H

7 8 9 10 11 12

ISLE OF SHEPPEY

KENT

Queenborough
-in-Sheppey

Sheerness

Minster-on-Sea

Sittingbourne

Faversham

Whitstable

Herne
Bay

Canterbury

Margate

Cliftonville

Broadstairs

Ramsgate

Sandwich

Deal

Walmer

Isle of Thanet

Ashford

Tenterden

Rye

Hastings

Romney
Marsh

New
Romney

Hythe

Folkestone

Dover

STRAIT OF DOVER

Isle of Oxney

Rother Levels

Walland Marsh

Winchelsea

Rye Bay

43

Wales & the Welsh Borders

LOWER BROCKHAMPTON

National Trust holdings in Wales and the Border counties include some of the finest coast and countryside estates in Britain. These apart, the Trust's most notable properties are perhaps the dozen or so great houses, largely of the seventeenth and eighteenth centuries, which so splendidly illustrate contemporary spacious living and taste. Here leading architects and decorators rewarded their wealthy patrons with country mansions whose handsome exteriors were matched by similarly fine interiors. The delicate plasterwork and other interior decoration still delight and, as in the past, these houses are home to a wealth of exquisite furniture, *objets d'art* and pictures. National Trust gardens, too, are outstanding, some, such as Bodnant and Hidcote, enjoying an international reputation.

But splendid though the great houses are, there are also numerous more modest properties reflecting the life of their times. Bath's Assembly Rooms evoke Jane Austen, dovecotes are a reminder that pigeons were once valued as winter fresh meat, and massive tithe barns recall past imposts.

Medieval times are well and contrastingly represented by attractive manor houses such as Horton Court and Lower Brockhampton as also by the ruins of Skenfrith and Cilgerran

The Trust owns about half the great ridge of the Shropshire Long Mynd (Welsh mynydd = mountain). This is Carding Mill Valley.

castles and of the once prosperous abbey of Hailes. Farther back in time, Segontium with its museum tells of the Roman military presence, while something of Romano-British domestic life can be pictured at Chedworth Villa. National Trust lands are also rich in prehistoric sites. The most obvious are the many Iron Age defensive earthworks – Little Solsbury Hill and Croft Ambrey are outstanding – while the cultures of Bronze and Stone Age peoples survive in the scattered traces of their burials.

Coast & Countryside

The National Trust owns a total of over 80,000 acres in Wales and its border counties, made up of around 130 large and small individual properties. These include some 500 miles of Welsh coast, much of it of wild and rugged grandeur, and scenery as diverse as the high bare mountains of Snowdonia, glorious woodland threaded by impatient streams, the open rolling uplands of the Brecon Beacons and of Shropshire's Long Mynd, and the rich farming land to be found throughout the region.

Ignoring the north-east with its succession of popular resorts, caravan parks and holiday camps, as also the largely industrial Bristol

The spectacular Henrhyd Falls lie hidden in a deep ravine in Graigllech Woods, just north of Coelbren, Powys.

The impressive massif of the Brecon Beacons, Powys, is good walking country with spectacular views from the higher ground.

WALES AND THE WELSH BORDERS

Channel east of Swansea, the Welsh coast divides into five regions, all scenic and all in part owned or otherwise protected by the National Trust. From north to south these regions are Anglesey, Lleyn, the great crescent of Cardigan Bay, south-western Dyfed, and Gower. Many areas are accessible only on foot.

The principal Anglesey properties, together providing some 375 acres of cliff, bay and agricultural land, form a group at the island's north-west corner, here being **Cemaes, Cemlyn** with a nature reserve and bird sanctuary, and **Dinas Gynfor**, this last the northernmost point of Wales and including part of an Iron Age promontory fort (60 A3).

The Lleyn peninsula, its coast officially designated an Area of Outstanding Natural Beauty, projects some thirty miles south-westward to separate Caernarfon Bay and Cardigan Bay. Here the Trust's properties form two groups, those close to Aberdaron near the tip of the peninsula (60 H1) and those of the Plas-yn-Rhiw estate (60 G2) a short distance to the east. Beyond Aberdaron will be found the open, green and steeply sloping cliffland of **Braich y Pwll**, below which from the fifth or sixth century onwards pilgrims embarked for Bardsey (not National Trust). Bardsey is an island of such sanctity that it is said that three pilgrimages here equated with one to Rome. On Braich y Pwll a holy well and the site of a chapel recall those times, while Bardsey is also well seen from the Trust's clifftop acres of **Pen y Cil** a short way to the south.

To the east of Aberdaron Bay, along an outstandingly lovely stretch of coast, the **Plas-yn-Rhiw** estate provides seven National Trust properties in addition to the parent manor house. These include **Porth Ysgo**, with a sandy beach, cliffs and a waterfall; the rock, bracken and heather moor of **Mynydd-y-Graig**, site of a hill-fort and of megalithic remains and rising 800 feet above the west side of Porth Neigwl, a large arc of sand and cliffs known also as Hell's Mouth; the cliffs of **Mynydd Cilan** guarding the eastern arm of Porth Neigwl; and **Foel Felin Wynt** (Windmill Hill) to the north of Abersoch, a high point (700 feet) commanding long views seaward and towards Snowdonia (60 G2). Other properties on Lleyn, all along the south coast and very different from those just described, are **Tywyn-y-Fach**, nineteen acres of sandhills on the northern edge of Abersoch (60 G3); **Ynysgain** near Criccieth, an area of farmland and shore crossed by the railway (60 F4); the golf course and dunes of **Morfa Bychan** just south-west of Porthmadog (60 F5); and in Porthmadog itself **Ynys Towyn**, a modest small site where a rocky knoll provides a view across the Glaslyn estuary (60 F5).

Around Cardigan Bay, a crescent some eighty miles in length between Porthmadog and Cardigan, little is owned by the National Trust.

The Llyn Ogwen valley lies in the heart of the wild, mountainous country of the Trust's great Carneddau estate in north Wales.

However, one property, **Dinas Oleu** (58 A2), high above Barmouth and the Mawddach estuary (described by Wordsworth as 'sublime'), is of interest for being the first to come to the Trust, in 1895 the year of its founding, and an adjoining piece of land, **Cae Fadog**, was acquired in 1980. Farther south, there are five properties between New Quay and Cardigan, most of them farmland but with public access to quiet beaches (55 A7 to 54 B5).

From the mouth of the Teifi near Cardigan (54 B5) starts the Pembrokeshire Coast National Park's coastal path. This runs for 168 scenic miles, rounding the bold promontory of St David's Head, skirting St Bride's Bay and Milford Haven, and finally winding above the magnificent cliffs to the south-west of Pembroke to end at Amroth on Carmarthen Bay (54 F5). Along or close to this path there are three important groups of National Trust properties: those around St David's and along the north shore of St Bride's Bay; those on the peninsula forming the southern arm of the bay; and the clifftop sites to the south. Within the first group the Trust owns over fifteen miles of coast and protects another eight. Among the properties are **St David's Head** itself, mentioned by Ptolemy as *Octopitarum Promontarium* and with some prehistoric remains, and parts of **Whitesand Bay**, traditionally the site of St David's first monastery. **Marloes** and **Kete**, forming the second group, command striking views towards Skomer and Skokholm islands (not National Trust; nature reserves

The red sandstone cliffs of Manorbier, Dyfed, typify the wild and rugged grandeur of the Pembrokeshire coast.

and bird sanctuaries). Finally, along the cliffs to the south of Pembroke, there are **Stackpole**, an estate of nearly 2,000 acres made up of woods, cliffs, beaches, farmland and lakes, the striated red sandstone cliffs of **Manorbier** (the name deriving from Maenor Pyr, the manor of Pyr, first abbot of Caldy), and **Lydstep Headland**, below which there are caves.

The long sweep of Carmarthen Bay is bounded on its southern side by the popular **Gower Peninsula** (55 H7/8/9) on which the National Trust owns sixteen scattered areas, all on or close to the coast and together embracing a remarkable variety of scenery – cliffs, sand burrows, salt marsh, commons, downland and rocky headland. There are caves below many of the cliffs, but access can be difficult. They are of interest only because the bones of animals such as lions and rhinoceros were found in them, while in 1823, in a cavern below **Paviland** (west of Port Eynon), were discovered the bones of a young man, subsequently radio-carbon dated to about the seventeenth millennium BC. Other Trust properties on Gower include earthworks, probably of the Iron Age, on **The Bulwark** and on **Thurba Head**; **Worm's Head**, with a cave and a blow hole, jutting seaward as the southern arm of the fine curve of the beach of Rhossili Bay; while above, on the grass and bracken covered hill of **Rhossili Down**, can be found burial chambers known as Sweyne's Houses (Howes), traditionally the resting place of the Viking who may have given his name to Swansea.

Of the National Trust's many inland country-side properties perhaps the most impressive is the **Carneddau** in Snowdonia (60 C/D6), a huge estate (15,860 acres) of breathtaking scenery which includes Carnedd Dafydd and much of Carnedd Llewelyn, mountains both well over 3,000 feet and named after the brother princes who stood against Edward I. Other features of this estate are the striking rocky pyramid of Tryfan, south of Llyn Ogwen, and, at the head of the steep Nant Ffrancon Pass, Cwm Idwal and the lake of the same name, a sombre place which is romantically associated with Prince Idwal who is said to have been drowned here, but more practically known as a nature reserve important for its Alpine flora. Other important properties in northern Wales are the precipitous wooded **Aberglaslyn Pass** to the south of Beddgelert (60 E5); the vast **Ysbyty Ifan** estate south of Betws-y-Coed (61 E/F7), with 25,820 acres of wooded hills and valleys, upland farming and moorland, and beautifully situated Llyn Conwy, source of the river of the same name; and farther south, but still in the county of Gwynedd, **Dolmelynllyn** (60 H6) where a short footpath ascends the Gamlan stream to Rhaiadr Ddu, one of the finest cascades in Wales, and **Cregennau**, near Arthog (58 A2), a fine open space of 705 acres embracing lakes, hill farms and mountain.

In the south of the principality there are important properties in Dyfed, Powys and Gwent. **Dolaucothi** at Pumpsaint (55 C10) includes ancient gold mines, principally exploited by the Romans but possibly in use even earlier and also worked intermittently through to modern times; nearby are an ancient standing stone and a mound of disputed origin. In the county of Powys the Trust owns much of the **Brecon Beacons** including the principal summits of Pen y Fan and Corn Dû (56 B3), both only a little under 3,000 feet in height. Open upland and crossed by many tracks, one of these a Roman road, the Brecon Beacons are one of the most visited walking districts in Wales. To the east, above Abergavenny in Gwent, roads and tracks ascend towards the two bare peaks of **Sugar Loaf** and **Skirrid Fawr** (56 B6) – alternatively Ysgyryd Fawr – both commanding views of the lovely Usk valley.

The National Trust has many countryside estates scattered throughout the border counties – farm, wood, moor and downland. Some properties are remote, but many are concentrated around urban centres, such as Bristol, Bath, Stroud, and Birmingham. The largest and most notable comprises nearly 5,000 acres of the high moor of the **Long Mynd** in Shropshire (59 C9/10). Crossed by a narrow road ascending sharply westward out of Church Stretton, and notable for its extensive views across Shropshire and Cheshire and towards the Black Mountains of Wales, Long Mynd is also known for its many prehistoric barrows, three lengths of defensive earthworks, and a section of the Port Way, a track used by Stone Age traders and in more modern times marking parish boundaries.

Houses, Gardens & Parks

Aberconwy House, Gwynedd Dating from the fourteenth century, Aberconwy House survives as an example of the better type of dwelling once common in Conwy. It now contains an exhibition illustrating life in Conwy from Roman to modern times.

Conwy, at the junction of Castle Street and High Street (61 B7)

Attingham Park, Shropshire The mansion was designed in 1782 by George Steuart for Noel Hill, later the 1st Lord Berwick. On Hill's instructions Steuart had to incorporate the earlier house, but this was almost wholly demolished in 1840 while an earlier and more significant alteration was that of 1805 when, to house the 2nd Lord Berwick's collection, largely the result of a visit to Italy in 1792, John Nash inserted the picture gallery and a new staircase. In 1827 Lord Berwick was forced to sell most of his collection, but his successor, who served as ambassador to Sardinia, Savoy and Naples, built up fresh collections of both pictures and Neapolitan furniture. Among the artists whose works hang today in the house are Angelica Kauffmann, Lawrence, Romney, Kneller and Sickert. The interior decoration of the mansion is notable, especially that of the boudoir, late eighteenth-century work attributed to the Frenchman Louis Delabrière and among the most delicate surviving examples of its period.

After much planting by Thomas Leggett between 1769–72, the park was greatly altered by Humphry Repton in 1797. The estate occupies part of the site of the Romano-British town of Viroconium and is crossed and bounded by Roman roads.

Atcham, 4M SE of Shrewsbury, on A5 (59 A11)

Benthall Hall, Shropshire On the site of a much earlier house, today's hall was probably built in the late sixteenth century, although tradition gives a date of 1535. As early as 1583 there seems to have been considerable alteration, and in the seventeenth century a wing was added on the north-east. But the estate and its family name are of far greater antiquity, traced by records back to 1100 and with indirect evidence suggesting a pre-Norman ownership. Except for the period 1844–1934, the estate was held by the same family until given to the National Trust in 1958. The carved stone decoration on the porch, possibly alluding to the five wounds of Christ, and the several hiding places within the house suggest that in Elizabethan times the family was Catholic in sympathy.

In local sandstone, with mullioned and transomed windows and moulded brick chimneys, Benthall is an attractive example of the domestic style of its period. The best feature of the interior is the carved main staircase, thought to date from 1618; also noteworthy are the late eighteenth-century Welsh pewter, the oak panelling of *c.*1610 in the dining room, the plasterwork of the drawing room ceiling (*c.*1630), and, in both the drawing and dining rooms, the mantelpieces designed in 1756 by T. F. Pritchard.

Broseley, 4M NE of Much Wenlock   (59 B12)

Berrington Hall, Hereford and Worcester The present hall and park are the result of the association in the late eighteenth century between the then owner of the estate, Thomas Harley, 'Capability' Brown and the younger Henry Holland. Brown almost certainly advised on the commanding site of the house, enjoying a wide view and above a valley in which he fashioned a lake and island. Holland began work in 1778, achieving this imposing mansion – a rectangle with offices at the rear around a courtyard – the rather austere exterior of which contrasts with the rich internal decoration.

Beyond the marble hall, fairly typical of its period, the drawing room is the most splendid of the rooms, with a chimneypiece of Carrara marble and one of the most elaborate ceilings designed anywhere by Holland in which the central medallion and surrounding roundels are probably the work of Biagio Rebecca, who was also almost certainly responsible for work in the business room and the library. On Harley's death the estate passed to his daughter, wife of the eldest son of Admiral Rodney, a naval association recalled by the large battle paintings (three by Thomas Luny) in the dining

The picture gallery at Attingham Park in a watercolour of 1810. The ceiling is notable for its early cast-iron window frames.

room. Around the courtyard are the nineteenth-century laundry and the original dairy.

3M N of Leominster to W of A49   (59 F10)

Bodnant Garden, Gwynedd First laid out from 1875 onwards by Henry Pochin, Bodnant now ranks among the finest gardens in Britain. With backgrounds of large native trees and with views across the Conwy valley to Snowdonia, the garden is in two main sections. The upper, around the house, formed by lawns and a series of terrace gardens, is largely the achievement of the 2nd Lord Aberconway (grandson of Henry Pochin) between 1905 and 1914. The lower, known as the Dell and with a pinetum and wild garden, is along the valley of a stream.

8M S of Colwyn Bay on A470   (61 C7)

Chirk Castle, Clwyd This massive border fortress was completed in 1310 by Roger Mortimer to whom Edward I had given the estates of Chirk in 1282. Thereafter ownership changed frequently until 1595 when the estate

A flight of garden steps at Bodnant, showing some of the roses which are one of the garden's major summer attractions.

was bought by the merchant adventurer Sir Thomas Myddelton (Lord Mayor of London in 1614), the property then belonging to this family until 1977 (the Myddeltons still live in the castle). The design is a square around a courtyard. The south wing had become a house by Tudor times and the outline of the many Tudor gables can still be traced on the filling-in carried out during the eighteenth century. The interior of the east wing, now a private house, was much altered during the nineteenth century by Augustus Welby Pugin. The west range, with its deep dungeon, survives largely untouched since 1300, while the state rooms occupy the north wing. Entered through a hall by Pugin, the rooms are notable for their elaborate decorative work of the sixteenth to the early nineteenth centuries and contain fine furniture, portraits and Mortlake tapestries. The park, which is crossed by Offa's Dyke (*c.*784), is entered from Chirk town through superb iron gates completed in 1721, the work of the Davies brothers.

1M W of Chirk off A5   (61 F12)

Clevedon Court, Avon A once partly fortified manor house, with a twelfth-century tower and a thirteenth-century hall. The interior houses collections of Nailsea glass and of Eltonware, the product of Sir Edmund Elton's Sunflower Pottery, established at Clevedon in 1880. The gardens are terraced, and planted with rare shrubs.

1½M E of Clevedon, on B3130   (57 G7)

Croft Castle, Hereford and Worcester Held by the Croft family from Norman times until 1745, again from 1923 until the 1950s, and today still occupied by them, Croft Castle has outer walls and corner towers of the fourteenth and fifteenth centuries but was later much modified, especially in about 1765 when it was given a new internal structure with Gothick features, notably the staircase and ceilings where much

The Welsh name for Chirk Castle, Castell y Waun (Meadow Castle), aptly describes its beautiful setting in the Welsh borderlands.

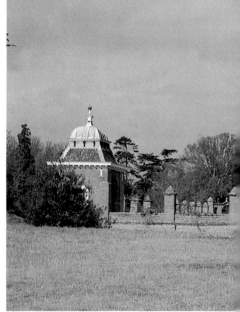

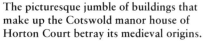

The picturesque jumble of buildings that make up the Cotswold manor house of Horton Court betray its medieval origins.

The medieval church in the grounds of Dyrham Park is one of the few owned by the Trust. It contains Blathwayt monuments.

The stilt garden at Hidcote Manor (named after the hornbeam hedges on stems), looking down the red border to the old garden.

of the decorative work is by T.F. Pritchard. Among the portrait painters whose works hang in the rooms are H.R. Morland, Gainsborough, Lawrence, Archer-Shee, Beetham and Phillip de Laszlo. Beside the castle stands a small fourteenth- and fifteenth-century church containing the impressive tomb of Sir Richard Croft (d.1509) and his wife (who was governess at Ludlow to the sons of Edward IV).

The grounds are known for their oak, beech, lime and Spanish chestnut avenues, the last perhaps dating back to 1588, and also for the large Iron Age fort of Croft Ambrey, occupied from the fourth century BC until the arrival of the Romans in AD 50. (*See also under Archaeological Sites.*)

5M NW of Leominster, approached from B4362 (59 F10)

Cwmmau Farmhouse, Hereford and Worcester A timber-framed and stone-tiled farmhouse of the early seventeenth century.

4M SW of Kington, to the W of A4111 (59 G8)

Dudmaston, Shropshire The estate probably existed as such as early as the twelfth century, but today's Dudmaston Hall, although incorporating Tudor fragments, dates from 1695 to 1701 and is attributed, though on circumstantial evidence, to the architect Francis Smith of Warwick; alterations, notably to the roof-line with the addition of pediments and a parapet, were made in the early nineteenth century and the south wing was heightened in the 1890s.

Dudmaston is visited principally for its varied collections of pictures, sculpture, furniture and applied art, much of the material having been assembled in recent years by Sir George and Lady Labouchere, who still live in the house. The collection of Dutch flower

The staircase in Croft Castle, with its delightful plasterwork, shows clearly the influence of the Gothick movement.

pictures in the library and dining room includes works by eighteenth-century artists such as Jan van Os, Jan van Huysum, Johannes Linthorst and Rachel Ruysch, while in the gallery devoted to botanical art there are examples of the skill of P.J. Redouté, P. Reinagle and, from our century, John Nash. Also to be seen are topographical watercolours, many of them Shropshire scenes, and an important collection of twentieth-century paintings and sculpture, including works by Barbara Hepworth, Henry Moore, Ben Nicholson, Sonia Delaunay, and Spanish painters such as A. Tàpies and L. Muñoz.

Quatt, 5M SE of Bridgnorth on A442 (88 C1)

Dyrham Park, Avon Dyrham is an ancient name (*deor-hamm*: deer enclosure), the site of the battle of 577 in which the Saxons defeated the early Welsh, thus cutting the latter off from their kinsmen in the West Country and confin-

ing them within their present borders. The estate existed in pre-Norman times and from about 1100 onwards was owned by two family lines, the break coming in 1571 when George Wynter bought it. In 1686 Dyrham passed by marriage (with Mary Wynter) to William Blathwayt, a successful public servant who became Secretary of State to William III and between 1692–1704 so extensively remodelled the Tudor manor that effectively he built a new

left The design of the dignified entrance front of Hanbury Hall reflects the influence of William Talman.

below This red japanned bureau-bookcase in the state bedroom at Erddig is described in the inventory of 1726.

house. Two architects were concerned. The earlier was a Frenchman, S. Hauduroy, responsible for the west front, at that time with the entrance. The other, slightly later, was William Talman, who designed the east front. Sheltered below a steep escarpment, the house and its park command good views westward.

The interior well illustrates the Dutch influence on taste at the close of the seventeenth century, with tapestries, panelling, leather-hung walls, Delftware, and pictures by such masters as David Teniers the Younger, Melchior d'Hondecoeter, Abraham Storck and Samuel Hoogstraeten, two of whose perspective paintings are here.

8M N of Bath on A46, 2M S of M4, Tormarton (57 G10)

Erddig, Clwyd The house dates from two periods: the central portion of 1684–7 was built by a mason called Thomas Webb, and wings were added in 1724 by John Meller who bought the property in 1716. Later, in the 1770s, James Wyatt was associated with the stone facing of the west front, while in 1826 Thomas Hopper designed the neo-classical dining room. Meller, a successful lawyer of both means and taste, may well himself have designed his new wings and it was certainly he who enriched the house with the splendid furniture that is still Erddig's outstanding feature. The many paintings are also notable and include portraits by Gainsborough, Cotes and Kneller.

Erddig is also known for its range of outbuildings and domestic rooms complete with contemporary equipment. The various workshops (joiner's, blacksmith's), the stable, the bakehouse, servants' hall and kitchen, together with a remarkable series of portraits of estate and household staff, combine to give a perhaps unique picture of the domestic history of a great house of the period. The garden has been restored to its eighteenth-century formal design, and there is an agricultural museum in the park at Felin Puleston.

1M S of Wrexham, E of A483 (61 E12)

The Greyfriars, Hereford and Worcester is a timber-framed and tiled house, mainly of the late fifteenth century but with early seventeenth- and late eighteenth-century additions.

Friar Street, Worcester (88 G2)

Hanbury Hall, Hereford and Worcester Recorded in the Domesday survey, and belonging to the bishops of Worcester until seized by Queen Elizabeth, the Hanbury estate was purchased by the Vernon family in 1631, the present substantial brick house, by an unknown architect, being completed in 1701 for Thomas Vernon, a successful barrister. The formal gardens laid out at the same time by George London were broken up in the late eighteenth century as being no longer fashionable, their place being taken today by some splendid lawns. The orangery dates from soon after 1732.

The outstanding feature of the interior is James Thornhill's painted staircase with its great classical scenes (c.1710). Thornhill also carried out the ceiling paintings in the Long Room, today a gallery displaying the R.S. Watney collection of English porcelain figures and Flemish, Dutch and French flower paintings; the collection also includes eighteenth-century English furniture shown both here and in other rooms.

2½M E of Droitwich, N of B4090 (88 F3)

Hidcote Manor Garden, Gloucestershire An extensive series of small and mostly formal gardens, separated from one another by hedges of different species and containing many rare trees, shrubs, plants and bulbs. The garden was the creation between about 1908 and 1948 of the horticulturist Major Lawrence Johnston.

4M NE of Chipping Campden, E of A46 (88 H5)

Horton Court, Avon This Cotswold manor house, although restored and somewhat altered during the nineteenth century, preserves its mainly twelfth-century Norman hall (an interesting architectural link between the Saxon 'aula', known only from illuminated manuscripts, and the typical medieval manor hall), built by Robert Beaufeu, the first prebendary of the see of Salisbury. A later owner of the estate was William Knight (1476–1547), a diplomat serving Henry VIII, and it was he who built the house's porch with its early Renaissance carving and also the unique detached ambulatory in the style of the Italian loggia.

3M NE of Chipping Sodbury, W of A46 (57 F11)

Lower Brockhampton, Hereford and Worcester A secluded and pleasantly situated late fourteenth-century, half-timbered moated manor house, approached through an attractive and rare detached fifteenth-century gatehouse. Close by are the ruins of a twelfth-century chapel. The house lies deep in an estate of 1,895 acres of hilly farming land and woods.

2M E of Bromyard, off A44 (59 G12)

Morville Hall, Shropshire A modest Elizabethan house to which two wings were added during the eighteenth century. (Visits by appointment.)

3M W of Bridgnorth, off A458 (59 C12)

Penrhyn Castle, Gwynedd The Penrhyn estate, dating back to the thirteenth century, in 1765 came through marriage to Richard Pennant, the man who developed the slate quarries above Bethesda. His successor, through the female line, was G. H. Dawkins Pennant, who in 1827 commissioned Thomas Hopper to rebuild the Gothick house (by Samuel Wyatt, c.1800) which he had inherited. The result was this huge neo-Norman Penrhyn Castle which virtually obliterated Wyatt's house, although today's drawing room represents his great hall, itself modelled on a medieval predecessor. Hopper was allowed a free hand – his responsibility embraced the interior decoration and even the furniture – and with both the exterior and interior he achieved the spacious yet solidly massive effect that was his highly personal interpretation of Norman. At the same time, modern details included a hot air heating system and water closets.

Main features of the interior are the plasterwork and the elaborate stone and wood carving, and also the unusual craftsmanship in slate, the staircase being one of the most extraordinary features in any interior in Britain. The castle contains a collection of about 1,000 dolls and an industrial railway museum, with locomotives dating back to 1848, interesting pictures and examples of slate work.

2M E of Bangor, at junction of A5 and A55 (60 C5)

Plas Newydd, Gwynedd The seat beside the Menai Strait of the marquesses of Anglesey, Plas Newydd as seen today is the result of the work carried out between 1783 and 1809, principally by James Wyatt and Joseph Potter, which both externally and internally converted an early sixteenth-century manor into a stately mansion; at the same time Humphry Repton advised on the layout of the grounds. Some alteration, notably remodelling of the north wing, took place in the 1930s.

Of the house's many elegant rooms the largest and most splendid is the music room, occupying roughly the position of the hall of the earlier house and very possibly incorporating something of its structure. Plas Newydd is rich in furniture and pictures, much of both coming from Beaudesert, the family's Staffordshire home which was demolished in 1935.

Among the artists whose works may be seen are Snyders, Hoppner, Romney, Lawrence, and Rex Whistler. Whistler was a close friend of the family and in addition to portraits and other works now collected here Plas Newydd houses one of his last and largest murals (1937). There is also a museum largely devoted to the 1st Marquess, who as Lord Uxbridge lost a leg while commanding the cavalry at Waterloo (1815). In the grounds, with views across the Menai Strait towards Snowdonia, large boulders mark the remains of a prehistoric burial chamber.

Anglesey, 3M SW of Menai Bridge on A4080 (60 C4)

Plas-yn-Rhiw, Gwynedd A small, part-medieval manor house with Tudor and Georgian additions; woodland and ornamental gardens. The estate includes several coastal and inland properties owned by the National Trust. (Visits by appointment.)

Lleyn peninsula, 3½M NE of Aberdaron on S coast road (60 G2)

Powis Castle, Powys Still inhabited after some 700 years, the present castle dates from the late thirteenth century when Edward I granted Gruffydd ap Gwenwynwyn the barony of De la Pole. In 1587 the castle was bought by Sir Edward Herbert who added the Long Gallery and did much internal remodelling; there was further reconstruction during the seventeenth to nineteenth centuries, the architects being William Winde, T. F. Pritchard and Robert Smirke, while the beginning of our century saw extensive remodelling of the interior and exterior by G. F. Bodley. Among features of the interior are the panelling and plasterwork; the

carved late seventeenth-century staircase and the State Bedroom, probably by Winde; ceilings and murals by Lanscroon; Mortlake and Brussels tapestries; early Georgian furniture; many portraits by, amongst others, Romney, Reynolds and Gainsborough; a miniature by Isaac Oliver; a view of Verona by Bellotto; and Indian works of art collected by Clive of India and his son, who married the Powis heiress and was created Earl of Powis in 1804.

The late seventeenth-century formal garden, very likely the work of William Winde and a unique survival in original form, has four terraces nearly 200 yards in length; outstandingly developed since 1700, and especially in this century, it is now one of the finest gardens in Britain.

1M S Welshpool, on A483 (59 B7)

Snowshill Manor, Gloucestershire The Snowshill estate is an ancient one, owned by Hailes Abbey from 821 until 1539 when, at the

Plas Newydd (*above*) **looks over the Menai Strait. The view from the house inspired Rex Whistler's** *trompe l'oeil* **mural in the dining room** (*below*)**.**

A view along one of the famous terraces at Powis Castle, showing the early eighteenth-century lead statues. The southerly aspect permits rare and tender shrubs to be grown.

Castles, Abbeys & other Buildings

Dissolution, it passed to the Crown. The rambling Cotswold manor house, dating mainly to *c.*1500, belongs only to the closing years of this long tenure; altered and enlarged in *c.*1600, the house was given a classical south front in about 1700. The last owner (1919–51) was Charles Wade, an eccentric whose hobby was to collect whatever took his fancy, and the astonishing results of this hobby – material as disparate as musical instruments, Japanese armour, clocks, toys, bicycles, oriental masks, spinners' and weavers' equipment and much else – cram the house.

3M S of Broadway (84 A2)

Tudor Merchant's House, Dyfed In part perhaps dating from the fourteenth century, but considerably rebuilt in the fifteenth, this house survives as a rare local example of a merchant's home. The interior frescoes, discovered only in the late 1960s under something like twenty-eight coats of lime wash, are contemporary with the rebuilding and typical of the interior decoration of the time.

Quay Hill, Tenby (54 G5)

Tŷ Mawr, Gwynedd A seventeenth-century farmhouse, successor to the one in which Bishop William Morgan, first translator of the Bible into Welsh, was born in 1541; his work, dedicated to Elizabeth I in 1588, became one of the foundations of Welsh literature and, as revised by Bishop Parry in 1620, remains in all essentials the Welsh Bible in use today.

3½M SW of Betws-y-Coed, best approached from B4406 through Penmachno (61 E7)

The Weir, Hereford and Worcester A garden with views of the river Wye and the Welsh mountains. The house (not open) dates from 1784.

Swainshill, 5M W of Hereford on A438 (59 H10)

Westbury Court Garden, Gloucestershire Laid out between 1696 and 1705, this formal water-garden with canals and yew hedges is an early example of its kind and something of a rarity because most such gardens were broken up when they became unfashionable in the eighteenth century.

Westbury-on-Severn on A48 (57 C10)

Wilderhope Manor, Shropshire Standing in a remote valley, Wilderhope is a late sixteenth-century house built of local limestone and little altered. The seventeenth-century decorated plasterwork ceilings are the principal attraction of the interior, that in the hall bearing the initials of Francis and Ellen Smallman who built the house.

7M E of Church Stretton off B4371 (59 C11)

Williamston Park, Dyfed In medieval times one of the deer parks of Carew Castle, and much quarried during the eighteenth and nineteenth centuries, the park is now a nature reserve. (Managed by the West Wales Naturalists' Trust. No parking; access only by footpath.)

The promontory between the Cresswell and Carew rivers, SE of Lawrenny (54 F4)

Arlington Row, Gloucestershire A row of early seventeenth-century stone cottages. (Cottages not open.) *Bibury, on S side of A433* (84 D2)

Ashleworth Tithe Barn, Gloucestershire A barn of the fifteenth century, 120 feet long with a stone roof and two porch bays.

6M N of Gloucester, E of A417 (57 B11)

Assembly Rooms, Bath, Avon Built by the younger John Wood in 1771 when Bath was at its most fashionable, these elegant rooms are frequently mentioned by Jane Austen and also feature in Dickens's *Pickwick Papers*. The rooms as seen today were rebuilt after being gutted by a fire bomb in 1942, with redecoration (1979) in late eighteenth-century style. (The Rooms are leased to the City Council and used for public functions. The Museum of Costume is not National Trust.)

Alfred Street, Bath (57 H10)

Blaise Hamlet, Avon A group of ten cottages in differing styles around a green, built in 1809 by John Nash for John Harford to house his estate pensioners. (Cottages not open.)

4M N of central Bristol, W of Henbury and just N of B4057 (57 F9)

Bredon Tithe Barn, Hereford and Worcester A fourteenth-century barn 132 feet in length and unusual for having a stone chimney serving the bailiff's room over the easternmost porch. Seriously damaged by fire in 1980 and being restored, it will *not* be open until repairs are completed.

3M NE of Tewkesbury, N of B4080 (57 A12)

Chipping Campden Market Hall, Gloucestershire A Jacobean market hall of 1627 with pointed gables and an open arcade.

Chipping Campden, opposite the Police Station (88 H5)

Cilgerran Castle, Dyfed The ruins of a thirteenth-century castle, built on the site of an earlier one by William Marshall, son of the Earl of Pembroke. Marshall's work was short-lived and by 1326 the castle was recorded as a ruin, though later there was rebuilding from time to time and the Vaughan family lived here until the early seventeenth century.

Strikingly perched on rock above the Teifi, the ruins have inspired such artists as Turner and Richard Wilson. They comprise outer and inner wards, separated by a rock-cut ditch. Entered through a gatehouse which stood beyond a drawbridge over the ditch, the inner ward preserves lengths of curtain wall, round east and west towers and a very ruined rectangular north-west tower, this last a fourteenth-century addition. Only fragments recall the domestic buildings that would have leaned against the inner walls. Two short sections of wall – one just north-west of the gatehouse, the other on the cliff edge at the north-east – are remnants of the twelfth-century castle. (Under the guardianship of the Secretary of State for Wales.)

3M S of Cardigan, 1½M E of A478 (54 C5)

Clytha Park, Gwent The estate includes a hilltop mock castle of 1790 and a nineteenth-century house. (Picnic site. Castle not open. House open by appointment.)

4M SE of Abergavenny, on A40 (57 C7)

The Fleece Inn, Hereford and Worcester Dating in part from the fourteenth century, this half-timbered house was first licensed as an inn in 1848. It is still an inn today.

Bretforton, 4M E of Evesham on B4035 (88 H4)

Hailes Abbey, Gloucestershire The extensive excavated remains of a Cistercian abbey founded with great pomp in 1246 by Richard, Earl of Cornwall. Richard was buried here and the abbey was long famous for its relic of the Holy Blood, mentioned by Chaucer in his *Pardoner's Tale*. The seventeen cloister arches are the main surviving feature and the site includes a small museum. (Under the guardianship of the Department of the Environment.)

8M NE of Cheltenham, near Winchcombe, 1M E of A46 (84 A2)

Superbly positioned on a rocky promontory above the gorge of the Teifi River, Cilgerran Castle is almost unassailable on two sides.

Hawford Dovecote, Hereford and Worcester Sixteenth-century and half-timbered.

3M N of Worcester, ½M E of A449 (88 F2)

The Kymin, Gwent A hill over 800 feet high with a tower called the Round House, built by a dining club in 1794, and a 'naval temple' put up by the same club in 1800 in honour of the Royal Navy, commemorating sixteen admirals and crowned with a statue of Britannia. Nelson breakfasted here in 1802. (Buildings not open.)

1M E of Monmouth between A466 and A4136 (57 C8)

Little Fleece, Gloucestershire A modest Cotswold town house, probably seventeenth-century. (Let as a bookshop.)

Painswick, 4M N of Stroud, off A46 (57 C11)

Middle Littleton Tithe Barn, Hereford and Worcester A barn 140 feet in length and dating from the thirteenth or fourteenth century.

3M NE of Evesham, E of B4085 (88 G4)

Paxton's Tower, Dyfed A folly of 1811 built by Sir William Paxton as a memorial to Nelson. (Not open. Car park with view.)

7M E of Carmarthen, S of B4300 (55 E8)

Skenfrith Castle, Gwent An unusually small ruined castle with a raised round keep standing within a roughly square curtain wall. Although there was probably a primitive fortress here as early as 1071, what is seen today was largely built by Hubert de Burgh between 1201 and 1239, the design being interesting for the way in which the keep is deliberately set on a mound of spoil so that defenders could fire on targets beyond the curtain. The west range of buildings, contemporary with the rest of the castle, was discovered only in 1954. With White and Grosmont (neither National Trust), Skenfrith was one of three castles known as the 'Welsh Trilateral', granted by King John to Hubert de Burgh. (Under the guardianship of the Secretary of State for Wales.)

6M NW of Monmouth on B4521 (57 B8)

Town Walls Tower, Shrewsbury, Shropshire Built in the fourteenth century, this is Shrewsbury's only surviving watch-tower. (Not open.)

Shrewsbury, Town Walls on S of the inner town (59 A10)

Tu Hwnt i'r Bont, Gwynedd The 'House over the Bridge' is a fifteenth-century stone building

Skenfrith Castle. With Grosmont and White Castle, it formed a line of defence for the Norman Lords Marcher (the 'Welsh Trilateral').

which in turn served as a courthouse and two cottages. (Let as a tea-room.)

Llanrwst, at W end of the bridge of 1636 (61 D7)

Westbury College Gatehouse, Avon The fifteenth-century gatehouse of a college of priests of which John Wiclif was a prebend. The college was founded in the thirteenth century on the site of an earlier Benedictine monastery.

Westbury-on-Trym, 3M N of central Bristol, key from 44 Eastfield Road (57 G9)

Wichenford Dovecote, Hereford and Worcester Seventeenth-century and half-timbered.

5½M NW of Worcester, N of B4204 (88 F1)

Archaeological & Industrial Sites

Breinton Springs, Hereford and Worcester Much of this farm and woodland is the site of a medieval village, the misnamed Breinton Camp in fact being a homestead enclosure. Footpath.

2M W of Hereford, left bank of the Wye (59 H10)

The Bulwark, West Glamorgan A complex Iron Age hill-fort.

Gower (55 H8)

Bushey Norwood, Avon Farmland with the

site of a field system and of a walled courtyard. The property is bounded on the north by part of a hill-fort. Footpath.

2M SE of Bath *(57 H11)*

Cadbury Camp, Avon An Iron Age hill-fort with a double rampart.

2½M E of Clevedon *(57 G8)*

Chedworth Roman Villa, Gloucestershire The extensive remains of a large Romano-British country house, occupied between about 180 to 350 and discovered and excavated in 1864. Some thirty-two rooms have been identified, including two sets of baths, one of these the damp heat type and the other the later dry system. There are some mosaic floors and the hypocaust system is well seen. Local material is shown in a site museum.

Near Yanworth, 8M SE of Cheltenham *(84 C2)*

Crickley Hill, Gloucestershire A Cotswold escarpment on which is part of an Iron Age fort.

6M E of Gloucester, just N of A417 *(57 C12)*

Croft Ambrey, Hereford and Worcester This large Iron Age fort above Croft Castle was first occupied in the fourth century BC, at that time being no more than a small defensive enclosure of some eight acres. When the Romans threatened in AD 43, the camp was much enlarged by second and third banks and outer defences, but was abandoned about seven years later after the defeat of Caractacus.

Croft Castle, 5M NW of Leominster, approached from B4362 *(59 F10)*

Dinas Gynfor, Gwynedd Part of an Iron Age fort on the northernmost point in Wales.

Cemaes, Anglesey, N of Llanbadrig *(60 A3)*

Dolaucothi, Dyfed A large property on which are the aqueducts, opencasts and shafts of gold mines, worked perhaps in prehistoric times but principally exploited by the Romans and also on and off since then. Close by (picnic site), the ancient Five Saints (Pumpsaint) Stone bears indentations, possibly the result of Roman rock-breaking but traditionally and more romantically left by five saints who used the stone as a pillow.

Pumpsaint on A482 *(58 H2)*

Haresfield Beacon and Standish Wood, Gloucestershire The Beacon (713 feet) may be the site of a hill-fort, and there is a Neolithic long barrow in Randwick Wood on the south.

2 to 3M NW of Stroud between A419 and A46 *(57 C11)*

Leigh Woods, Avon Woodland in which is the Iron Age hill-fort of Stokeleigh Camp.

Left bank of the Avon by Clifton suspension bridge *(57 G9)*

Little Solsbury Hill, Avon An Iron Age hill-fort with ramparts still faced with dry-stone walling.

2½M NE of Bath between A46 and A4 *(57 G11)*

Long Mynd, Shropshire On this large tract of upland moor there are some fifteen barrows, three stretches of defensive earthworks, and a length of the Port Way, a prehistoric track, later a drovers' road.

W of Church Stretton (A49) *(59 C9)*

Midsummer Hill, Hereford and Worcester An Iron Age hill-fort with hut sites.

Malvern Hills, N of A438 *(88 H1)*

Minchinhampton Commons, Gloucestershire Amberley Camp and Minchinhampton Bulwarks are Iron Age defences, and there are also remains of a long barrow.

N of Nailsworth and E of A46 *(57 D11)*

Mynydd-y-Graig, Gwynedd Iron Age hill-fort and megalithic remains.

Plas-yn-Rhiw, Lleyn *(60 G2)*

Pointz Castle, Dyfed A Norman motte.
5M E of St David's, S of A487 *(54 E2)*

Rainbow Wood Farm, Avon Iron Age field enclosures. Footpath.

Claverton Down, just SE of Bath *(57 H11)*

Rhossili Down, West Glamorgan The highest point in Gower, with the remains of two prehistoric burial chambers known as Sweyne's Houses (Howes), traditionally the grave of Sweyne Forkbeard, the Viking to whom Swansea is said to trace its name.

Gower, above Rhossili Bay *(55 H7)*

Rodborough Common, Gloucestershire Part of the site of an Iron Age enclosure.

1M S of Stroud between A46 and A419 *(57 D11)*

St David's Head, Dyfed The *Octopitarum* of Ptolemy. A stone rampart across the base may be Iron Age in origin. Near the headland there is a burial chamber, and there are remains of others in the area. *NW of St David's* *(54 D1)*

Sand Point, Kewstoke, Avon Here 'Castle Batch' is probably a Norman motte, while a mound to the east is the remains of a round barrow. (Leased to Axbridge Rural District Council.)

5M N of Weston-super-Mare *(56 H6)*

Segontium, Gwynedd A Roman fort probably built in AD 78 by Agricola for auxiliaries and occupied until about 380. What is seen is the ground plan, this including something of the defensive enceinte and gates, the barracks, and some administrative buildings, among them the commander's house. The excellent museum covers not only this site but also general aspects of Roman military life. Segontium is by tradition associated with Magnus Maximus (d.387), the Roman commander in Britain who was proclaimed emperor by disaffected troops and who lives in Welsh legend as Macsen Wledig. (Under the guardianship of the Secretary of State for Wales.)

SE outskirts of Caernarfon beside A487 *(60 D4)*

Telford Bridge, Gwynedd A suspension bridge across the Conwy completed by Thomas Telford in 1826 to replace the ferry. Telford exhibition in the Old Toll House.

Conwy *(61 C7)*

Telford's Conway Suspension Bridge was a major technical achievement of its time. Conwy Castle stands at the southern end.

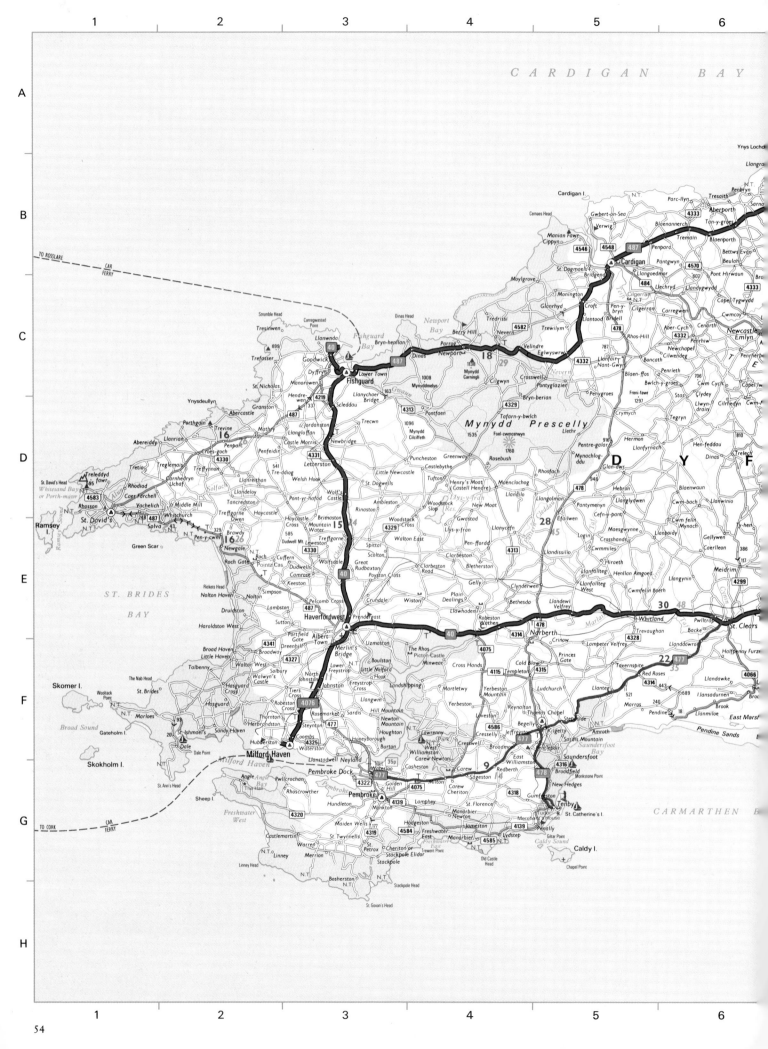

C A R D I G A N   B A Y

Ynys Lochd
Llangra
Penbryn
N.T.
Parc-llyn
Tresaith
Sarna
Aberporth
Gwbert-on-Sea
Verwig
4333
Tan-y-groes
Cemaes Head
Manian Fawr
Cippyn
4546 **4548** **487**
Cardigan
Blaenannerch
Penpard
Tremain
Blaenporth
Bettws Evan
Beulah
Moylgrove
St. Dogmaels
Bridgend
Llangoedmor
4570
807
Pont Hirwaun
484
Llechryd
Llandygwydd
4333
Brd
Monington
Glanrhyd
Llantood
Croft
Pen-y-bryn
Bridell
Cilgerran
N.T.
Carregwen
Cwmcoy
Aber-Cych
Cenarth
Cwm
Strumble Head
Carregwastad
Point
Dinas Head
Newport Bay
Berry Hill
Nevern
4582
Trewilym
Velindre
Eglwyswrw
4332
Rhos-Hill
Newcastle
Emlyn
Penrherb
Tresinwen
Llanwnda
40
Fishguard Bay
Bryn-henllan
Parrog
Newport
18 **29**
Crosswell
4332
Llanfair
Nant-Gwyn
Boncath
Penrhiw
Newchapel
Cilwendeg
Capel Ll
699
Goodwick
Dyffryn
Lower Town
Dinas
487
1138
Mynydd
Carningli
Cilgwyn
Pontglazier
Penygroes
706
Cwm Cych
Clydey
Freni-fawr
Trefasser
Fishguard
Llanychaer
Bridge
163
1008
Mynyddmelyn
Bryn-berian
Penrieth
1297
Stap
Llwyn-y-
drain
Cilrhedyn
Cwm
St. Nicholas
Hendre-
wen
4219
437
Scleddau
4313
Pontfaen
4329
Mynydd Prescelly
Llethr
Hermon
Llanfyrnach
916
Tegryn
Manorowen
Sealddau
Trecwn
1096
Mynydd
Cilciffeth
Tafarn-y-bwlch
Foel-cwmcerwyn
Pentre-galar
Mynachlog-
ddu
Hen-feddau
Dinas
810
Ynysdeullyn
Granston
Castle Morris
Newbridge
4331
1535
1760
Rosebush
Rhosfach
Glan-dwr
948
Hebron
Blaenwaun
Cwm-bach
Llanwinio
Porthgain
Trevine
16
Penparc
Llanglofan
Letterston
Little Newcastle
Castlebythe
Greenway
Maenclochog
Llangolman
478
Llanglydwen
Cwm-felin
Mynach
Ty-hen
Abercastle
Mathry
Treffynnon
Penfeidir
Tufton
Henry's Moat
(Castell Hendre)
Llandilo
Llanfallteg
Efailwen
Crasshands
Gellywen
Caerlleon
Abereiddy
Llanrian
4330
Croes-goch
Treglemais
Treffynnon
Welsh Hook
St. Dogwells
New Moat
28
Loginv
Cwmmiles
Llanboidy
386
117
Ynysdeullyn
Tretio
Rhodiad
Tre-ddiog
Wolf's
Castle
Woodstock
Slop
4329
45
Llandissilio
Llanfallteg
West
Hiraeth
Henllan Amgoed
Meidrim
St. David's Head
Treleddyd
fawr
85
Caerfarchell
Pont-yr-hafod
Brawdy
Ambleston
Rinaston
Woodstock
Cross
Gwastad
Llys-y-fran
4313
Llangynin
4299
*Whitesand Bay
or Porth-mawr*
4583
Rhosson
Vachelich
Middle Mill
Treffgarne
Owen
Haycastle
15 **14**
Walton East
Pen-ffordd
Llandewi
Velfrey
Llanfallteg
Cwmfelin Boeth
Ramsey
I.
St. David's
248 **487**
Whitchurch
Solva
43
Pen-y-cwm
Brimaston
Haycastle
Cross
Mountain Water
Great
Rudbaxton
Clarbeston
Road
Bethesda
30 **48**
Whitland
Backe
St. Clears
Green Scar
16 **26**
Newgale
Roch
Pointz Cas
585
541
Dudwell Mt.
4330
Treffgarne
Leweston
Spittal
Scolton
Clarbeston
Bletherston
Llandewi
Velfrey
Trevaughan
Pwlltrap
St. BRIDES
BAY
Rickets Head
Nolton Haven
Nolton
Simpson
Cuffern
Dudwells
Camrose
40
Poyston Cross
Crundale
Wiston
Plain
Dealings
Llawhaden
Robeston
Wathen
Marlan
Lampeter Velfrey
Llanddowror
Halfpenny Furze
Druidston
Lambston
Pelcomb Cross
Haverfordwest
Prendergast
Gelly
Clynderwen
Llandewi
Velfrey
Crinow
4328
22 **477**
35
Skomer I.
The Nab Head
Haroldston West
Sutton
Portfield
Gate
Dreenhill
Albert
Town
Prendergast
Uzmaston
40
The Rhos
Picton Castle
Minwear
Narberth
4314
Princes
Gate
Tavernspite
Red Roses
Llandawke
4066
Broad Haven
Little Haven
4341
4327
Merlin's
Bridge
Boulston
Little Milford
Cross Hands
4075
Cold Blow
4315
Llanteg
4314
443
Llansadurnen
Brook
East Marsh
Woollack
Point
St. Brides
Broadway
Walton West
Solbury
North
Johnston
Lower
Freystrop
Hook
Landshipping
Templeton
4115
Ludchurch
521
240
Marras
Pendine
18
Llanmiloe
Broad Sound
Gateholm I.
Talbenny
Walwyn's
Castle
7
Johnston
Freystrop
Cross
Llangwm
Hill Mountain
Martletwy
Yerbeston
Reynalton
Thomas Chapel
689
Pendine Sands
Marloes
93
St. Ishmael's
Sandy Haven
Thornton
Herbrandston
4076
Rosemarket
Sardis
Newton
Mountain
Houghton
Yerbeston
Mountain
Loveston
Begelly
4586
Kilgetty
Stepaside
Amroth
Sardis Mountain
N.T.
Dale
Dale Point
Steynton
477
Burton
Honeyborough
Lawrenny
Park
Cresselly
Broadmoor
477
Jeffreyston
Sanderlerton
Saundersfoot
Skokholm I.
Coombs
Waterston
4325
Cosheston
West
Williamston
Carew Newton
9
East
Williamston
478
4316
Broadfield
Monkstone Point
Milford Haven
Milford Haven
Llanstadwell
Neyland
TOLL
Waterloo
35p
Carew
Sageston
Redberth
New Hedges
Pembroke Dock
4322
Golden
Hill
4075
Milton
St. Florence
4318
Gumfreston
Tenby
Angle
Angle Bay
The Hall
Pwllcrochan
Rhoscrowther
4320
Pembroke
Hundleton
Monkton
4139
Lampey
Manorbier
Newton
St. Florence
Manorbier
4139
St. Catherine's I.
Giltar Point
Penally
CARMARTHEN B
Sheep I.
Freshwater
West
Castlemartin
Maiden Wells
4319
St. Twynnells
St. Petrox
Hodgeston
4584
Freshwater
East
Jameston
4585
Lydstep
Trewent Point
Old Castle
Head
Caldy Sound
Caldy I.
Chapel Point
Linney
Warren
Merrion
Cheriton or
Stackpole Elidor
Stackpole
Linney Head
N.T.
Bosherston
N.T.
Stackpole Head
St. Govan's Head

TO ROSSLARE
CAR
FERRY

TO CORK
CAR
FERRY

54

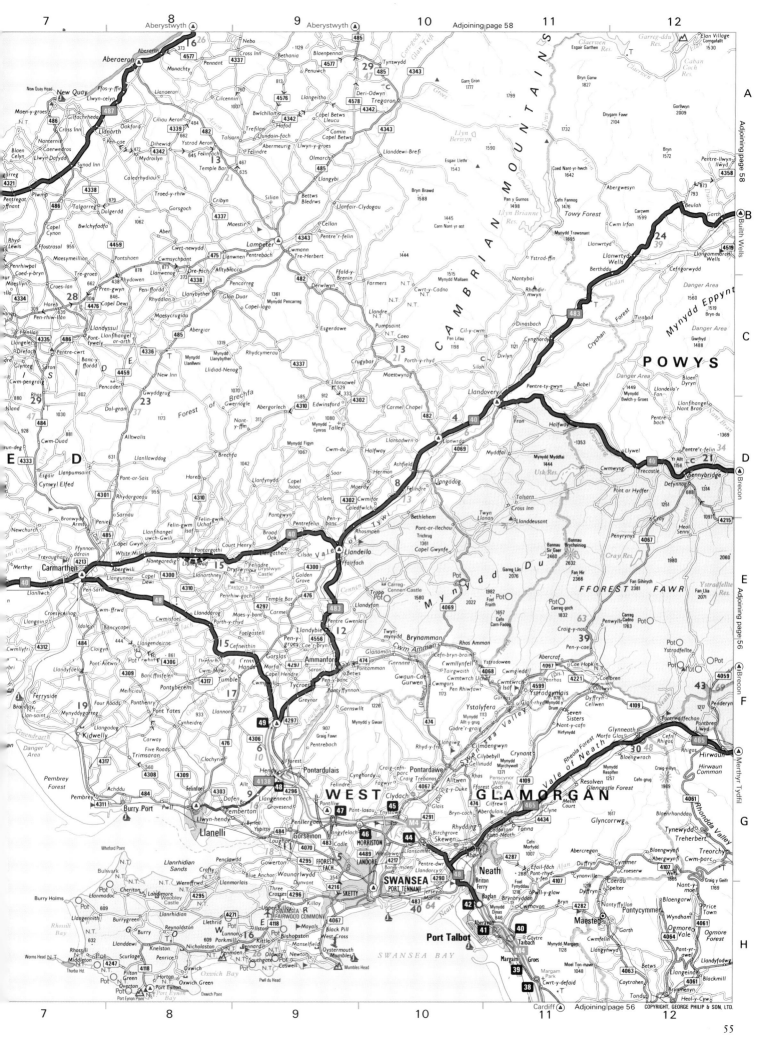

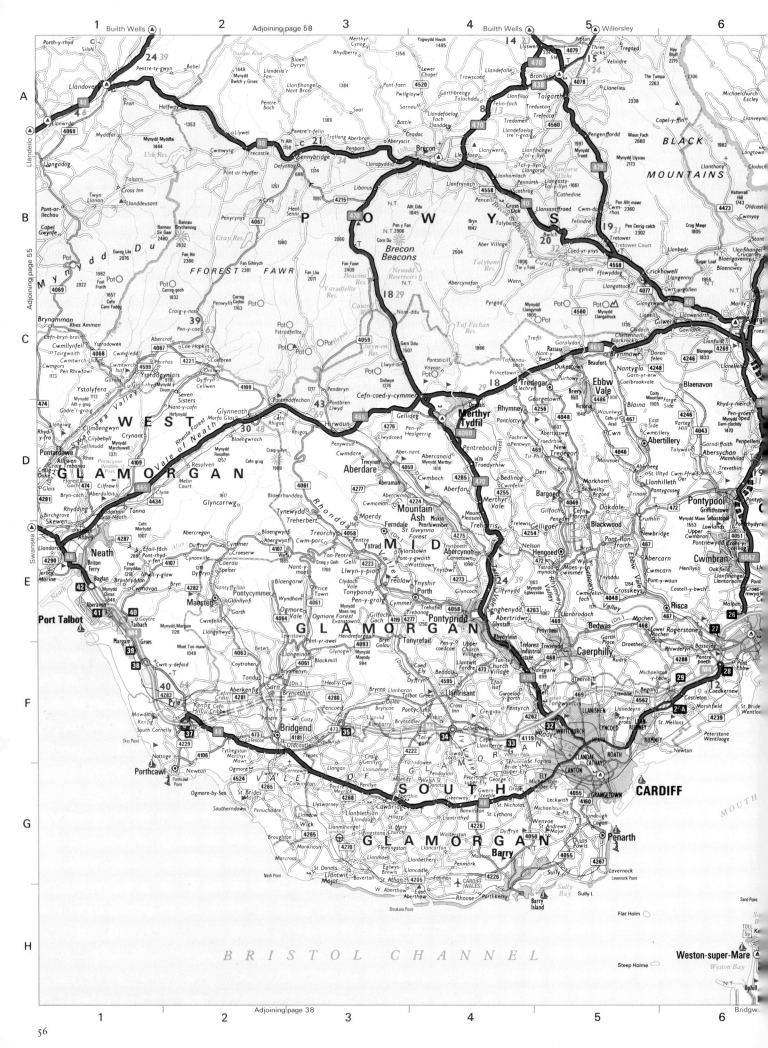

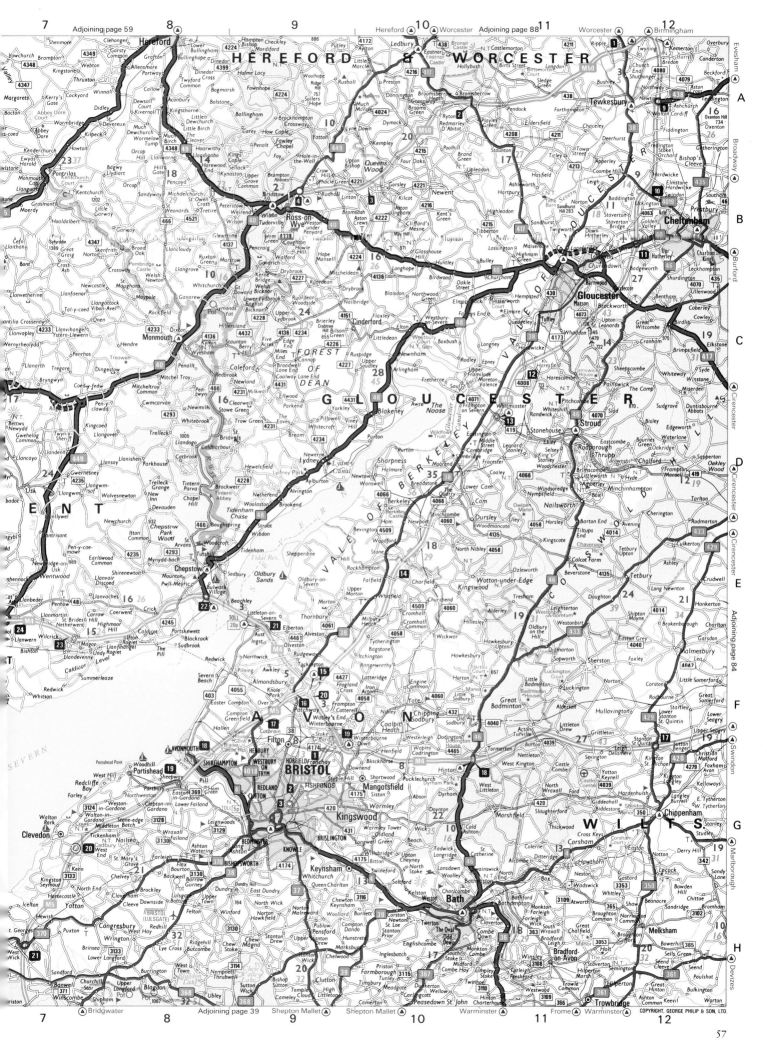

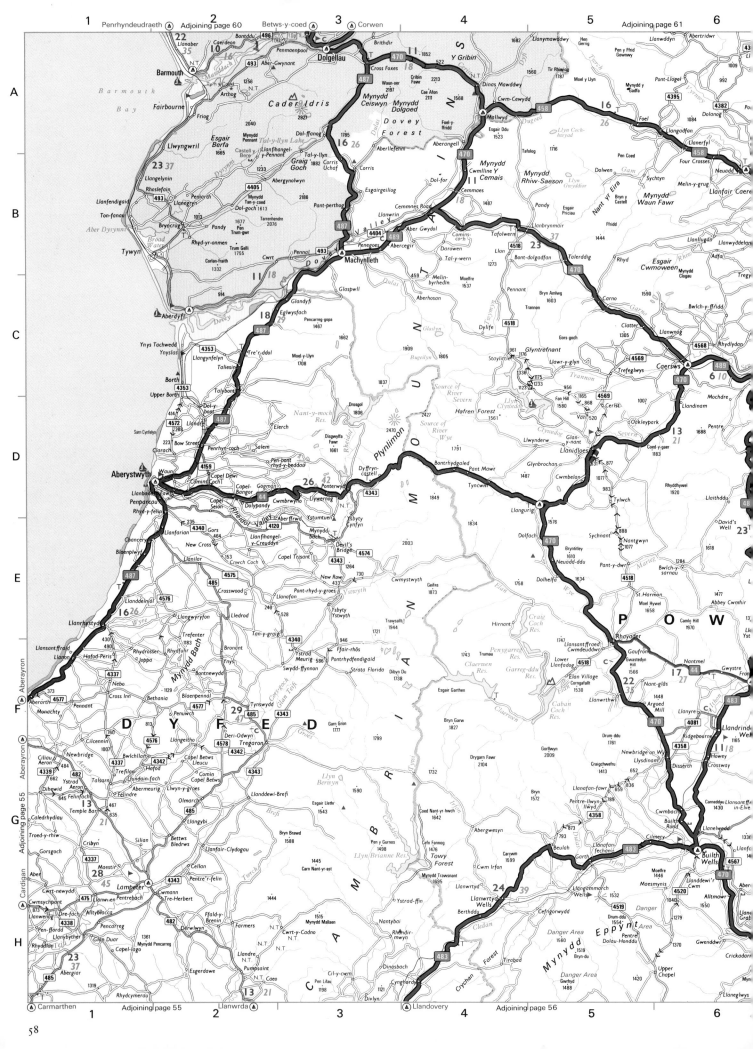

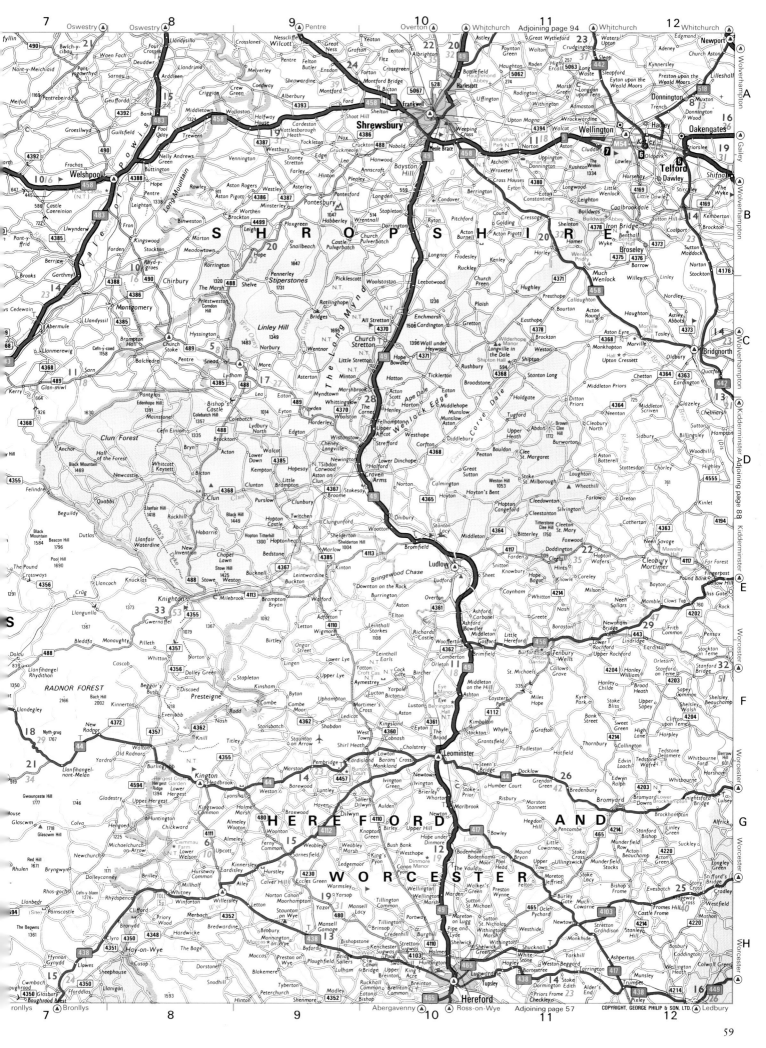

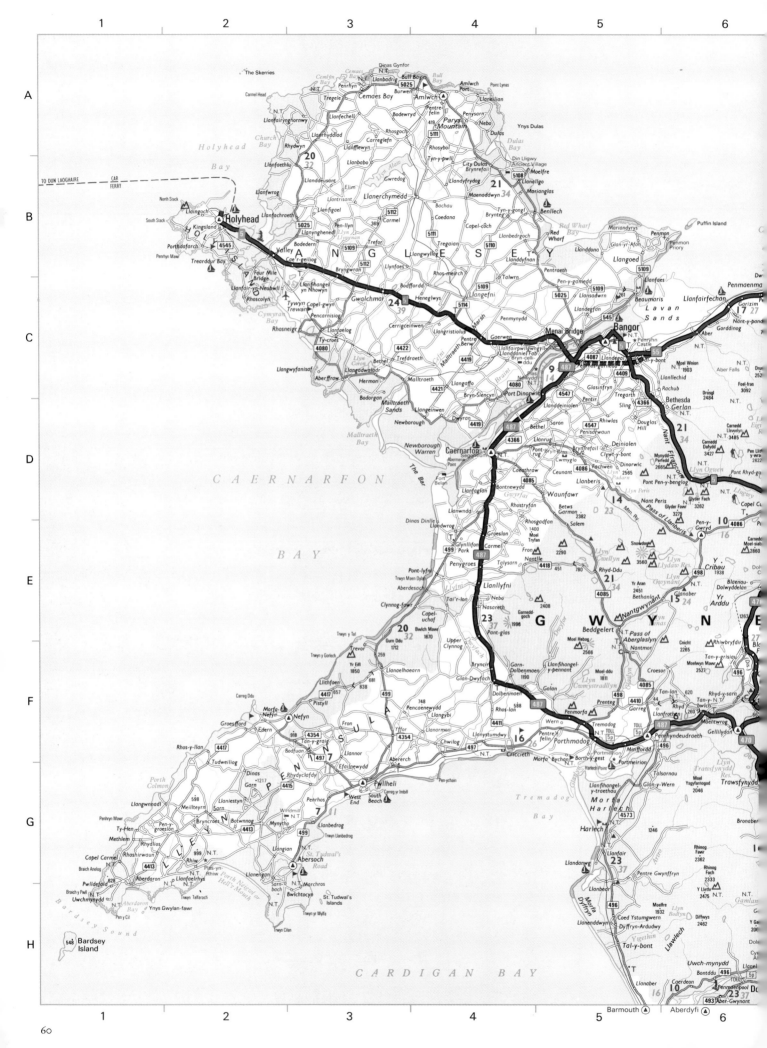

London, Thames Valley & Chilterns

PITSTONE WINDMILL

Here lovers both of open country and of elegant houses are well served by the Trust. It owns considerable areas on the breezy chalk hills, with their exhilarating views along the ridges and over the extensive plains, and others in the gentler Thames valley (a number of them, surprisingly unspoilt, in the northward loop of the river around Cookham). At the same time it owns some great houses – houses which seem largely to match the calm landscape and to reflect the spirit of their former occupants: urbane, civilized, and confident. Only the earthworks of ancient hill-forts recall times of constant fear and strife; the Trust owns no later castles here – indeed with the notable exception of Windsor there are very few in the whole region.

Some who enjoy visiting houses are more interested in the personalities that pervade them than in their architecture, decoration, or contents for their intrinsic worth. For them Carlyle's House (Thomas Carlyle), Hughenden Manor (Benjamin Disraeli), and Shaw's Corner (Bernard Shaw) will hold a special appeal, although on all the important houses the previous owners have left their mark.

Variety is a characteristic of the Trust's properties everywhere. Those in this region include four villages, two inns, a moated gatehouse, a huge and remarkable dovecote, a seventeenth-century windmill, a duck decoy, a 'Roman bath', and a monastic barn considered by William Morris to be 'as noble as a cathedral'.

Countryside

The dominant features of this part of Britain are the ring of chalk hills – the Berkshire Downs and the Chilterns – to the west and north of London, and the River Thames, which breaks through the chalk at Goring Gap. The hills bear numerous signs of early human habitation, and of having provided in prehistoric times the chief highway across this part of the country.

The Trust cares for some of the most spectacular heights and viewpoints on these chalk uplands. **The Clappers, Sharpenhoe (85 A11)**, is a dense beech clump at the northern end of the Chilterns; the steep flanks of the hillside are clothed in trees and scrub covered with Traveller's Joy, or Old Man's Beard. There is an easy approach to it on foot (half a mile) from the car park to the south. **Dunstable Downs**

left The Ashridge Estate (north of Berkhamsted) includes much fine woodland.

below The view to the west from Dunstable Downs, a 285-acre property on the Chilterns. Ivinghoe Beacon, also National Trust, is in the left background.

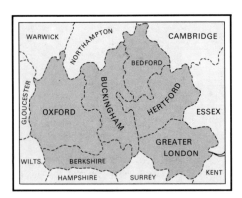

(85 B10/11), partly Trust property, is another steep ridge commanding long views over the Midland Plain. **Ivinghoe Beacon** (85 B/C10) is perhaps the best-known viewpoint, while **Coombe Hill**, further west (85 C9), is, at 852 feet, the highest; from here one looks north-east back to Ivinghoe, north to Mentmore Towers, north-west to Aylesbury, and west to the distant line of the Cotswolds beyond Oxford, while at the head of a valley a mile or so to the south stands Chequers, the Prime Minister's country residence. Beyond the chalk ridge of the Chilterns, the beech wood known as **Badbury Hill** (84 E4), above the village of *Coleshill*, covers an Iron Age fort, from the edge of which is a good and very distant view across the Upper Thames valley. These viewpoints are exhilarating; but seekers after solitude should turn elsewhere, even, surprisingly, to **Cock Marsh** (85 E9), on the south bank of the Thames facing Bourne End, one of the Trust's many properties in the Cookham and Maidenhead area. Here from a chalk ridge affording a superb view over the Thames and the town of Marlow a footpath descends to an enormous flat green expanse stretching to the river.

A countryside property of a different kind is to be found at Whipsnade (85 B11), where from the edge of the village green a footpath leads to the **Tree Cathedral**, with deciduous trees and conifers enclosing glades of quiet and mystery. Another is at **Finchampstead Ridges** (85 H9), a steep ridge of sand and heath covered with birch and sweet-smelling pine, with long southward views through the gaps in the trees.

. Prehistoric sites abound in these counties. **Uffington White Horse** (84 E/F4) is an ancient landmark (*see below under Archaeological and Industrial Sites*); there are many Iron Age forts on the hills, notably on Ivinghoe Beacon, while in **Maidenhead Thicket** between the A4 and the A423 (85 F9) are the remains of an ancient British settlement.

An interesting survival is the **Boarstall Duck Decoy**, a stretch of water, acquired by the Trust in 1980, near *Boarstall Tower* (85 C7). Decoys were introduced into England from Holland by Charles II. Ducks are decoyed into

netted-over funnels of water, called 'pipes', by a dog controlled by a decoyman. Nowadays they are, once caught, ringed for purposes of scientific study; in former times, however, they were killed and sent to market. At Boarstall there are also woodland walks in the vicinity of the lake; notes are supplied to help visitors interested in studying the local flora and fauna.

The traveller in these regions who likes gardens and parks will be well rewarded. Former landowners cherished their grounds as much as their houses, from Sir Francis Dashwood at *West Wycombe*, Ferdinand de Rothschild at *Waddesdon*, and the various owners of *Cliveden*, to Carlyle in his 'poor sooty patch' in Chelsea. The Trust, in the far from easy circumstances of today, strives to maintain the tradition.

Houses, Gardens & Parks

Ascott, Buckinghamshire People come here to see a lovely garden and an important collection of pictures, furniture, and Chinese porcelain. The house itself is a half-timbered building of the 1870s incorporating a farmhouse dating from the early seventeenth century.

Ascott was bought in 1873 by Baron Mayer de Rothschild of nearby Mentmore, and taken over as a hunting-lodge by Leopold de Rothschild, who employed the architect George Devey to transform and enlarge the old house. In 1937 Ascott passed to his son, the late Anthony de Rothschild, who with his wife was responsible for the present interior, and who gave Ascott and its great collection to the Trust in 1949.

The thirty-acre garden, laid out by Leopold de Rothschild, is remarkable for its specimen trees and shrubs. There are also fountains, sculptures, a sunken flower garden, a lily pond and an evergreen sundial – not to mention the

cricket ground, still very much in use.

Indoors, the Ascott collection includes excellent examples of French and English furniture, of English, Dutch, French and Italian paintings, and of Chinese porcelain, particularly of the Ming dynasty (1368–1644) and of the K'ang Hsi period (1662–1722) collected by Anthony de Rothschild.

2M SW Leighton Buzzard, entrance on A418 (85 B9)

Ashdown House, Oxfordshire The fascination of this house lies in its lonely situation, its unusual – even bizarre – appearance, and the story of the man who built it, William, 1st Earl of Craven (1608–97), and his single-minded devotion to Elizabeth ('The Winter Queen'), sister of Charles I.

The house, built about 1663, probably by William Winde, is without any external ornamentation, and looks, even with its flanking pavilions, somewhat too tall and narrow. Inside, however, the rooms are light and well-proportioned, while from beside the cupola above there is a splendid view of the rolling chalk downs among which the house stands.

Although the 1st Earl of Craven died a bachelor, Ashdown House remained in the Craven family until 1956, when, little altered structurally but virtually empty and almost derelict, it was given with an endowment to the Trust. It was fortunate indeed when in 1968 twenty-three portraits from the large Craven collection of pictures were presented to the Trust by the Treasury to be hung here – portraits of the first owner, of the lady whose cause he championed and her large family, and of some of the people with whom they were both acquainted during the turbulent years of the seventeenth century.

2½M S Ashbury on B4000 (84 F4)

Basildon Park, Berkshire Basildon was built between 1776 and 1783 by the Yorkshire architect, John Carr, for Sir Francis Sykes, also a Yorkshireman, who had made his fortune in India. It has had a chequered history: from 1910 until the outbreak of World War II it stood empty, and was then requisitioned; in 1952 it was bought by Lord and Lady Iliffe, who restored and furnished it with great skill, using items acquired from another Carr house which was being demolished.

Notable features are the recessed portico of the west front, with its four tall Ionic columns, and the Octagon Drawing Room, whose three great windows look out across the Thames valley to the beechwoods beyond; but it was not until about 1840 that the interior decoration of this room was completed by J. B. Papworth during the ownership of James Morrison, a haberdasher who built up his large

Ashdown House, set off by a restored seventeenth-century formal garden, looks like an enormous doll's house.

fortune on the principle of 'small profits and quick returns', but who was also a man of taste and discernment.

The house contains much good plasterwork, and a splendid collection of pictures, particularly Italian pictures of the eighteenth century, acquired by Lord Iliffe. The spacious park and gardens set off the house to perfection.

7M NW Reading, on A329 (85 F7)

The Blewcoat School, London was founded in 1688, and moved here in 1709, when the house was built. The statue of a boy in a blue tunic stands in a niche above the front door. The handsome schoolroom is shown to visitors. (Open by prior arrangement.)

In Caxton Street, near St James's Park Underground station (see map below)

Buscot, Oxfordshire This property includes the village of Buscot and part of the surrounding countryside; Buscot Park, housing the Faringdon Collection of works of art; and Buscot Old Parsonage, an early eighteenth-century house of Cotswold stone.

Buscot Park was built shortly before 1780 by the then owner of the manor, Edward Loveden Townsend, probably acting as his own architect. The main façade was considerably altered in the nineteenth century by a later owner, Alexander Henderson, 1st Baron Faringdon, a renowned connoisseur and collector. In the 1930s it was restored to its original appearance by the 2nd Lord Faringdon, advised by the architect Geddes Hyslop, who also designed the two pavilions that now stand east and west of the house.

Within, there is an outstanding collection of paintings of the Italian, Dutch, Flemish, Spanish, and English Schools, and of English and French furniture. There are also some excellent examples of Chinese porcelain.

The formal water-garden, which blends so well with the house and park, was laid out early in the twentieth century by Harold Peto for the 1st Lord Faringdon.

(Buscot Old Parsonage open by appointment with the tenant.)

Between Faringdon and Lechlade, on A417 (84 D/E3)

Carlyle's House, London This modest eighteenth-century house, where Thomas Carlyle (1795–1881), writer and philosopher, lived from 1834 onwards, has about it the aura of this great man and of his lively and intelligent wife.

The kitchen in the basement and the sitting room on the ground floor – 'unfashionable in the highest degree', wrote Carlyle, 'but in the highest degree comfortable and serviceable' – look much as they did in the Carlyles' time. Most of the furniture now in the library or drawing room was theirs too.

Upstairs in what for a time was Mrs Carlyle's bedroom is her famous 'red bed', its red hangings long since decayed. In the dressing room stands a mahogany washstand, given by Carlyle to 'the neatest of all Women'. And at the top of the house is the Attic Study, which was intended to be sound-proof but turned out not to be. The 'poor sooty patch of garden', on the other hand, where Carlyle cut the grass with a sickle, provided some solace.

Note: Certain rooms have no electric light. Visitors wishing to make a close study of the interior should avoid dull days early and late in the season.

24 Cheyne Row, Chelsea (see map below)

97–100 Cheyne Walk, London Comprises most of Lindsey House, built in 1674 on the site of Sir Thomas More's garden, and much altered in the mid eighteenth century. (Not open.)

Just W of the N end of Battersea Bridge (86 F3)

Claydon House, Buckinghamshire From 1620 Claydon was the seat of the Verney family, of violently fluctuating fortunes. The present house dates almost wholly from the mid eighteenth century, the creation of the improvident 2nd Earl Verney, and is decorated in flamboyant rococo style. The Earl built a huge rotunda attached to the north side of the surviving west wing, with another identical wing beyond, but both proved to have inadequate foundations and had to be demolished shortly after the Earl's death.

What remains, however, is quite enough to satisfy the most demanding student of architecture and interior design. The North Hall, with swirling designs on walls and ceiling; the saloon, equally magnificent but more restrained; the library, with its superb ceiling and frieze; above all the Chinese Room and the great staircase – these are some of the delights of Claydon.

In Victorian times Florence Nightingale (whose sister was the wife of Sir Harry Verney, the 2nd Baronet) was a frequent visitor here; the bedroom she always occupied is shown, as are a number of letters and relics.

In the grounds are three lakes, and, less than fifty yards from the house, the church of Middle Claydon.

3½M SW Winslow, near the village of Middle Claydon (85 B8)

Cliveden, Buckinghamshire This great house, standing above a beautiful reach of the Thames, was built in the Italianate style in 1851 by Sir Charles Barry, chief architect of the (quite different) Houses of Parliament. But there had been a house on the site from soon after 1666, when the 2nd Duke of Buckingham commissioned William Winde to design the terrace and on it to build a four-storeyed brick house.

Carr's great staircase at Basildon Park is unusually lit by giant semi-circular windows. The delicate plasterwork repeats neo-classical themes established in the hall.

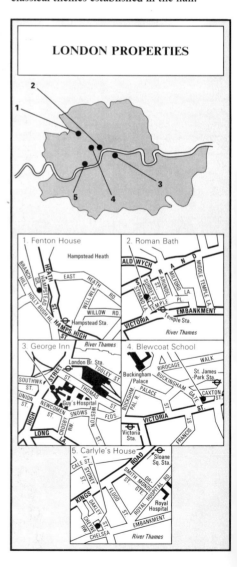

above The Chinese Room, Claydon House, decorated by Luke Lightfoot, reflects the eighteenth-century fashion for chinoiserie.

below left The formal water garden at Buscot Park was laid out by Harold Peto early in this century.

below The beds of the magnificent parterre at Cliveden are now bordered with box and planted with lavender and *Senecio*.

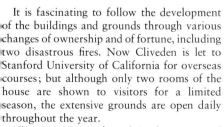

It is fascinating to follow the development of the buildings and grounds through various changes of ownership and of fortune, including two disastrous fires. Now Cliveden is let to Stanford University of California for overseas courses; but although only two rooms of the house are shown to visitors for a limited season, the extensive grounds are open daily throughout the year.

The grounds are formal in character, and contain two eighteenth-century buildings by Giacomo Leoni (the architect of *Clandon Park* in Surrey and *Lyme Park* in Cheshire) as well as

some good examples of classical Roman sarcophagi and of Italian Renaissance statuary collected by the 1st Viscount Astor, a former owner.

On N bank of the Thames 2M N Taplow, off B476 (85 F10)

Dorneywood Garden, Buckinghamshire A garden with pleasant lawns and many flowering shrubs. The house (not open) is the residence of a Secretary of State or a Minister of the Crown. (Garden open at certain times in August and September on written application.)

2M N Burnham (85 F10)

Eastbury House, London Typical Elizabethan brick manor house in the middle of a twentieth-century housing estate. (Not open.)

In Eastbury Square, Barking, ¼M W of junction of A123 and A13 (86 F4/5)

Fenton House, London Probably built in 1693, when Hampstead was still a country village, Fenton House is a large William and Mary house, much altered in Regency times. It is not known by whom or for whom it was built, but we know that in 1707 it was bought by Joshua Gee, friend of William Penn and champion of protectionism, whose writings had considerable influence in their time.

In 1793 the property was acquired by Philip Fenton; it was his son, James, who after 1807 carried out Regency-style alterations inside and out, moving the main entrance from the south side to the east, and perhaps giving the house its present name. Despite (or possibly because of) many later changes of ownership, it has hardly been touched since.

The last owner, Lady Binning, left to the Trust not only the house but also the collection of pictures, furniture, and outstanding English, Continental and Chinese porcelain that graces its elegant rooms. Here too is the beautiful Benton Fletcher Collection of early keyboard instruments, formerly kept at Old Devonshire House, which was destroyed by bombs in World War II.

300 yards N of Hampstead Underground Station, on W side of Hampstead Grove (see map p. 64)

Greys Court, Oxfordshire From the 1080s to the 1930s, with only two short breaks, Greys Court belonged to but three families: de Grey, Knollys, Stapleton. Today, the Tudor house of the Knollyses, with eighteenth-century improvements by the Stapletons, stands within the medieval courtyard of the de Greys. Visitors to Greys Court who enjoy architectural detective work will not find it hard to fill in the main details.

Merely to list some of the features of the place gives a hint of its flavour: the great medieval tower of the de Greys; the Dower House; the Cromwellian stables; the early-Tudor wheelhouse, containing the largest surviving example of a donkey wheel; the even older well, 200 feet deep. In the gardens is a stupendous tulip tree and a weeping ash, and one of the oldest larch trees in England; a rose garden, a wistaria garden, a nut avenue and an avenue of cherries, and a Chinese bridge leading

over a ha-ha to irises and shrubs.

In the house itself, modest and unassuming, are some delightful examples of late seventeenth- and eighteenth-century furniture, mainly English, and a drawing room with beautiful eighteenth-century plasterwork on ceiling and walls.

3M NW Henley-on-Thames (85 F8)

Hughenden Manor, Buckinghamshire Hughenden was the country home of the Conservative leader Benjamin Disraeli from 1847 to his death in 1881. The plain eighteenth-century brick house was drastically Gothicized for the Disraelis in the fashion of the time by the architect E. B. Lamb in 1863. The gardens and grounds were also much altered.

The main interest of the house derives from its connection with the great statesman, who was Prime Minister in 1868 and from 1874 to 1880. It contains many portraits and busts of Disraeli, of members of his family, and of his distinguished contemporaries (his 'Gallery of Friendship'). The library (the only room to retain its eighteenth-century fireplace and plaster ceiling) reflects the literary tastes of a man who was both politician and novelist. 'I have a passion', he wrote, 'for books and trees . . . When I come down to Hughenden I pass the first week in sauntering about my park and examining all the trees, and then I saunter in the library and survey the books.' The drawing room, with its Gothic architectural features, is typically Victorian, as is the rather sombre dining room. The study remains much as Disraeli left it.

1½M N High Wycombe on A4128 (85 E9)

33 Kensington Square, London Built in 1695, this narrow but attractive brick house was the home of the actress Mrs Patrick Campbell (1865–1940). (Not open.)

At NW corner of the square (86 F2/3)

Osterley Park, London An Elizabethan house transformed by Robert Adam in 1761–80 (after a start had been made by Sir William Chambers). The design, decoration, and furnishing of the state rooms remain almost entirely as originally carried out by Adam, or by John Linnell under Adam's general supervision.

The architecture throughout is characteristically cool, dignified, meticulous. The rooms were designed for show rather than for comfort, with the furniture standing against the wall in the eighteenth-century manner, and at Osterley each piece is placed, so far as possible, where Adam intended. The result is superb, and we are surely more likely to agree with Horace Walpole's opinion of the drawing room, for instance – 'worthy of Eve before the Fall' – than of the Etruscan Dressing Room – 'a profound tumble into the Bathos'.

After Adam's almost overwhelming perfection the comparatively rustic stable block, perhaps the original Tudor manor house, comes as something of a relief. To north-west of it is Adam's semi-circular garden house; facing this across the lawn is the Doric Temple, possibly by Sir William Chambers. In the park are three lakes and some huge cedar trees.

Just N of Osterley Station (London Transport) on A4, access from Syon Lane or from Thornbury Road (85 F12)

Princes Risborough Manor House, Buckinghamshire Elegant red-brick house of about 1670 with spectacular oak staircase rising by an open stair-well from the hall. Good seventeenth-century panelling. (Hall and drawing room shown by appointment only.)

Opposite the church near town centre (85 D9)

40, 42, 44 Queen Anne's Gate, London Part of a row of Queen Anne houses, and the headquarters of The National Trust. No 42 is of stone and stuccoed, while nos 40 and 44 are of brick. (Not open.)

On S side of St James's Park (86 F3)

Rainham Hall, London Brick house of 1729 with stone dressings, a typical example of the period. It has a beautiful porch, concealed cupboards under an archway in the hall, and a large garden. (Open on written application to the tenant.)

Rainham, just S of the church (86 F5)

Shaw's Corner, Hertfordshire This unpretentious house at the south-west end of Ayot St Lawrence was for forty-four years (1906–50) the home of the great Irish writer and dramatist, George Bernard Shaw. All the rooms shown are full of Shaw relics and are arranged very much as they were during his lifetime. His famous hats hang in the hall, above his glove

Shaw's Corner is full of Shaw relics. The desk in his study (shown here) remains exactly as he left it.

box and walking-sticks; the desk he worked at is in the study, with filing cabinets alongside – one of the drawers labelled 'Keys and Contraptions'. The drawing room next door was almost entirely Mrs Shaw's room. In the dining room Shaw would read during his vegetarian lunch (which consequently might last for as long as two hours); here too, after his wife's death in 1943, he was wont to sit in the evenings. From the dining room, which contains many personal relics, the visitor passes into the garden, with its revolving summer-house in which Shaw did much of his work. After his death at the age of ninety-four his ashes were scattered in this garden.

Like *Bateman's* in East Sussex, this place breathes the very spirit of a famous and most individual writer.

Ayot St Lawrence, 3½M W Welwyn (86 B2)

Waddesdon Manor, Buckinghamshire This house is a huge mansion of Bath stone built for Baron Ferdinand de Rothschild in the French Renaissance style between 1874 and 1889, by the French architect Destailleur. The grounds were laid out by the French landscape gardener Lainé. The hilltop on which the house stands had first to be levelled. The Bath stone and other materials were brought halfway up by special steam tramway, and hauled the rest of the way by teams of horses. The bare hillside was planted with hundreds of fully grown trees, the largest requiring as many as sixteen horses to shift.

The house contains much of Baron Ferdinand's collection of eighteenth-century French pictures and English portraits, and paintings by earlier Dutch and Flemish masters; of Miss Alice de Rothschild's collection of Sèvres china and of arms and armour, and Baron Edmund de Rothschild's equally important collection of pictures, furniture, carpets, and china.

The grounds of 160 acres include a large aviary in the eighteenth-century style and a

Francis was equally concerned. On an island in the lake, from which issues a cascade flanked by reclining nymphs, stands the Temple of Music. Three more temples are disposed around, while from the side of the lake opposite the cascade a broad walk passes through woods where serpentine streams run, crossed by footbridges.

The Trust also owns most of West Wycombe village, which extends east from the gates of West Wycombe Park and contains many old cottages. On Church Hill to the north is an Iron Age fort. The mausoleum and caves are not Trust property.

2M W High Wycombe on A40   (85 E9)

Castles, Abbeys & other Buildings

Boarstall Tower, Buckinghamshire Intriguing fourteenth-century moated gatehouse, with later alterations, of a manor house demolished in the eighteenth century (open by prior appointment with the tenant). *Boarstall Decoy (see Countryside section)* lies a few fields away to the north.

Midway between Thame and Bicester, 2M NW Oakley, off B4011   (85 C7)

Bradenham Village, Buckinghamshire A huge green slopes down from the church and the seventeenth-century brick manor house, where Disraeli's father once lived. The village is set amongst rolling hills, woods and cornfields.

4M NW High Wycombe on E side of A4010 (85 D9)

Chantry Chapel, Buckinghamshire Fifteenth-century building incorporating a good Norman

The Norman doorway is the most interesting feature of Buckingham Chantry Chapel and probably predates the building itself.

top **The centrepiece of this fountain pool is part of a fine collection of garden sculpture at Waddesdon Manor.**

above **West Wycombe Park reflects Sir Francis Dashwood's personal genius. The tapestry room shown here is hung with Flemish arras.**

herd of Sika deer. There is also a play area for young children. A huge Italian fountain dominates the approach from the south.

Children under 12 not admitted to house.

6M NW Aylesbury, entrance in Waddesdon village, on A41   (85 B8)

West Wycombe Park, Buckinghamshire This eighteenth-century house owes its character to that of its presiding genius, Sir Francis Dashwood, the 2nd Baronet.

The Dashwoods acquired the estate in 1698.

(Most of the 4,000-acre estate, together with the contents of the house, still remains in the family today.) From 1739 onwards Sir Francis transformed the Queen Anne house built by his father into one which, although it may broadly be described as Palladian, cannot be placed in any neat architectural pigeon-hole. Fortunately it has hardly been altered since. 'If the total effect . . . is one of a series of stage sets rather than an entity that is perhaps part of the secret of its charm.'

As interesting as the house, with its pictures, furniture and sculpture, and its impressive façades, are the grounds, with which Sir

south doorway. Much restored in 1875. Key obtainable in accordance with notice at the site.

In the narrow part of Market Hill, Buckingham, near its junction with West Street (85 A8)

Coleshill Village, Oxfordshire Handsome village of Cotswold stone houses and farm buildings running down to the River Cole, where Wiltshire begins. *Badbury Hill (see Countryside section)* is just up the road towards Faringdon.

On B4019 3M SW Faringdon (84 E3)

Falkland Memorial, Berkshire Nineteenth-century obelisk commemorating Royalists killed in the 1st Battle of Newbury (1643), especially Lord Falkland. Wordy inscription, supplemented by quotations from Thucydides, Livy, and Burke.

Beside A343 1M SW Newbury (84 H5)

Gray's Monument, Buckinghamshire Massive monument commemorating the writer of the famous *Elegy*. Erected in 1799, it stands on the edge of a field east of the churchyard.

Stoke Poges, 1½M N Slough on B473 (85 F10)

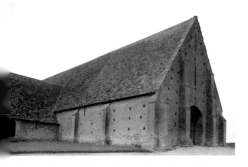

Great Coxwell Barn dates from the mid thirteenth century and belonged to the Cistercian monks of Beaulieu Abbey.

Willington Dovecote was built in the sixteenth century and is lined with nesting boxes for 15,000 pigeons.

The George Inn, London This is the only galleried inn left in London. It was built soon after the Southwark fire of 1676, replacing a former inn, burnt in the fire, which had stood there at least since the middle of the previous century. The George became a well-known coaching terminus during the eighteenth and early nineteenth centuries. Sadly in 1889 much of the galleried part was demolished. Since 1937 the inn has been cared for by the Trust; it is still very much an inn, providing food and drink – but not accommodation – for weary travellers. Shakespeare's plays are occasionally performed in the courtyard.

The George is referred to more than once in literature, notably by Dickens in *Little Dorrit*, but also in the works of E. V. Lucas, H. V. Morton, and the American writer F. Hopkinson Smith. The old, pre-fire, inn features in a poem published in 1655, unkindly entitled 'Upon a Surfeit caught by drinking evill Sack at the George Tavern at Southwark'.

Southwark, on E side of Borough High Street, near London Bridge station (see map p. 64)

Great Coxwell, Oxfordshire: The Great Barn Immense thirteenth-century monastic barn of stone, roofed with Cotswold stone tiles. The main oak timbers have lasted with only minor renewal for over 700 years.

2M SW Faringdon (84 E4)

The King's Head, Aylesbury, Buckinghamshire Lovely old hostelry, partly fifteenth-century, with cobbled courtyard. In a lounge of the hotel is a specially interesting fifteenth-century window with stained-glass armorials.

Off NW corner of Market Square (85 C9)

Long Crendon Courthouse, Buckinghamshire Fourteenth-century staple hall at the end of the picturesque High Street. Only the large upper room is open. It has remarkable roof timbers and a most uneven floor.

2M N Thame, via B4011 (85 C8)

Priory Cottages, Oxfordshire Range of fourteenth-century houses, formerly monastic buildings. South Cottage only is shown; it includes the great hall of the priory, and a small inner courtyard.

On corner of The Causeway and Mill Street, Steventon, 4M S Abingdon (84 E5/6)

Willington Dovecote and Stables, Bedfordshire Large sixteenth-century stone dovecote with curious stepped gables, and, across a farm lane, the stables, with rooms above for the men. (Open by written appointment only.)
7M E Bedford, N of A603 (91 K2)

Archaeological & Industrial Sites

Maidenhead Thicket, Berkshire Wooded area between two main roads, containing **Robin Hood's Arbour**, an ancient British enclosure of roughly one acre probably dating from about the time of Christ. Re-inhabited in World War II by the bodyguard of Queen Wilhelmina of the Netherlands.

Between A4 and A423, 2M W Maidenhead (85 F9)

Pitstone Windmill, Buckinghamshire One of Britain's oldest post mills, bearing the date 1627. In working order, except that it cannot be revolved to face the wind.

In a large field just S of Ivinghoe (85 C10)

'Roman' Bath, London An archaeological puzzle, although almost certainly not Roman, and probably not a bath. The most likely date is thought to be the seventeenth century, but evidence is scanty. Viewable from the pavement. (The 'bathroom' interior can be visited by arrangement.)

5 Strand Lane, accessible from The Strand via Surrey Street and Surrey Steps, or from The Embankment via Temple Place (see map p. 64)

White Horse Hill, Oxfordshire This property includes the White Horse hill figure, an ancient barrow or burial mound just above it, and Uffington Castle, a large hill-fort probably of the Iron Age. It can be reached by car from the B4507, or on foot from the Ridgeway to the south.

The Uffington White Horse, 360 feet long and 130 feet high, is one of the most ancient landmarks in England, although its origin is unknown. It is a lively representation of a horse cut in the chalk of the Downs, over 800 feet up. From the seventeenth century or earlier 'The Scouring of the White Horse' became an occasion for merrymaking by the people of the Vale, when a fair was held within the earthen ramparts of Uffington Castle. The last such ceremonial cleaning was in 1857.

On the knob below, known as Dragon Hill (also Trust property), St George is supposed to have slain the Dragon, the bare patch being caused by the spilling of the Dragon's blood. (Under the guardianship of the Department of the Environment.)

S Uffington, 6M W Wantage, on S side of B4507 (84 E/F4)

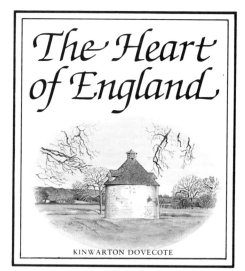

The Heart of England

KINWARTON DOVECOTE

The heart of England has an irregular beat. There could hardly be a greater contrast than that between the ruggedness of the Derbyshire Peak and the gentle meadowland of Northamptonshire, or between the bustling streets of Birmingham and the leafy lanes linking Preston Bagot with Wootton Wawen where a youthful Shakespeare may have roamed.

National Trust properties in the heart of England reflect this almost infinite variety. Ten minutes driving separates the Tudor charm of Little Moreton Hall on the Cheshire Plain from the starkness of Mow Cop Castle, an eighteenth-century folly high up on the western edge of the Pennines looking out across wild moorland to the pastoral plain beyond.

These two properties exemplify not only the variety but also the two main strengths of the Trust in the region: houses and scenic viewpoints. The houses provide a lesson in the development of large-scale domestic buildings.

Baddesley Clinton, a recent acquisition, is a splendid example of a late medieval moated manor house. The simplicity of Little Moreton and the opulence of Hardwick tell us much about contrasting Tudor building styles and

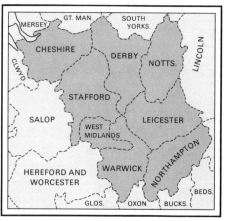

Tudor attitudes. Sudbury and Shugborough display the increasing elegance of seventeenth- and eighteenth-century interiors; Wightwick Manor the lavishness of late Victorian times. Dunham Massey, another newly-acquired property, is a mixture of sixteenth- and early eighteenth-century styles. Like its comparatively close neighbour Lyme, it stands on the edge of the Peak, an area where the Trust owns a sizable slice (nearly ten per cent of the Peak Park) of some of the finest, most varied scenery in the region.

Countryside

The heart of England has no coastline, but it can offer almost every other kind of scenery. Some of the finest (and some of the best viewpoints) lies within the Peak District National

The dramatically beautiful gorge of Dovedale is one of the most popular spots in the Peak District.

The wild moors of the Longshaw estate, only eight miles from Sheffield, typify the upland landscapes of Derbyshire.

Bare grit and shale on Mam Tor, the 'shivering mountain', fringes the view towards Lose Hill Ridge.

Park at the southern end of the Pennines in Derbyshire and the adjoining counties of Staffordshire, Cheshire and South Yorkshire. The National Trust acquired its first purely scenic property in Derbyshire in 1930. This was **Alport Height** (95 E11), 1,032 feet above sea-level, from which it is possible to see across half Derbyshire and the width of Staffordshire to the Wrekin in Shropshire. Fifty years later the Trust held well over 20,000 acres, with a further 3,000 acres protected under covenant.

More than half of this total is contained in one vast parcel of land listed under the generic title of **Hope Woodlands**. Most of this is not woodland at all but wild peat moorland which includes parts of the plateaux of Kinder Scout and Bleaklow (both reaching 2,000 feet) and a short section of the Pennine Way (95 A/B9). Close by lie nearly 2,000 acres of **Edale**, including Mam Tor, the Shivering Mountain, so called because of its sliding strata of grit and shale, and the Winnats Pass, a steep and narrow defile between towering limestone sides which is now a Site of Special Scientific Interest. Just to the east, a further stretch of heather-covered moors and woodland around **Longshaw** (95 B/C11) runs almost up to the Sheffield boundary.

South of these gritstone moorlands of the Dark Peak, the Trust now owns virtually all **Dovedale** (95 D/E9/10), arguably the most beautiful, and certainly the most popular, of the limestone dales of the White Peak, as well as the greater part of the connecting valleys of the **Manifold** and **Hamps** across the county boundary in Staffordshire. For all but short sections of the Manifold and Hamps, the delights of these valleys are denied to motorists, and therefore are all the more loved by walkers.

Motorists, however, can enjoy the views from **Alderley Edge** (95 B7), just west of the

The attractive pink brick gatehouse of Charlecote Park on whose walls Shakespeare is said to have written ribald verses.

Peak, or from **Mow Cop** on its western fringe (95 D7), without moving far from their cars. This higher northern portion of the region naturally possesses most of the more spectacular viewpoints, but by no means all. From **Kinver Edge** (88 D2), in that unexpectedly attractive salient of south-west Staffordshire that pushes down from the Black Country with the borders of Worcestershire and Shropshire close on either flank, one looks out across the Severn Valley to the Shropshire hills to enjoy a view of 'coloured counties' to challenge those that Housman enjoyed from Wenlock Edge or Bredon. Below the wooded escarpment a cave-dwelling known as Holy Austin Rock – possibly once a hermitage – has been hewn out of the sandstone. Other 'rock cottages' were occupied well into the nineteenth century. They are some of the most bizarre dwellings in National Trust ownership.

Staffordshire, indeed, is a much maligned county containing fine stretches of country off the usual tourist routes. One of these is **Downs Banks** (95 G7), north of Stone, where the

National Trust owns 166 acres of undulating moorland with a stream running through its centre. Another is **Hawksmoor** (95 F9), a larger stretch of woodland with open spaces on the edge of the delightful Churnet Valley. Much of this is a nature reserve founded by Mr J. R. B. Masefield, a cousin of the poet John Masefield, and there are interesting relics of its industrial past as well as glimpses through the trees of modern industry in an unusually attractive setting.

Houses, Gardens & Parks

Baddesley Clinton, Warwickshire 'The perfect medieval manor house' is Sir Nikolaus Pevsner's opinion of this recently-acquired property in a secluded setting in a remnant of Shakespeare's Forest of Arden. The present house dates predominantly from the mid fifteenth century, but the wide moat surrounding it may have encircled the earlier fortified manor house of the Clintons. The grey stone entrance front, approached across the moat by a Queen Anne brick bridge, was erected by the Bromes, who inherited the estate about 1438, but the entrance tower with its tall porch and fine Elizabethan window to light the banqueting hall were alterations made by the Ferrers family who owned the house from 1509. The Elizabethan fireplaces were theirs, as presumably were the numerous hiding places, including one by Nicholas Owen, the leading hide-builder, below the level of the lake. Panelled rooms, tapestries and heraldic glass add to the medieval atmosphere of a house which Pevsner says 'could not be better'.

5M SE Knowle, off A41 (88 E6)

Charlecote Park, Warwickshire Queen Elizabeth I slept here for two nights on her way to Kenilworth in 1572, but there is no evidence for the tradition that young William Shakespeare was caught poaching deer in Charlecote Park by Sir Thomas Lucy and took revenge by portraying Sir Thomas as Justice Shallow in *The Merry Wives of Windsor*.

Sir Thomas Lucy built the present house on the site of an earlier one in 1558, and it retains its basic plan though much altered and enlarged in the nineteenth century. The gatehouse in mellow red brick with polygonal angle-turrets, stone balustrade and oriel window was built slightly earlier than the house and remains unaltered, as do the stables, and brewhouse and the two-storied Renaissance porch of the house. Much of the collection of furniture, ceramics and lacquer came from the sale of William Beckford's Fonthill collection. (William Beckford (1760–1844) was a wealthy eccentric who built himself an extravagant Gothic revival

Wood was still plentiful when Little Moreton Hall was built in the sixteenth century. This fantastic house is perhaps the most famous example of half-timbering.

top The avenue of elms which once framed the front of Coughton Court are now no longer.

above The beautifully-proportioned north front of Dunham Massey is seen here reflected in the waters of the moat.

mansion, Fonthill Abbey in Wiltshire, now demolished.) The principal rooms are decorated in the Elizabethan Gothic revival style by Warwickshire craftsmen, and there are good collections of books and pictures.

The Lucy deer still roam the park, laid out in its present form by 'Capability' Brown. There is also a flock of Jacob sheep.

4M E Stratford-upon-Avon, on B4086 (88 F6)

Clumber Park, Nottinghamshire Early in the eighteenth century the Duke of Newcastle created the largest estate in the Dukeries, ten miles in circumference. Clumber Park was described as 'a black heath full of rabbits . . . with a small boggy close or two' within Sherwood Forest. Of its 3,800 acres, about 2,000 are woodland and over 600 acres heathland. The ducal mansion of 1770, designed by Stephen Wright, was demolished in 1938, except for the Smoke Room, or Duke's Study, now housing an exhibition, and the stable block (which probably pre-dates the house), but Wright's fine bridge, Doric temples and lodges remain, as does the eighty-acre lake. The two-mile double lime avenue was planted in the nineteenth century.

Near the lake is G. F. Bodley's ornate Victorian Gothic church, in the style of fourteenth-century Decorated and built for the

7th Duke between 1886 and 1889. It contains exquisite limewood carvings to the designs of the Rev. Ernest Geldhart, stained-glass windows by C. E. Kempe and some first-class metalwork, much of it wrought by estate blacksmiths.

2½M SE Worksop, via A57 or A614 (96 C3)

Coughton Court, Warwickshire Throckmortons have remained at Coughton since 1409, despite suffering the penalties imposed on Roman Catholic families after the Reformation. They were closely involved in the Throckmorton Plot of 1583 but not directly in the Gunpowder Plot of 1605, though it was at Coughton that Lady Digby and her companions awaited news from London on the night of 5 November, the house having been lent to Sir Everard Digby while Throckmorton was abroad.

The splendid early Tudor gatehouse is the most substantial portion of the fabric to have survived from that time. It is now flanked by battlemented Gothic wings of 1780. A wide archway in the gatehouse leads through what is now an entrance hall into a courtyard flanked by half-timbered north and south wings, the east wing having been destroyed by Protestant rioters in 1688. A secret hiding place reached from the tower room is a reminder of those

stormy times. There is a fine collection of family portraits, particularly outstanding being that of Sir Robert Throckmorton, 4th Baronet, by Nicolas de Largillière. This hangs above a Tudor fireplace in the drawing room where tradition says Lady Digby and her ladies waited for Catesby's servant to bring her news from Westminster.

2M N Alcester on E side of A435 (88 F4)

Dunham Massey, Cheshire In the reign of Elizabeth I, Sir George Booth built himself a moated courtyard house close to the site of a Norman castle of which only the motte remains. A later George Booth, 2nd Earl of Warrington, whose daughter and heiress married the 4th Earl of Stamford, rebuilt it in the first half of the eighteenth century. It is basically this house which stands today, though it was altered and redecorated by J. C. Hall for the 9th Earl between 1905 and 1909. It was acquired by the Trust under the will of the 10th and last Earl in 1976.

The house contains a series of portraits of the Grey family, Earls of Stamford, kinsfolk of Lady Jane Grey, as well as some outstanding early eighteenth-century furniture and Huguenot silver.

Within the deer park stands an Elizabethan mill in working order, two ranges of handsome early Georgian stables and a deer house bearing the date 1740. A row of dogs' tombs north of

Sixteenth-century tapestries hang below a painted frieze in Hardwick Hall.

the house have dates of death ranging between 1702 and 1836.

3M SW Altrincham off A56   (94 B6)

Farnborough Hall, Warwickshire This honey-coloured, classical stone house on a 'little hill of ferns' looking out to Edge Hill three miles away was acquired in 1684 by the Holbech family (who still live here). William and Francis Smith of Warwick probably built the early eighteenth-century west front, but the rest of the house was reconstructed around 1750, almost certainly to the design of the skilful amateur architect Sanderson Miller, who lived close by at Radway.

The interior of the house is notable for the exuberant rococo plasterwork by William

Perritt. The splendid dining room was planned to house large views of Rome and Venice by Panini and Canaletto (now replaced by copies).

A most attractive feature of Farnborough is the gently curving terrace walk along the ridge to the south-east. This leads to an obelisk three-quarters of a mile from the house where there is a magnificent view across to Edge Hill. The obelisk, and a temple and oval pavilion along the walk, are again probably by Sanderson Miller.

6M N of Banbury, ½M W of A423   (89 G8)

Hardwick Hall, Derbyshire A complete late Elizabethan mansion built by Bess of Hardwick shortly after the death of her fourth and most influential husband, the Earl of Shrewsbury, as her initials and coronets on the six towers remind us. The house is important architecturally for the innovations introduced by Bess and her locally-born architect Robert Smythson. These include the ground plan H-shape instead of the conventional arrangement round a courtyard; a great hall at right angles to the façade instead of running parallel to it; windows becoming progressively taller to suit the interior arrangement of servants' quarters on the ground floor, family apartments on the first floor and state rooms on the second floor reached by a magnificent stone staircase soaring up through the house.

The High Great Chamber, described by Sir Sacheverell Sitwell as 'the finest room not only in England but in all Europe', was evidently built to take eight pieces of Brussels tapestry depicting a hunting scene bought by Bess in 1587. These fit perfectly between dado and painted plasterwork frieze. Similarly, the long gallery must have been planned to take a set of thirteen pieces of Flemish tapestry telling the story of Gideon. On them hang an interesting series of early family portraits.

Most of the excellent craftsmanship was the work of local men using local materials mainly from the Hardwick estate, from which also came the fabric of the house, though the marble comes from elsewhere in Derbyshire. The ruins of Bess's earlier house stand close by.

6½M NW Mansfield, 9½M SE Chesterfield, approach from M1 (junction 29)   (96 D2)

Ilam Park, Staffordshire Eighty-four acres of thick woodland and park on both sides of the River Manifold adjacent to the National Trust's Dovedale and Manifold valley properties. Within the park the Manifold emerges from a subterranean course before passing below St Bertram's Bridge to join the Dove. Paradise Walk (twelve acres of woodland alongside the Manifold) contains the remains of a Saxon cross. Dr Johnson, who refused to believe that the river ran underground, used this area as the setting for *Rasselas*.

The surviving portion of Ilam Hall, a battlemented, turreted sham-Gothic mansion rebuilt 1821–6 and partly-demolished 1935, is

a youth hostel and not normally open to the public.

4½M NW Ashbourne   (95 E9)

Little Moreton Hall, Cheshire An idyllic, much loved, moated, half-timbered manor house. Ralph Moreton, whose family held the land for over six centuries, began building the house about 1480, and John Moreton virtually completed it about 1580. Apart from minor additions and modifications it has remained untouched since, mainly because the Royalist Moretons had little money after the Civil War for more than careful maintenance. They let the house to farmers for two centuries before it passed to a cousin, Bishop Abraham, who with his son gave it to the National Trust in 1937.

A bridge over the moat leads to the gatehouse, built around 1580, beyond which the original H-shaped house of 1480 forms the north side of an irregular quadrangle open to the west. The Great Hall, entered through an ornate porch, remains the focal point of the house. Much of the sixteenth-century character of Little Moreton comes from the patterned glazing of the windows and from the elaborate joiner's and carpenter's work. The painted panelling in the parlour was discovered during alterations in 1977–9.

4M SW Congleton, on E side of A34   (95 D7)

Lyme Park, Cheshire For 600 years until 1946, Lyme was the home of the Leghs, eleven of whom were christened Peter (or Piers). Sir Peter Legh VII greatly enlarged an existing house about 1560, but his sizable Elizabethan house is now partly hidden behind Giacomo Leoni's vast Palladian mansion of around 1725 with early nineteenth-century additions by Lewis Wyatt. The north (entrance) front is Elizabethan, though partly disguised by later sash windows and end bays, but the more imposing south front, with its three-storey Ionic portico, is by Leoni.

One of the most remarkable rooms in the

A detail of Gibbons' carvings in the saloon at Lyme Park.

house is the oak wainscoted Elizabethan drawing room, darkened in Victorian times by stained glass from Disley Church and heavy varnishing. The fine Baroque ceiling over the grand staircase was carved by a local craftsman, and another local man, an estate carpenter, made the present ceiling to the Elizabethan long gallery. Family tradition attributes the magnificent limewood carvings in the saloon to Grinling Gibbons.

Beyond the formal gardens, the deer park stretches on to the wild Peakland moors. Lyme Cage, a stone building on a ridge in the park, is probably an Elizabethan hunting tower rebuilt by Leoni, but its name suggests that it may also have been used as a poachers' prison.

(The whole estate is managed for the National Trust by the Metropolitan Borough of Stockport and Greater Manchester Council.)

6½M SE Stockport, entrance on S side of A6 on W edge of Disley (95 B8)

Lyveden New Bield, Northamptonshire This extraordinary atmospheric shell of a stone-built house is set in a rolling, empty landscape of cornfields and woodlands half a mile from the nearest minor road. Started in 1594 as a lodge to Lyveden Manor House – the 'Old Bield' – it was probably incomplete when its owner, Sir Thomas Tresham, died in September 1605 shortly before his son's arrest for complicity in the Gunpowder Plot, and it may never have been intended to be finished.

The cruciform shape of the house and the inscriptions and symbols on the frieze of the upper entablature illustrate the twin themes of the Passion of Christ and the Mother of Christ, recalling the symbolism of Tresham's better-known Triangular Lodge at Rushton, also in Northamptonshire.

To reach the house, two fields (half a mile) have to be crossed. The National Trust guide book, obtainable from the nearby cottage, is fairly essential reading for an understanding of Sir Thomas Tresham and his house.

4M SW Oundle via A427 (1½M from Oundle, bear left), 3M E of Brigstock (A6116) by road from its S end. (There is a small lay-by for cars.) (91 G1)

Moseley Old Hall, Staffordshire Charles II slept here for three nights after the Battle of Worcester in 1651. They must have been uncomfortable nights as the secret hiding place below what is now the King's Room is only five feet long and Charles was a tall man. He stayed here after his two days at Boscobel, nine miles away, and before his five weeks' circuitous journey to safety in France.

Victorian brick has unfortunately encased the original late-Elizabethan half-timbering, but the shape and the chimneys are unmistakably Elizabethan. Some early seventeenth-century panelling in the parlour has survived mining subsidence and a long period of neglect.

The house contains contemporary portraits

Sir Thomas Tresham's Lyveden New Bield, representing the Passion, illustrates the Elizabethan love of symbolism and stands as a monument to the Catholic faith.

of Charles and some of those who aided his escape, including his host Thomas Whitgreave and Whitgreave's chaplain Father John Huddlestone, who thirty-four years later administered the last rites to Charles.

The reconstruction of a seventeenth-century garden includes the then popular quince, mulberry and medlar trees, as well as knot and herb gardens.

4M N Wolverhampton, ¾M W of A460 (88 B3)

Packwood House, Warwickshire Charmingly situated in a clearing in the Forest of Arden, Packwood is famous for its gardens, particularly for its yew topiary work said to represent The Sermon on the Mount. A raised walk is flanked by twelve yews known as The Apostles, with four larger ones, The Evangelists, in the centre. A spiral walk leads to The Mount, crowned by a single yew, The Master. The layout probably dates from 1650–70, but the

Packwood House (*centre above*) is a fine example of domestic Tudor architecture but is best known for its topiary garden (*above*) representing The Sermon on the Mount.

clipped yews representing The Multitude lower down the garden may be a nineteenth-century addition.

The house and red-brick stable block form a delightful group. The main block of the house dates from the mid sixteenth century, but its original timber frame has been rendered over. Its preservation owes much to Alfred Ash, who bought it in 1905, and his son Graham Baron Ash, who carefully restored it before giving it to the National Trust in 1941. Graham Baron Ash created a new great hall, which had been used as a cow-byre and barn, and linked it to the house by a new long gallery. Queen Mary's Room commemorates the Queen's visit in 1927. Ireton's Room is the one occupied by General Henry Ireton on the eve of the Battle of Edge Hill in 1642.

1½M E Hockley Heath, off A34 (88 E5)

The principal feature of the garden at Moseley Old Hall is a copy of a seventeenth-century knot garden, using coloured gravels and beds edged with dwarf box.

Shugborough, Staffordshire This imposing, white-fronted country house stands in a large park owned by the Anson family from 1624 to 1960, and the 5th Earl of Lichfield (Patrick Lichfield) still occupies part of the house. The present house was started in 1693, enlarged around the mid eighteenth century and further enlarged by Samuel Wyatt from 1794 to 1806. Its contents include much that was brought back by Admiral Sir George Anson (later Lord Anson) from his circumnavigation of the world and other voyages, as well as a great amount of French furniture. The extensive picture collection includes two portraits by Reynolds.

The gardens and park are famous for their monuments, mainly by James (Athenian) Stuart in the neo-Greek style which he made fashionable. The Doric Temple, Lanthorn of Demosthenes and Triumphal Arch are outstanding. The Arch is a copy of Hadrian's Arch in Athens and honours the memory of Lord and Lady Anson.

Staffordshire County Council, who administers and maintains the property, has a folk museum in the stable block and a farming museum, with rare livestock breeds, around the Georgian farmstead in the park.

5½M SE Stafford on A513, entrance at Milford (95 H8)

Sudbury Hall, Derbyshire The extravagance of Charles II's reign is exemplified at Sudbury, the most richly decorated surviving house of the period. George Vernon spent most of the second half of the seventeenth century in building and decorating it. At first he employed mainly local craftsmen, like William (later Sir William) Wilson of Leicester who was responsible for the frontispieces on the two main fronts, the outstanding features of the exterior.

Later he turned to London men: Grinling Gibbons and Edward Pierce as carvers, Robert Bradbury and James Pettifer as plasterers, and the Frenchman Louis Laguerre for the decorative paintings in the dome and over the Great Staircase, which is considered the finest staircase of its period *in situ* in any English country house. The fine long gallery is a surprising feature in a house built as late as Charles II's reign.

Sudbury continued in Vernon ownership until acquired by the Trust in 1967, but in 1840 it was leased for three years to Queen Adelaide, William IV's widow, and her instructions for her own funeral are framed beside the bed in the Queen's Room.

Sudbury also houses a museum of childhood exhibits in the Victorian servants' wing.

6M E Uttoxeter, off A50 (95 G10)

Tatton Park, Cheshire Tatton is an ideal centre for family parties because of the variety of attractions within its 2,000-acre park. The colourful sixty-acre garden contains a small beech maze, one of only two on National Trust properties; a large mere is a haunt of wildfowl and of sailing enthusiasts, and nearby a former manor house is being restored by Cheshire County Council – who finance and manage the property in close consultation with the National Trust – and is open to the public along with a tithe barn and the site of the deserted village of Tatton.

At the heart of the park stands the stone-built mansion of the Egertons, who owned the estate from 1598 to 1958. The house is largely the work of the Wyatts, Samuel and his nephews Jeffry and Lewis, who worked here between 1774 and 1825. Most of the exterior, and the interior decoration, were designed by Lewis Wyatt between 1808 and 1813. Gillow of Lancaster, the cabinet makers, were responsible for the execution of much of his interior decorations and for most of the exquisite furniture and fittings.

The Egertons built up interesting collections of pictures, silver and books as well as furniture, but the 4th and last Lord Egerton had even wider tastes. Beyond the kitchens and servants' quarters, which are of great interest to students of social history, he built in 1935 the Tenants' Hall to house a remarkable collection of souvenirs of his astonishingly full life and extensive travels.

3½M NW Knutsford, entrance on A5034 just N of junction of A5034 and A50 (94 B6)

Upton House, Warwickshire Standing slightly back from the edge of the ridge less than a mile south of the battlefield of Edge Hill, Upton was bought by the 2nd Viscount Bearsted in 1927 to house his magnificent collection of works of art, which is particularly outstanding in the fields of ceramics and paintings. The ceramics collection is especially strong in the eighteenth-century soft-paste porcelains of Sèvres and

The eighteenth-century porcelain at Upton House includes this rare Chelsea yellow ground tea service with panels of chinoiserie figures dating from *c.* 1760.

These William de Morgan tiles illustrate the Pre-Raphaelite influence at Wightwick Manor.

Chelsea. More than 250 paintings cover a wide range of artists and subjects, with English sporting and country scenes of the eighteenth and early nineteenth centuries particularly well represented.

The house dates from the late seventeenth century, but was extensively remodelled by Percy Morley Horder in 1927 to provide a suitable setting for the collection.

The garden makes charming use of the natural landscape. One notably felicitous feature is a lake formed in the mid eighteenth century more than a mile from the house. This has a small classical temple in the style of Robert Adam on its eastern bank.

1M S Edge Hill, 7M NW Banbury, on W side of A422 (89 G7)

Wightwick Manor, West Midlands Here is Victorian splendour on the edge of Wolverhampton. The house was built in two portions in 1887 and 1893 by Liverpool architect Edward Ould for Theodore Mander, paint and varnish manufacturer, and its furnishings have been heavily influenced by Ruskin and the Pre-Raphaelites. It has William Morris wallpaper, tapestries and tiles, Kempe glass and Pre-Raphaelite pictures, though some things were brought in after 1935 when Sir Geoffrey and Lady Mander decided to make it a treasure house of the period.

The earlier, western, range has a black-and-white timber upper storey over a ground floor of Ruabon red brick. The eastern half, inspired by the Tudor houses of the Welsh marcher country, is predominately timber resting on a low plinth of local stone. The Great Parlour rises impressively through two storeys in the Tudor fashion. The drawing room has a superb Italian Renaissance fireplace and one of the several imitation Jacobean plaster ceilings by L. A. Shuffrey.

A charming, secluded garden, with yew hedges and topiary work, slopes down to a lake.

3M W Wolverhampton, on A454 (88 B2)

Castles, Abbeys & other Buildings

Colston Bassett Market Cross, Nottinghamshire The National Trust's earliest property in Nottinghamshire, the Cross was given by the Society for the Protection of Ancient Buildings in 1933. The Doric shaft on a medieval moulded base was put up to commemorate William IV's coronation in 1831, but its square head surmounted by a ball dates from the eighteenth century.

10M SE Nottingham, 5M S Bingham, 2½M E of Fosse Way (96 G4)

Duffield Castle, Derbyshire Only the foundations of the keep on a mound remain of the Norman castle of the powerful Ferrers family. The rest was destroyed in 1266 by Prince Henry, nephew of Henry III, in the Barons' War. The keep, commanding the Derwent Valley, measured 95 feet by 93 feet and had walls 15 feet thick, figures comparable with those of Colchester, Dover and the White Tower of London.

The site was given to the National Trust in 1899 and it is thus the oldest of the Trust's properties in Derbyshire. (It is managed for the National Trust by Duffield Parish Council.)

½M N Duffield station, 2½M S Belper on W side of A6 (95 F11)

Easton-on-the-Hill: Priest's House, Northamptonshire Pre-Reformation priest's lodge in village street of originally stone-built village. (Open only by appointment.)

3M SW Stamford, off A43 (90 E1)

Kinwarton Dovecote, Warwickshire This fourteenth-century circular stone dovecote stands in a field at the end of a lane beyond a charming group of buildings – church, rectory and farm – that make up the hamlet of Kinwarton. Its interior retains its *potence* (French for gallows), a rare feature nowadays. This is a vertical beam in the centre of the building to which are attached several horizontal beams at varying heights. The vertical beam pivots so that all the 500 nesting boxes can be reached from ladders fixed to the end of each horizontal beam. The birds nesting there were probably pigeons rather than doves. In the Middle Ages pigeons could be kept only by the lord of the manor, here probably the Abbot of Evesham.

1½M NE Alcester, just S of B4089 (88 F4)

Staunton Harold Church, Leicestershire 'In the yeare: 1653 When all thinges sacred were throughout ye nation Either demollisht or profaned Sr Robert Shirley Barronet Founded this Church Whose singular praise it is to haue done the best thinges in ye worst times And hoped them in the most callamitous The righteous shall be had in everlasting remembrance'.

So runs the inscription over the west doorway of Staunton Harold Church. Sir Robert Shirley went to the Tower of London for his act of defiance in illegally building this church – one of very few erected during the Commonwealth period – and died there aged 29.

The exterior is in the then outmoded Gothic style, but the interior is pure seventeenth-century and has changed little since. A painted ceiling signed 'Samuell Kyrk 1655' depicts the Creation. The wrought-iron altar rail and grille over the chancel screen are by the local craftsman Robert Bakewell. There is rich panelling on walls and piers, a Father Schmidt organ – older than the church – box pews, a sumptuous altar cloth and other draperies on the altar and in the pulpit in velvet. The seventeenth-century separation of the sexes in church is maintained at Staunton Harold, where the men sit on the south side of the aisle and the women on the north.

The church forms part of a charming group with lake and hall. The hall is now a Cheshire Home, but Group Captain Leonard Cheshire VC gave covenants over it to the Trust in 1956.

5M NE Ashby de la Zouch, just W of B587 (95 H12)

Winster Market House, Derbyshire This charming old building stands at the centre of a long main street in a ruggedly attractive ancient lead-mining village. Its stone-built ground floor with pointed arches was originally open but is now filled in, supporting an upper floor of brick with gable ends, and windows with single mullions and transoms. It dates from the late seventeenth or early eighteenth century, and was bought by the National Trust in 1906 after repairs from funds raised locally by Mrs Childers Thompson.

4M W Matlock, on S side of B5057 (95 D11)

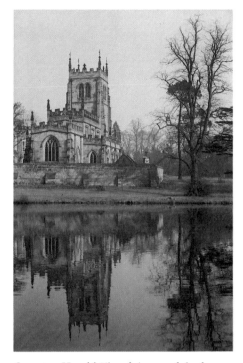

Staunton Harold Church is one of the few built between the outbreak of Civil War and the Restoration.

Archaeological & Industrial Sites

Letocetum, Wall, Staffordshire The excavated bath-house of a Roman posting station on Watling Street close to its intersection with Ryknild Street. The bath-house is attached to a dwelling which may have been a resting place for official travellers. A small museum contains finds from the site as well as some from another Roman site (at Shenstone, one and a half miles south-east). (The property is under the guardianship of the Department of the Environment.)

2M *SW Lichfield, on N side of A5* *(88 A4)*

Nether Alderley Mill, Cheshire This sixteenth-century corn mill is built of warm red local sandstone and set into a picturesque wooded bank. Water from a small stream was reinforced from reservoirs behind the mill to drive the two wheels.

Lath and plaster have replaced the original wattle and daub in the half-timbered gables, but the original mullion remains in a blocked-up window. The framed woodwork – all of oak – inside the building is as old as the mill,

left **Nether Alderley Mill is built right up against the dam of its reservoir; hence the unusual sweep of the roof.**

below **The cotton industry was the first in which rural cottage production was replaced by a factory system. Quarry Bank Mill, Styal, was built in 1784.**

but the machinery was renewed about a century ago.

The mill continued to work until 1939. The fabric was restored about 1950, and the machinery repaired and put back into working order in 1967. It is now grinding corn again.

1½M *S Alderley Edge, on E side of A34* *(95 C7)*

Stratford-upon-Avon Canal, Warwickshire The property comprises the southern section of the canal from Kingswood Junction, Lapworth, to the Royal Shakespeare Theatre gardens in Stratford-upon-Avon. It includes thirty-six locks, twenty-one cast-iron split bridges and impressive cast-iron aqueducts at Wootton Wawen (built 1813 on tapering brick piers) and Edstone. Construction of the canal began in 1793, but it did not reach Stratford until 1816. It passed into railway ownership in 1856 and eventually became completely derelict. It was the object of a pioneer restoration by volunteers and prison labour after being leased by the National Trust in 1960, and was reopened by Queen Elizabeth the Queen Mother in July 1964.

There is access to the River Avon by a wide-beam lock, with an attractive steel bridge made in Wormwood Scrubs gaol, and to the Grand Union Canal at Kingswood Junction. Throughout the thirteen miles in National Trust ownership, the canal passes through pleasant countryside.

(88 E5 to F5)

Styal, Cheshire A complete Industrial Revolution colony in 252 acres of well-wooded parkland in the Bollin valley. Samuel Greg built his Quarry Bank cotton mill in this narrow, isolated valley in 1784, attracted by the power of the stream. To this handsome Georgian mill, surmounted by a cupola, he, and later his son Robert Hyde Greg, added further buildings, including a warehouse and weaving sheds in the 1820s and 1830s. Before that – in 1790 – he had built an apprentice house near the mill to house the pauper children who formed the bulk of the labour force, for Styal was a small scattered place where little labour was available. Later it became necessary to recruit workers from farther afield, and to provide houses for them.

These houses form the major portion of the village of Styal, along with a shop, a school and the Norcliffe Unitarian Chapel (built in 1822). The chapel was given to the National Trust in 1979 by the chapel trustees to whom it has been leased back, but most of the rest of the estate has been National Trust property since 1939.

Much of the mill is now open to the public and is being developed as a charitable trust museum by Quarry Bank Mill Trust to illustrate the role of the textile industry in the north-west by means of many galleries and working exhibits. Part of the estate is now designated a country park.

1½M *N Wilmslow* *(95 B7)*

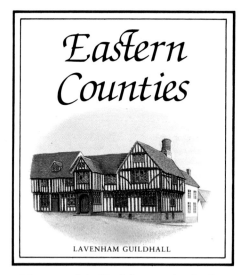

Eastern Counties

LAVENHAM GUILDHALL

Until quite recent times East Anglia was very remote. Even in the last century the fens, on the westernmost edge of the region, were not completely drained, and river crossings in the fens are still comparatively few. The coast, hospitable enough on a windless summer day, can be virtually unapproachable in winter, and those famous East Anglian skies tend to dwarf even grand country houses that in softer, more cosy countryside would dominate their setting.

Of all the Trust's properties in these Eastern Counties it is, coincidentally, probably the most recent major acquisition of real note that is outwardly most impressive. Wimpole Hall, near Royston, commands a low hill and, being seen to best advantage from the south, enjoys correspondingly superb views from its south-facing rooms. Such houses are comparatively few in this part of Britain, and their distance from each other and from main centres of population lends enchantment.

Appropriately, the National Trust owns examples of two types of property that sum up some essential characteristics of the region's history. One reflects the importance of the wool trade in the fifteenth and sixteenth centuries and includes the Guildhall at Lavenham and Paycocke's, in Coggeshall, the other the region's importance as a grain producer, with no fewer than three preserved mills among the properties owned.

There are also a number of properties that are built over or incorporate remains of abbeys or monasteries. These too are evidence of the isolation that the region has long enjoyed.

Coast & Countryside

The north Norfolk coast, part of which is officially an Area of Outstanding Natural Beauty, belies its comparatively easy access to London. British Rail trains run as far as Sheringham and the North Norfolk Railway, operated privately by steam enthusiasts, runs between Sheringham and Weybourne. That railhead roughly marks the western boundary of that part of the Norfolk coast that has been colonized by caravanners and the beginning of a wilder terrain where wildfowl are more numerous than holidaymakers.

On the south side of The Wash the coast is exposed and, in winter, exceptionally bleak, though in the height of summer it throngs with holidaymakers who know something of the underrated charms of one of the country's most remarkable sandy coastlines. The Trust is responsible for two of the best parts of the Norfolk coast – Blakeney Point and Scolt Head. **Scolt Head** (92 A1), the most northerly point of the Norfolk coast, is an island, and though it is ostensibly accessible across the marshes at low tide, these are dangerous, and the only safe access is by boat. Owned by the Trust since 1923, Scolt Head is rich in rare bird life – oystercatchers, gannets, kittiwakes, Arctic skuas, among others – a distinction matched only by the varieties of rare freshwater and saltwater plant species.

Blakeney Point (92 A3), Wells-next-the-Sea, was acquired by the Trust in 1912. The sand dunes and mud flats here, which are accessible on foot from Cley (pronounced Cly) at low tide or by boat at high tide, make a natural bird sanctuary: the long shingle beach is a barrier, and behind it are high dunes out of the reach of anything but exceptional tides. Many rare birds are regularly seen here, including Lapland buntings and long-tailed duck, and as many as 263 different species have been recorded, thirty-three breeding.

More easily accessible is the beach at **Brancaster**, a little over 2,000 acres of tidal foreshore, sand dunes, marsh and saltings (92 A1). The beach, while submerged at high tide, is one of the widest, most sandy and unspoilt on the Norfolk coast. The Trust also owns land on the **Stiffkey Saltmarshes**, between Wells and Blakeney (92 A3), with access off the A149 at both ends of Stiffkey village, and about two miles of the south shoreline of Blakeney harbour between Stiffkey and Blakeney. Ten miles west of Blakeney, the Trust owns just over 100 acres of heathland south of West Runton (92 A5). This includes the highest point in Norfolk and **Beeston Regis Heath**, a ridge of wooded and open heathland with good views of the coast. About twenty miles to the south-east, only a barrage of sand dunes divides **Horsey Mere** (92 C7), the most salt of all the Norfolk Broads, from the North Sea. Because

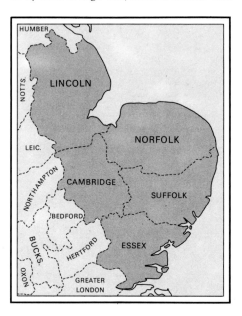

Wicken Fen is noted for its insect, plant and bird life and is visited by ecologists from all over the world.

of its brackishness, the plant and marine life is unusual and rare birds, including bitterns, can be seen. The 120-acre mere is part of a total holding of 1,734 acres.

The fen country that makes up a large part of Cambridgeshire is often dismissed as dull and uninspiring. **Wicken Fen**, near Soham (91 H7), however, is an exceptional and haunting place. The last substantial remnant of the Great Fen of East Anglia, this is one of Europe's most important 'wet' nature reserves. Surrounded by drained fenland, composed mainly of peat which contracts as it dries, Wicken is undrained and is therefore more prominent, a kind of island in an inland sea. The property consists of about 730 acres of exceptional sanctuary for rare insects, spiders, birds and plants, with, for example, 700 kinds of butterflies and moths alone. There is an imaginative display in the Thorpe Building at the access point to the Fen.

The wild and lonely stretches of Scolt Head are rich in marine flora and contain large nesting colonies of sea-birds.

In Essex the National Trust owns two properties in the remnants of Epping Forest, which once covered almost the whole country. **Blakes Wood** (87 C7), between Danbury and Little Baddow, is one of the few areas of true woodland left. It is best known for hornbeams, chestnuts and wild flowers and is well served by public footpaths. More usually, the Forest is represented by little pockets of heath and scrub, like the 200 or so acres that make up **Danbury and Lingwood commons** (87 C/D7/8) situated on a ridge between Chelmsford and Maldon. Danbury is more open, more typical of the common land on which 'commoners' could graze their cattle and sheep, while Lingwood is more forested, with open glades and clearings. Both are rich in unusual flora.

Similar to Epping Forest, though consisting only of about a thousand acres, **Hatfield Forest** (86 B5) was a Royal hunting ground even before the Norman Conquest. Here there are still fallow deer, foxes, badgers and, among the bird population, woodpeckers, hawfinches and grasshopper warblers. On the lake and the adjoining marsh are snipe, grebe and water-hen,

among other wildfowl. There are hornbeams among the trees, but the most famous tree of all is the Old Doodle Oak, which 'died' over a hundred years ago.

Only six miles north-west of what is now Southend, a fortress was created almost a thousand years ago by cutting off access to a spur of land jutting out from the **Rayleigh Hills** (87 E8), and though nothing except impressive earthworks remains of what was a primitive motte-and-bailey castle, further defended by ditches and stockades, this is an imposing site. The Domesday Book of 1086 mentions the castle.

The Trust's most important properties in rural or coastal Suffolk are at **Dunwich Heath** (93 H/J7/8), just over 200 acres of sandy cliff and heathland forming a coastal beauty spot, and **Flatford Mill** (93 M4). Though neither the mill, which belonged to John Constable's father, and where John himself worked for a time, nor the nearby Willie Lott's Cottage, are open, they are worth visiting for their setting.

Houses, Gardens & Parks

Angel Corner, Suffolk In a Queen Anne house acquired by the Trust in 1943 is the John Gershom Parkington Memorial Collection of Time Measurement Instruments. Housed in the principal rooms in the building, the collection is perhaps best known for the 'Atmos' clock, which operates by changes in temperature. A change of only 2°F provides enough energy to run the clock for forty-eight hours.

Angel Hill, Bury St Edmunds   (93 J2)

Anglesey Abbey, Cambridgeshire Little remains of the Augustinian priory that was founded here in 1135 except for a crypt under the present house that dates from about 1235, parts of the chapter house – much altered before 1600 and embedded in the core of the present building – and the vaulted Canon's Parlour, now the dining room. Outwardly Anglesey Abbey looks like a typical Elizabethan manor house of local greyish stone, with bay windows, mullions, dormer windows and a steep tiled roof, partly covered by creeper.

The house is best known for being surrounded by one of the most remarkable gardens in East Anglia, with a layout dating roughly from 1926, when Lord Fairhaven bought the abbey. He planted herbaceous borders, rare flowers and trees and planned woodland walks that still have not reached full

The lake in Hatfield Forest was created in the eighteenth century; it is now a favourite haunt of water-birds.

Oxburgh Hall, rising sheer from its formal moat, was built at a time when protection was needed against widespread unrest.

maturity – all of them part of a grand and intricate geometric pattern rarely seen since Elizabethan times.

Inside the house there is a cornucopia of treasures, an Aladdin's cave of priceless furniture, silver, paintings, porcelain, from Ming Dynasty lacquered effects to Egyptian *objets d'art*. The statuary in the garden includes busts of Roman emperors and lions couchant.

The house that Lord Fairhaven saved and recreated was once owned by Thomas Hobson, the carter from whose name the phrase 'Hobson's Choice' derives, and Sir George Downing, whose name lives on in Cambridge University's Downing College, which he founded.

6M NE of Cambridge on B1102 Cambridge to Mildenhall Road (91 J6)

Blickling Hall, Norfolk This exceptional house, both beautiful and historic, is enhanced by the spacious hamlet in which it is situated. Set well back from the road, its red-brick Jacobean façade contrasts with the dark, high yew hedges that border the wide approach drive. Between these hedges and the house itself are harmonious and elegant outbuildings, partly creeper-clad, with ornate Dutch-style gables and 'Elizabethan' chimneys.

Blickling Hall was built between 1616 and 1625 by the Hobart family, who became the Earls of Buckinghamshire. It then passed to the Marquesses of Lothian, and was bequeathed to the Trust by the 11th Marquess, who died in 1940, along with 4,500 acres.

Though much of the exterior is original the interior has been radically changed, and the best of it owes much to the eighteenth century, when the Hall was owned by the 2nd Earl of Buckinghamshire. He was ambassador to St Petersburg in the 1760s, and had one room redesigned in the classical style to accommodate a tapestry given to him by Catherine the Great. Other remarkable rooms include the Chinese Bedroom and the long gallery, with an exquisitely plastered ceiling.

The garden, though partly reorganized in modern times, is largely Georgian in layout: a rare survival, with wooded walks, an orangery, a pre-1730 'temple', topiary and now-mature rare trees.

1½M NW of Aylsham, off B1354 (92 C5)

Felbrigg Hall, Norfolk Felbrigg combines an almost perfect, unaltered Jacobean exterior (built in the 1620s, at roughly the same time as *Blickling Hall*) with a sumptuous and beautiful eighteenth-century interior: the best of two elegant worlds. The house was built by the Windham family and is the result of 300 years' growth and change. William Windham I added

This exquisite bureau by Roentgen at Anglesey Abbey was made for Tsar Paul I. The Regency clock is by James McCabe.

Blickling Hall is a splendid Jacobean house, seen here across the formal garden.

Gunby Hall, built of beautiful rose-red brick, is a good example of a country house in William III's reign.

With its chimneys and turrets, Melford Hall is a typical mid sixteenth-century building.

The rotunda at Ickworth is the centrepiece of an extraordinary building.

a new wing in 1670 in symmetrical Reformation style and is also responsible for the fine plaster ceilings that can be seen in the drawing room and cabinet. He was a forester and it was he who planted the great chestnuts that today shield the house from winds off the North Sea, and many other trees in the great park.

His son, William Windham II, was largely responsible for the decoration and contents of the Georgian rooms. After his return from the Grand Tour in 1741, he began to refurbish the house in contemporary style and created a new dining room, staircase and Gothick library. The Georgian rooms remain largely unaltered today and are the most notable aspect of the house. Among later changes was the addition in about 1825 of battlemented stables in the revived Gothic style.

3M Cromer, W B1436   (92 B5)

Grantham House, Lincolnshire This is a mainly seventeenth- and eighteenth-century house, which does however retain some traces of its fifteenth-century origins. With quiet gardens that border the River Witham, Grantham House is a pleasant, comfortable-seeming marriage of different styles both internally and externally.

Opposite the parish church, in Castlegate, Grantham   (96 G6)

Gunby Hall, Lincolnshire Gunby was one of the country houses acquired by the Trust during World War II. At first sight it could be a town house built by Wren, and it was probably designed by a master builder with knowledge of London. It was commissioned in 1700 by Sir William Massingberd, whose family had already been associated with Lincolnshire for 300 years. Built of a distinctive dark red brick fired from clay actually dug from the estate, the house is set off by formal gardens that do not follow the original design but do contain,

The half-timbered front of Paycocke's, showing the richly-carved bressummer and the oriel windows on the upper storey.

within the walled garden, rare original fruit trees. Among the comparatively small rooms inside the house, several of them oak panelled, is a dining room added in 1873 that has the elegant Queen Anne ambience of the house as a whole.

Gunby has some associations with Dr Johnson: the dining room has a portrait of Bennet Langton, a friend of Johnson, who brought to Gunby a drawing of Boswell and one of only six autographed copies of Boswell's *Life of Johnson*.

7M W of Skegness, on S side of A158, the Lincoln/Skegness road   (97 D11)

Ickworth, Suffolk Remarkable both for its unusual shape and for the fact that today, almost 200 years since it was built, it is not quite finished, Ickworth was conceived by the immensely wealthy Frederick Hervey, 4th Earl of Bristol and Bishop of Derry, as a storehouse for treasures collected during his continental tours. The two wings on either side of the massive, three-storeyed and domed rotunda which makes Ickworth so unusual were intended to house Hervey's paintings, silver, furniture and sculpture, most of which he acquired in Italy. But before many of these could reach Ickworth they were impounded by French armies invading Italy. The present collection is nevertheless impressive, comprising Hogarth, Gainsborough and Velasquez paintings in the library and drawing room, and silver (mainly in the West Corridor) collected by the 1st and 2nd Earls and including priceless pieces made by early eighteenth-century Huguenot refugees.

The Rotunda was completed in the 1820s. Intended as a grand reception, entertainment and exhibition room, it is linked to the two rectangular pavilions by the semi-elliptical wings. After the death of the Bishop, his son, the 5th Earl and later 1st Marquess, considered demolishing Ickworth, but did in fact virtually complete it, and adapted the East Pavilion for living quarters.

The 2,000-acre park was laid out by 'Capability' Brown. The grounds are particularly distinguished by massive oak and cedar trees.

3M SW of Bury St Edmunds, off A143   (93 J1)

Melford Hall, Suffolk This is an outstandingly well-preserved warm red-brick house, more typical of the Tudor era than the more flamboyant Elizabethan one. It was probably complete by 1578, when Queen Elizabeth was royally entertained by Sir William Cordell who had built the house after acquiring the land around 1550 after the Dissolution of the Monasteries. Sir William's family retained Melford Hall, except for a period in the mid seventeenth century, until the last quarter of the eighteenth century, when it was sold to the Parker family. Parker and Cordell family portraits are displayed in the two-storeyed

banqueting hall. This and the library contain many treasures of historical as well as aesthetic interest: Restoration furniture, oriental ceramics, paintings of naval actions in which the 5th Baronet and his second son, Sir Hyde Parker (one of Nelson's admirals), took part. There is a portrait of Nelson himself. In the Blue Drawing Room are Sèvres china, and rare seventeenth- and eighteenth-century furniture, among other treasures.

Beatrix Potter was related to the 11th Baronet, and there are displays in the Hall of some of her paintings, drawings and other mementoes.

Long Melford, 3M N of Sudbury on A134 (93 K2)

Oxburgh Hall, Norfolk From the top of Oxburgh Hall's great and distinctive gatehouse – a rare, virtually untouched example of fifteenth-century architecture and brickwork – it is possible on a clear day to see the outline of Ely Cathedral, eighteen miles away. Not only has the gatehouse escaped the modernization and remodelling suffered by most of the building, but the superb King's Room inside the gatehouse, which gets its name from Henry VII's stay here in 1487, is also intact. In a room nearby are wall hangings with sections worked by Mary, Queen of Scots, and Bess of Hardwick (whose own *Hardwick Hall* is remarkable for its tapestries). There are also letters from Tudor kings to the family living in Oxburgh Hall, and wood carvings by Grinling Gibbons.

Oxburgh Hall was threatened with demolition just after World War II, but survived and was presented to the Trust in 1952. Apart from the gatehouse, much of the best of the interior was created in the 1830s, notably the library, dining room and drawing room. These rooms also contain mementoes of the family that has been associated with Oxburgh Hall for most of the house's existence – the Bedingfelds, who in 1661 were granted a Baronetcy by Charles II.

7M SW of Swaffham, on Stoke Ferry road (90 E8)

Paycocke's, Essex Paycocke's is an outstanding example of the fine, half-timbered houses that were built by successful tradesmen and merchants in the Middle Ages, often from fortunes made in the wool trade. Originally the fabric between the timber frames would have been of wattle and daub, slats of wood woven basket-style and filled in with dung, clay and horsehair, but it is now of brick. The house, which has been much restored, is named after Thomas Paycocke, whose family is represented by four tombs in Coggeshall's parish church.

Upstairs there are five identical gables, each with an oriel window, above an intricately carved 'bressummer', a horizontal wooden beam, and this first floor juts out slightly above the ground floor.

West Street, on W side of Coggeshall   (87 B8)

Peckover House, Cambridgeshire Peckover House, built in 1722, is just one of several imposing town mansions in Wisbech along the north bank of the River Nene. When Wisbech was a port there was much trade with Holland, and the Dutch influence on the Georgian architects of Peckover House and its neighbours is easy to see. The house was built by Jonathan Peckover, a banker from a prominent Quaker family. Though the hallway and the main reception rooms at the front of the older part of the house are not large, the way the house opens out on to magnificent mature gardens gives a sense of spaciousness. The garden was laid out in Victorian times and retains its original plan, enhanced by summer houses, hothouses and serpentine, wooded paths.

Wisbech, N bank of River Nene   (90 D6)

4, South Quay, Great Yarmouth, Norfolk The elegant, early nineteenth-century exterior of this house actually masks a much older building – an Elizabethan house believed to date from 1596. Much of the interior is original, particularly the chimneypieces and some of the oak panelling. It is now a local museum.

(92 E8)

Wimpole Hall, Cambridgeshire The biggest house in Cambridgeshire and a very recent acquisition (bequeathed in 1976 and opened to the public in 1979), its position on a low hill in fairly flat countryside emphasizes its grandeur.

The original house, of which some internal walls are incorporated in the present mansion, was built in the mid seventeenth century, and for the next 200 years the house and the grounds were frequently and radically altered. 'Capability' Brown extended the Park in about 1767 and in the last decade of the century Sir John Soane designed the domed Yellow Drawing Room.

Between 1740 and 1894 Wimpole was owned by the Earls of Hardwicke, and it was the 4th Earl who, in the 1840s, made the last large-scale additions to the house. It was his son, known as 'Champagne Charlie', who sold Wimpole Hall which in due course was bought, in 1938, by Captain George Bambridge, whose wife Elsie was Rudyard Kipling's daughter.

Peckover House is the most imposing of the merchant's houses along the River Nene.

She, after demolishing some of the later and less harmonious additions to the house, bequeathed it, along with 3,000 acres, to the Trust.

Though from the south especially Wimpole Hall seems immense and palatial, several of the elegant rooms are surprisingly intimate – especially the Book Room which leads into the great library of 1719, planned by James Gibbs and containing over 50,000 volumes. The same atmosphere is sensed in the ante-room, between the entrance hall (exceptional partly because of its remarkable views over the Park) and the South Drawing Room. Soane's Yellow Drawing Room and Gibbs's Chapel decorated by James Thornhill are just two more of the many jewels in this country treasure-house.

1M E of A14 Royston to Huntingdon road, 6M N of Royston   (91 K4)

Woolsthorpe Manor, Lincolnshire Tucked unobtrusively behind rows of twentieth-century houses, in a low-lying situation overlooking farmland, Sir Isaac Newton's former home gives few outward clues to its famous associations: it is small for a 'manor house', and might pass for a rather charming seventeenth-century farmhouse.

Woolsthorpe was a fairly new house when Isaac, son of Isaac and Hannah, was born there on Christmas Day 1642. The record of his baptism is still in the parish church of St John the Baptist, which also contains a sundial made by Newton at the age of nine. Visitors can see the room in which the great scientist and mathematician was born, and, in the garden at the front of the house, what is said to be a direct descendant of the apple tree from which Newton saw an apple fall when he 'discovered' gravity. Newton left Woolsthorpe for Cambridge as a teenager but returned for about a year and a half when the Great Plague of 1665 reached the city, and the study in which he did much of his creative work during that stay is on view. New evidence concludes that his spectrum experiments were carried out there during his 'evacuation' from the Plague.

½M NW of Colsterworth and 7M S of Grantham on B6403   (96 H6)

The Guildhall, Lavenham, Suffolk Dominating the market place in this remarkably well-preserved medieval 'wool town', the Guildhall is an exceptional timber-framed building.

It was built in the 1520s by the Guild of Corpus Christi, one of three guilds that locally controlled the all-important wool industry. The Guild was dissolved soon after Henry VIII's Dissolution of the Monasteries. Over the centuries the building has been a proxy-church, a magistrates' court, a priory, a Town Hall, a workhouse, an almshouse, a restaurant, a home for wartime evacuees and a nursery school. During its period as a prison, in the seventeenth century, it was the main place of confinement in Suffolk, and a pillory, whipping post and stocks were set up in the market square immediately outside. It now contains a collection of local bygones and archaeology.

The building has some interesting examples of wood carvers' skill, particularly on the doorposts of the porch and on the carved corner post. It has been heavily restored, but is still one of the most remarkable buildings in a remarkable small town.

Market Place, Lavenham   (93 K2)

Ramsey Abbey Gatehouse, Cambridgeshire The Benedictine monastery of Ramsey was founded in the Saxon period, in the year 974. It was founded by St Oswald, Archbishop of York, with the help of Eolwin, foster brother of the Saxon King Eadgar. (Eolwin's remains lie here in a marble tomb of about 1230.) Little remains of the abbey, which, like Ely, once stood on an island in undrained and virtually impenetrable fen country. But the gatehouse, which was built around 1500, still stands. Even this is incomplete, because after the Dissolution of the Monasteries by Henry VIII in about 1538 it was partly dismantled and used as building stone. Enough still stands of the gatehouse, however, to indicate how richly carved and ornate the abbey buildings must have been, with panelled buttresses and decorative friezes carved in the stone around the doorway and the oriel window. There are some remains, too, of the Lady Chapel.

Ramsey, 10M SE of Peterborough   (91 G4)

St George's Guildhall, King's Lynn, Norfolk The largest surviving medieval Guildhall in England, now used as a theatre, but retaining many of its original fifteenth-century features. Open for performances etc, particularly during the King's Lynn Festival.

On W side of King Street   (90 C/D7)

Sun Inn, Essex An antique shop, formerly an inn, that dates from the fifteenth century but has seventeenth-century pargetting, an exterior plaster decoration commonly found in Essex and other East Anglian counties. (Not open.)

At the junction of Church Street and Market Hill, Saffron Walden (91 L6)

Tattershall Castle, Lincolnshire The impressive red-brick tower that is all that remains of Tattershall Castle is the highest point for many miles around: from it there are lovely views across the fen country and to the Lincolnshire Wolds to the north-east. On a clear day, both Lincoln Cathedral and the Boston 'Stump' can be seen.

Tattershall Castle is an outstandingly good example of the fortified house which appeared during the Wars of the Roses that dominated the early and mid fifteenth century. In contrast to the great spartan castles of the Normans, these were comparatively comfortable to live in. Many of the architectural details, such as the machicolated gallery, suggest Continental influence of the late fourteenth and fifteenth centuries.

The original Castle was built by Robert de Tatershale in 1231, but only vestiges remain. The red-brick keep, built by Ralph Cromwell, Henry VI's Lord Treasurer, between 1434 and 1445, now stands alone, but it was once inside the castle's enclosed inner ward. Although Tattershall's plan followed that of castles built in the twelfth century, architectural and domestic details still intact show that it was really much more of a country house than a castle proper: there is a decorative roof-gallery unlike anything found in more purely functional buildings; there are unusually large and therefore vulnerable windows, deep window recesses, cosy turret rooms.

The carved stone chimney-pieces in the empty and echoing rooms that the visitor enters as he climbs up to Tattershall's highest levels are original, but were reinstated after being retrieved on their way to the United

States in the nineteenth century. They were traced by Lord Curzon, who bought Tattershall in 1911 after it had stood in ruins since about 1695. He bequeathed Tattershall to the Trust in 1926.

3½M SE of Woodhall Spa, off the A153 Sleaford to Louth Road (97 D9)

Theatre Royal, Bury St Edmunds, Suffolk Built in 1819, restored 1962–63, and an outstanding example of the Regency period. Leased from Greene King, the nearby brewers. Open for performances etc.

In Westgate Street (93 J2)

Tattershall Castle is a country mansion masquerading as a medieval defensive keep.

Dutch influence on the design of Bourne Mill shows clearly in the gables.

Bourne Mill, Essex Bourne Mill was built as a fishing lodge by Sir Thomas Lucas in about 1590, using materials from the ruined Abbey of St John, which had been razed by Henry VIII half a century earlier. The design shows considerable Dutch influence and it is thought Sir Thomas may have employed Dutch Protestant refugees. It is also believed that the pond might originally have been a stockpond for the monks.

The Lucas family paid during the Civil War for their Royalist sympathies. The property was confiscated and passed to Dutch refugees (an interesting twist of fate) who used it for weaving. By 1860 it had become a flour mill, and the machinery, recently restored, can still be seen.

1M S of Colchester, just east of the B1025 Mersea road (87 B10)

Burnham Overy Mill, Norfolk This is unusual in that a complete complex of late eighteenth-century mill buildings and outbuildings has survived intact: the three-storeyed mill itself, the barn, maltings, miller's house and mill-hands' cottages. It is a pretty setting, where warm red brick is well set off by white paint-work. Many of the original features of the mill survive, including the windows (louvred to aid ventilation) on the maltings, and cantilevered 'lucams', which project from either side of the roof and which housed the lifting gear that enabled grain to be raised to storage areas high in the driest and best ventilated part of the building. A wooden windmill stands nearby.

½M SW of Overy Staithe, on SE side of A149 Hunstanton to Wells road (92 A1)

Houghton Mill, Cambridgeshire It is said that a mill has existed here, on an artificial island in the River Ouse, for over a thousand years. When Eolwin built Ramsey Abbey in 974 he presented the mill and an adjacent meadow to the monks; the miller retained water rights over the local inhabitants, and tenants of the abbey had to have their corn ground at the mill.

After the dissolution of the abbey the mill became Crown property. The present building dates from the seventeenth, eighteenth and nineteenth centuries, and, having ceased to operate as a mill in 1930, is used as a Youth Hostel. Originally thatched, it now has a slate roof. 2½M *from St Ives, S of A1123 (91 H4)*

The wooden tower of Burnham Overy windmill set against a dramatic East Anglian sky.

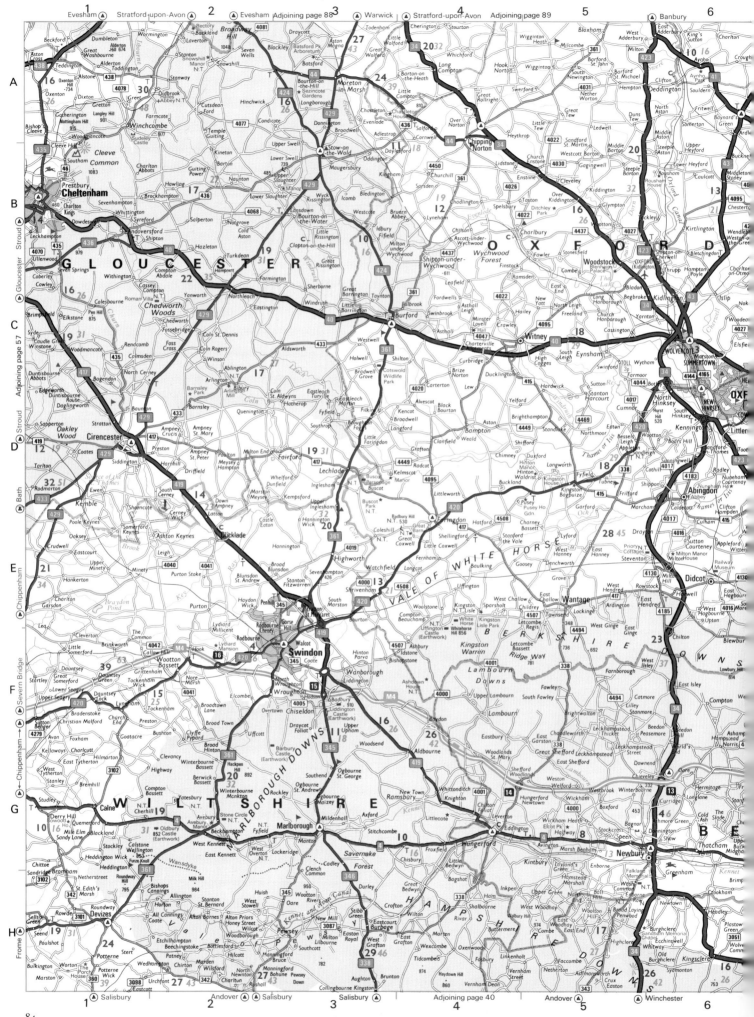

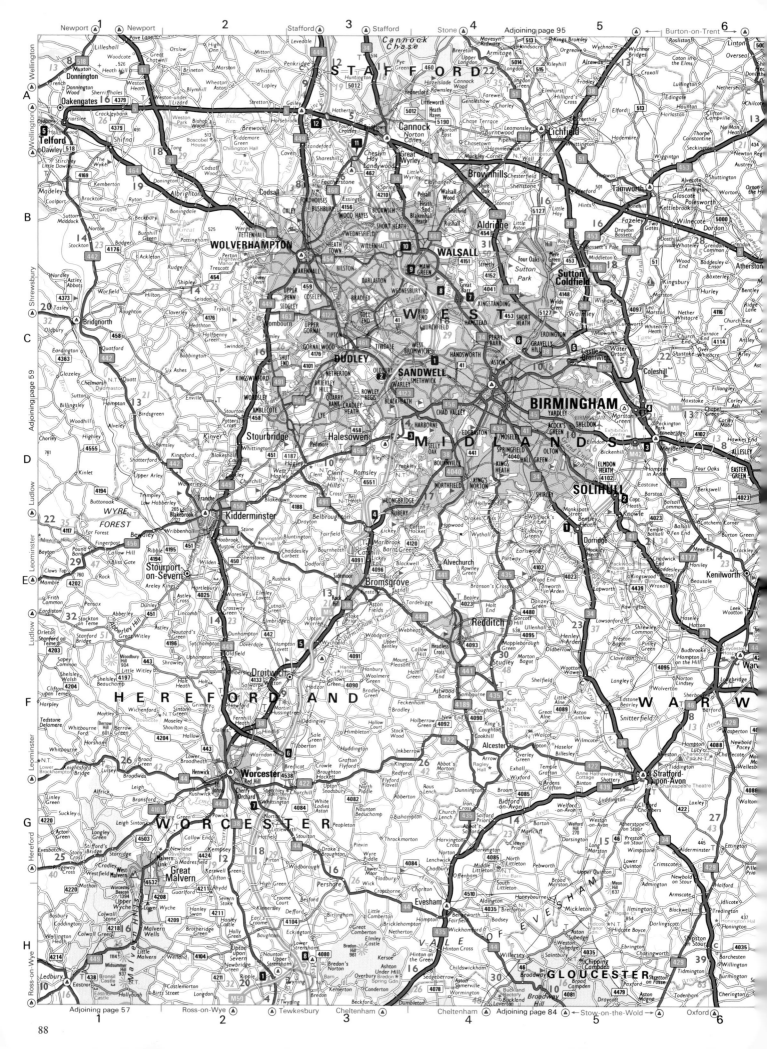

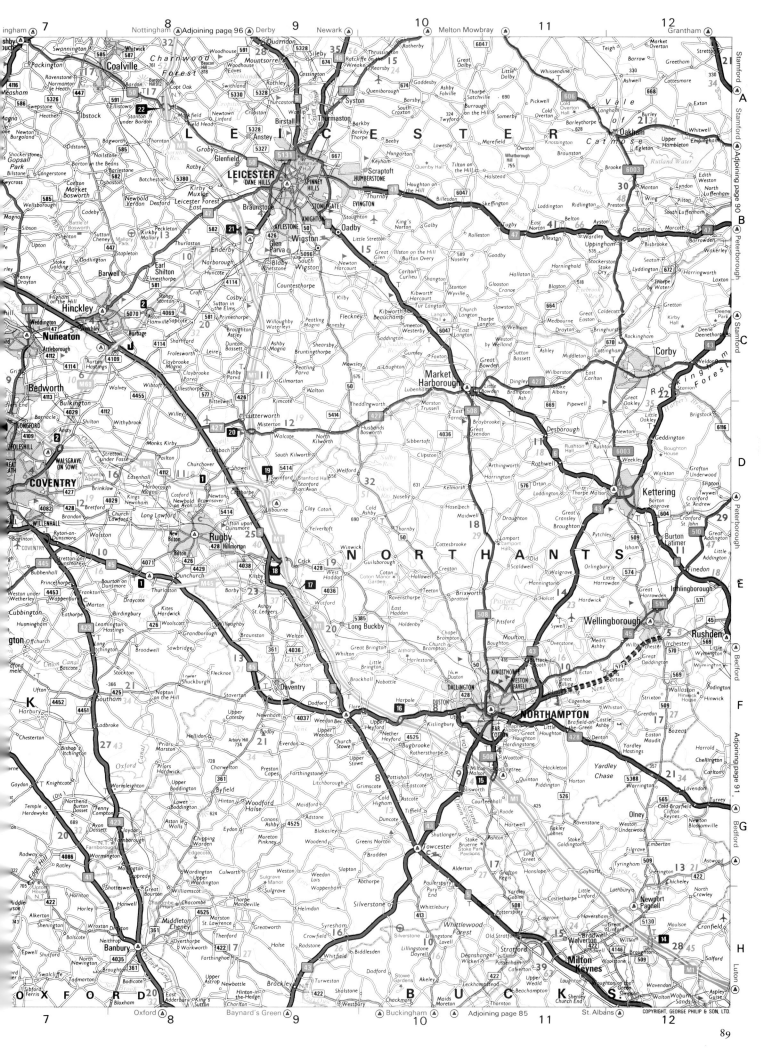

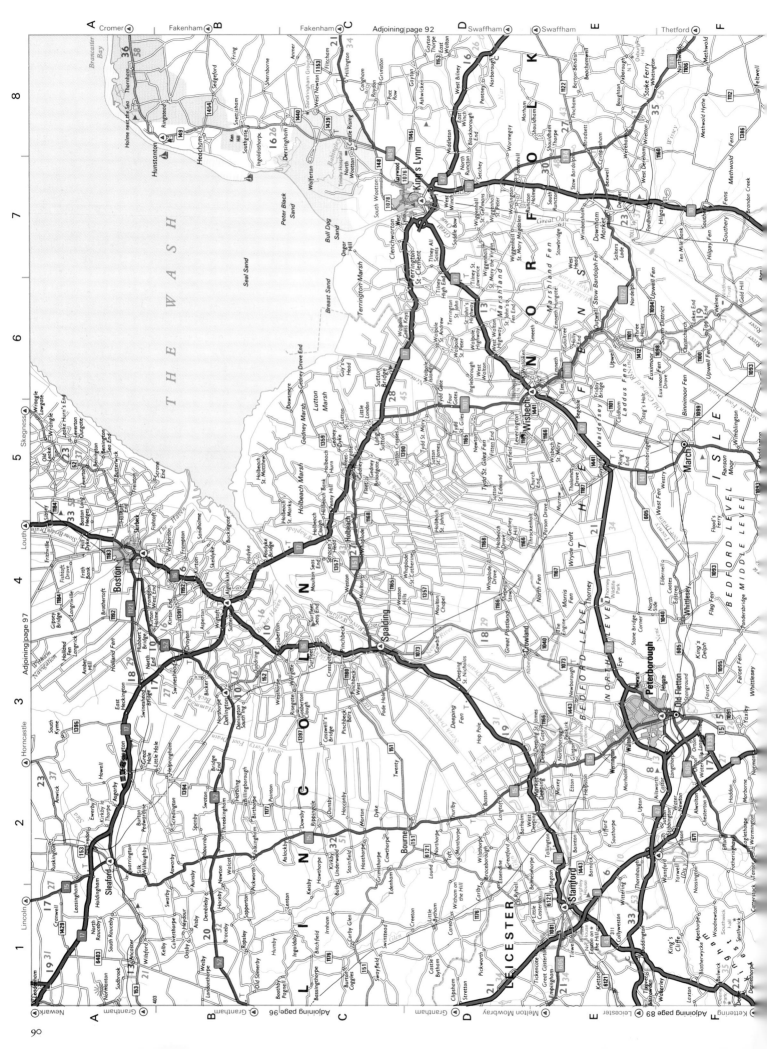

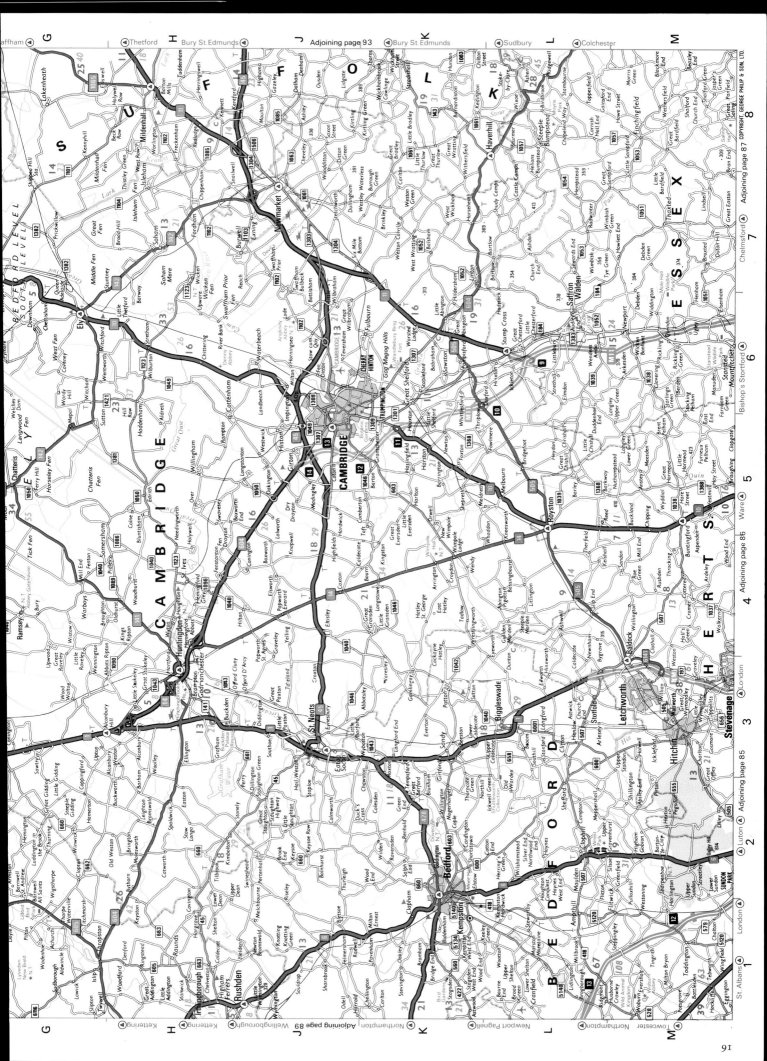

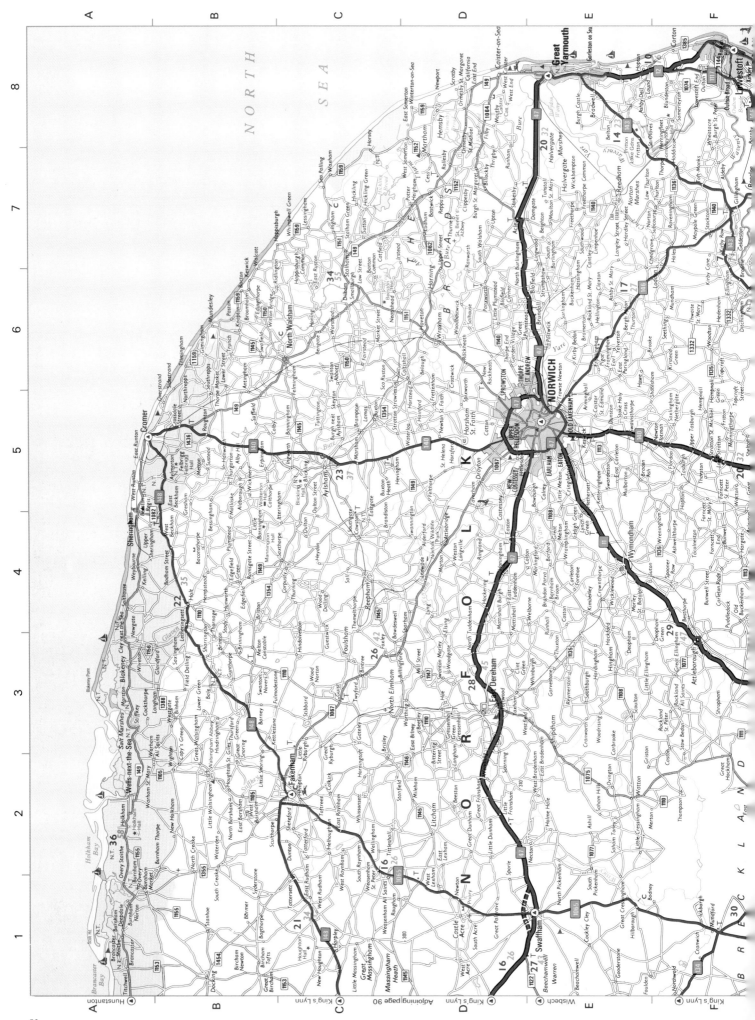

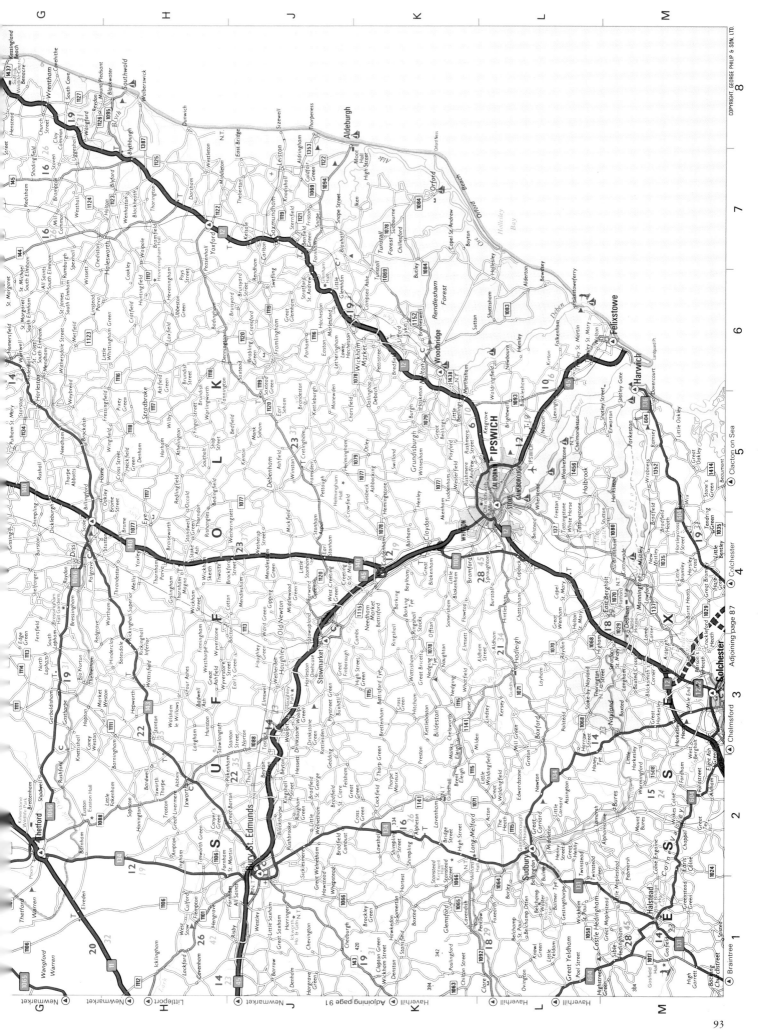

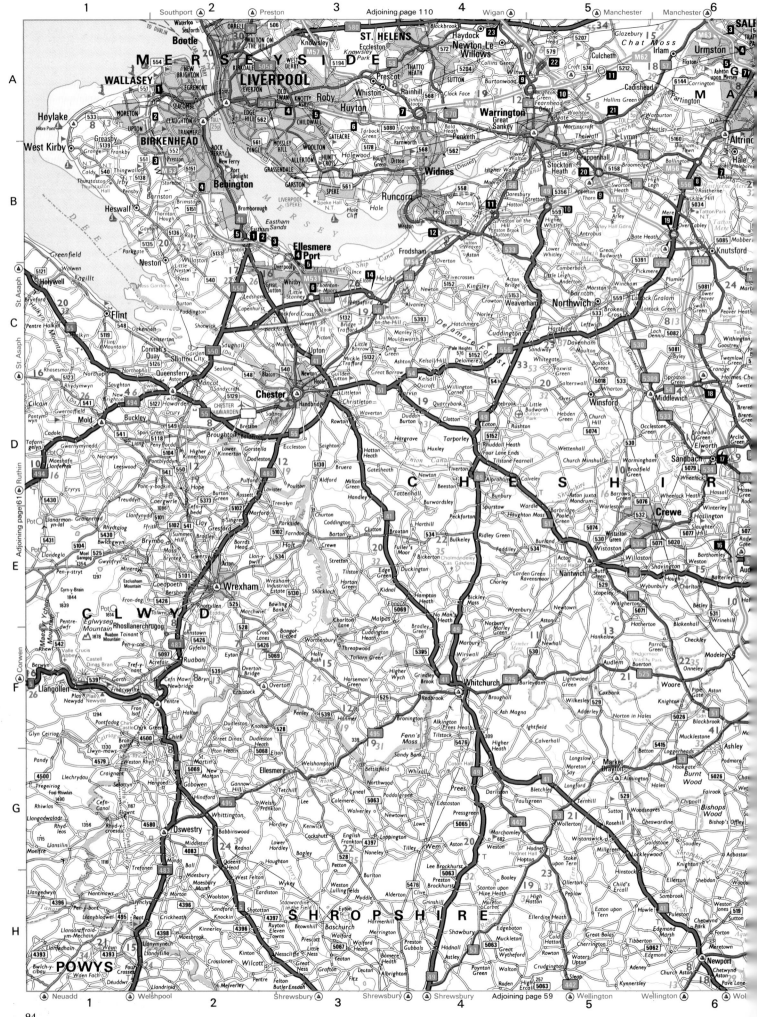

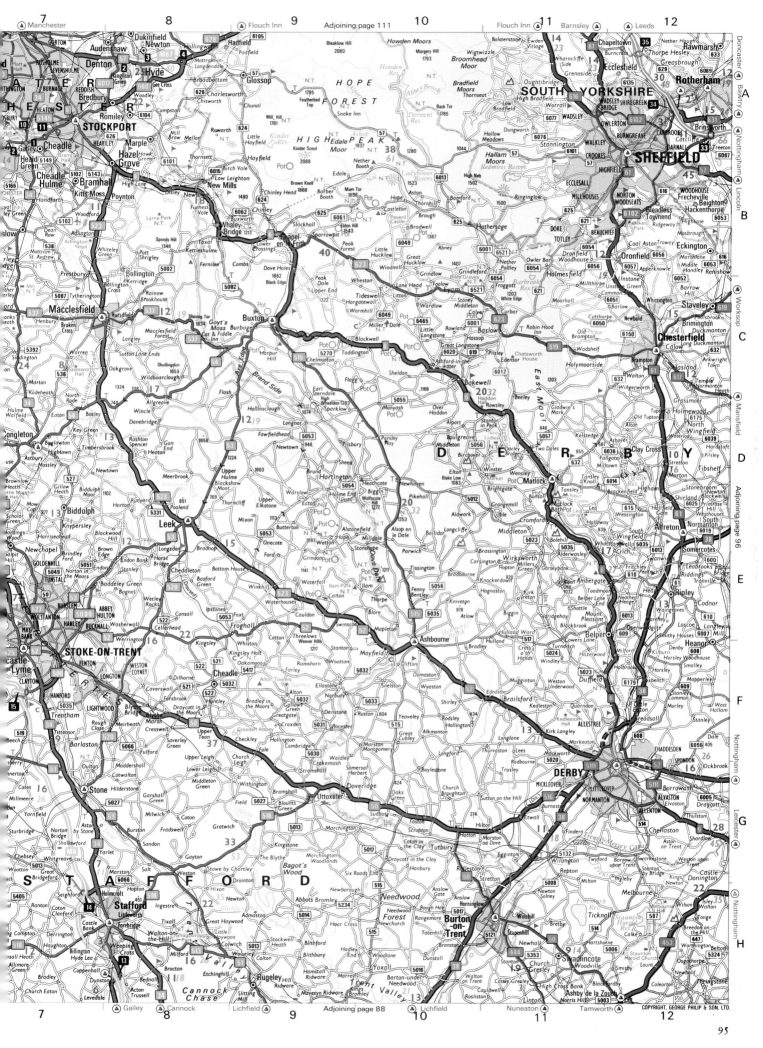

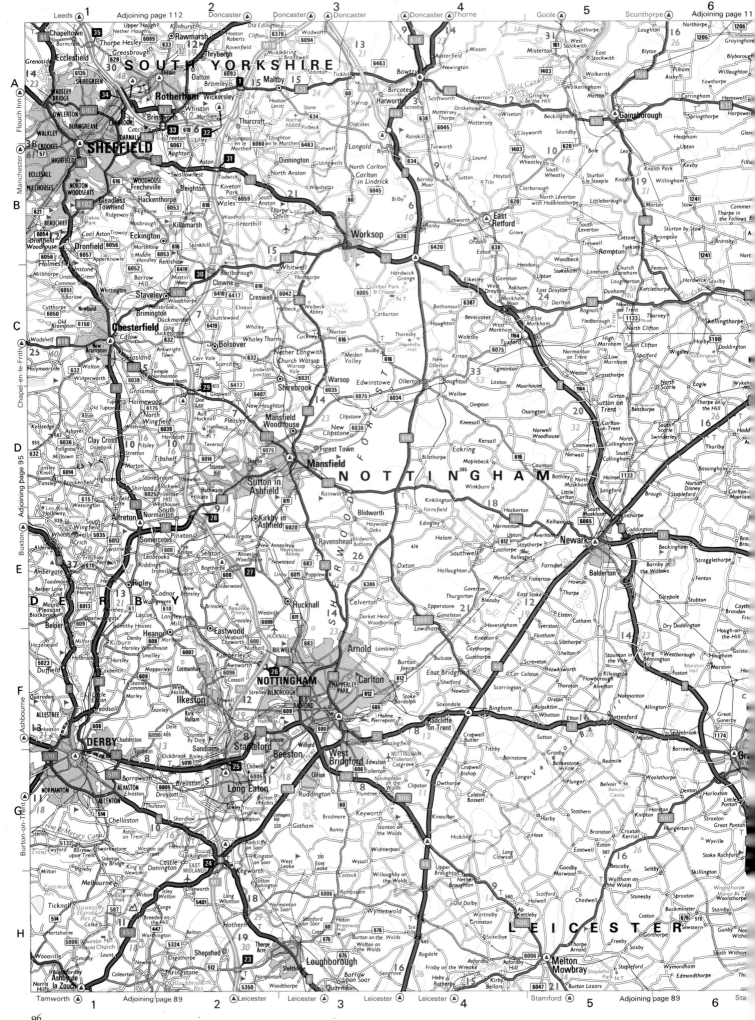

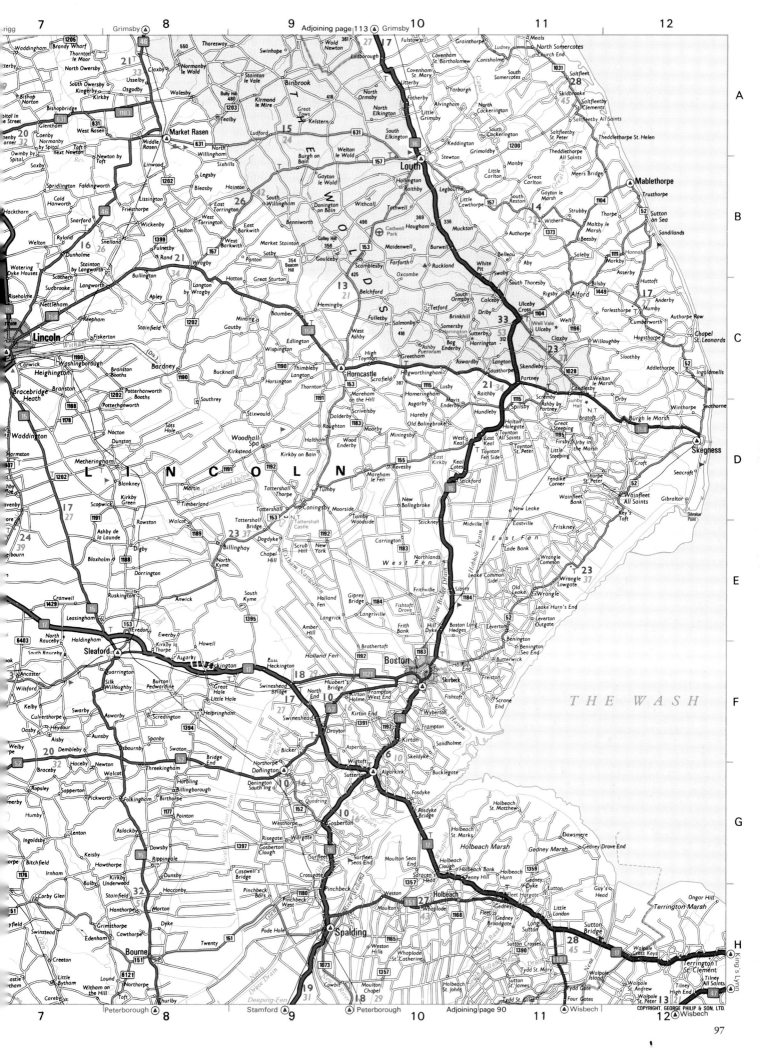

North-West England

GAWTHORPE HALL

Extending from the Dee estuary to the Solway Firth, from the Pennines to the Irish Sea, north-west England presents landscapes and seascapes of immense variety. With modern industry and urban growth concentrated in the southern half of the region the Trust's properties there, though few, assume a greater significance. Pockets of attractive countryside such as commons and woodlands in the Wirral, and dunes on the Lancashire holiday coast, are safeguarded. So, too, are two of England's finest half-timbered houses, Speke Hall and Rufford Old Hall.

But it is in Cumbria that the National Trust plays its most powerful preservationist role, owning or protecting about a quarter of the Lake District National Park. From its first purchase in 1902 of Brandelhow on the western shore of Derwentwater, to its largest, recent acquisition of the Leconfield Commons – 32,000 acres of magnificent fell country in the west of the Lake District – the Trust has, over seventy-five years, fulfilled many of the hopes expressed by one of its founding fathers, Canon Rawnsley. The unmatched beauty of many lakes and shores, of valley-heads with their farms, fields and surrounding fells, as well as all the highest land in the centre of the Lake District, is now safeguarded for the nation.

The Trust's Cumbrian properties reflect Lakeland history. Fourteenth-century pele towers contrast with the comfortable functionalism of seventeenth-century 'statesmen's' farmhouses, while the modestly elegant birthplace of the Lake District's greatest publicist, Wordsworth, provides an interesting comparison with Hill Top, Sawrey, home of Beatrix Potter, one of the most generous of the Trust's many Lake District benefactors.

Coast & Countryside

With fine views across the estuary of the Dee to the Clwydian Hills, **Thurstaston Common** (94 B1) is the largest and best-known of Trust properties in the Wirral peninsula, with pleasant paths and picnic places among sandstone outcrops and gorse. Woodland and watermeadows at **Harrock Wood**, east of Irby (94 B1), and Scots pine at **Burton Wood** (94 C2) farther south are welcome scenic contrasts. If these are important open spaces on Merseyside's doorstep, even more critical is **Medlock Vale** (111 G8), Greater Manchester, now part of the Daisy Nook Country Park, a refreshing ribbon of rural peace among quiet pastures within a few hundred yards of the suburbs of Oldham and Ashton under Lyne.

On the Lancashire coast, midway between Liverpool and Southport, is a different kind of oasis. **Formby Dunes** (110 F2), an Enterprise Neptune acquisition in 1967, comprises 472 acres of splendid sand-dunes, inhabited by shelduck, oystercatchers and species of wading birds. Rare plants among the brushwood and pines may have originated from grain swept off merchant ships berthing in Liverpool that was gradually washed northwards on the tides.

Seventy-five miles away across the sea the Trust safeguards the **Calf of Man** (114 H1). This is an important nature reserve, where Atlantic seals breed, together with large colonies

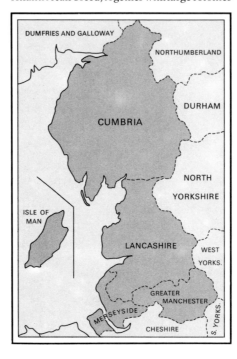

[Map showing: DUMFRIES AND GALLOWAY, NORTHUMBERLAND, CUMBRIA, DURHAM, NORTH YORKSHIRE, ISLE OF MAN, LANCASHIRE, WEST YORKS., GREATER MANCHESTER, MERSEYSIDE, CHESHIRE, S. YORKS.]

Formby dunes is a unique stretch of unspoilt coastline between Liverpool and Southport. Red squirrels can still be seen here.

of sea-birds including guillemots, kittiwakes, puffins and razorbills. Bona-fide naturalists and day visitors are welcome at the farmhouse that now serves as a bird-observatory, wardened during the summer months.

Lancashire's long coastline ends at Morecambe Bay, by the mudflats, marshes and sheltered woods of Silverdale. Here, the Trust owns **Eaves Wood** (115 H7), where venerable oaks and yews mingle with beech, hornbeam, and larch planted last century. Hazel is still coppiced, spring flowers add their carpet of colour, and in association with Lancashire Naturalists' Trust a rewarding two-mile nature trail has been established, which includes a section of limestone pavement and culminates on **Castlebarrow**, a rocky outcrop with extensive views. Even wider views are enjoyed from **Arnside Knott** (115 G7), two miles to the north, in Cumbria. Inviting tracks through bracken, gorse, and silver birch lead easily to the wooded 500-feet high summit, with a superb panorama, particularly northwards across the Kent estuary to the mountains of the Lake District.

About a quarter of all the land owned by the National Trust is in the Lake District, where it is now one of the largest landowners. Canon Rawnsley, Vicar of Crosthwaite (Keswick), one of the three co-founders of the Trust, and

for twenty-five years its first Honorary Secretary, was the dynamic driving force who ensured that the Lake District became so closely associated with the aims and ideals of the National Trust. Initially, the greatest concern was for the lake shores, and in 1902 the Trust bought its first Lake District property, **Brandelhow** (114 C5), 100 acres of woodland and rocky bays on the west side of Derwentwater. Over the next quarter century a further 100 acres at **Manesty** at the south end of the lake (114 C5) were added. Today a delightful woodland track links these two pioneer properties, with glorious views across the lake to Skiddaw and Blencathra, and motor launches

call regularly at the landing-stages on the shore of the lake.

The Trust now owns the western half of Derwentwater, much of the western shore, and the wooded part of the eastern shore and islands near Keswick, from **Calf Close Bay** to **Friar's Crag** (114 C5), that rocky headland yielding a memorable view towards Borrowdale, always associated with the early conservationist John Ruskin. If Derwentwater was for early tourists to Lakeland the quintessential aesthetic experience, only marginally less so was the charm of Ullswater, long, sinuous, and naturally divided into three distinctive reaches. **Gowbarrow Park** (114 C6), above the western shore, with **Aira Force** and **Aira Crag**, was the Trust's foothold here, quickly followed by **Glencoyne Wood** and **Stybarrow Crag** (114 C6) nearer to Glenridding, thus ensuring for public enjoyment an important three-mile stretch of the lake's western shore and adjoining woodlands by the main Penrith road. It was by the lakeside, near Lyulph's Tower, a neat Gothick folly, that Wordsworth saw the field of daffodils which inspired one of his best-known poems.

Windermere is the largest of the lakes, the first one seen by Victorian travellers arriving at Windermere station after the railway came in 1847, and the first seen by today's motorist a few miles after leaving the A6 at Kendal. As long ago as 1900 Canon Rawnsley and the Trust successfully opposed the idea of a tramway along the eastern shore of Windermere between Bowness and Ambleside. At the head of the lake, **Borrans Field** (114 E6), adjoining the Brathay outlet, with the remains of a Roman fort, Galava, was an early Trust acquisition. Round on the western shore beyond **Wray Castle**, Low Wray (114 F6), whose landscaped grounds are freely open, the Trust owns three miles of **Claife's** (114 E6) ancient woodlands where oak, ash, alder and hazel were cultivated centuries ago by Furness Abbey monks. Now, as far as Ferry Nab they offer quiet walks and good access to the lake shore.

At the opposite end of the lake, the Trust's land at **Fell Foot** (114 F6) has become a very popular country park, with extensive car-parking, launching facilities for boats, picnic

Derwentwater, looking towards Skiddaw. Derwent Isle, off this shore, was Beatrix Potter's 'Owl Island' in *The Tale of Squirrel Nutkin*.

and bathing facilities, an information centre and café, and the riot of colour of rhododendrons in late spring. The latest Trust attraction at nearby Coniston Water is the restored Victorian steam-yacht *Gondola*, operating from **Monk Coniston** (114 E5) at the lake's northern end, and the Trust safeguards extensive areas of wooded shore on both eastern and western sides.

No powered boats are allowed to disturb the tranquillity of **Buttermere** (114 D4), **Crummock Water** (114 C4) and **Loweswater** (114 C4), in the west of the Lake District. These three lakes occupy a long, glacial valley, enclosed by steep-sided, craggy mountains so darkly dominant in the view from Honister Pass, Fleetwith Pike, or Haystacks, but, towards Loweswater, more pastoral and wooded. Lakeside paths encourage exploration away from the road that threads their eastern margins, and for many lovers of the Lake District the Buttermere valley is a special paradise. The appeal of **Wastwater** (114 D/E4) is different: an incomparable amalgam of mystery and majesty, where screes 2,000 feet high tumble dramatically into the lake's eastern side, and the road opposite yields increasingly impressive views as it winds tortuously towards the Lake District's grandest valley head, at **Wasdale Head** (114 D4). There, towering mountains overlook the tiny, wall-enclosed fields first farmed by Norse settlers a thousand years ago; and now by tenant farmers of the Trust.

The Trust has been concerned for many years with the upper reaches of vulnerable valleys, and, through gift and purchase, now owns many dalehead farms. Thus, the Trust has assumed the landowning role of the Lake District's 'statesmen' of three or four generations ago, in a hill-farming economy, based on sheep, where the tradition is continued of 'heafed' flocks, which are let to tenants of the farms. The Trust owns nearly 30,000 sheep in the Lake District, mainly the local Herdwicks,

so familiar in the scene of fells and farms. Typical of dalehead farms and their walled intakes are those at the head of **Great Langdale** (114 E5), running up to Langdale Fell, whose mountain backcloth of the Langdale Pikes, Bowfell and Crinkle Crags is one of the best-loved and most majestic scenes in Britain. Much of **Little Langdale** (114 E5), too, is safe in Trust hands, while across the hills to the west, over the exciting passes of Wrynose (half National Trust) and Hardknott (entirely National Trust), Trust ownership of many farms in **Eskdale** ensures that the rare beauty of that exquisite valley will remain sacrosanct.

The neighbouring **Duddon Valley** (114 E4), beloved by Wordsworth and now heavily afforested, retains a sylvan character, with river scenery unequalled in the Lake District. This makes it a particular favourite for discerning visitors who appreciate the quiet miles of excellent walking, rather than climbing, which it offers. Many of the farms in the head of the valley are owned by the Trust.

But it is Borrowdale (114 D5) which probably claims first place in the affections of many walkers and climbers, for generations of whom **Stonethwaite** and **Seathwaite** (114 D5) have seen the beginning and the end of memorable days among the noblest mountains in England. Above the valley farms and intake pastures are the great upland commons of the central Lake District, thousands of acres of tawny hillsides, frowning crags, proud peaks, chuckling becks and lonely tarns that mirror the changing sky. All the central mountain summits belong or are on lease to the Trust – **Scafell Pike**, **Lingmell**, **Kirkfell**, **Great End** and **Great Gable** (114 D4/5). In addition, the **Lonsdale** and **Leconfield Commons** (114 D/E5 and 114 C/D4) bring under Trust protection further huge areas of wild mountainous country in a broad swathe from Seat Sandal at the southern end of the Helvellyn range to

Bowfell, and westwards from Derwentwater to Wastwater.

Lesser hills should not be forgotten. Here, youngsters experience the joys of discovery that only the Lake District can give. Their more modest slopes can still challenge older limbs, and a summit at 1,000 feet can be as exciting and rewarding as one three times higher. Lakes and hills are still in perfect proportion, as **Loughrigg's** (114 E6) broad, knobbly summit reveals, west of the road between Ambleside and Grasmere. Above Borrowdale, and forming its eastern wall, **Grange Fell's** (114 D5) rocky outcrops among grass, heather and bracken afford a sense of achievement with the rewards of glorious views of Derwentwater, matched, perhaps, by the irresistible challenge of **Catbells'** (114 C5) friendly slopes to the west of the lake. Overlooking Grasmere from the north, **Helm Crag** (114 D6) has the most famous profile in the Lake District, a rocky crest whose pinnacles can be reached only by a careful scramble, yet its summit is under 1,300 feet.

Among the lesser hills quiet tarns abound. Some, like **Burnmoor** (114 E4) above Eskdale, are forever lonely mirrors of the hills; others, like **Tarn Hows** (114 E6), north-west of Hawkshead, have become justifiably popular beauty spots, where the Trust provides well-screened carparks. Yet not far away, two miles north of Coniston, above the unique enchantment of **Tilberthwaite** (114 E5), are little-known jewels on **Holme Fell** (114 E5), capturing in miniature those magic elements that make the Lake District, for many people, beloved over all – water, rock, grass, trees, bracken, and the everlasting hills.

Nearer to the northern Pennines than to the Lake District hills, **Wetheral Woods** (132 H3), in the lower Eden valley, is one of the Trust's lesser-known Cumbrian properties.

In marked contrast, the Trust also protects 1,800 acres of commonland along a dozen miles of the **Solway shore** (132 G1/2), mainly at Burgh Marsh and farther west between Bowness-on-Solway and Anthorn. Across the mudflats and shining sands, where the tide comes in, as Scott described, like a galloping horse, are the hills of Galloway and Scotland.

above The wooded northern shore of Rydal Water, in the view from Loughrigg looking towards Rydal Fell.

below There are glorious views over Derwentwater from the ridge of Catbells to the west of the lake.

Houses, Gardens & Parks

Acorn Bank, (Temple Sowerby Manor), Cumbria Dorothy Una Ratcliffe, the Yorkshire dialect poet and travel writer, lived in this beautifully-situated house built of local red sandstone. Used now as a Sue Ryder home, the house can be visited only on application. The garden, however, is open, and is renowned for its spring bulbs, herbaceous border and herb garden.

6M E Penrith, off A66   (115 B8)

Gawthorpe Hall, Lancashire An unusual house built 1600–05 for the Rev. Lawrence Shuttleworth, possibly by Robert Smythson. Rare for a Jacobean house in having neither wings nor courtyard, its compact plan is emphasized by

An eighteenth-century painting of Gawthorpe Hall shows what may be the remnants of a formal seventeenth-century garden.

its three storeys. The original medieval fortified tower round which the later building was designed was heightened in the middle of the last century by Sir Charles Barry, who made other elaborate changes at the same time.

Gawthorpe's essential Jacobean character survives, as incidentally do its complete building accounts. The ground floor drawing room and top floor gallery are outstanding for their rich panelling and stucco ceilings, and contain many rare pieces of furniture. In former Victorian nurseries are displayed selected exhibits from Rachel Kay-Shuttleworth's remarkable collection of treasures and textiles from all over the world, including embroideries, laces, costumes and ceramics.

(The house is let to Lancashire County Council and forms part of the Nelson and Colne College of Further Education, with the Jacobean dining hall now a lecture room, and basement serving as kitchen and refectory.)

3M W Burnley, on N of A671 (111 D7)

Hill Top, Cumbria From 1905 to 1913 the home of Beatrix Potter. It is a typical, modest seventeenth-century Lake District farmhouse. It is heavily over-visited, to the detriment of the house and the peace of the village. The National Trust would be grateful to all those who can bear to forgo a visit.

Near Sawrey, 2M S Hawkshead, on B5285 (114 F6)

Rufford Old Hall, Lancashire This home of the Heskeths shows three phases of building spanning 350 years. Originally a typical H-shaped house of Tudor times, only the central part of this survives – the magnificent timbered old hall of the fifteenth century facing down the approach drive. Studding, quatrefoils and wood-mullioned windows are the impressive outer display of an interior whose exuberance is unmatched in England. A noble hammer-beam roof spans a room whose rich decorative detail is emphasized by its being above window level and thus well illuminated. Unique among the furniture is an enormous, finely carved contemporary, movable screen.

The Carolean wing of 1662 was added at right-angles to the medieval hall, its brick contrasting with the older timberwork, and in 1821 an ingenious architectural addition in place of the old office wing linked the two, and provided more comfortable living accommodation for the family. This part also contains the main staircase, giving access to a large, elegant drawing room on the first floor.

A feature of the house is the fine collection of seventeenth- and eighteenth-century furniture of the Hesketh family. This is displayed throughout and includes many superb court-cupboards, chests, tables and chairs, mainly in oak, several dated and crested. Also shown is the Hesketh armour, while part of the 1821 and Carolean wings house the Philip Ashcroft Museum of local life.

7M N Ormskirk, on A59 (110 F3)

The drawing room at Rufford Old Hall has an apparently sixteenth-century roof and yellow wallpaper made specially for it.

Sizergh Castle, Cumbria This home of the Strickland family for 700 years looks impressive from any angle. Glimpsed first at a distance across its mature parkland, a closer view of its north-western front reveals the various additions made through the centuries to the fortress at its heart. This large, three-storey, massive pele tower of 1350 is characteristic of Border refuges built to withstand Scottish raids. Adjoining it is a Tudor great hall, re-modelled during Elizabethan times and again in the eighteenth century, an Elizabethan gabled corner block next to it, with two long sixteenth-century wings projecting so that a three-sided courtyard results.

Apart from the persona which continued occupation by one family imparts to a house, Sizergh is outstanding in having a wealth of fine quality early Elizabethan woodwork, including benches, chairs and panelling, with the oak linenfold work in a passage room upstairs dating from Henry VIII's time. Five exceptional chimney-pieces from 1563–75 are carved with a remarkable delicacy. A collection of the more interesting Strickland family treasures, including a number of Stuart relics, is housed in the top floor of the pele tower.

3½M S Kendal, close to A6/A591 interchange (115 F7)

Speke Hall, Merseyside Sandwiched between industrial buildings and a runway of Speke Airport is this astonishing survival – one of the finest English half-timbered houses. Although started by Sir William Norris in 1490, the present quadrangular form of Speke Hall, surrounding a flagged, yew-gloomy courtyard, is largely the work of Sir Edward Norris between 1598 and 1606 and the outside appearance has scarcely changed since then. Structurally one of the least altered of Tudor houses, with contemporary panelling and elaborate plasterwork in a series of quite small rooms, it is also unusually well supplied with secret hiding places and observation holes associated

with the recusant activities of the Norris family in the early seventeenth century.

The great hall, with its marvellously incongruous chimney-piece and fine Flemish wainscoting, and the great parlour with its sumptuous stucco ceiling, are perhaps the most memorable rooms in this remarkable house.

Richard Watt, a wealthy Liverpool merchant, acquired Speke in 1795, and he and his family restored it, most of the furniture and fittings introduced in mid Victorian times being a revival of styles which prevailed during the sixteenth and seventeenth centuries. Thus Speke successfully juxtaposes Tudor and nineteenth-century influences, each complementing the other.

(The house is let to Liverpool Corporation.)

8M SE Liverpool, S of A561   (94 B3)

Stagshaw Garden, Cumbria Overlooking the northern end of Windermere lake, this steeply-sloping woodland garden is renowned for its unique collection of rhododendrons, azaleas, camellias and spring bulbs.

½M S Ambleside, on A591   (114 E6)

Townend, Cumbria The Brownes lived at Townend from the reign of Henry VIII until 1944, and their house, built in 1623, is a remarkably intact, unchanged survival of the home of successive generations of Lake District 'statesmen'. These were yeoman-farmers who emerged as a rural middle-class in Tudor times, enjoying the right at death to hand on their estates to their next-of-kin, even though they may have been tenants of a lord. Having customary tenure of land more akin to freehold

than copyhold, they eventually became freeholders.

Townend's roughcast, white-washed walls, slate roof, round chimneys and mullioned windows typify Lake District vernacular building. The Brownes had a passion for carving and, inside, panelled walls and carved oak furniture, much of it with family initials, and canopied bedsteads, combine into a homely record of a yeoman family. The library reflects the tastes of literate people, with books accumulated and used over many generations. Locally-woven fabrics provide evidence of a cottage industry of the seventeenth-century and there are old household utensils, now obsolete. Across the road is a magnificent ramp-entrance barn, with wooden galleries, of the same date as the house.

Troutbeck, 3M SE Ambleside, off A592 (114 E6)

Wordsworth House, Cumbria In 1766 John Wordsworth, agent to Sir James Lowther, moved into this modest, rather austere house which had been completed about twenty years earlier. His second son, William, was born here in April 1770, and his daughter, Dorothy, the following year. In the secure atmosphere of a happy family home the children grew up, loving the house and its garden which fringed the River Derwent. There, Dorothy first influenced her brother, nurturing a relationship which became one of the most creative in English literature, a fact recognized in the poet's own words:

'She gave me eyes; she gave me ears;
And humble cares, and delicate fears;
A heart, the fountain of sweet tears;
And love, and thought, and joy.'

above Sizergh Castle, seen across the lake and the eighteenth-century terraces. The pele tower is on the right.

right With its slate roof, roughcast walls and mullioned windows, Townend typifies traditional Lake District architecture.

The stone, many-windowed house retains original fireplaces, brass door fittings, a handsome staircase with elegant balusters and softwood panelling in a number of rooms. Among the poet's own pieces are a Crown Derby dinner service, a bureau bookcase with some first editions, a late Georgian longcase clock, and a set of Georgian chairs which belonged to Wordsworth's friend Robert Southey.

Main Street, Cockermouth, off A66   (114 B4)

Castles, Abbeys & other Buildings

Bridge House, Cumbria One of the smallest but best-known of all National Trust buildings, this whimsical little early sixteenth-century garden house on a stone bridge over Stock Beck in the middle of Ambleside is now used as a Trust Information Centre.

In Ambleside (A591)   (114 E6)

Cartmel Priory Gatehouse, Cumbria Apart from the fine monastic church, this is the only surviving building of the Augustinian Priory. Built 1130–40, with the character and appearance of a fortified tower, after the Reformation it became a courthouse and then a grammar school. It is now used as a shop.

4M S Newby Bridge   (114 G6)

Cautley: Cross Keys Inn, Cumbria A whitewashed, stone-built Temperance Hotel at the foot of the steep eastern slopes of the Howgill Fells, dating from about 1600, but extensively altered in the eighteenth and nineteenth centuries. A carved inscription above one of its inside doorways quotes William Blake's lines:
'Great things are done when men and
    mountains meet:
These are not done by jostling in
    the street.'

5M NE Sedbergh, on A683   (115 F9)

Dalton Castle, Cumbria A fourteenth-century pele tower in the former regional capital of Low Furness, dating from about 1350, and formerly the Court House of Furness Abbey. Upper floors are reached by a spiral staircase within the thickness of the walls, and retain some original Gothic windows. Others are nineteenth-century insertions. Inside is a collection of armour, old documents, and items of local historical interest.

In Dalton-in-Furness, on A590   (114 H5)

Hawkshead Courthouse, Cumbria A fifteenth-century building surviving from the days when the manor of Hawkshead was owned by Furness Abbey. Manorial courts were traditionally held in the upper room which now houses a museum of local rural life, jointly managed with the Abbot Hall Art Gallery, Kendal.

In Hawkshead, on B5285   (114 E6)

Keld Chapel, Cumbria This modest, rubble-built chapel, probably of the early sixteenth

above **Bridge House, the smallest dwelling owned by the Trust, has been a teahouse, a weaving shop and a cobbler's shop.**

below **Hawkshead Courthouse is one of the few secular buildings of the medieval period to have survived in the Lake District.**

century, may have been a chantry chapel, or erected by the abbot of nearby Shap Abbey for his tenants in Keld village. Services are occasionally held in the chapel.

1M W Shap (A6)   (115 D8)

Tower Bank Arms, Cumbria Next door to Beatrix Potter's home, Hill Top, and formerly called 'The Blue Pig', this inn is illustrated in *The Tale of Jemima Puddle-Duck*. Keeping its 'real ale' cool in old cellars, and containing oak furnishings in 'Lakeland vernacular', it is one of three inns not only owned but managed by the Trust, and provides accommodation and refreshments in a comfortable, homely atmosphere.

At Near Sawrey, 2M S Hawkshead, on B5285 (114 F6)

Archaeological & Industrial Sites

Castlerigg Stone Circle, Cumbria An almost complete stone circle, about one hundred feet across, of thirty-eight stones of various shapes and textures, dating from the Bronze Age. Apart from its prehistoric significance, the circle is dramatically and beautifully situated on a plateau, with surrounding hills forming an impressive amphitheatre.

2M E Keswick, off A591   (114 C5)

Castlerigg stone circle is at its most dramatic in stormy or wintry weather, when curtains of rain or snow sweep the fells.

Steam Yacht 'Gondola', Cumbria After lying derelict for many years at the southern end of Coniston Water, this 85-feet long steam yacht has been renovated and is in full working condition, operating a passenger service from the pier at Monk Coniston at the northern end of the lake. Commissioned originally by the Furness Railway Company in 1860, her two ornate saloons carried thousands of passengers during her eighty years of service, an enterprise now happily revitalized, so that once more a beautiful steam yacht adds its own unique distinction to Coniston Water.

1½M NE Coniston, on B5285   (114 E5)

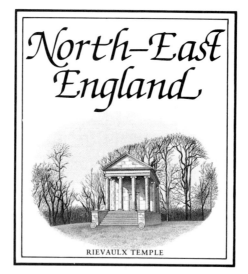

North-East England

RIEVAULX TEMPLE

The landscape of the north-east is one of great beauty and variety. It is a land of farms and mineral exploitation, of castles and monasteries, of industry and fine houses and parks. It sweeps down from the tops of the bleak Pennines to the wild coasts of Northumberland, and from the Cheviots on the Scottish border to the flats of Humberside.

Well-dispersed through the area, National Trust properties epitomize many aspects of the life and history of the region.

Hadrian's Wall and Housesteads Fort recall the might of Rome, while castles are later reminders of Northumberland's frontier position. Mount Grace Priory, the finest Carthusian ruin in England, is in striking contrast to the great eighteenth-century houses of Wallington and Nostell Priory, with their collections of furniture and china; and Beningbrough Hall makes a perfect setting for the eighteenth-century portraits loaned by the National Portrait Gallery.

York is a handy centre for exploring the grotesque shapes of Brimham Rocks and the classical landscapes of Rievaulx Terrace and Temples, and The Treasurer's House in the city itself is a fine repository of seventeenth- and eighteenth-century furniture.

Three buildings neatly point the area's links with industry: George Stephenson's Cottage at Wylam; James Paine's coolly elegant Gibside Chapel – built on and from the wealth of coal – and Cragside, one of the architectural peaks of Victorian imagination and self-confidence, home of the industrialist and inventor William Armstrong.

Coast & Countryside

Three National Parks, together with part of a fourth, display the varied scenery of this part of Britain. Rivers flow eastwards from the Pennines; austere gritstone moors give way to lush upland pastures on the limestone of the Yorkshire Dales. East of the Vale of York chalk wolds and heather moorland reach towards an exciting coastline. Beyond the Tyne, Northumberland's spacious uplands with their

castles and pele towers recall a troubled past, and on the coast a Christian culture flowered thirteen centuries ago.

In the northern part of the Peak District National Park the undulating moorlands of the **Derwent Estate** (111 G/H10) overlook the Ladybower, Derwent and Howden reservoirs, while to the north-west, within easy reach of Huddersfield, the peat hags and heather of **Marsden Moor** (111 F9), crossed by the Pennine Way, typify the sombre solitudes of gritstone uplands.

In sharp contrast, near the southern edge of the Yorkshire Dales National Park, are the finest limestone landscapes in Britain, around Malham, where stone walls, fissured 'pavements', and great natural cliffs gleam white in sunlight. North of the horseshoe-shaped Malham Cove is **Malham Tarn** (111 A7), one of the few natural lakes in the Dales and a Site of Special Scientific Interest. The nature reserve is leased to the Field Studies Council, but on the 4,000-acre estate there is access to the southern shore. Also, there are many public footpaths

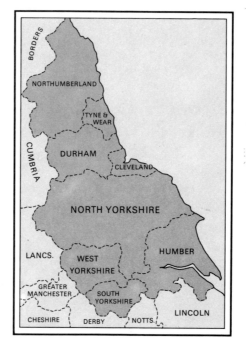

and tracks in the surrounding countryside, where monastic flocks of Fountains Abbey grazed in medieval times, their fleeces the foundation of the Yorkshire wool trade.

In later centuries the wool trade was centred on Halifax, and near Hebden Bridge to the west are many survivals of the domestic industry of the seventeenth and eighteenth centuries, including farms, cottages and a mill in **Hebden Dale** (111 D8), a steep-sided oakwood valley with miles of fine walks, gay with bluebells in spring.

Wind and weather carve gritstone outcrops into strange shapes, none more fantastic than those among the heather and silver birches at **Brimham Rocks** (111 A10), on the eastern margin of the Dales, where giant rock towers form one of the most remarkable natural scenic wonders in England. **The Bridestones**, (117 F9), on the North Yorkshire Moors to the east (two miles off the A169), are similar, though smaller and less spectacular. At the western edge of the moorland plateau **Scarth Wood Moor** (116 E5), north of Osmotherley,

Shags (nesting) and kittiwakes are among the sea-birds that frequent the Farne Islands.

provides a superb viewpoint, with the Cleveland Way passing through its bracken and heather.

A spectacular stretch of coastline at **Ravenscar** (117 E9/10) on the southern end of Robin Hood's Bay is now safeguarded by the Trust, with steep access to a rocky shore. A few miles to the south, **Hayburn Wyke** (117 E10), recently acquired, incorporates woodland walks, access to the shore and a nature reserve.

From the north of the Coquet to the estuary of the Tweed the Northumberland coast is one of outstanding beauty, where sandy, dune-backed bays alternate with rocky outcrops and headlands. The four-mile stretch between **Craster** and **Low Newton by-the-Sea** (133 A10) is characteristic, and is owned or protected by the Trust. Car-parking facilities at each end

encourage access to one of the most enjoyable coastal walks in the north-east. The Trust's observation hide at Newton Pool provides good opportunities for watching the wide range of breeding birds which use it during the year.

The Farne Islands (133 D12), known to St Aidan and St Cuthbert, are an important nature reserve, breeding-place for grey seals and huge colonies of many species of sea-birds. Best visited in late spring they are reached by boat from Seahouses, landing being restricted to Inner Farne and Staple Island. Prominent in the seaward view from **St Aidan's Dunes** (133 D12), two miles south-east of Bamburgh, the Farne cliffs are a distant highlight when seen from **Ross Castle** (133 A9), a heathery hill-top forming part of an Iron Age fort above Chillingham, many miles inland, and one of the finest viewpoints in Northumberland.

Malham Tarn is a natural lake formed by a dam of glacial moraine. The bare limestone landscapes of the North Yorkshire moors stretch away on every side.

Houses, Gardens & Parks

Bellister Castle and Pele Tower, Northumberland A large, seventeenth-century farmhouse adjoins the grey stone ruins of an older pele tower, all on a semi-artificial mound. Three farms, cottages in nearby Park village, and parts of the South Tyne river also belong to the estate. (Not open.)

1M SW Haltwhistle, off A69 (132 G5)

Beningbrough Hall, North Yorkshire Beningbrough's welcoming façade of fine rubbed red brick with stone quoins is little changed from 1716, when it was completed for John Bourchier. A York carpenter-architect, William Thornton, supervised the building of this outstanding house, probably with some advice from the better-known Thomas Archer.

Its cool, dignified architecture is enriched by decorative detail of superb quality, exemplified by Thornton's elaborate wood-carving. The central Great Hall, rising through two storeys, is one of the most beautiful of English Baroque interiors, with restrained plasterwork, elegant arches, and fluted pilasters.

Though it came to the Trust with few contents, Beningbrough has been enriched with generous loans and gifts, especially of furniture and oriental porcelain, and it provides an ideal setting for about a hundred paintings from the National Portrait Gallery. The state rooms of the ground and first floors display famous contemporaries of the Bourchiers between 1688 and 1760, including Kneller's noted portraits of members of the Kit-cat Club.

The top floor has been skilfully adapted to display, using modern exhibition techniques, various aspects of English society in the eighteenth century as revealed by portraits and architectural styles, and examples of owner's collections. An audio-visual presentation in the stable block sets the scene for a tour of the house; another one in the Bell Tower of the laundry courtyard supplements it. Beningbrough is not just a superbly restored mansion, it is an experience.

8M NW York, off A19 (112 A3)

Braithwaite Hall, North Yorkshire This late seventeenth-century farmhouse, containing some Jacobean furnishings, is open on prior application to the tenant at Braithwaite Hall.

2M W East Witton, off the A6108 (116 G1)

Hebden Dale includes survivals of the domestic wool industry, such as this mill.

Cragside (*above*), set against a sea of sombre conifers, is dramatically Victorian. The inglenook fireplace in the dining room (*right*) has Pre-Raphaelite stained glass by Morris & Co.

Cragside, Northumberland This dramatic Victorian country mansion was built between 1864 and 1895 for the Newcastle industrialist Sir William (later the first Lord) Armstrong. At first an unexciting stone villa, it was continually added to by Richard Norman Shaw from 1870 to 1884 to create a building large enough to be a family home and showy enough to impress visiting clients.

A contrived approach through the now heavily wooded estate suddenly reveals Shaw's 'Old English' style in a bewildering array of timber-framed gables and tall chimney stacks and towers. Most of the living rooms are sited to enjoy superb views to the west.

This remarkable house has retained most of its original fittings. Shaw himself designed some of the furniture, and the remainder represents a mixture of eighteenth-century revival and the Arts and Crafts Movement. The library survives as one of the best Victorian interiors still intact, with furniture by Gillow and stained-glass made by William Morris & Co. from a design by Rossetti. In 1880 this room became the first in the world to be lit by electricity powered by a hydro-electric generator. This was in the grounds and invented by Sir William.

The drawing room – Shaw's last great addition to the house – shows Victorian opulence at its most magnificent. The room is dominated by a massive carved marble chimney-piece and inglenook, designed by Lethaby and made by the firm of Farmer and Brindley.

The grounds of Cragside form a 900-acre country park, with steep, rocky hillsides, artificial lakes, several million trees, and a single-track driveway of five miles, best seen in June when it is ablaze with rhododendrons and azaleas.

15M NW Morpeth, entrance on B6344 (133 C9)

Wheeling gulls recall Lindisfarne Castle's links with the sea and its past importance in coastal defence.

The Chinese wallpaper in the state bedroom at Nostell Priory is decorated with every sort of bird, from peacocks to pheasants.

East Riddlesden Hall, West Yorkshire Most of this impressive house was built about 1648 for James Murgatroyd, a Halifax clothier. Although the masonry is sadly darkened, both main façades are remarkably impressive, with mullioned windows, gables, finials, and great porches with circular windows. The main part of the house lies to the left of the north entrance, with the banqueting hall to the right. Beyond that, to the west, only the façade of the Starkie wing of 1692 remains, its classical appearance a contrasting foil to the rest of the house.

The stone-flagged kitchen contains furniture and domestic items from the seventeenth and eighteenth centuries. In the dining room and drawing room, oak panelling and moulded plaster friezes and ceilings are contemporary with the house, with seventeenth-century furniture, portraits and Delftware contributing to the fine period flavour.

Adjoining the visitors' car park is the timbered barn. Stone built, of eight bays, with two cart entrances, this is contemporary with the house, and is outstanding for its oak pillars and tie-beam roof with king-posts. It now houses a collection of agricultural bygones.

1M NE Keighley, on A650 (111 C9)

Lindisfarne Castle, Northumberland Clinging to a crest of hard dolerite rock, the castle was completed by 1550 as a fort to protect English merchantmen and naval vessels using Holy Island's sheltered anchorage. It was garrisoned until the end of the Napoleonic Wars, then used by coastguards, and finally fell into disuse. Edward Hudson, founder and editor of *Country Life*, bought it in 1902, and engaged Edwin Lutyens to restore and convert it into a private house.

Imaginatively exploiting the unusual site,

The entrance front of East Riddlesden Hall, with the façade of the Starkie wing on the right.

Perseus and Andromeda, one of the mythological frescoes painted by Borgnis in the Ionic Temple at Rievaulx (exterior p. 104).

Lutyens transformed the derelict shell into a comfortable country home. Inside the lower part of the building he created a modern entrance hall of low arches on strong round piers, and passages, hewn from the rock, leading to two beautiful vaulted chambers, formerly the castle's magazines, their masonry very little changed from the original. Upstairs, a timbered and brick-floored long gallery, of typical Lutyens design, links a series of bedrooms with beamed ceilings and windows looking out to the sea and along Northumberland's coast.

English and Flemish oak furniture, together with a good collection of prints, are in complete harmony with this delightful miniature castle.

5M E Beal across causeway, off A1   (133 B12)

Maister House, Humberside Built by a Hull merchant, Henry Maister, in 1744 to replace a house destroyed by fire the previous year. Behind its plain brick façade, the hall and staircase are open to visitors. A wrought-iron balustraded stone staircase rises round three sides of the richly-ornamented hall lit from above by a glazed octagonal lantern. The coved and plastered ceiling completes a picture of Palladian perfection.

160 High Street, Hull   (113 D8)

Moulton Hall, North Yorkshire A compact stone house of 1650, with large Dutch gables and a very fine carved wood staircase. (Open only by prior arrangement with the tenant.)

5M E Richmond, off A1   (116 E3)

Nostell Priory, West Yorkshire People visit Nostell to see an almost unchanged example of eighteenth-century architecture, with superb decoration and furniture reflecting contemporary tastes of successive generations of the Winn family. The young James Paine designed the main block from about 1736, and Robert Adam, called in thirty years later to complete work on the interior, also added the north wing.

Paine's two noble staircases, dining room and state bedchamber all show rococo exuberance, with magnificent plasterwork by Joseph Rose the elder. Furniture by Chippendale, who served part of his apprenticeship here, is one of Nostell's greatest glories, the house being one of only three where his complete accounts survive. There is also a superb Palladian doll's house standing in the hall which may be the earliest surviving example of Chippendale's work.

Adam's contribution is cool, meticulous, and elegantly neo-classical. The saloon, top hall, library and tapestry room all contain fine plasterwork by the younger Rose, with decorative painting by Zucchi. An overall sumptuousness of quality characterizes the rooms of Nostell, from the grandest items such as Chippendale's library table down to the smallest details like door handles and escutcheons, all made to Adam's design. He was also responsible for two wings of the elegant stable-block.

6M SE Wakefield, on A638   (111 E12)

Nunnington Hall, North Yorkshire This large stone manor house in the gentle Ryedale countryside is essentially of two dates and styles. The Tudor west range is now the entrance front with a modern porch, while the main south front shows a characteristic late seventeenth-century façade to the neat lawns and gardens. Robert Huickes, who leased Nunnington from the Crown in the mid sixteenth century, was physician to Henry VIII, Edward VI and Elizabeth I. A century later the house was commandeered for Parliamentary troops, who left it in a sorry state.

Inheriting the house in 1685, Richard Graham, first Viscount Preston, removed the old north wing and remodelled the south front, giving it a classical entrance. He was also responsible for much of the fine panelling throughout the house.

Contemporary furniture, tapestries and porcelain include items probably presented to Lord Preston when he was Charles II's ambassador to Louis XIV. The Carlisle Collection of miniature rooms fully furnished in different period styles is in the attics.

4½M SE Helmsley, off B1257   (117 G7)

Ormesby Hall, Cleveland The architect of this modest house, built for Dorothy Pennyman about 1750, is not known. Its plain façade suggests an earlier date, and probably reflects provincial conservatism in style. Inside, there is an unexpected opulence of design and decoration indicative of high-quality craftsmanship.

Ionic columns in the entrance hall, together with Palladian motifs there and in the library, are clearly of the middle of the century. The drawing room and dining room, decorated in the 1770s, reveal in the classical delicacy of their stuccowork an Adamesque influence. Carr of York is said to have designed the plasterwork of the ceilings. The most remarkable feature of the house is a first-floor gallery across the middle, with rooms along each side, with elaborately pedimented doorcases.

To the north of the house, a handsome stable-block with cupola tower and open courtyard is attributed to Carr, and is leased to the Mounted Police.

3M SE Middlesbrough, W of A171, but access only from A174   (116 C5)

Rievaulx Terrace and Temples, North Yorkshire Above the wooded valley of Ryedale, a level grass terrace follows a gently serpentine course for half a mile, with a classical temple at each end, both of dressed sandstone, and dating from about 1760. The whole concept is one of Britain's most imaginative pieces of eighteenth-century landscaping, the work of Thomas Duncombe.

A woodland walk parallel to the terrace leads visitors to the southern Rotunda encircled by its Doric colonnade. The return by the terrace reveals a succession of planned views of the ruins of Rievaulx Abbey far below, each framed by hanging woodlands, with moorland beyond.

The Ionic temple, pedimented and with a portico of six columns, contains elaborate plasterwork and a superb painted ceiling by Giovanni Borgnis. Enhancing this elegance, furniture on loan from the Treasury includes William Kent settees, George II tables, and a magnificent Worcester dinner service. In the basement a display illustrates the significance of the terrace in English landscape design.

2½M NW Helmsley, on B1257   (116 G6)

The Treasurer's House, York Bases of Roman columns in the cellars suggest that a house has occupied this site for almost 2,000 years. Successive Treasurers of York Minster lived here from 1100 to 1547, but the present building is mainly of the seventeenth and eighteenth centuries. The garden front and centre range are Thomas Young's work of 1630, while the Venetian windows and Dutch gables were added a century later when the house was subdivided. When Frank Green bought it in 1897 it was three dwellings, and today's structure owes much to his réstoration work.

Apart from the medieval character of the great hall and its staircase leading to a half-timbered gallery, the flavour of the house is essentially Palladian and early Georgian. Throughout there is a rare quality of decorative detail, with outstanding examples of plasterwork and panelling, and elaborate chimney-pieces.

The quality of furniture matches its elegant setting. Two centuries of craftsmanship are represented, covering a remarkable range of items augmented by collections of early English china, pottery and glass, while the paintings include a number of English and Flemish portraits from the sixteenth to eighteenth centuries.

Chapter House Street, behind York Minster (112 B4)

Wallington, Northumberland Set in remote Northumberland countryside this square, dignified and elegant house of local sandstone

Wallington's sober exterior gives no hint of the elaborate decoration within, as seen here in the staircase hall.

dates from 1688. Sir Walter Calverley Blackett extensively re-modelled it in the 1740s, and it was his artistic taste and creative talents which resulted in the superb quality of decoration in the main rooms. Plasterwork, panelling, furniture, portraits and collections, especially of fine porcelain, all reveal eighteenth-century craftsmanship at its best.

If the Blacketts gave Wallington its architectural flavour, successive generations of Trevelyans made no less distinguished a contribution. Sir John Trevelyan, nephew of Sir Walter Blackett, inherited the estate in 1777, and it remained in the family until Sir Charles transferred it to the National Trust in 1941.

Sir Walter Trevelyan, a man of wide knowledge and interests, who inherited in 1846, and his artistically talented wife Pauline, enclosed the central hall in 1853. To Wallington came poets and painters, including Millais, Ruskin, Swinburne and Augustus Hare. Lady Trevelyan actively supported the Pre-Raphaelites, and engaged young William Bell Scott to paint eight canvases for the hall depicting episodes of Northumbrian history. Her parlour contains Ruskin drawings and Turner watercolours. The working collection of Lord Macaulay, the historian, is housed in the library, a comfortable, homely, well-used room.

Other attractions at Wallington include a famous collection of dolls' houses, a handsome stable-block, and extensive gardens, grounds and woodlands.

12M W Morpeth, on B6342 (133 E8)

Washington Old Hall, Tyne and Wear Saved from demolition in 1936, this small manor house is an object lesson in Anglo-American cooperation. Washingtons had lived at the Old Hall from 1183, finally selling the manor to the Bishop of Durham in 1613. The present house, of local sandstone, dates from this sale, though parts of the earlier house are incorporated.

At the west end of the stone-flagged great hall, two arched doorways of the original house lead into the kitchen. In the east wing is some excellent Jacobean panelling. Most of the furniture is seventeenth-century, much of it and other items being bought by the Trust with money given by Americans.

Genuine George Washington relics include a bust by Houdon, who visited Mount Vernon in 1785, and the fan given to Martha Washington by General Lafayette.

On the second floor, one room is furnished as a bedroom, with an interesting seventeenth-century bed and other furniture of the same date. A picture presented by President Carter on his visit to the Hall in 1977 hangs here.

Two other rooms on this floor are in daily use as a community centre, and the property is leased to, and maintained by, Sunderland Borough Council.

5M W Sunderland in the old village of Washington New Town (signposted District 4). The Old Hall is on the E side of The Avenue, which runs through the village (133 G11)

Castles, Abbeys & other Buildings

Dunstanburgh Castle, Northumberland Approached only by a mile's walk, from Craster to the south or Embleton to the north, Dunstanburgh's gaunt ruins crown a rocky headland on a hauntingly beautiful coast. Built about 1314 by the Earl of Lancaster, and extending over eleven acres, the castle was largely destroyed during the Wars of the Roses. Only its gentler southern slopes made a curtain wall necessary; this survives, together with two towers and the massive, unusual gatehouse-keep which completely dominates the coastal scene. (Under the guardianship of the Department of the Environment.)

9M NE Alnwick, off B1339 (133 A10)

Gibside Chapel, Tyne and Wear Gibside Chapel is the main building to have survived on the large Gibside estate of a wealthy eighteenth-century landowner, Sir George Bowes. He planned it as the family mausoleum to face along an avenue of trees to the British Liberty statue on its tall column. Designed by James Paine, work started on Gibside Chapel in 1760 but money shortages delayed its completion until 1812.

James Paine's chapel, in the form of a Greek cross, is very much influenced by Palladio's Villa Rotonda at Vicenza, and only internally is its ecclesiastical character revealed.

The outside is beautifully proportioned, with a classical portico of Ionic columns supporting a pediment, and a central dome behind. Fine-quality sandstone is tooled and carved with superb craftsmanship.

Inside, the central altar is surrounded by communion rails. A three-decker pulpit, and box-pews curved to fit the semi-circular apses, are of mahogany and cherrywood. Together with excellent plasterwork they create an impression of exquisite, restrained dignity.

6M SW Gateshead, A694, then B6314 (133 G10)

left The interior of Gibside Chapel, showing the central altar, the rare mahogany three-tier pulpit and the cherrywood box pews.

right Hadrian's Wall runs across northern England for 73 miles. Housesteads, shown here, is the best preserved of its forts.

below The special nature of the Carthusian rule is particularly well seen in the layout of Mount Grace Priory.

Lady's Well, Northumberland This large trough in a tree-shaded grove was probably used by nuns of the twelfth-century Augustinian priory. Walled-in during medieval days, repaired in 1780, with a wheel-head cross added last century, it continues to supply Holystone village with clear, fresh water.

Holystone, 7M W Rothbury, off B6341 (133 C8)

Mount Grace Priory, North Yorkshire Beneath the wooded western edge of the Cleveland Hills are the most important Carthusian ruins in England. Founded in 1398 and quietly surrendered in 1539, the priory passed into lay hands, part of it becoming a country house.

Monks' individual two-storey cells, each twenty-seven feet square with walled garden behind, were spaced round the Great Cloister, an irregular quadrangle with a longest side of 272 feet. Ruins survive of the simple, narrow priory church, with its later tower and side-chapels. Monks met here for services, but most of their life was spent in seclusion. Tranquillity pervades this rare Carthusian priory in its enchanting setting. (Under the guardianship of the Department of the Environment.)

6M NE Northallerton, off A19 (116 E5)

Penshaw Monument, Tyne and Wear Splendidly incongruous, a roofless Doric temple crowns a windy hill, visible for miles across industrial landscapes. Built in 1844 as a memorial to the first Earl of Durham, its honeyed sandstone, now darkened and sombre, adds a touch of magic to the skyline.

5M SW Sunderland, E of A183 (133 G11)

Ripon: Sanctuary Cross, North Yorkshire The stump remains of the only surviving cross which marked the limits of sanctuary associated with St Wilfrid's Abbey.

Sharow, ¾M NE Ripon, off A61 (116 H3)

George Stephenson's Cottage, Northumberland A stone cottage, built about 1750, and the birthplace in 1781 of George Stephenson, the 'Father of Railways'. Appropriately it adjoins the track of the old Wylam colliery wagonway, now a riverside walkway. (The room in which Stephenson was born is open at any reasonable time, April–September, by appointment with the lessee.)

½M E Wylam village, 8M W Newcastle-upon-Tyne, off B6528 (133 F9)

Beadnell Limekilns, Northumberland An imposing group of late eighteenth-century limekilns overlooking the tiny, west-facing harbour of Beadnell.

½M SE Beadnell, off B1340 (133 E12)

Hadrian's Wall Estate and Housesteads Fort, Northumberland Striding confidently over the hackled crests of lonely hills, this defensive structure is Britain's most impressive Roman monument, begun by Emperor Hadrian in AD 122, subsequently strengthened with forts, milecastles and turrets, and flanked by a ditch and vallum. The Trust owns about four miles of the most spectacular section, from east of Housesteads Fort westwards to Winshields Crag, including milecastles and turret sites, and Housesteads itself, best-preserved of all the forts. (Housesteads, and its associated museum of Roman finds, is in the guardianship of the Department of the Environment.)

Plainly visible at Housesteads (*Vercovicium*) are the remains of ramparts and gateways, barracks and headquarters blocks, granaries and latrines, and a nearby milecastle is well-preserved. A walk along the Wall westwards from Housesteads follows the route of part of the Pennine Way, over Cuddy's Crags, Hotbank Crags, Milking Gap, and high above the reed-fringed waters of Crag Lough to Peel Crags and Winshields. Wide views extend northwards to Northumberland's forests, southwards to the gentler landscape of the South Tyne valley, while to east and west the Wall's own sinuous, surging course leads the eye to far horizons.

4M NE Haltwhistle, off B6318 (132 F6)

Stainforth Bridge, North Yorkshire This graceful, single-arch, seventeenth-century packhorse bridge spans the river Ribble in a beautiful wooded valley.

2½M N Settle, off B6479 (115 H10)

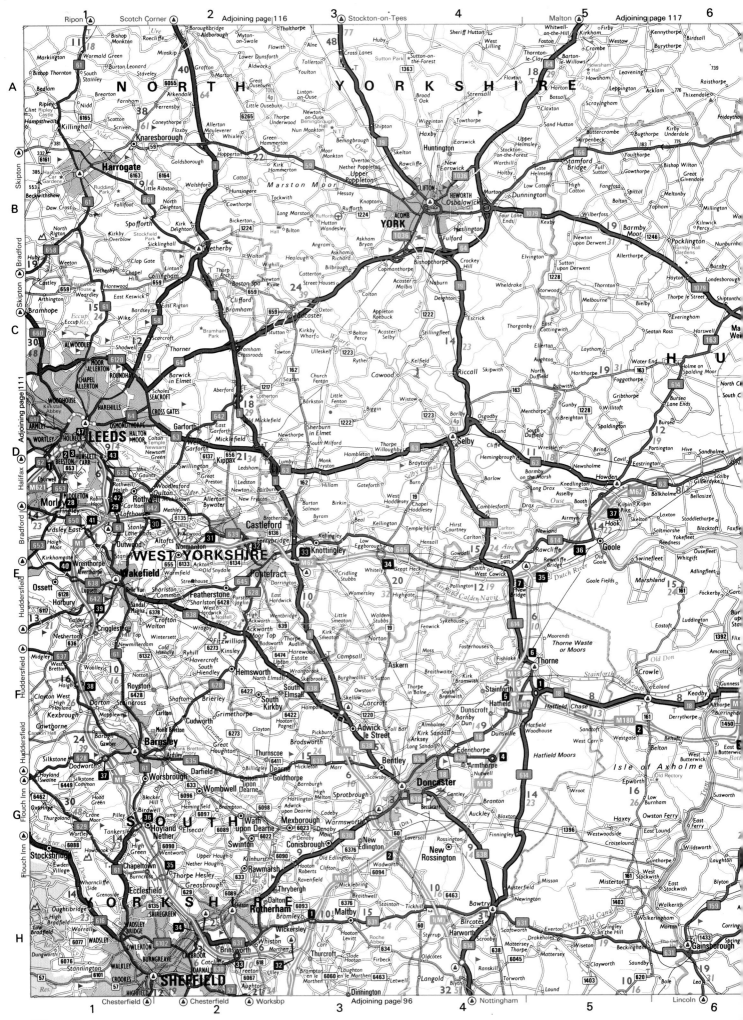

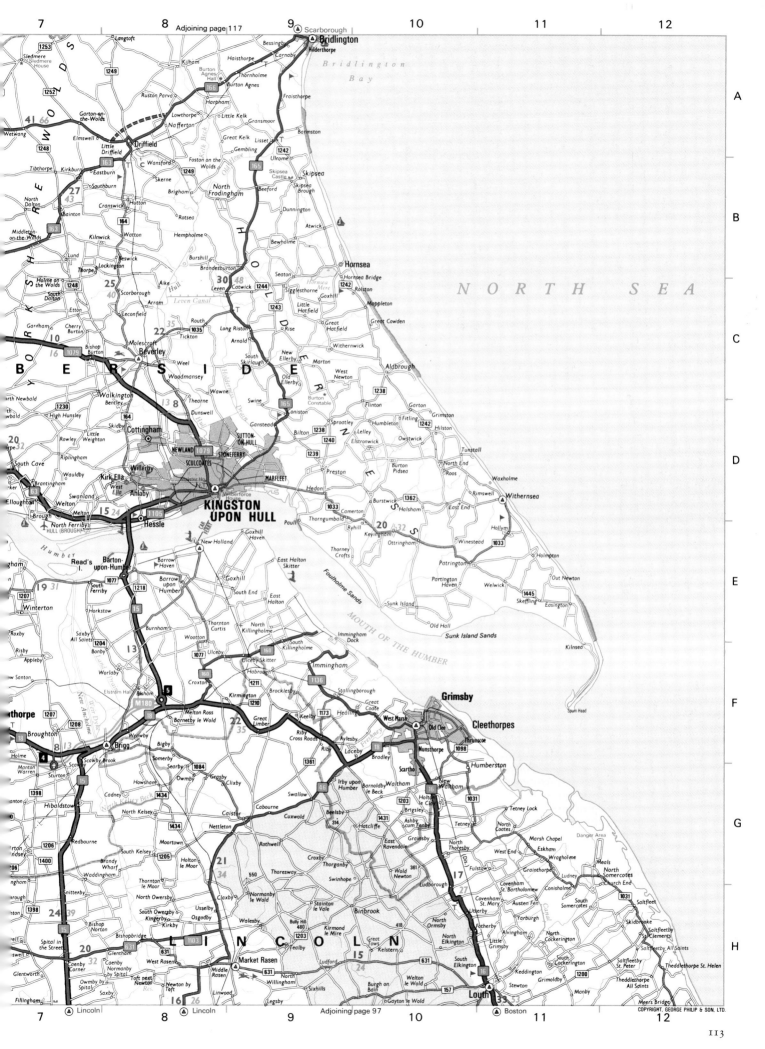

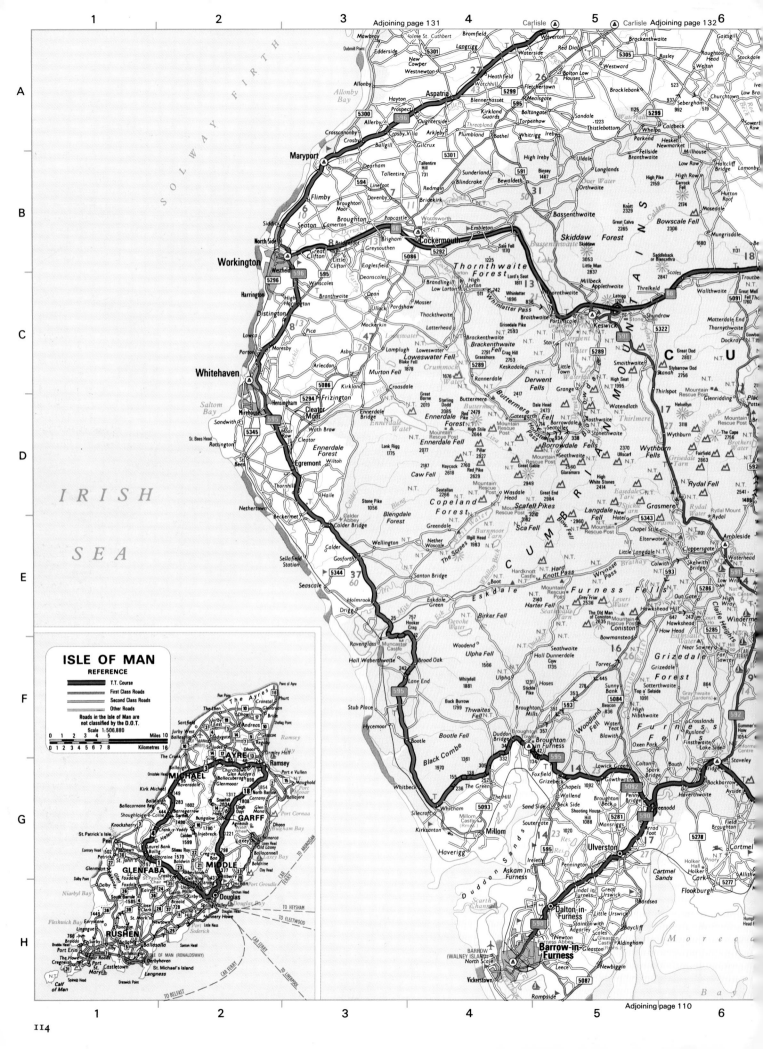

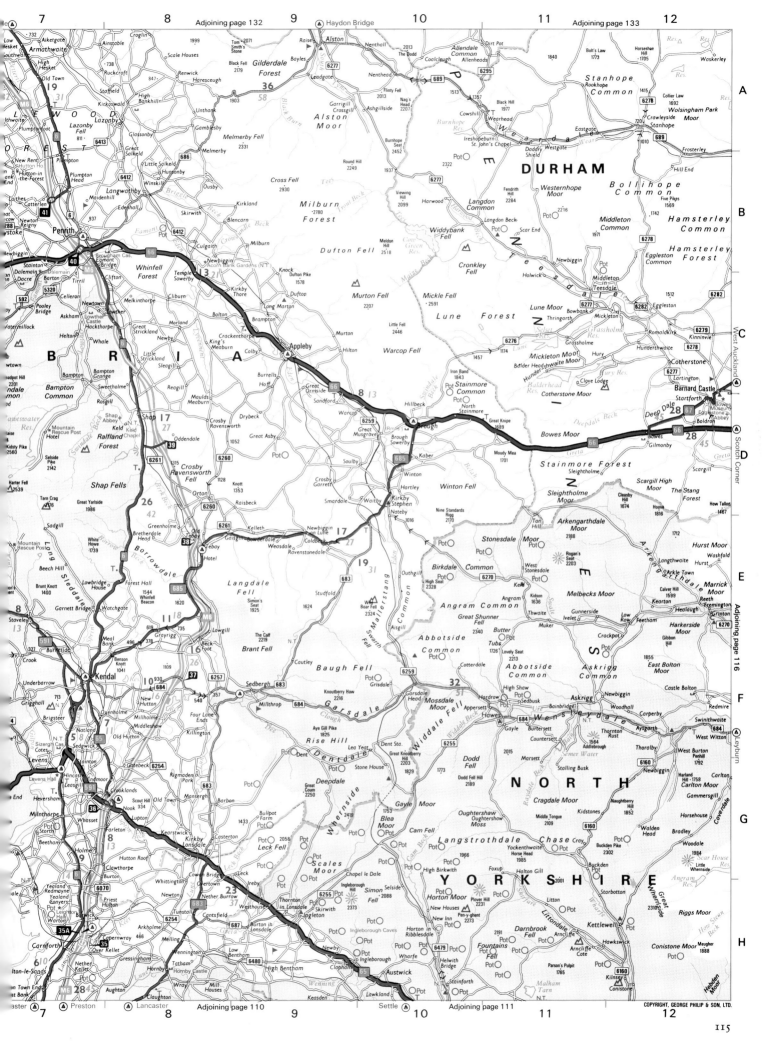

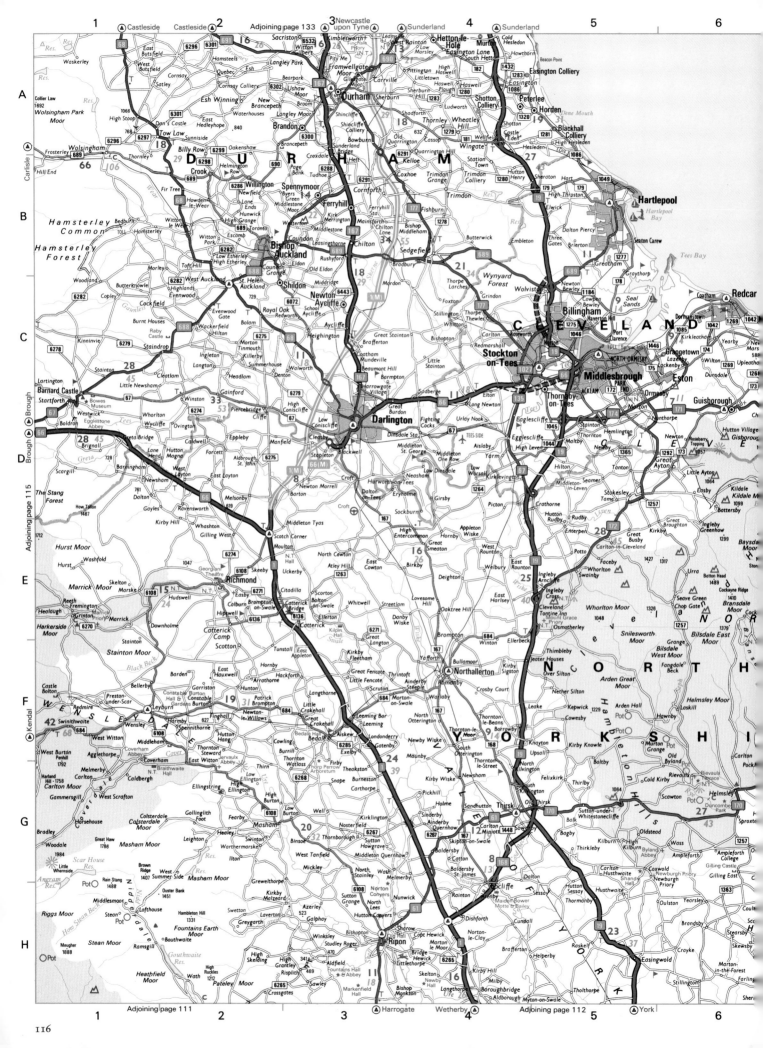

N O R T H

S E A

Saltburn-the-Sea
Brotton
546
174
Skinningrove
Carlin How
North
Skelton
Kilton
Loftus
Easington
Boulby
Staithes
Dalehouse
Port Mulgrave
174
Lingdale
Stanghow
Liverton
1366
Roxby
Newton
Mulgrave
Ellerby
Hinderwell
Runswick
Kettleness
Goldsborough
Moorsholm
Scaling
Mickleby
West
Barnby
East
Barnby
Lythe
488
Sandsend
171
821
616
W
774
1266
17
27
Danby Low
Moor
Roxby High
Moor
Ugthorpe
Dunsley
Newholm
174
Whitby
Saltwick Bay
22
35
Beacon
Hill
Lealholm
Moor
988
Stonegate
171
Aislaby
Ruswarp
Briggswath
Sneaton
Stainsacre
High Hawsker
1410
Danby
Houlsyke
Lealholm
Egton
Sleights
Ugglebarnby
1447
Ness Point or
North Cheek
Westerdale
Church
House
Glaisdale
Egton
Bridge
Grosmont
Littlebeck
Sneaton
Thorpe
171
Raw
368
N.T.
Robin Hood's Bay
Ainthorpe
Street
945
Fylingthorpe
Castleton
Danby High
Moor
1419
Glaisdale
Moor
Egton High Moor
Beck Hole
1416
Old Peak or
South Cheek
425
Rosedale
Moor
1071
Goathland
N.T.
Ravenscar
1258
Hill
Cottages
169
Goathland Moor
959
Fylingdales Moor
20
Blakey Ridge
Thorgill
Hunt Ho.
Wheeldale
Moor
171
Falcon
Inn
32
Staintondale
Rosedale
Abbey
1134
952
Allerston
High Moor
812
Harwood
Dale
Cloughton
Newlands
N.T.
Cloughton
Wyke
Spaunton Moor
TOLL
Stape
N.T.
Langdale
Forest
Broxa
Forest
Cloughton
Cromer Point
Lastingham
Keldy
Castle
IDLL
Levisham
N.T.
Silpho
Burniston
Hutton-
le-Hole
Spaunton
Pot
Newton-
on-Rawcliffe
Lockton
Staindale
Langdale
End
Broxa
Suffield
Hackness
Scalby
165
Newby
Barrowcliff
Fadmoor
Pot
Cropton
Cawthorne
Dalby Forest
Wykeham
Forest
Everley
Scarborough
Appleton-
le-Moors
169
Low Dalby
Scalby
Falsgrave
Kirkbymoorside
Keldholme
Sinnington
Aislaby
Wrelton
Middleton
170
Sawdon
West Ayton
East
Ayton
Hutton
Buscel
Irton
170
64
Eastfield
Osgodby
Cayton Bay
Kirkby
Mills
Welburn
Great
Edstone
Marton
Pickering
Thornton-
Dale
Wilton
Ebberston
Ebberston
Hall
Ruston
Wykeham
Seamer
1261
Cayton
165
Southfield
Normanby
170
Allerston
1415
1258
218
Snainton
Brompton
T
Lebberston
1261
Gristhorpe
1039
Muscoates
Salton
Little
Barugh
169
High
Misperton
Yedingham
29
18
Willerby
Staxton
Folkton
1039
Muston
Filey
17
Filey Brigg
Filey Bay
Great
Barugh
8
13
Low
Marishes
Sherburn
Ganton
Willerby
Hertford
1039
Flixton
West Ness
East Ness
Brawby
Kirby
Misperton
East
Knapton
1258
East
Heslerton
Potter
Brompton
Hunmanby
27
Primrose Valley
South
Holme
Great
Habton
Ryton
West
Knapton
West
Heslerton
22
35
1249
Fordon
Reighton Gap
Slingsby
1257
Amotherby
Barton-
le-Street
Wykeham
Rillington
Scampston
64
Wold
Newton
Reighton
Speeton
Broughton
Old Malton Moor
Thorpe
Bassett
Wintringham
Place
Newton
Foxholes
Burton
Fleming
1229
Buckton
Appleton-
le-Street
Swinton
Old Malton
1255
Bempton
North Moor
1255
Flamborough
1259
Flamborough Head
Coneysthorpe
1257
Malton
Scagglethorpe
Settrington
1248
North
Grimston
654
High
Mowthorpe
West
Lutton
East
Lutton
Helperthorpe
Octon
Weaverthorpe
Butterwick
Rookdale
Wold
Newton
HUMBERSIDE
Thwing
Grindale
165
1255
Sewerby
Hall
Castle Howard
18
29
Norton
64
High Hutton
Low Hutton
Firby
Langton
Kirby
Grindalythe
363
322
Duggleby
West
Lutton
1253
Burton
Fleming
Boynton
Sewerby
41
68
Bridlington
30
Bulmer
Welburn
Whitwell-
on-the-Hill
Kennythorpe
Wharram le Street
Langtoft
Rudston
1253
Bessingby
Kingston
upon Hull

YORK MOORS

Glaisdale

Rosedale

E

PICKERING

VALE OF

Hills

Scotland

PRESTON MILL

The rich variety of properties now in the care of the National Trust for Scotland not only embraces much of the country's grandest scenery (Glen Coe, Torridon and Kintail are but three examples) but also provides an insight into a colourful past.

Pride of place must go to that synthesis of comfortable home and minor castle, the tower-house. The Trust owns several of these ranging from twelfth-century Drum through simple Scotstarvit to the sixteenth- and seventeenth-century castles of Mar (Castle Fraser, Craigievar and Crathes). All are splendid examples of a local style which crowned otherwise stern keeps with elaborate yet purely decorative defensive features. The following century was that of the Adams, Scotland's most distinguished family of architects. Of their achievements the Trust owns the houses of Haddo and Dun by William the father, while the more renowned Robert is represented by Culzean and Edinburgh's Charlotte Square. More modest properties include the Bachelors' Club and Souter Johnnie's Cottage, both associated with Robert Burns; 'doocots', those providers of winter meat; the birthplaces of Carlyle, Barrie and the geologist Hugh Miller; the small houses of Dunkeld and Culross; and the weaver's cottage at Kilbarchan.

The Trust's many gardens include Inverewe, Threave and Pitmedden, all widely known, while for the lover of more intimate places there is a fine choice scattered throughout much of the country.

Lastly there are the many visitor centres, some introducing the great mountain estates, some describing towns where the Trust has been active with restoration, some associated with great houses or gardens, while Bannockburn, Culloden, Glenfinnan and Killiecrankie tell their own dramatic stories.

Coast & Countryside

The National Trust for Scotland owns many coast and countryside properties together amounting to some 85,000 acres and descending in size from the great tracts of mountain which make up estates such as Glen Coe and Dalness, Kintail and Morvich, and Torridon down through a rich choice of other places which, though smaller, are almost all of scenic worth. Among these smaller properties there are a number of islands, including **Iona**, landing place of Columba in 563 and hallowed in the story of Scotland's early Christianity (the Trust does not own the abbey and other sacred and historic buildings); **Fair Isle**, Britain's most isolated inhabited island and of international renown in the study of migrating birds; and remote **St Kilda**, a group of islands and rocks some fifty miles west of the Outer Hebrides, uninhabited since 1930 when the thirty-five people still there were evacuated at their own request (leased to the Nature Conservancy Council).

Much of Scotland's grandest scenery lies along or behind the country's north-western coast and here too will be found many of the Trust's most splendid coast and countryside estates, the most northern (apart from

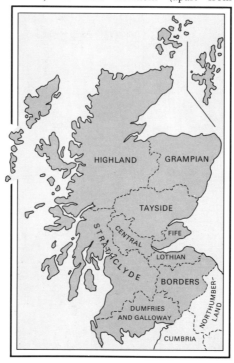

Inverewe), beside the A835 to the south of Ullapool, being **Corrieshalloch Gorge** (148 H3). A mile long and 200 feet deep, this steep and narrow cleft is known for the Falls of Measach which plunge 150 feet into its depths. Some twenty-five miles to the south-west the great mass of **Torridon** towers high above the glen and sea loch of the same name; in the loch lies the Trust's island of **Shieldaig** whose thirty-two acres are almost entirely covered in Scots pine (142 D2). A tract of over 14,000 acres of some of the best mountain scenery in Scotland, and with several heights of over 3,000 feet, Torridon is a magnet as much for walkers and climbers, and naturalists and geologists, as for those content simply to enjoy the place's scenic grandeur. The principal heights are Liathach (a string of summits extending over some five miles) and Beinn Eighe which forms the Trust's boundary. Both are made up of crags, corries and high ridges and both also illustrate the estate's best-known geological feature of white quartzite summits, some 500 million years old, crowning a mass of rather older red sandstone. Wildlife, though sparse and not easily seen, includes red and other deer, wildcat, pinemarten, buzzards and the golden eagle. There is a visitor centre, with a deer museum, at the junction of the A896 and the road to Diabaig (142 D3).

A total contrast is provided by the **Balmacara Estate** filling most of the promontory between lochs Carron and Alsh opposite Skye (143 G2). Here the countryside is one of winding roads, villages, woodland and constantly changing glimpses of sea, loch and islands. Not far inland, though, the road running east (A87) forms the southern boundary of the Trust's huge **Kintail and Morvich** estate. Together with the land around the **Falls of Glomach** to the north this provides some 15,000 acres of remote and magnificent Highland scenery. The chain of abrupt, sharp peaks known as the Five Sisters hangs an almost sheer 3,000 feet above the road (143 H3), a barrier behind which extends first the lonely country of Kintail, home of red deer and feral goats, and then, as a narrow finger of Trust land, the southern approach to the Falls of Glomach, one of the highest and wildest waterfalls in Britain (143

above Fair Isle, where the summer sun never sets, is Britain's most isolated inhabited island.

right The houses in the village street of Hirta, St Kilda, are being gradually restored by volunteer work parties.

G4). The best access to the mountains is from Morvich (visitor centre) off the A87 at the eastern end of Loch Duich. There is also a Trust information board farther east beside the road below the Five Sisters, maps and plans here describing the estate and also explaining a skirmish fought nearby in 1719 as part of an attempt to put the Old Pretender on the throne.

Glen Coe, a name with infamous historical associations but today almost synonymous with awesome mountain grandeur, ascends some twelve miles from sea-level at Loch Leven to a watershed at just over 1,000 feet (139 B8); it is a place which will probably never wholly lose its reputation for sombre gloom, earned partly because this can indeed be its effect, especially when descended in lowering weather, but also perhaps because of its ever-present association with the treachery and massacre of February 1692 as also through the influence of the paintings and writings of romantically imaginative travellers of the eighteenth and nineteenth centuries. But whatever its reputation and whatever its mood, Glen Coe is a splendid mountain wilderness towering above the rushing River Coe, a glen moreover which can readily be enjoyed by all (because a road runs its length) yet which at the same time offers walks and challenging climbs to the more ambitious.

As to the massacre – the worst of which occurred in the lower glen, outside the boundary of the Trust lands – it is the smell of treachery both here in Glen Coe and in London that lingers. Very briefly what happened was that the government set the last day of 1691 as

The Five Sisters of Kintail from a viewpoint high above the north side of Loch Duich. The highest peak is 3,505 feet.

the final date for submission by the Highlanders to William and Mary. Glencoe delayed but recorded his oath on 2 January. Meanwhile in London the Master of Stair, William's ruthless Scottish minister who was determined to inflict an example on the Highlands, wrote to the Commander-in-Chief in Scotland that he was glad that Glencoe did not 'come in within the time prescribed' and that it would be a great advantage to the nation if 'that thieving tribe were rooted out and cut off'. On 1 February a company under the command of Campbell of Glenlyon moved into the glen and was warmly received by the unsuspecting Macdonalds; on 12 February the order was received that all under the age of seventy should be put to the sword, and early the next morning Glenlyon and his men turned on their hosts, shooting the elderly chief in the back and butchering some thirty-eight people while as many more died of exposure and starvation on the mountains.

The Trust's Glen Coe lands of over 14,000 acres were acquired between 1935 and 1937 and are thus one of its earliest properties. Embracing the scenic best of the glen, the estate is also of considerable and varied geological interest (an aspect well explained and illustrated in the Trust's booklet) although, largely because it is so bare, it is not rich in either fauna or flora. Nevertheless there are attractions for the specialist, and the ordinary visitor may with luck see a soaring eagle or a herd of red deer, while wildcat have their home on the heights. The road ascends the left bank of the Coe, soon reaching the beautifully situated visitor centre, built by the Countryside Commission for Scotland but operated by the Trust; from here easy paths lead to Signal Rock, traditionally the place from which the signal was given to start the massacre, and to An Tor, a hill commanding a good view up the glen. Ascending, the road crosses the river just below Loch Achtriochtan to reach its grandest stretch, to the north being the rock-face of jagged Aonach Eagach and to the south Aonach Dubh on which is Ossian's Cave, legendary birthplace and home of that shadowy early bard. Some four miles above the visitor centre the Study (*studdie*: anvil) is reached, a terrace offering a view down the glen and also marking the limit of Trust property on the north. On the other side, though, the Trust cares for a huge tract of mountain, the limits being roughly marked by this road (A82), Glen Etive on the south as far as Dalness, and a line running north-west across Bidean nam Bian (3,766 feet) back to the visitor centre. A road descends the right bank of the Etive below the mass of Buachaille Etive Mór, known for its rock climbs.

At Scotland's centre **Ben Lawers** (140 C1), rising to nearly 4,000 feet above the north shore of Loch Tay and commanding views of both coasts, is another mountain range of geological interest, in this case because an overfold has brought the oldest rocks to the surface. The Trust owns 8,000 acres of the summits and southern slopes, the property, famed for its Alpine flora, being a national nature reserve under the joint control of the Trust and the Nature Conservancy Council. A road climbs

above The Grey Mare's Tail waterfall cascades down a rugged gorge. The area around is rich in wild flowers.

right The spectacular promontory of St Abb's Head is an important locality for cliff-breeding sea-birds.

from the loch shore to a visitor centre at 1,400 feet from where start a nature trail and a path to the summit.

Three other sizable countryside properties merit mention, the first two being on islands. On Mull, **The Burg** (138 E2) embraces 1,525 acres of the Ardmeanach promontory (five miles rough walk) and includes a petrified tree set in the basalt cliffs and perhaps fifty million years old, while on Arran the Trust owns **Goatfell** (134 F5), 2,866 feet and the highest point on the island, Cir Mhor, adjacent and only slightly lower, and part of Glen Rosa which provides an approach towards the mountains from the south. The third large property, in Scotland's south-west off the A708 near Moffat, is **Grey Mare's Tail** (136 H4), a site of nearly 2,400 acres named after the 200-foot waterfall which is the principal feature.

Among more modest coast and countryside properties are **Linn of Tummel**, fifty acres with a nature trail along the rivers Tummel and Garry below the Killiecrankie visitor centre (140 A4); **Craigower**, a beacon-hill 1,300 feet high above Pitlochry (140 A4); **Bucinch** and **Ceardoch**, two small islands in Loch Lomond (139 H11); **Dollar Glen**, a wooded walk which offers an attractive approach to Castle Campbell (140 G4); **Blackhill**, three miles west of Lanark, a viewpoint over the valley of the Clyde (136 E1); **Threave Wildfowl Refuge**, on the Dee near Castle Douglas and known for its many species of wild geese and duck (131 E8); and, by the Solway shore near Dalbeattie, the bird sanctuary of **Rough Island** and the fifty acres of coastline known as **Muckle Lands and Jubilee Path** (131 F9). Finally, and acquired only in 1980, there is **St Abb's Head** on Scotland's south-east coast not far above the border (137 B11), a grand headland named after Ebba, a

seventh-century Northumbrian princess who founded a nunnery here, reputedly in gratitude for surviving shipwreck. It was destroyed by Vikings two centuries later. The cliffs rise to 300 feet and the headland is of considerable botanical and ornithological importance.

Houses, Gardens & Parks

Abertarff House, Highland Long a town residence of the Lovats, Abertarff dates from 1593 and is one of the oldest houses in Inverness. (Let to the Highland Association – An Comunn Gaidhealach.)

Church Street, Inverness (144 E2)

Bachelors' Club, Strathclyde A seventeenth-century house in which Robert Burns and some friends formed a club in 1780 and where in the following year he became a Freemason. Period furnishings.

In Tarbolton (on B744 off A758), 7½M NE of Ayr (135 G9)

Barrie's Birthplace, Tayside The modest home in Kirriemuir, the 'Thrums' of his books, in which J. M. Barrie (1860–1937) was born, the son of a handloom weaver who at the time of his son's birth still worked on the premises. Personal and literary material is shown.

9 Brechin Road, Kirriemuir (141 B8)

Branklyn Garden, Tayside A garden of two acres, the personal achievement from 1922 onwards of the late Mr and Mrs J. T. Renton. The outstanding collection of plants includes alpines and also many of specialist interest.

Dundee Road, Perth (140 E6)

Brodick Castle and Country Park, Strathclyde In 1503 James IV appointed the 2nd Baron Hamilton royal justiciary in Arran (with the title Earl of Arran). Brodick then remained a seat of the Hamiltons until 1895 when it passed to the Duchess of Montrose, only child of the 12th Duke. The castle is of several periods, the oldest masonry being the remnants of a round tower of the later thirteenth century. These remains are within the tower-house built by the 2nd Earl of Arran in about 1558 and now forming the eastern end. In 1653, when in English hands after the defeat of Charles II at Worcester, the castle was enlarged by a western block, and finally, in 1844, the architect Gillespie Graham was commissioned to add a major extension to the west, the western terminal becoming a tower of four storeys.

The beautifully decorated interior houses notable collections of furniture, silver (including specially-commissioned items by great craftsmen), porcelain and paintings. Many of these treasures derive from the wealthy connoisseur William Beckford (*see Charlecote Park*) who, on his death in 1844, bequeathed them to his daughter Susan Euphemia, who married the 10th Duke of Hamilton. Among

The drawing room at Brodie Castle is part of the extension begun in the 1820s.

the artists whose works hang here are Van Dyck, Fragonard, Watteau, Gainsborough, Kneller, Winterhalter, Pollard and Turner.

The country park was formed in 1980 and is managed by the Trust in conjunction with Cunninghame District Council. It includes the gardens and grounds of the castle, while Goatfell and its neighbouring hills, although not a part of the park, will be managed in association with it.

The gardens of about sixty-five acres comprise two principal areas, a walled formal garden dating from 1710 and a large woodland garden which was started by the Duchess of Montrose in 1923 and is internationally famous, especially for its rhododendrons.

Brodick, Isle of Arran (134 F5)

Brodie Castle, Grampian Malcolm IV gave these lands to the Brodies in 1160, but although

The north side of Charlotte Square, Edinburgh, is Robert Adam's urban masterpiece.

the present house may well incorporate something of an earlier building it is basically of 1567, much modified and extended in later centuries and especially after 1824 when the architect William Burn was involved in extensive rebuilding. Features of the interior are the rich seventeenth-century plasterwork ceilings, the drawing room designed by Burn, the Victorian kitchen, and an important collection of paintings which includes Dutch works (Van Dyck, Jacob Cuyp and others), English and French Impressionists and early English watercolours. There are also important collections of French furniture and Chinese export porcelain. In the grounds are a woodland walk, a wildlife observation hide, an adventure playground and a picnic area.

Between Nairn and Forres, off A96 (144 D5)

Carlyle's Birthplace, Dumfries and Galloway The house in which Thomas Carlyle (1795–1881) was born. It was built by his father and uncle, both master masons. Letters and other personal articles are shown in a contemporary setting. (*See also Carlyle's House, London.*)

Ecclefechan, on A74 (131 D12)

Castle Fraser, Grampian Castle Fraser is one of the most splendid of the great houses in this district, historically the lands of Mar. Built between 1575 and 1636, the castle is the work of two well-known local families of master masons, Bel and Leiper. Among noteworthy features of the granite exterior are the corner turrets reaching through two floors, the blind machicolation, the rope design of the mouldings, and the magnificent heraldic panel (signed I. Bel) on the north side. In the grounds a formal garden occupies what was the old walled garden.

16M W of Aberdeen, 3M S of Kemnay, off B993 (146 F5)

Charlotte Square and Georgian House, Edinburgh Charlotte Square was designed by Robert Adam in 1791 and its superb north side is widely accepted as one of his most distin-

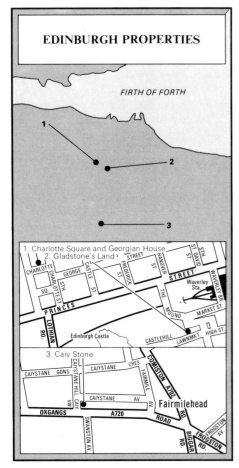

Central Edinburgh (see map above)

Craigievar Castle, crowned with a profusion of corbels, turrets and cupolas, is an outstanding example of the contemporary Scottish Baronial style.

guished urban achievements. Later much altered to meet Victorian tastes, the north side was largely restored to its original form during the 1920s and 1930s, one feature of the restoration being the return of the first-floor window levels to their correct eighteenth-century height. Eleven houses are contained within a single façade; No 5 is the headquarters of the National Trust for Scotland, No 6 the official residence of the Secretary of State for Scotland, and No 7 what is now known as the Georgian House. The upper floors of No 7 are the residence of the Moderator of the General Assembly of the Church of Scotland, while the lower ones have been furnished to illustrate the interior, family and domestic, as it may have been during the period c.1790 to 1820. During this period the house was owned by John Lamont of Lamont, eighteenth chief of the clan of that name.

Central Edinburgh (see map above)

Craigievar Castle, Grampian It is recorded that men of Craigievar fought for the Earl of Mar at Harlaw in 1411, and known too that by 1457 these lands belonged to the Mortimers who are thought to have started to build the castle around the end of the sixteenth century. However, by 1610 financial difficulties forced the family to sell, the purchaser being an Aberdeen merchant called William Forbes. By the time his home was finished in 1626 it stood as an outstanding example of the contemporary local Scottish Baronial style, a tall tower-house, plain below but on top crowded with turrets, corbelling, cupolas and other decorative features. With the great hall typically occupying the main part of the first floor, the castle's interior is notable for the plasterwork of the ceilings, a choice which at this period was superseding painted decoration in popularity, and also for the magnificent carved Royal Arms of the United Kingdom over the hall's fireplace, a decoration to which William Forbes was entitled as a tenant-in-chief holding his lands direct from the Crown. The architect of Craigievar may well have been that same I. Bel whose name appears on the heraldic panel at *Castle Fraser*.

On A980, 6M S of Alford (146 F3)

Crathes Castle, Grampian Crathes seems to have been started in about 1553 by Alexander Burnett of Leys, the head of a family granted lands here by Bruce in 1323. Progress was slow, partly because of frequent deaths in the succession, and it was not until the last decade of the century that the house was occupied. A typical Scottish Baronial tower-house of the district and time, plain below but turreted in its upper part, Crathes is best known for the decorative work of its interior and especially for its splendid painted ceilings with their allegorical figures, among the last of their kind before plasterwork became popular, and for the ribbed and carved ceiling of the long gallery, unique in Scotland for being of oak. The grounds of nearly 600 acres are made up of woodland, fields and a garden area of about six acres in which there are several individual gardens, each on a particular theme. The yew hedges dating from 1702 may be survivals of a formal garden, and there are four nature trails.

3M E of Banchory on A93 (147 H5)

Crathes Castle is best known for its painted ceilings, illustrating an art of which few examples have survived.

The Study in Culross is so called because of the small withdrawing room at the top of the tower.

Culross, Fife Ever since its formation the Trust has been active here and Culross is now preserved as an unspoilt example of a small Royal Burgh of the sixteenth and seventeenth centuries, at which time it thrived through its trade in salt and coal fostered by its enterprising laird Sir George Bruce.

The principal building owned by the Trust here is Culross Palace, which stands virtually unaltered since it was built by Sir George Bruce between 1597 and 1611. The earlier date with the simple initials GB appears on the building on the west of the courtyard, while SGB (Sir George Bruce) and the date 1611 on a pediment on the building on the north side of the courtyard indicate that this newer part of the house was completed after its owner had been knighted. The most important feature of the interior is the painted woodwork of the walls, ceilings and beams, much of this found dismantled and scattered when the house was taken over by the Office of Works in 1932 but since carefully reassembled. (The Palace is under the guardianship of the Scottish Development Department, Ancient Monuments.)

Two other houses in Culross can also be visited: the Town House of 1626, with a clock tower and façade of 1783 (visitor centre); and the Study, built for a merchant in 1633 and with a small room used as a study by Bishop Leighton of Dunblane (1611–84). Several other Trust buildings can be viewed from the outside.

12M W of N side of Forth road bridge, off A985 (136 A3)

Culzean Castle and Country Park, Strathclyde This estate was owned by the Kennedy family (earls of Cassillis) from the fourteenth century, but Culzean Castle as seen today, apart from some alterations of the nineteenth century, is the achievement of Robert Adam working for the 10th Earl between 1777 and 1792. Adam designed and built the castle in three stages. The first was the conversion of the existing sixteenth-century tower-house into an elegant and comfortable mansion facing southward; the second involved the replacement of the old domestic buildings on the north by a wing of rooms along the rim of the cliff, including the unique round drawing room with windows sheer above the sea; and in the third stage the old courtyard which still survived between the new mansion and the cliff-top wing became the site of the Oval Staircase, generally accepted as one of Adam's most ingenious creations. Completed, Culzean successfully combined Georgian symmetry, romantic mock fortification and also Italianate elements. Since the castle's acquisition by the Trust in 1945, the interior decoration has been the subject of much carefully researched restoration and, since 1972, nearly all the original eighteenth-century colour schemes have been restored.

The country park of 560 acres, run by the Trust on behalf of local authorities, includes the walled garden, swan pond, deer park, woodland walks and picnic places, and also a Park Centre (restaurant, shop, exhibition) occupying the restored and adapted Adam home farm.

On A719, 12M S of Ayr (130 A3)

Drum Castle, Grampian The castle was built in three separate stages. The tower-house is believed to have been built in 1286 by Richard Cementarius, the royal mason; a brewhouse was added to the tower's north wall during the fifteenth century, and a Jacobean mansion built on by the ninth laird in 1619. Later changes included the addition of a central door and steps to the south front of the mansion in about 1800 and the construction in 1875 (to the design of David Bryce) of a hall and door on the north front within the courtyard. The tower-house is notable for being one of the oldest in Scotland, but Drum is also interesting for having been in the possession of the same family for 653 years, from 1323 when Robert Bruce gave these lands to his armour-bearer William de Irwin until 1976 when the estate came to the National Trust for Scotland.

The tower, its early origin suggested by the unusually high battlements, is a square keep with three vaulted storeys, the first of which, once the great hall, was converted into a library in about 1845, the large arched window on the east being thrown out at the same time. Above is a large upper hall, from which a modern wooden stair allows access to the battlements. In the mansion the rooms contain family portraits, porcelain, *objets d'art* and furniture mainly of the eighteenth and nineteenth centuries. The grounds of 400 acres include mixed woodland, an attractive picnic area and a chapel roughly contemporary with the mansion.

10M W of Aberdeen, off A93 (147 G5)

Dunkeld, Tayside Here the Trust owns twenty little houses along Cathedral and High streets. Most of these date from the rebuilding of the town after its destruction in 1689 during the battle in which the Covenanter Cameronians beat off the attacking Highlanders, thus reversing the decision of Killiecrankie and finally assuring the cause of William and Mary. From 1954 to 1965 the houses were restored by the Trust and now provide modern homes behind modest late seventeenth-century exteriors. The restoration is explained in photographs at a visitor centre. Nearby Stanley Hill is a mock fortification raised by the Duke of Atholl in 1730. (Houses not open. Visitor Centre run in conjunction with Dunkeld and Birnam Mercantile and Tourist Association.)

On A9 15M N of Perth (140 C5)

Falkland Palace and Garden, Fife There was a castle here as early as the twelfth century and by the fifteenth Falkland had become a favoured hunting-palace of the Stuarts. It was so popular

GLADSTONE'S LAND.

The garden at the Royal Palace of Falkland showing planting against the long retaining wall under the ruined East Range.

that James IV began a new palace sometime before 1500, this being completed and much embellished by James V who died here in 1542. Still technically the property of the sovereign, Falkland has for centuries been held in the care of a hereditary Keeper, the position of the Trust today being that of Deputy Keeper.

Most of the palace is in ruin but the South Range was restored by the 3rd Marquess of Bute who became Keeper in 1887. Built by James IV, this range's street façade, with long, narrow windows, buttresses and battlement, and twin-towered gatehouse, stands as an attractive example of Scottish Gothic. In contrast the early Renaissance courtyard façade, added by James V, is distinctive for the influence of French craftsmen, recalling that James married two French wives and that his reign marked the high point of the Scottish–French alliance. The range includes the Chapel Royal, with Falkland's only surviving original interior. The East Range housed the royal apartments and here the Trust has restored the King's Bedchamber.

In the grounds a rose garden occupies the site of the North Range, burnt down in 1654, while just to the north of this something of the outline of the early castle survives. The royal tennis court of 1539 is attached to the stables, and there is a visitor centre at the East Port.

11M N of Kirkcaldy on the A912 (141 F7)

Gladstone's Land, Edinburgh This tall, narrow building, completed by Thomas Gledstanes in 1620, is typical of those that once crowded old Edinburgh. The interior, with characteristic wall and ceiling paintings, has been in part

refurbished to seventeenth-century domestic style.

Lawnmarket, Edinburgh (see map p. 122)

Greenbank Garden, Strathclyde The garden and grounds of a Georgian house of 1763. The Advice Centre is likely to be of particular interest to owners of small gardens. (House not open.)

Clarkston, on B761 on S edge of Glasgow (135 D10)

Haddo House, Grampian This great house was designed for the 2nd Earl of Aberdeen in 1731 by William Adam, father of Robert, as successor to the House of Kellie, the mansion of the Gordons of Methlick until burnt down by Covenanters in 1644. With its simple and well-proportioned symmetry the house stands virtually unchanged apart from the front porch which was remodelled by the 7th Earl in 1880 to lower the entrance from the balcony to ground level. The 7th Earl was also largely responsible for the elegant 'Adam Revival' of much of the interior. The house is notable too for its portraits, outstanding among which is one by Lawrence of the 4th Earl (Prime Minister 1852–5), whose care and energy transformed a neglected inheritance into a thriving estate. The chapel of 1880, the last achievement of G. E. Street, contains a window by Burne-Jones.

The Trust owns the house and gardens, while about 180 acres of park are owned and managed by Grampian Regional Council as a country park. The Haddo Choral and Operatic Society ranks as one of Scotland's leading musical societies.

On A9005 near Methlick (146 D6)

Gladstone's Land is the most important example of seventeenth-century high-tenement housing to survive in Edinburgh.

Hamilton House, Lothian A house of 1628 built by John Hamilton, a wealthy citizen of Edinburgh. (Open only by prior arrangement.)

Prestonpans (136 B6)

Hill of Tarvit, Fife A seventeenth-century country house remodelled in 1906 by Sir Robert Lorimer and containing Chippendale, Jacobean and eighteenth-century French furniture, Flemish tapestries, Chinese porcelain and bronzes, Dutch paintings and portraits by, amongst others, Raeburn and Ramsay.

2½M S of Cupar, off A916 (141 F8)

House of The Binns, Lothian The site is thought to have been occupied in prehistoric times and it is known that there was a house here during the fifteenth century. In 1612 the estate was bought by Thomas Dalyell who had accompanied James VI/I to London and made money there, and between that date and 1630 he enlarged and decorated the house converting it to a comfortable mansion. Thomas's son, the colourful General Tam (who, amongst other exploits, escaped from the Tower of London, campaigned in Russia for the Tsar and on his return raised the Scots Greys), added a west wing. During the eighteenth and nineteenth centuries there were further modifications such as the addition of the morning and dining rooms, the reversal of the house (the front moving from the south to the north side) and the enlargement of the east and west ranges.

The interior is known for its moulded plaster ceilings, the best being those in the High Hall

The elegant rooms of Haddo House contain fine antique furniture and a notable collection of portraits.

The House of The Binns was built at a time when fortified houses were no longer essential in Scotland.

and the King's Room, both put up in 1630. The house also contains good Regency furniture, porcelain, and souvenirs of General Tam, while the artists represented include Jamesone, Wilkie and Kneller. The grounds include a nineteenth-century folly and a woodland walk to a view over the Forth.

15M W of Edinburgh, off A904 (136 A3)

House of Dun, Tayside This modest country house dates from 1730 and stands on the site of two earlier houses. It was designed by William Adam for David Erskine, Lord Dun, twelfth laird in a succession reaching back to 1375. The interior is notable for its plasterwork, chimney-pieces and panelling. The estate, which came to the Trust in 1980, includes some 800 acres of farm and woodland. (Not open until 1982–3.)

4M W of Montrose, off A935 (141 A11)

Inveresk Lodge Garden, Lothian The garden of a seventeenth-century house specializing in plants suitable for the small garden. (House not open.)

Just S of Musselburgh, 7M E of Edinburgh, on A6124 (136 B6)

Inverewe Garden, Highland Pleasantly situated on a small headland into a sea loch, this famous garden was the creation from 1862 on of Osgood Mackenzie. After his death in 1922 his work was continued by his daughter, Mrs Sawyer. Despite the northern latitude, many subtropical species are able to flourish on this secluded site washed by the warm North Atlantic Drift and there is normally colour throughout the year.

On A832, 6M NE of Gairloch (148 H1)

Kellie Castle and Garden, Fife Although called 'castle', Kellie is in fact a noteworthy example of Lowland Scottish domestic architecture. The house seen today was completed in about 1606, the last stage in development from a single tower of *c.*1360. Owned first by the Siwards, then by the Oliphants, Kellie was bought in 1613 by Thomas Erskine, later 1st Earl of Kellie. In 1876, by which date the place had long been virtually abandoned, Kellie passed first by lease and then by purchase to the Lorimers who over three generations restored and cared for it. The interior is particularly noteworthy for the painted panelling and the sixteenth-century tapestry in the dining room (formerly the drawing room), and, in the Vine Room, for a ceiling painting (*c.*1685) of Mount Olympus by Jacob de Wet the Younger. Additionally there are displays on the Lorimer family, notably Professor James, the jurist, who first leased Kellie in 1876, and his son Robert, the architect.

3M NNW of Pittenweem, off B9171 (141 G10)

Lamb's House, Edinburgh The combined home and warehouse of a wealthy merchant of the

late sixteenth or early seventeenth century. (Leased as an old people's day centre. Visits by appointment only.)

Water Street, Leith, Edinburgh (136 B5)

Leith Hall and Garden, Grampian The hall was started in 1649 by James Leith, the head of a family first recorded as landowners near Leith (Edinburgh) but who moved northwards in perhaps the thirteenth century and appear as Aberdeen shipowners by the fourteenth. The original design of the hall – a rectangle around a courtyard – has survived, although modifications and enlargements, notably the addition of further storeys, were made during the eighteenth and nineteenth centuries. The house contains portraits and personal souvenirs of the successive lairds, most of whom followed military careers in many parts of the world. The grounds of 236 acres include a bird observation hide, a picnic area and two country walks.

On B9002, 34M NW of Aberdeen (146 E3)

Linlithgow Houses, Lothian Two locally typical late sixteenth- or early seventeenth-century small town houses. (Not open.)

Nos 44 and 48 High Street, Linlithgow (136 B3)

Lochalsh Woodland Garden, Highland A system of footpaths covers most of the garden and woodland around Lochalsh House on the Balmacara Estate, and there is a small countryside interpretation centre in the coach house. (House not open.)

2M E of Kyle of Lochalsh (143 G2)

Leith Hall contains collections recording the family's political and military achievements.

Malleny Garden, Lothian The garden of a house of about 1635, last in a succession of houses on an estate dating back, though with many changes in ownership, to the fifteenth century. The house was probably built by Sir James Murray, Master of the King's Works. The shrub roses are a feature of the garden. Also, four magnificent yew trees survive from a planting of twelve to commemorate the Union of Crowns in 1603. (House not open.)

Balerno, off A70 (136 C4)

Pitmedden Garden, Grampian The main feature here is the interesting formal Great Garden, laid out in the second half of the seventeenth century by Sir Alexander Seton and recreated by the Trust. Terraces, formed when Seton had to level off a slope, allow a raised view of the four parterres (patterned beds). Three of these are to designs thought to have been used in 1647 for the gardens of Holyroodhouse in Edinburgh and the fourth has a heraldic theme derived from Sir Alexander's coat-of-arms.

A museum of farming life has recently been formed in the outbuildings at Pitmedden, based largely on the collection of Mr William Cook. A fascinating assortment of old farm imple-

right **Threave Garden is particularly known for its daffodils, as featured in this magnificent display near the house.**

below **The four parterres in the Great Garden at Pitmedden contain some 40,000 bedding plants, best seen in summer.**

ments and domestic artefacts is on display. Other local attractions are an exhibition on the development of the formal garden, woodland and farmland walks, rare breeds of cattle and a picnic area.

14M N of Aberdeen on A920   (146 E6)

Plewlands House, Lothian A small town house of 1643. (Not open.)

South Queensferry   (136 B4)

Priorwood Garden, Borders A garden specializing in flowers for drying. Visitor centre and picnic area.

Melrose, adjacent to the Abbey   (137 F8)

Provan Hall, Strathclyde A well-restored, fifteenth-century mansion (1450–71), considered to be the most perfect survival of its kind in Scotland. There are two buildings

either side of a courtyard, the original hall on the north and, on the south, an addition of the seventeenth and eighteenth centuries. (Let to Glasgow District Council.)

Auchinlea Road, eastern Glasgow   (135 C11)

Provost Ross's House, Grampian A town house of 1593, now converted into a maritime museum run by Aberdeen District Council.

Shiprow, central Aberdeen   (147 G7)

Sailor's Walk, Fife A group of seventeenth-century merchants' houses by the harbour. (Not open.)

Kirkcaldy   (141 H7)

Stenhouse Mansion, Edinburgh A town house built by a prosperous Edinburgh merchant in the early seventeenth century. (Not open.)

Gorgie Road, south-west Edinburgh   (136 B5)

Suntrap, Lothian A gardening advice centre at which instructional courses are available. (Administered in cooperation with Lothian Regional Council.)

Gogarbank, W of Edinburgh, between A8 and A71   (136 B4)

Threave Garden, Dumfries and Galloway An estate of some 1,500 acres made up of farms, woodland and a nineteenth-century house and

below **The domestic, agricultural and social history of Angus over more than two centuries is illustrated in the folk museum.**

garden of sixty-five acres. The house (not open) is the Trust's School of Gardening. Although especially known for its daffodils, the garden is of wide interest and includes separate rose, woodland, walled, nursery, peat, rock, vegetable, herbaceous and heather areas, while there is also a way-marked woodland walk.

1M W of Castle Douglas, S of A75   (131 E8)

Castles, Abbeys & other Buildings

Angus Folk Museum, Tayside Housed in a row of restored and adapted nineteenth-century cottages, the Angus Folk Collection (the achievement of Jean, Lady Maitland) is one of the most important of its kind in Scotland. Considerable expansion of the agricultural side was made possible by the construction of a new building in 1976.

Glamis, off A94   (141 C8)

Balmerino Abbey, Fife The ruins of a monastery founded in 1229 by Alexander II and his mother for Cistercians from Melrose and largely destroyed by the English in 1547. (Not open, but seen from outside.)

Balmerino, on the Firth of Tay, 5M SW of Newport-on-Tay   (141 E8)

Boath Doocot, Highland A seventeenth-century dovecote standing on the motte of a twelfth-century castle. There was a battle here in 1645 in which Montrose defeated a numerically greatly superior army of Covenanters under General Urry and this is well explained.

Auldearn, 2M E of Nairn   (144 D5)

Castle Campbell, Central Strikingly perched on a steep hillside and on a mound which may represent a Norman motte, Castle Campbell grew between the fifteenth to the late sixteenth or early seventeenth centuries. The oldest part is the north-east tower, almost certainly built by Colin Campbell, 1st Earl of Argyll, soon after 1481, and known to have been successor to an earlier structure. John Knox is believed to have preached here in 1556, and on the evidence of a letter from Monk to Cromwell it seems that the castle was burnt in 1654. The tower is the most complete and most interesting part. It contains a pit prison within the wall, the vaulted great hall on the first floor, and on the underside of the vaulting of the top floor two unusual late sixteenth- or early seventeenth-century grotesque masks from the mouths of which may have hung lamps. The attractive open loggia between the tower and the south range is also noteworthy. The castle may be approached on foot by way of the Trust's wooded Dollar Glen. (Under the guardianship of the Scottish Development Department, Ancient Monuments.)

Dollar, off A91 (140 G4)

Crookston Castle, Strathclyde The early fifteenth-century tower-house of a branch of the Stewarts (from about 1473 lords Darnley) standing on the site of a twelfth-century castle probably built by Sir Robert Croc. Mary, Queen of Scots, and Darnley stayed here after their marriage in 1565. In the basement there is a large room with a vaulted roof, and the great hall, also vaulted, is on the first floor. (Under the guardianship of the Scottish Development Department, Ancient Monuments.)

Crookston, SE of Paisley and SW of Glasgow, off A736 (135 C10)

The Hermitage, Tayside A minor folly built in 1758 by the future 3rd Duke of Atholl as a summer retreat in the wooded cut of the small river Braan. The site includes thirty-seven acres of woodland, mostly Douglas fir and Scots pine.

2M W of Dunkeld, off A9 (140 C5)

Hugh Miller's Cottage, Highland Built in about 1711 this cottage was the birthplace in 1802 of Hugh Miller, the stonemason who achieved fame as a geologist and writer. Material on both these activities is exhibited together with a period cottage kitchen and bedroom.

Church Street, Cromarty (144 C3)

Phantassie Doocot This dovecote, once with over 500 nests and probably of the seventeenth century, is of the round domed or 'beehive' type introduced by the Normans. It is unusual in Scotland for the way in which the top is sliced to form a south-facing slope, although this design is common in southern France as a means of giving weather protection. *Preston Mill* stands nearby.

East Linton, off A1 (137 B8)

The Pineapple, Central A strange garden retreat of 1761 built in the shape of a pineapple forty-five feet high. The sixteen acres of grounds include a walled garden, woodland and picnic area. (Leased to the Landmark Trust and let as a holiday home.)

Near Airth, 7M E of Stirling off A905, then B9124 (140 H4)

St Mungo's Chapel, Fife This ruined chapel of 1503 was built by Glasgow's Bishop Blacader on the traditional birthplace in 514 of St Mungo (or Kentigern), said to have been founder of the church which eventually became Glasgow cathedral. The story goes that the saint's mother, a Christian convert fleeing across the Forth from her pagan father, was driven ashore here.

On A985, just E of Culross (136 A3)

Scotstarvit Tower, Fife Probably built between 1550 and 1579, and in about 1611 the home of Sir John Scot, a distinguished lawyer and writer, Scotstarvit survives as one of Scotland's most complete and unspoilt examples of a simple tower-house. Designed for both resi-

Dovecotes, such as Phantassie Doocot here, were the prime source of winter meat before the advent of winter feed for cattle.

The Pineapple was built as a garden retreat in 1761 by an unknown architect.

---

dential and minor defensive purposes, the tower is a free-standing rectangular keep, its lines broken by a small side wing for the spiral stairway. The interior is of several levels, from the ground floor, used for storage, up to the parapet. The first floor was the most important, here·being the hall with its three windows and their flanking stone seats and also a garderobe. Above was the laird's private room. The parapet, still with gun-loops at its angles, was at one time battlemented, and above the door to the cap-house (the superstructure roofing the stair) can be seen the initials of Sir John Scot and his wife Dame Anne Drummond. (Under the guardianship of the Scottish Development Department, Ancient Monuments.)

S of Cupar, off A916 (141 F8)

Souter Johnnie's Cottage, Strathclyde Robert Burns (1759–96) spent the summer of 1775 in Kirkoswald, and it was here that he met the people from whom he drew the now famous characters of his poem *Tam o' Shanter*, notably Douglas Graham of Shanter and John Davidson, respectively the prototypes for Tam and Souter (cobbler) Johnnie. At this time, though, Davidson lived elsewhere, only building this cottage in 1785. The interior contains souvenirs of Burns, contemporary cobbler's tools, and also what is probably the actual cobbling chair used by Davidson. In the garden there are life-sized stone figures, carved in 1802 by James Thom, of Tam, Souter Johnnie, the innkeeper and his wife.

Kirkoswald, on A77 4M W of Maybole (130 A3)

Strome Castle, Highland This small ruin by the shore of Loch Carron, now little more than a confusion of stones, was long an outpost stronghold of the MacDonalds of Glengarry. It was also a constant challenge to the nearby Mackenzies of Kintail who finally blew it up in 1602. The story goes that some MacDonald women who had just fetched water from the well inadvertently emptied their buckets into the gunpowder vat; a Mackenzie prisoner overheard the women being upbraided, made his escape and told his chief, who was on the point of giving up the siege, that the defenders were now helpless.

N shore of Loch Carron (142 F2)

Threave Castle, Dumfries and Galloway This ancient and massive tower-house standing stark on a low island in the river Dee has played its part in the wars of Scotland and England. The castle was probably started soon after 1369 by Black Archibald the Grim, Lord of Galloway and later 3rd Earl of Douglas. When the Black Douglases rebelled in 1455 Threave was taken by James II in person, though only after a siege and artillery bombardment; in 1545, now owned by Lord

Maxwell who had sided with the Tudors, Threave was subdued by the Regent Arran; in 1588 the place was surrendered to James VI who had hastened to south-western Scotland when it seemed that the Catholic 8th Lord Maxwell was planning to aid a Spanish landing; and finally, in 1640 when held for Charles I by the Earl of Nithsdale, Threave was taken by the Covenanters and dismantled.

The keep is of several levels rising above a cellar area in which are the well and a dungeon. On the next two floors are the kitchen and then the hall, both with their garderobes and the latter with stone benches in the window bays. Above again would have been the lord's private rooms, while the garrison was quartered at the top. (Under the guardianship of the Scottish Development Department, Ancient Monuments.)

2½M W of Castle Douglas, N of A75   (131 E8)

Archaeological, Industrial & Historical Sites

Antonine Wall, Central and Strathclyde The Trust owns sections of this Roman wall built between the Forth and the Clyde in *c.*140 but abandoned by the end of the century. The wall is of turf on a stone base, with an outer mound and ditch on the north, a road along the south, and forts at intervals. The best preserved fort is Rough Castle which is Trust property. Here the above features are well seen, the road running through the fort while a confusion of earthworks marks the sites of the barracks (to the north of the road), the commander's house, granary and headquarters (to the south), and a bath house just east of the fort wall and south of the road. (Under the guardianship of the Scottish Development Department, Ancient Monuments.)

A803 and B816 from Bonnybridge   (136 A1)

Bannockburn Monument, Central It was near here in June 1314 that Robert Bruce routed England's Edward II and thus assured Scotland's independence. The Trust area includes an equestrian statue of Bruce (Pilkington Jackson, 1964), the Rotunda enclosing the Borestone site, traditionally Bruce's command post, and a visitor centre in which are displayed fragments of the Borestone in which Bruce is said to have planted his standard and where the wars of independence and the tactical details of the battle are explained.

2M S of Stirling, off M80   (140 H3)

The battlefield of Bannockburn, where the seal was set on Scotland's independence, is surveyed by a statue of Robert the Bruce.

Bruce's Stone, Dumfries and Galloway A boulder on Raploch Moss where Bruce won a skirmish with the English in 1307.

6M W of New Galloway by A712   (130 D6)

Caiy Stone, Edinburgh A prehistoric standing stone, probably on its original site and bearing traces of cup markings.

Oxgangs Road, southern Edinburgh (see map p. 122)

Culloden, Highland The site of the battle of April 1746 in which Prince Charles Edward, the Young Pretender, was defeated by the Duke of Cumberland. This battle, with Bannockburn, was one of the two most important in Scottish history; it not only destroyed the Stuart cause but, more important for Scotland, sounded the knell for a Highland clan way of life that had changed little over twelve or more centuries. The site embraces a memorial cairn; scattered stones marking the graves of the clans; the Well of the Dead where wounded Highlanders are said to have been killed while trying to drink; the Cumberland Stone where the duke may for a while have taken up position; Leanach farmhouse, now a museum; and a visitor centre.

5M E of Inverness, on B9006   (144 E3)

Glenfinnan Monument, Highland This tower topped by the figure of a Highlander stands at the head of Loch Shiel on the site where Prince Charles Edward, the Young Pretender, raised his standard on 19 August 1745. Put up in 1815 by MacDonald of Glenaladale, descendant of the man at whose house the prince had rested the previous night, the tower was given its Highlander, the work of John Greenshields, in 1834. A visitor centre describes the whole course of the campaign from the raising of the standard to the tragedy of Culloden and the prince's later wanderings.

On A830, 18M W of Fort William   (143 L3)

Mote of Mark, Dumfries and Galloway An Iron Age hill-fort.

7M S of Dalbeattie, off A710   (131 F9)

Pass of Killiecrankie, Tayside It was down this wooded gorge in July 1689 that the troops of William III fled in panic after their defeat about a mile to the north by Jacobite Highlanders under Claverhouse, Viscount Dundee. However, this Jacobite victory was both tragic and short-lived since Dundee was killed and twenty-five days later the Highlanders were in their turn defeated at Dunkeld.

Its historic interest apart, Killiecrankie is a renowned beauty spot and the visitor centre exhibitions feature not only the battle but also local natural history.

A9, 2½M N of Pitlochry   (140 A4)

Preston Mill, Lothian Dating from the sixteenth century and the oldest mechanically working water-driven meal mill in Scotland, Preston Mill's buildings form a picturesque group beside a stream. They occupy a site believed to have been home to a mill in medieval times, and the adjacent kiln may well belong to that period. Last used commercially in 1957, the mill's machinery has since been renovated by Messrs Rank Hovis McDougall Ltd. *Phantassie Doocot* stands nearby.

East Linton, off A1   (137 B8)

Stones of Clava, Highland An important prehistoric site of perhaps 2000–1500 BC made up of a small stone circle and three large burial cairns, two of the passage type and the third a ring cairn. All the cairns are surrounded by standing stones and the site is known for its many examples of cup and other markings. (Under the guardianship of the Scottish Development Department, Ancient Monuments.)

6M E of Inverness, off B851   (144 E3)

Weaver's Cottage, Strathclyde This cottage, built in 1723 and typical of those occupied by the handloom weavers of the eighteenth and nineteenth centuries, now serves as a memorial museum of this local industry. When it was at its peak in the 1830s Kilbarchan boasted some 800 looms. The industry survived until the 1950s, though by then the number of looms had dropped to four. In addition to looms and other weaving equipment, the museum shows local fabrics, shawls and domestic utensils and bygones of many kinds. The cruck construction of a part of the cottage is unusual for this part of Scotland.

Kilbarchan, 8M SW of Glasgow, off A737 (135 C9)

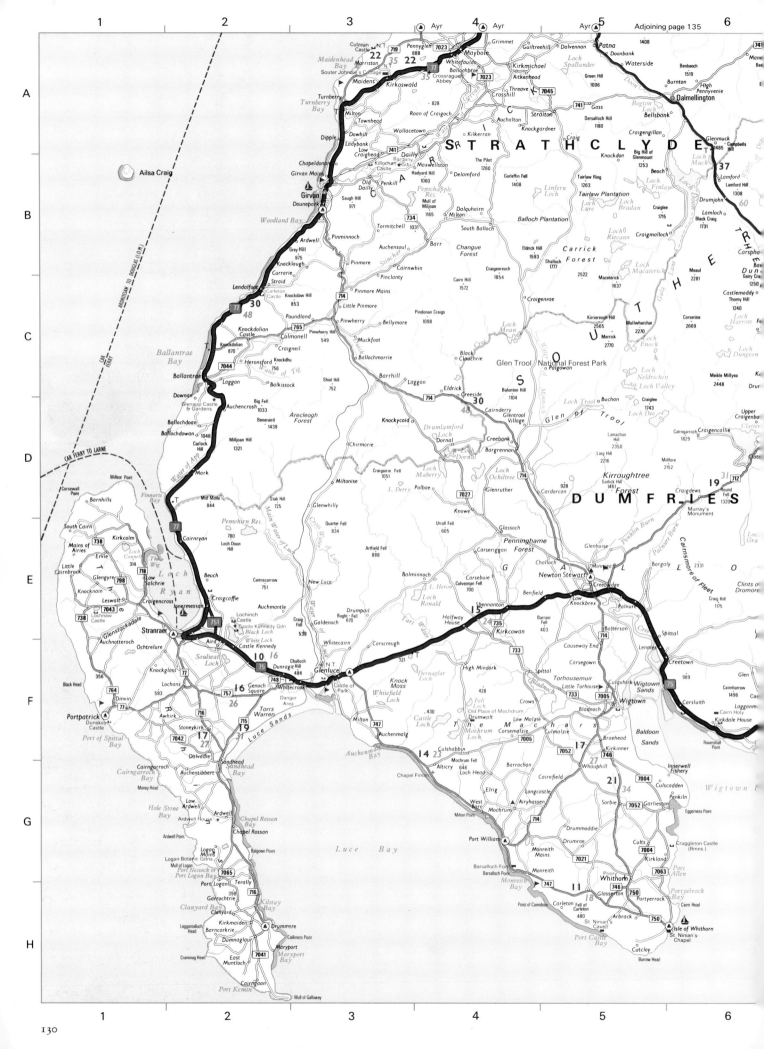

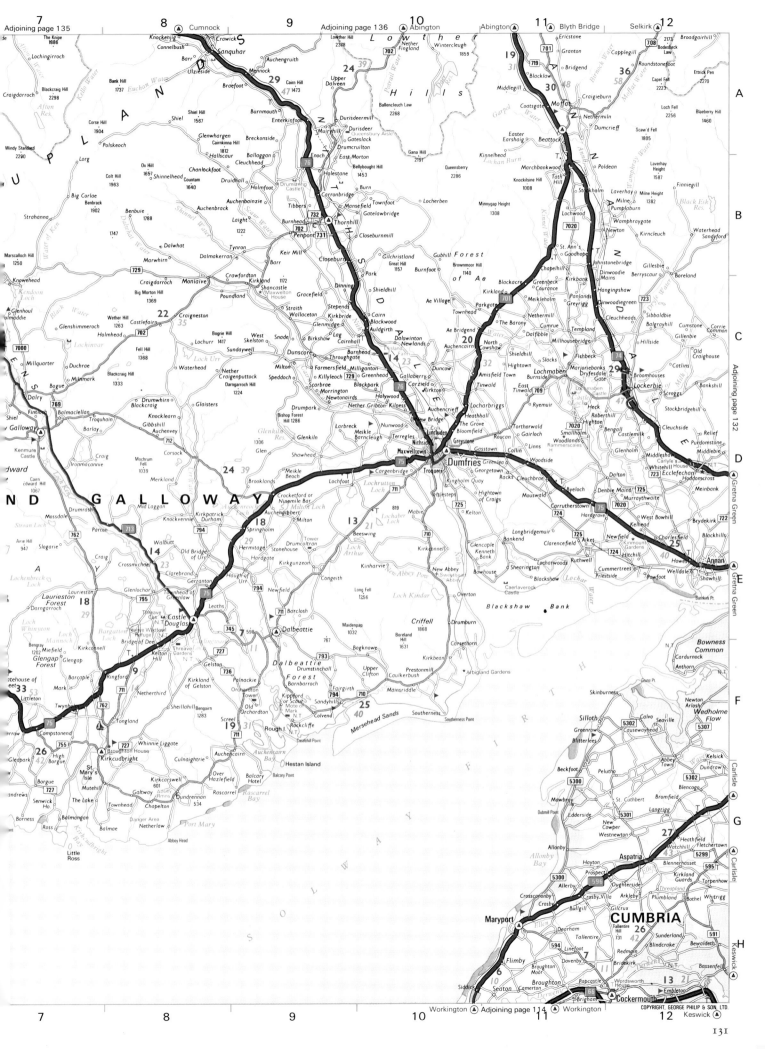

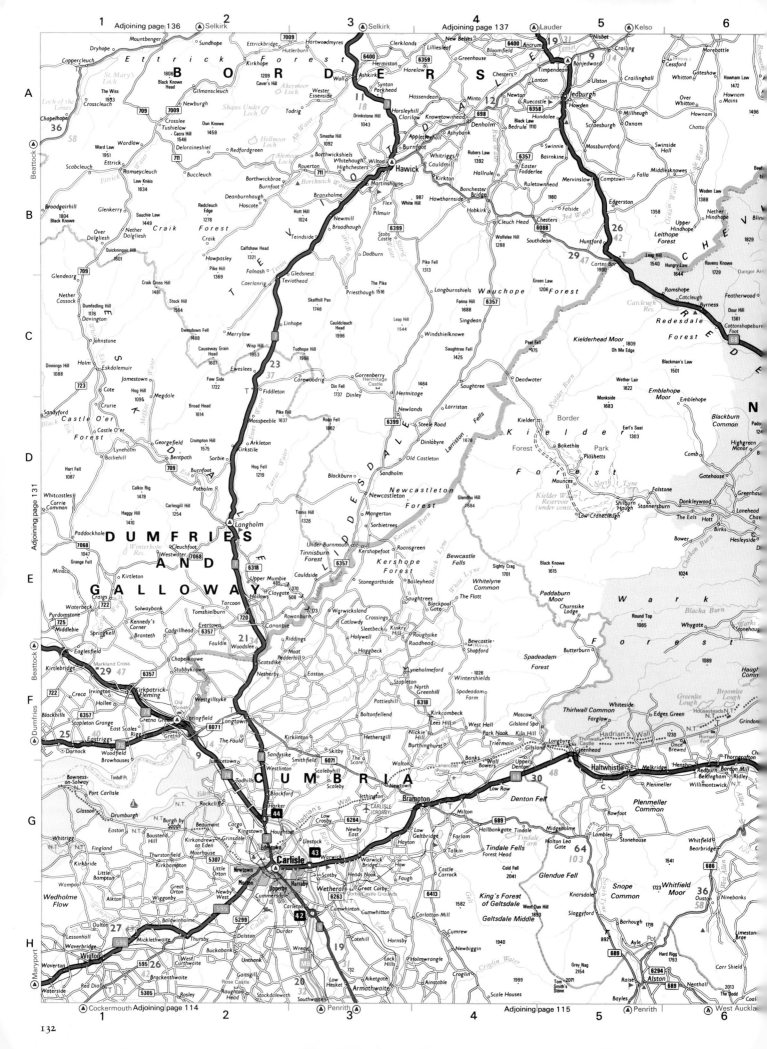

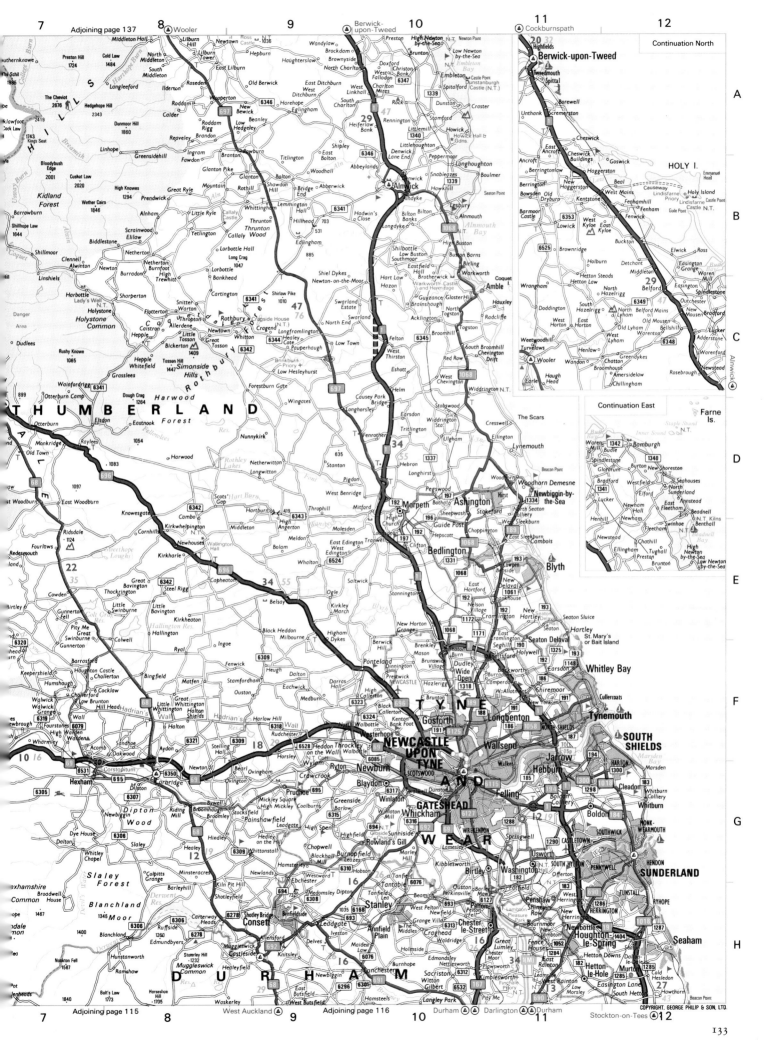

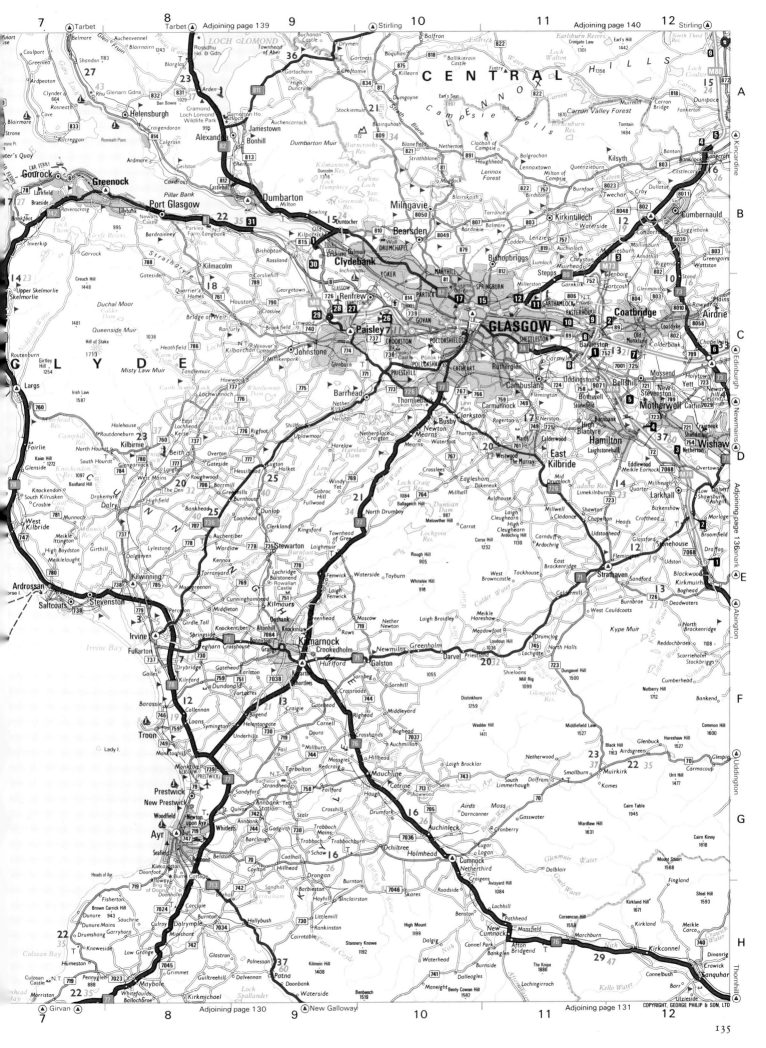

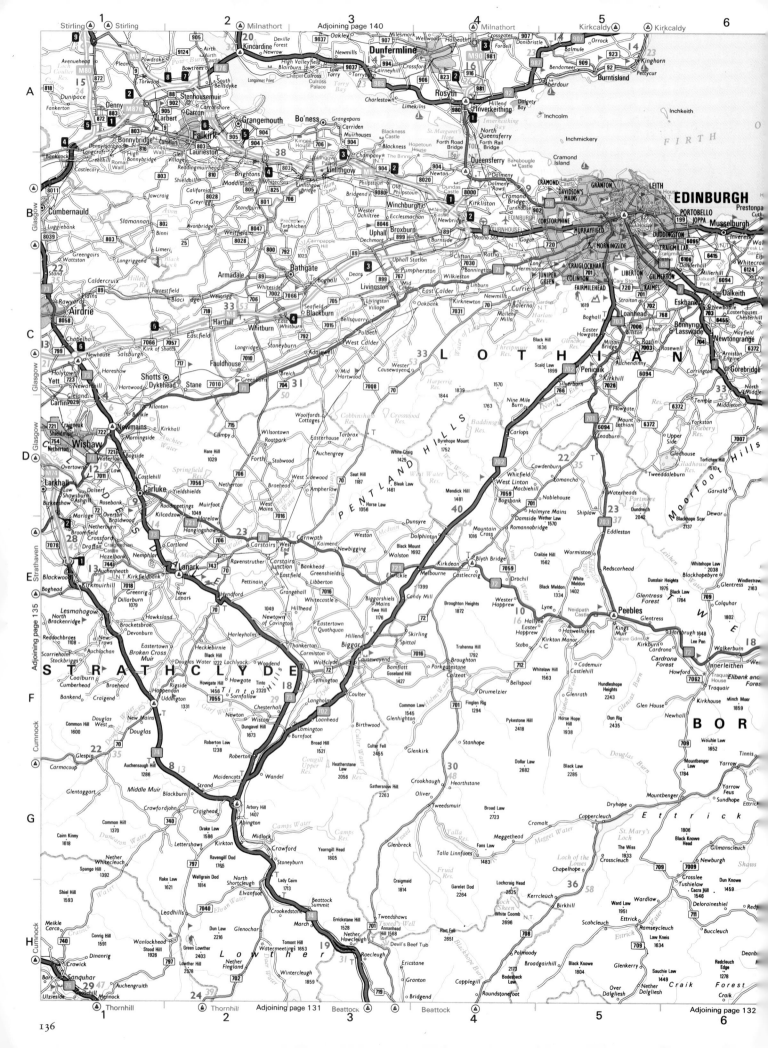

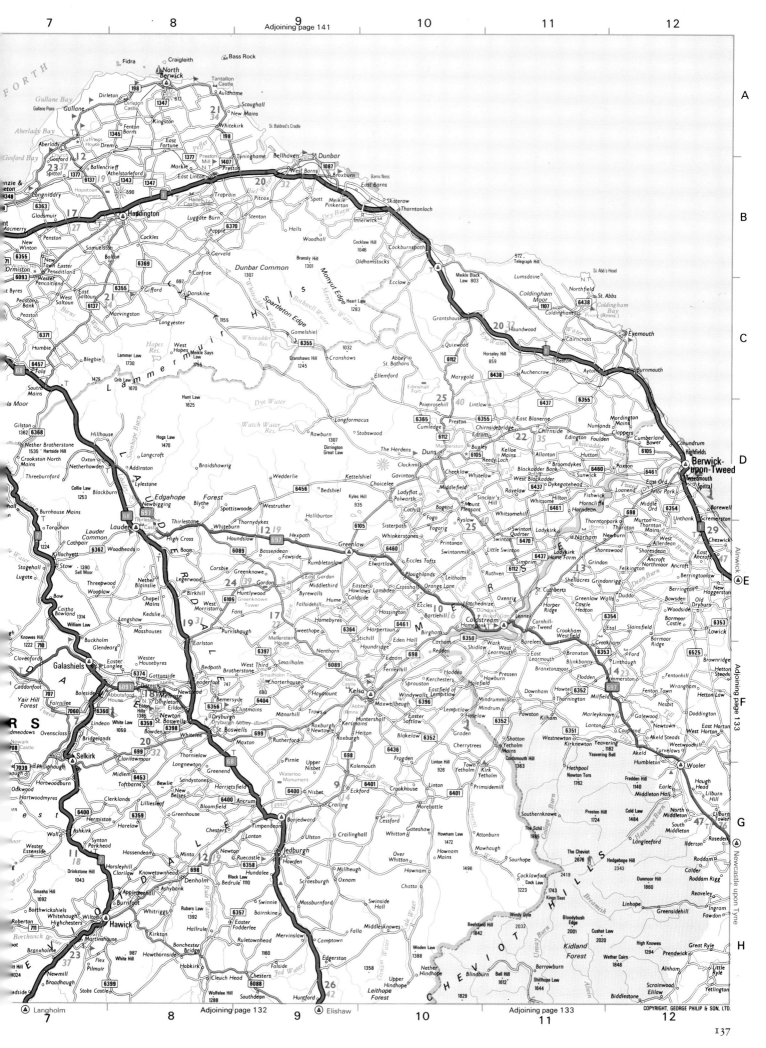

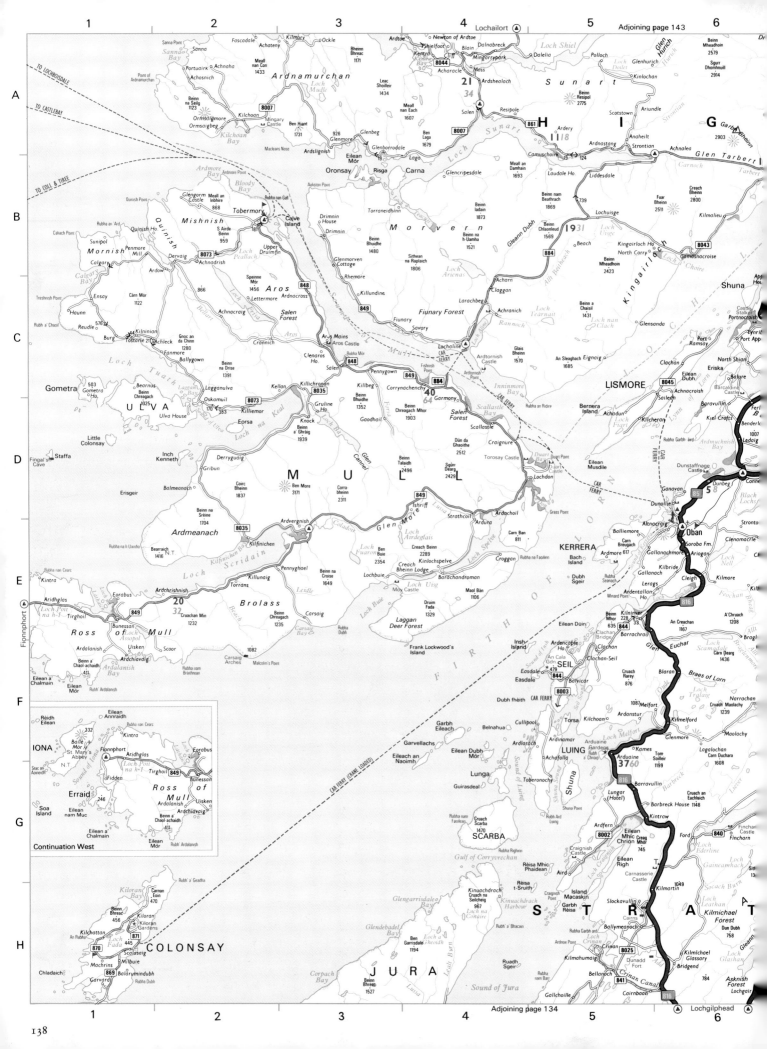

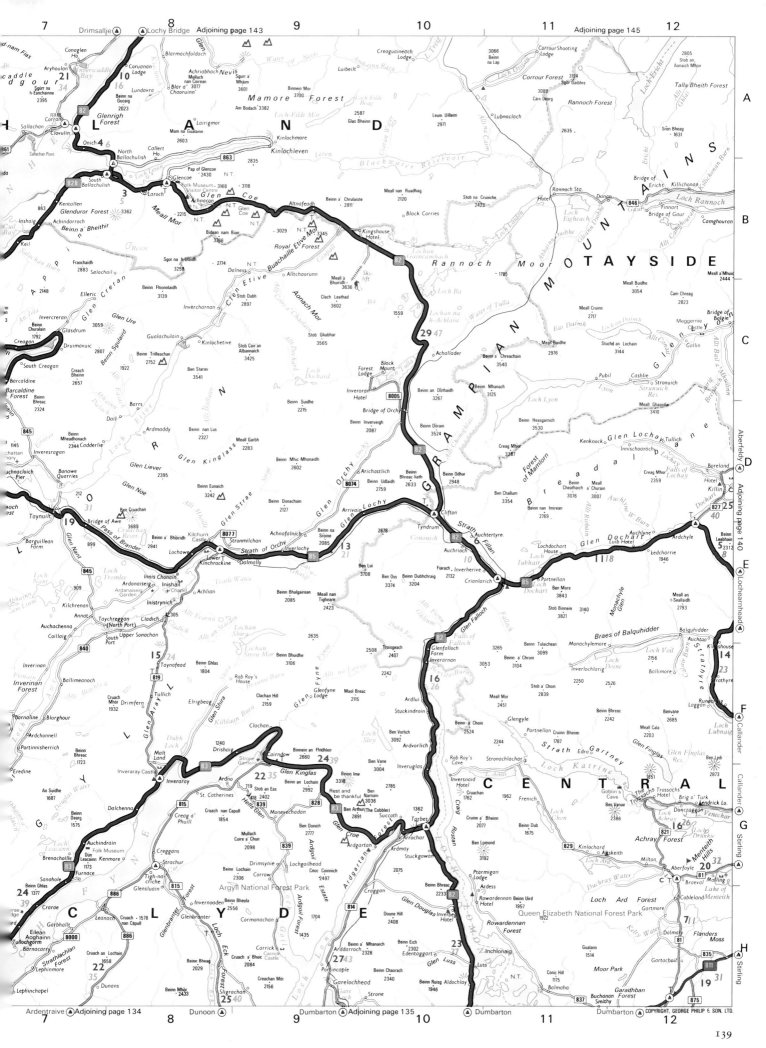

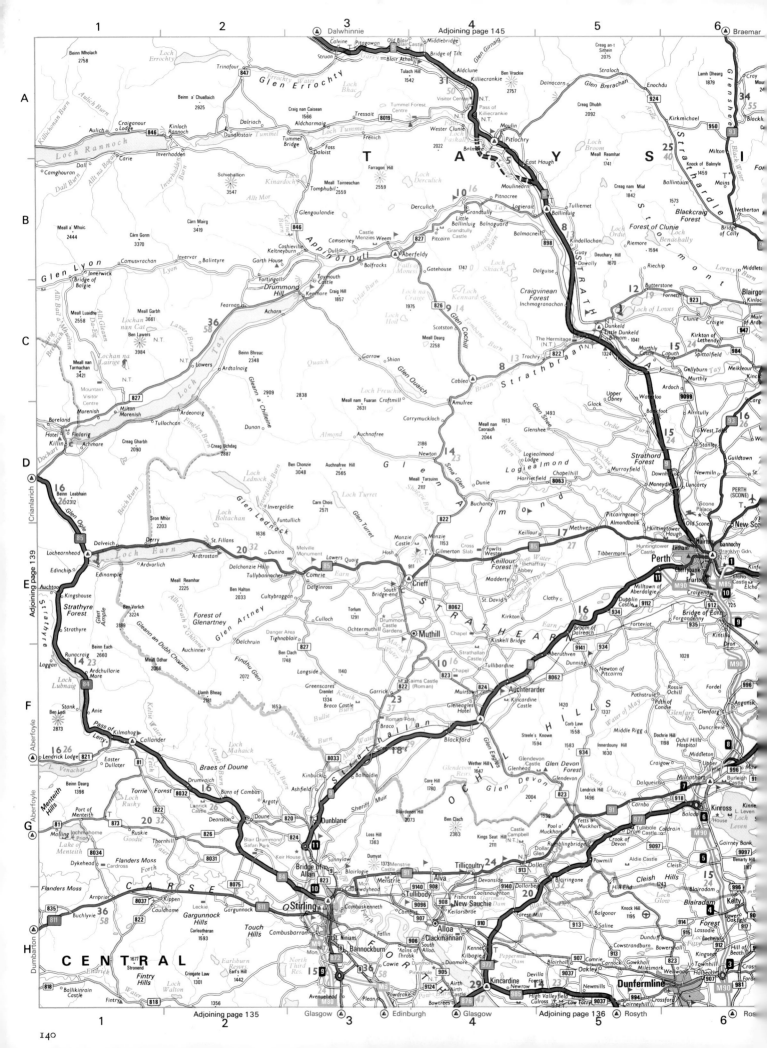

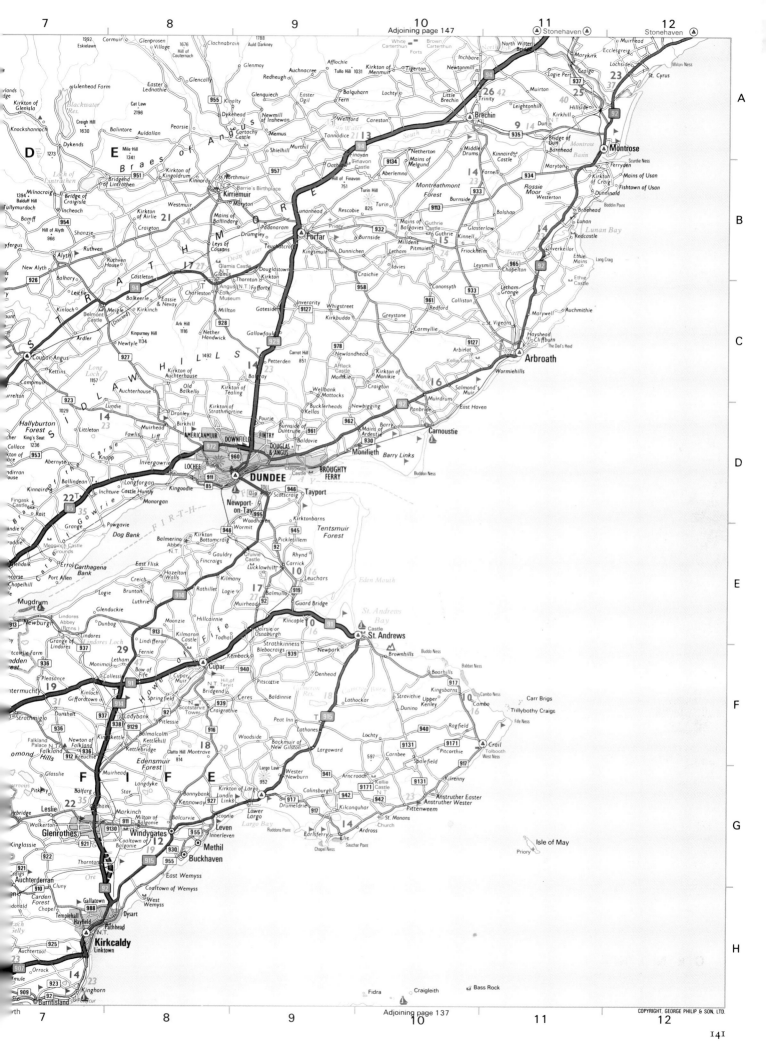

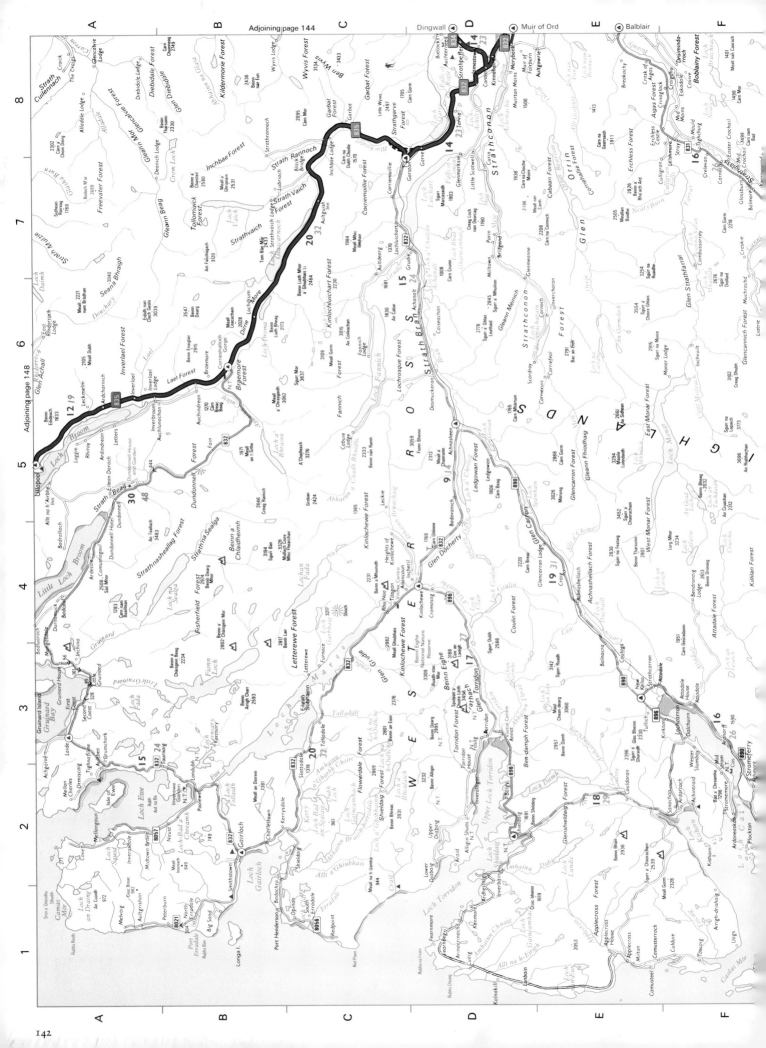

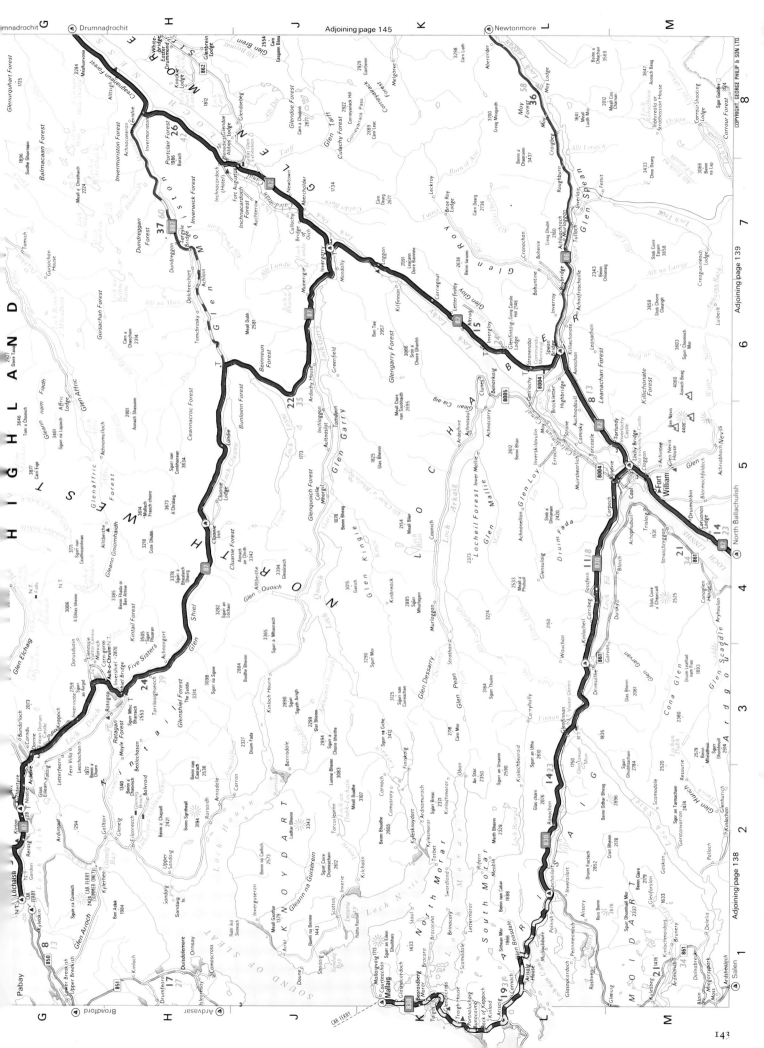

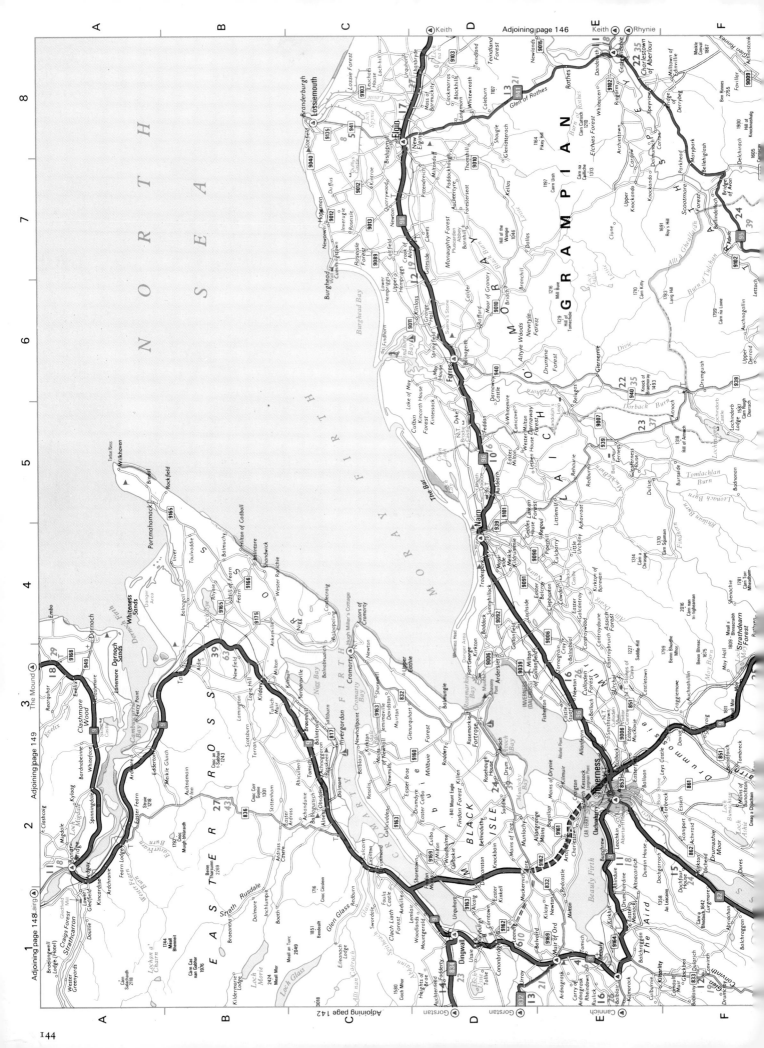

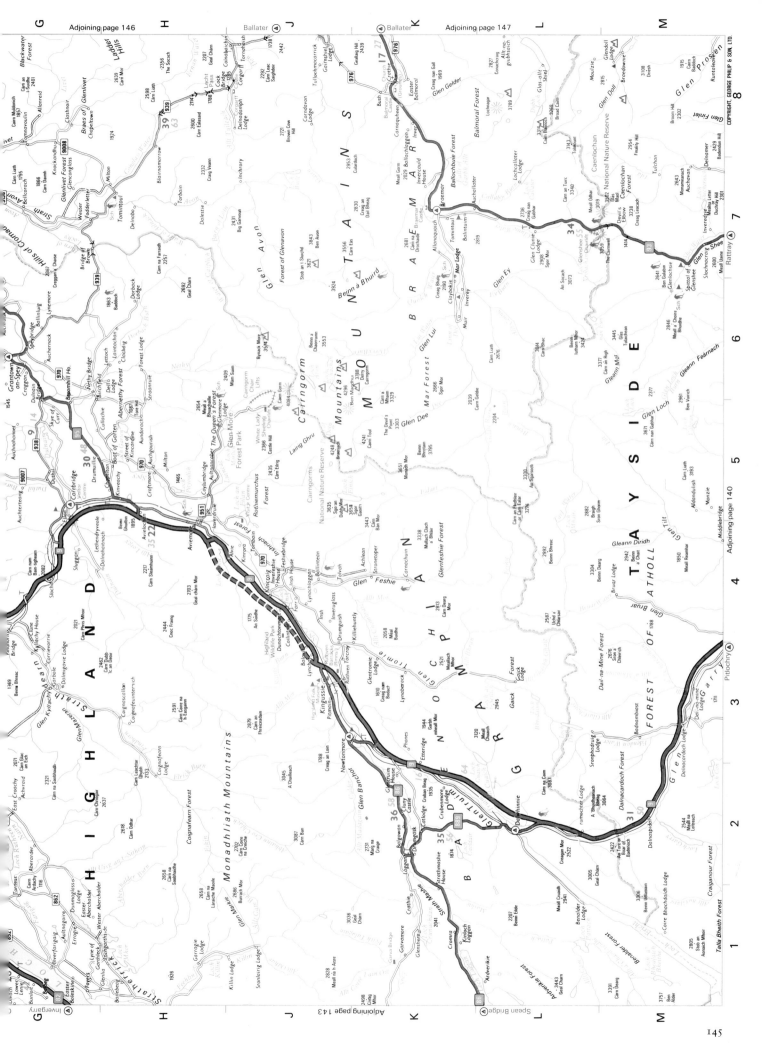

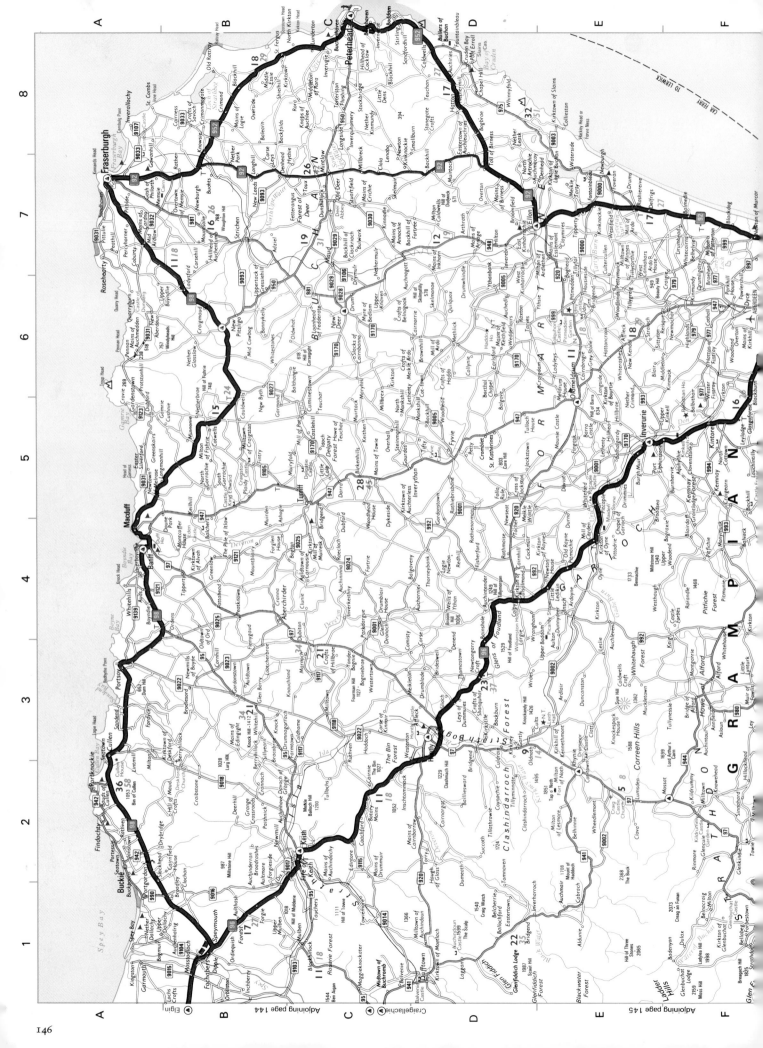

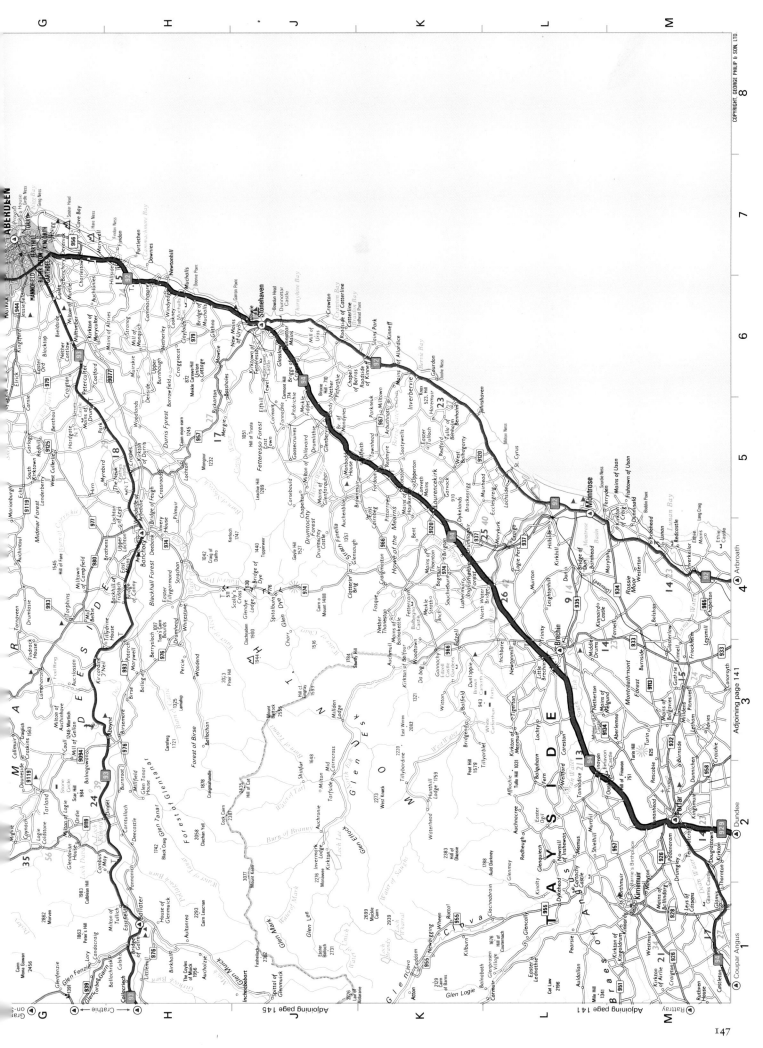

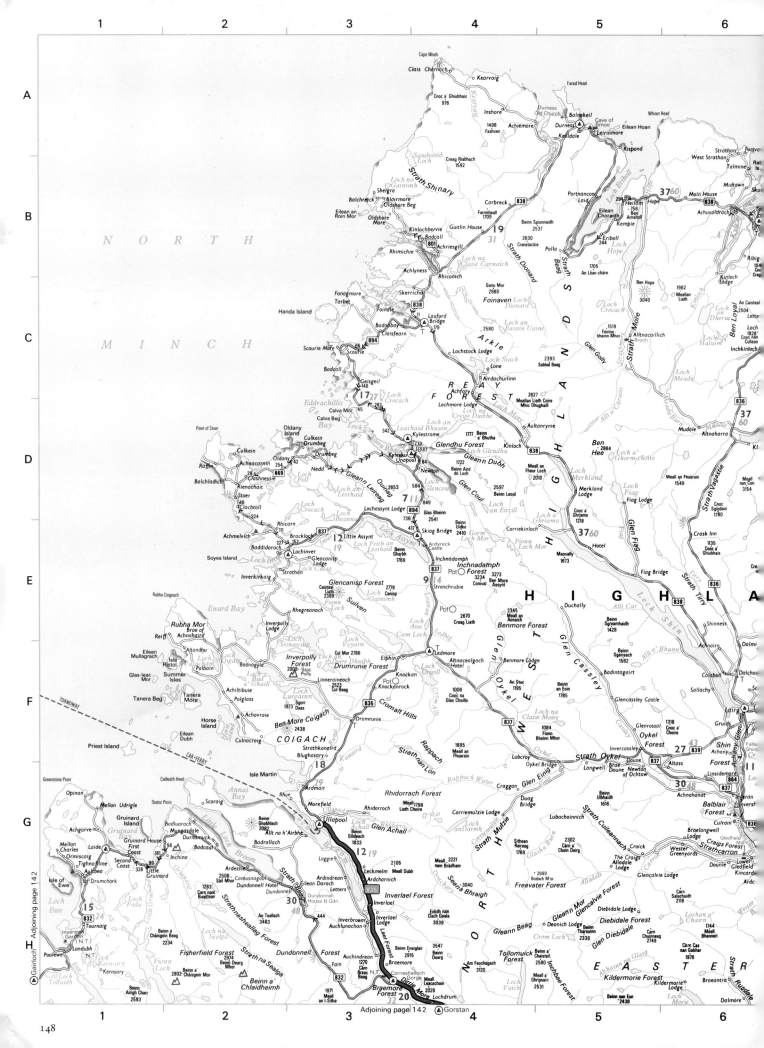

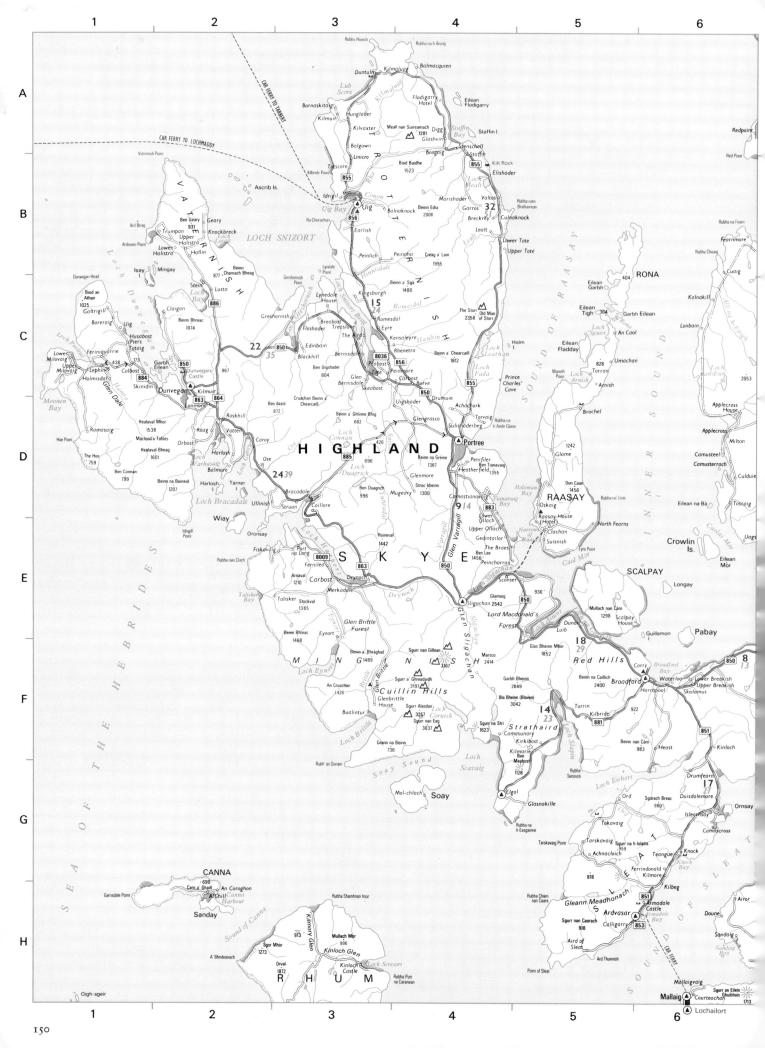

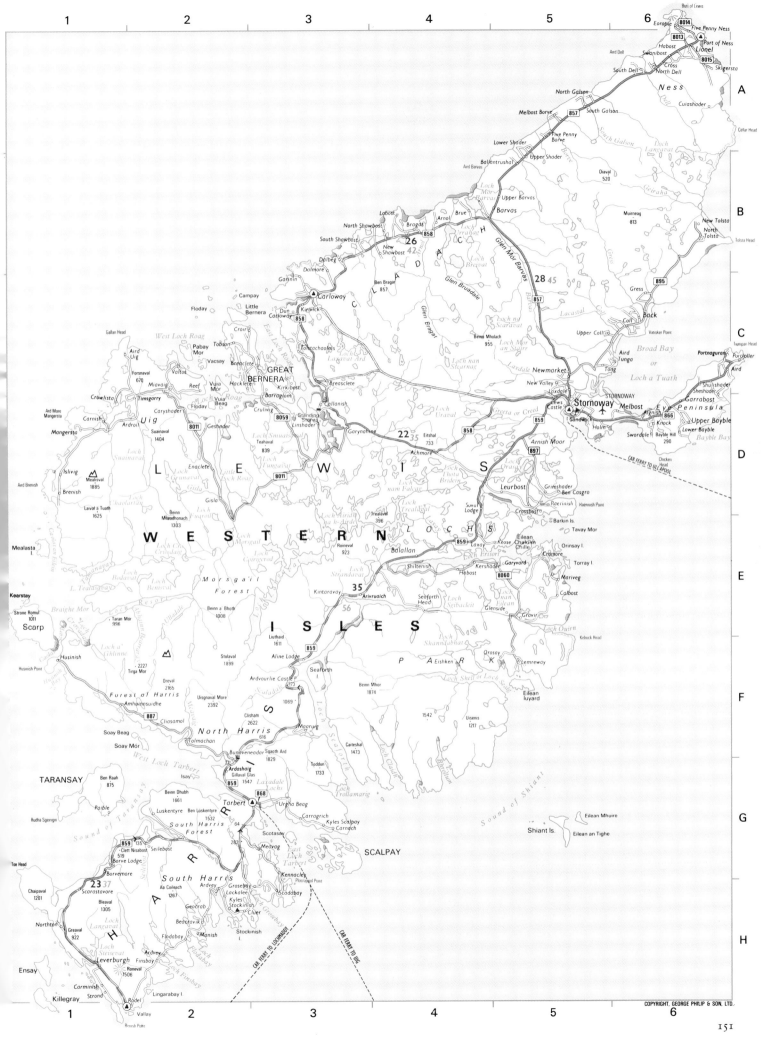

151

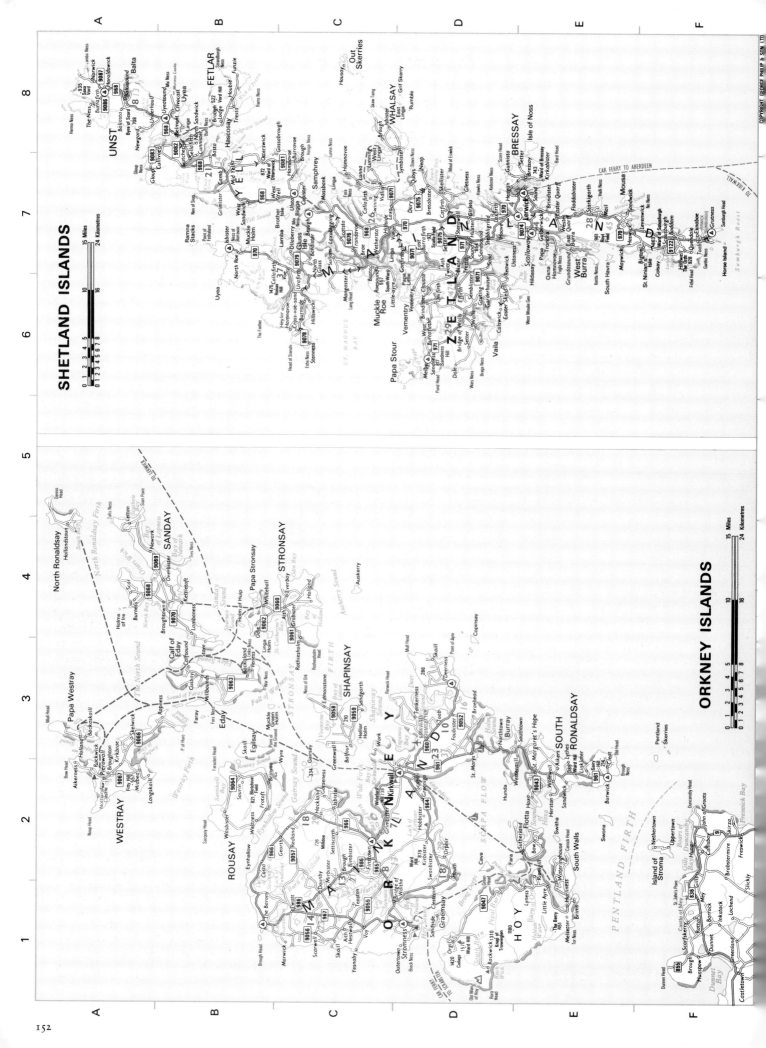

SHETLAND ISLANDS

ORKNEY ISLANDS

Northern Ireland

THE GIANT'S CAUSEWAY

Outside the conurbations of Belfast and Derry, Northern Ireland largely consists of unspoilt countryside, of a quiet and haunting beauty. Water, and the sea, are never far away however, and it is the sea which has shaped the history and the appearance of the province today, bringing invaders and taking emigrants away on its tides.

From the architectural point of view, the sixteenth- and seventeenth-century 'plantations' of Ulster with settlers from the north of England and Scottish Lowlands were decisive. Scottish town-houses, and later settlers' houses in the Anglo-Dutch style, like Springhill, replaced the medieval churches and abbeys whose remains are still to be seen in the south. Palladianism and neo-classicism became the accepted norms in the eighteenth century, culminating in masterpieces by English architects such as Wyatt's Castle Coole. But there is a streak of wholly Irish eccentricity to be found in the long-drawn-out entrance front of Florence Court,. the mixture of Gothic and classical at Castle Ward, or the 1830s Greek Revival interiors of The Argory – recently acquired by the Trust. Apart from country houses the Trust has a wide variety of other holdings in Northern Ireland, ranging from important gardens like those at Mount Stewart and Rowallane, and ruined castles like Dunseverick, to an early printing press and linen mill, an Adam mausoleum and a High Victorian pub. Had it not been for their rescue, most would not exist today, and Ulster's historic heritage would have been much the poorer.

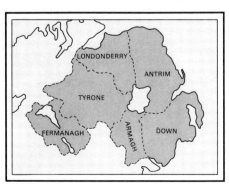

Island-studded Strangford Lough is best known for its wildfowl but is also important in the study of marine biology.

Murlough Bay, Co. Antrim, with its woodlands, is one of the most beautiful stretches of coast in Northern Ireland.

Coast & Countryside

Some of the finest and most varied natural scenery in the British Isles is to be found in Northern Ireland, from the soft green hedgerowed landscape of County Down to the dramatic cliffs of the north coast swept by Atlantic gales – from the lonely marshes and rush-beds which border the vast expanse of Lough Neagh, to the myriad islands, creeks and inlets of Upper Lough Erne.

Most of the 'places of natural beauty' held by the Trust in this region are coastal. Undoubtedly the best-known is the **Giant's Causeway** (159 A7), one of the most extraordinary natural phenomena in the world with its peninsula of basalt rock in the shape of faceted columns marching out into the sea – the result of volcanic activity some sixty million years ago. Enterprise Neptune has had some of its greatest successes in saving the coastline of north Antrim eastwards from the Giant's Causeway, including the ten-mile cliff-path from here to **Dunseverick** and **White Park Bay**, **Carrick-a-rede** with its famous rope bridge and salmon fisheries near Ballintoy, and **Fair Head** and **Murlough Bay** at the north-eastern extremity of Ulster, with views on a clear day as far as Islay and the Paps of Jura (159 A7/8/9).

Further south in County Down, the **Strangford Lough** Wildlife Scheme, established in 1966, has safeguarded the many species of wildfowl which frequent the broad mudflats of this inland sea from the combined effects of poaching and pollution (159 E/F10/11). Other stretches of coast here include two miles of foreshore at **Kearney** and **Knockinelder** (159 F11) east of Portaferry, the **Mourne coastal path** (159 G10), and Ulster's first national nature reserve at **Murlough Bay** (159 G10), near Dundrum. **Blockhouse** and **Green Islands** (159 H9) at the mouth of Carlingford Lough provide some important nesting sites for Arctic and Roseate terns.

Among the inland properties, the glen and waterfall at **Lisnabreeny**, near Newtownbreda, and **Minnowburn Beeches**, with its walks along the Lagan and Minnowburn river banks, are remarkable in being only two or three miles south of the centre of Belfast (159 E9/10).

Houses, Gardens & Parks

Ardress House, Co. Armagh A typical seventeenth-century manor house of the 'plantation' period, Ardress was completely transformed in 1770 by the Dublin architect George Ensor, who had married the heiress to the estate, Sarah Clarke, ten years earlier. On the garden

side he added curving screen walls with niches in the Palladian manner, and on the entrance front a bay at each end with urns set on the parapets, and a classical porch. Both façades are washed in a distinctive pale pink colour, which Ensor may also have introduced, and overlook an unspoilt 'natural landscape' framed by great beech trees on one side, and a terraced garden on the other, equally little changed since the eighteenth century.

The finest interior is the drawing room, with delicate plasterwork in the Adam style by the Dublin stuccadore Michael Stapleton. The other rooms, simpler in treatment, contain good Irish furniture of the eighteenth century, and the picture gallery in the centre of the garden front has an interesting collection of paintings on loan from the Earl of Castle Stewart.

7M W Portadown, on B28　　*(159 F7)*

The Argory, Co. Armagh The Argory is an unusually complete and evocative example of the way of life of the Irish gentry in the early nineteenth century. Built about 1820 by a barrister, Walter MacGeough Bond, it was designed by a firm of Dublin architects, A. and J. Williamson, in the newly-fashionable Greek Revival style, and retains most of its original contents. Out in the stable yard is the last surviving example in Northern Ireland of a working acetylene gas plant, and this still provides the house with lighting, by means of a series of bronze gasoliers throughout the main rooms. A magnificent cast-iron stove still exists in the central staircase hall.

The house stands on a hill overlooking a bend in the River Blackwater, with a walled

Castle Coole, perhaps the finest neo-classical house in Ireland, is set in a magnificent landscaped park.

Florence Court is known for its rococo plasterwork, shown here in the staircase hall. The staircase handrail is of tulipwood.

The battlemented Gothick façade of Castle Ward (*above*). The domestic offices of the house, such as the laundry (*left*), are concealed in a sunken courtyard.

pleasure ground to the north, a charming Victorian rose garden, and heavily-wooded parkland around it, adding to its sense of remoteness and isolation.

4M SE Moy, on Derrycaw road   (159 F7)

Castle Coole, Co. Fermanagh As the acknowledged masterpiece of James Wyatt, Castle Coole ranks as one of the finest neo-classical houses not just in Northern Ireland but in the British Isles. The Corry family settled here in 1656, later building a house near the lough with its famous colony of greylag geese. But it was Armar Lowry-Corry, 1st Earl of Belmore, who in 1788 decided to rebuild on a new site high above the lake.

The house was begun to designs by the Irish architect, Richard Johnston, who was only later superseded by Wyatt, and this explains the still Palladian layout of the main block and end pavilions linked by colonnades. But the scale and assurance of Wyatt's façades give an effect of austere magnificence that makes it a palace rather than a villa. The superb masonry and carving of the exterior is in Portland stone, brought from a specially-constructed quay on the coast, while inside the joinery and plaster-work are also of the highest quality. Wyatt's interiors, with ceilings by Joseph Rose (the

elder) and chimneypieces by Richard Westmacott, are now filled with elaborate Regency furniture bought by the 2nd Earl from the Dublin upholsterer John Preston. Castle Coole has been remarkably little changed since that date, and remains the home of the present Earl of Belmore.

1M SE Enniskillen, on A4   (158 F4)

Castle Ward, Co. Down Even for Ireland, Castle Ward is an eccentric house. Though built at one period, between 1762 and 1770, it has two strongly contrasted fronts: a classical entrance façade on the west, and a battlemented Gothick composition on the east. This curious arrangement is said to have come about because the builder, Bernard Ward (later 1st Viscount Bangor) and his wife, Lady Anne Magill, each favoured a different style of architecture. Nor was this the end of their differences for they were formally separated soon after the house was completed. The division between Gothick and classical goes right through the centre of the building – the saloon, the morning room, and Lady Anne's boudoir on the west are all decorated in a charming rococo Gothick style, while the hall, the dining room and Lord Bangor's library on the east are in a more conventional Palladian vein.

The house stands on an eminence with marvellous views over Strangford Lough, and with its domestic offices, including a fully-equipped laundry, carefully concealed in a sunken courtyard to the north. Near the shores of the lough are the old pele tower, built by

Nicholas Ward in 1610, the formal canal called the Temple Water (now a wildfowl reserve) and above it a little classical temple, again dating from about 1762.

7M NE of Downpatrick, on A25   (159 F11)

Derrymore House, Co. Armagh A late eighteenth-century *cottage ornée*, Derrymore was built for Isaac Corry, an MP and Chancellor of the Irish Exchequer, as an occasional summer lodge. The 'natural landscape' around it, with carefully-placed clumps of trees, undulating lawns and drives intended to give a variety of viewpoints, was laid out by John Sutherland, the most distinguished Irish landscape gardener of his day – and Sutherland may also have designed the house, which was apparently built in 1776. The thatched roof and rendered walls, Gothic quatrefoils and hood-moulded windows, show that it was conceived more as a picturesque incident in the tour of the grounds than as a full-blown country house.

The central pavilion, linked to two slightly smaller wings (all of one storey), contains the Treaty Room, so called because the Treaty of Union between England and Ireland is said to have been drafted here in 1801 by Isaac Corry, Lord Castlereagh and others.

1½M NW Newry, off A25   (159 G8)

Florence Court, Co. Fermanagh The first house on this wild and romantic site, looking west to the mountains of Cuilcagh, was built about 1710 by Sir John Cole, and named after his wife Florence, daughter and heiress of Sir Bourchier Wrey. Their son John, created Lord Mount Florence, built the present main block with its elaborate, and somewhat archaic, Baroque entrance front about 1750, traditionally to the designs of Richard Castle, though a master-mason using the pattern-books of Serlio, Palladio and Gibbs could equally have been responsible. The riotous rococo plasterwork of the staircase, the dining room ceiling and the Venetian Room on the first floor have been attributed to the Dublin stuccadore, Robert West.

In 1771, the 2nd Lord Mount Florence (later 1st Viscount Enniskillen) employed the Sardinian-born architect, Davis Ducart, to add the long colonnades and wings flanking the original entrance front, making a façade 350 feet in length. Much of the planting of the demesne was carried out at the same date, and in the early nineteenth century under the guidance of John Sutherland. It was here too that the celebrated Florence Court yew (*Taxus baccata* 'Fastigiata'), now generally known as the Irish Yew, was first discovered in 1767.

7M SW Enniskillen, off A32   (158 G3)

Hezlett House, Co. Londonderry A thatched cottage or 'long-house' probably built as a parsonage in 1691, the Hezlett House is of particular importance for the cruck-truss construction of its roof, fairly common at this date in Westmorland and Cumberland but rare in Northern Ireland. The house was acquired in 1761 by a family of well-to-do farmers, the Hezletts, who continued to live there for more than two hundred years and who made only minor additions and alterations to it. Some of the rooms contain simple eighteenth-century oak furniture, and there is a small display of early building and joinery techniques.

4M W Coleraine, on A2   (158 A6/7)

Mount Stewart, Co. Down The demesne was acquired by Alexander Stewart in 1744, but his original house was rebuilt by his son and grandson, the 1st and 3rd Marquesses of Londonderry, in the early nineteenth century. The 1st Marquess employed James 'Athenian' Stuart to design the octagonal Temple of the Winds on a promontory overlooking Strangford Lough in 1782–3, one of the architect's finest buildings and his only one in Ireland. But plans for James Wyatt to remodel the main house at this time came to nothing, and it was not till 1804–5 that the present west wing was built, using drawings sent from London by George Dance. The Music Room and the domed staircase behind it, with Stubbs' famous picture of the racehorse *Hambletonian* on the half-landing, both date from this period.

The rest of the house, including the entrance portico and two-storey hall, were added in the late 1830s by William Vitruvius Morrison, working for the 3rd Marquess, Castlereagh's half-brother. Much of the interior was redecorated and furnished a century later by Edith, Lady Londonderry, wife of the 7th Marquess. She also laid out the celebrated gardens which surround the house, filled with rare (many of them subtropical) trees and plants benefiting from the 'island' climate of the Ards peninsula.

5M SE Newtownards, on A20   (159 E11)

Rowallane, Co. Down The garden at Rowallane is largely the creation of Hugh Armytage Moore, who inherited the house in 1903 and devoted most of his life to its development, planting acres of large-leafed rhododendrons among the whinstone rock outcrops of the drive, converting the walled kitchen garden into a sheltered nursery for rare bulbs, plants, shrubs and trees, and creating a unique spring garden in an area of rocky pastures intersected by dry stone walls. The original chaenomeles, viburnum, hypericum, and the primula named after Rowallane, grow in the walled garden, and maples and dogwoods, birches, nothofagus, magnolia and hydrangea in the spring garden. It is at its best in March, April and May, and again in autumn when the colours are especially brilliant.

1M S Saintfield, on A7   (159 F10)

Springhill, Co. Londonderry Springhill is a simple 'planter's' manor-house, built by the Conyngham family who came from Scotland in the reign of James I and bought the estate in 1658. The house itself dates from the last quarter of the seventeenth century, but represents one of the earliest purely domestic buildings in Ulster, its original defensive barrier and fencework having disappeared. Roughcast and white-washed, it stands among old yew trees, the last trace of an ancient forest which once stretched to Lough Neagh. The lower wings with bay-windows flanking the entrance front are additions of 1765, but most of the original outbuildings – laundry, brewhouse, slaughterhouse, dovecote and stables – still survive. The interior of the house contains much

Rowallane has superb displays of azaleas and rhododendrons.

Stone dodos flank the ark on the dodo terrace in the gardens at Mount Stewart; many rare plants are grown here.

original panelling, an early eighteenth-century balustered staircase, a good library, and furniture of many different dates collected by the Conyngham family, while one of the outbuildings houses a wide-ranging collection of costumes.

Near Moneymore, on the B18   (159 D7)

Castles, Abbeys & other Buildings

Clough Castle, Co. Down The remains of a Norman castle consisting of a motte and bailey on the Inner Harbour above Dundrum, then an important strategic position, is leased by the Trust to the Historic Monuments Department of the Northern Ireland Government.

5M NE Dundrum, on A24   (159 G10)

The Crown Liquor Saloon, Belfast Perhaps the finest surviving example of a Victorian 'gin palace' anywhere in Britain stands on the corner of Great Victoria Street and Amelia Street in the centre of Belfast. The ground-floor façades are covered in brightly-coloured glazed tiles, with columns and pilasters, but it is the interior that takes the breath away: a riot of engraved and painted glass and mirrors, plasterwork garlands and festoons, tiles and mosaics. The 'snugs' or boxes have tall red oak partitions, elaborately carved and inlaid, to give complete privacy to their occupants. The designer of this Baroque fantasy is said to have been a Mr Flanagan, the son of the proprietor, who in the 1870s and 1880s obtained from Dublin and from London a vast array of manufacturers' stock items, which he then proceeded to put together with remarkable skill and bravura.

A great number of Belfast's splendid nineteenth-century public houses have been demolished or stripped of their original decoration in recent years, but it is some consolation that the Crown – acquired by the Trust in 1978 – has been saved for future generations.

Centre of Belfast, opposite the Europa Hotel (159 E9)

Cushendun, Co. Antrim The village of Cushendun lies at the mouth of a salmon river, the Dun, in the loveliest of the nine Glens of Antrim. With the old stone bridge spanning the estuary, the wide sandy bay beyond the green, the whitewashed and tile-hung cottages (some of them designed by Clough Williams-Ellis, the creator of Portmeirion, Gwynedd), it is picturesque without being self-conscious – like the poetry of its own bard, Moira O'Neill. Behind her house, Rockport, lies the ruined Keep of Castle Carra, where in 1567 the

MacDonnells fêted Shane O'Neill before striking him down and sending his head to Dublin. A cairn further up the hillside on the road to Torr Head marks his grave.

4M N Cushendall, on B92 (159 A9)

Dunseverick Castle, Co. Antrim Part of a ruined watch-tower and curtain wall poised dramatically on a rocky peninsula of the north Antrim coast is all that now remains of one of the oldest and strongest fortified places in Ireland. Said to be the spot where Deirdre of the Sorrows landed on her return from Scotland two thousand years ago, it was stormed by the Vikings in the ninth and tenth centuries, and later became a stronghold of the MacDonnells and the O'Cahans. The remaining fragments are part of the sixteenth-century castle, burnt out by Cromwellian troops in 1642, when the last O'Cahan owner lost both his life and lands.

3M E Giant's Causeway, off B146 (159 A7)

Mussenden Temple, Bishop's Gate and Black Glen, Downhill, Co. Londonderry Downhill was the creation of that colourful character, Frederick Hervey, Bishop of Derry, and 4th Earl of Bristol, known as the Earl-Bishop. The great house, now a ruin, was begun in about 1772 on a bleak and treeless headland overlooking the mouth of Lough Foyle and with superb views along the Donegal and Antrim coasts. Behind it, on the very edge of the cliff, is the Mussenden Temple, a domed rotunda based on the Temple of Vesta at Tivoli, and called after his cousin, Mrs Mussenden, who died shortly before its completion in 1785. The interior was originally furnished as a library, where the Bishop could study with only the roar of the wind and the crash of the waves below as accompaniment. The temple, executed by the Irish architect Michael Shanahan (though originally proposed by James Wyatt) also illustrates the Bishop's obsession with circular buildings – to blossom fully in his two other main houses, Ballyscullion on Lough Beg, and *Ickworth* in Suffolk.

The Bishop's Gate, once the main entrance to the demesne, is in the form of a triumphal arch, again strictly neo-classical in style, with Coade stone ornaments. It leads into Portvantage (otherwise called the Black) Glen, a steep wooded valley leading northwards to the house and temple.

1M W of Castlerock, on A2 (158 A6)

Templetown Mausoleum, Co. Antrim The quiet graveyard at Castle Upton, next to the home farm buildings, and not far from Robert Adam's castellated stables, contains one of the finest monuments the architect ever designed: a perfect little neo-classical temple decorated with Coade stone plaques. The mausoleum was built in 1789 in memory of the Hon. Arthur Upton, who had died over twenty years

previously, but it also contains plaques to later members of the Upton family, holders of the title of Lord Templeton.

At Templepatrick on A6, the Belfast–Antrim road (159 D9)

Archaeological & Industrial Sites

Coney Island, Lough Neagh, Co. Armagh Traces of Neolithic settlements have recently been found on this thickly wooded island of about eight acres, once joined to the mainland by a causeway. Later, St Patrick is thought to

Mussenden Temple, where the Earl-Bishop studied to the accompaniment of waves breaking on the rocks below.

Wellbrook beetling mill is a reminder of the days when linen manufacture was the most important industry in Ulster.

have used it as a retreat, while a ruined tower remains from the sixteenth-century stronghold of the O'Neills of Tyrone. The island is also an important nesting place for wildfowl.

Reached by boat from Maghery on B196 (159 E7)

Gray's Printing Press, Co. Tyrone In the late eighteenth century Strabane was an important publishing centre with two newspapers and at least ten printing concerns. John Dunlap, printer of the American Declaration of Independence in 1776, and founder of the first daily newspaper in the United States, is said to have learned his trade at Gray's Press before emigrating – like many other Strabane publishers and printers who set up in America and the Colonies. The works were housed in the upper storey of the long whitewashed buildings, now arranged as a museum with various early nineteenth-century presses, while the old bow-fronted shopfront still survives below.

In High Street, Strabane (158 C4)

Rough Fort, Co. Londonderry An impressive rath or Celtic ring fort, surrounded by Scots pines, oaks and beeches, this has as yet remained unexcavated, but may date from the first or second centuries BC.

1M W Limavady, on A2 (158 B6)

Wellbrook Beetling Mill, Co. Tyrone 'Beetling' is the last stage in the manufacture of linen, traditionally Northern Ireland's most famous industry, and involves the pounding of the cloth with heavy timbers to give it its final sheen. The process was originally carried on by hand but in the eighteenth century water-mills were built to make it quicker and more efficient. That on the little trout stream known as the Wellbrook was built in 1765, and continued in operation until 1965, three years before it came to the Trust. In collaboration with the Landmark Trust, it has now been put back into working order, retaining all its original mechanism. The upper floor with its louvred windows still has the airing racks where the pounded cloth was hung to dry.

3M W Cookstown, A505 (158 D6)

White Park Bay, Co. Antrim As well as being one of the most beautiful stretches of coastland on the north Antrim coast, this is one of the most important Neolithic sites in Ulster. Excavations have yielded large amounts of flints and pottery, five or six thousand years old, including a clay figurine of a 'Mother Goddess', the only one of its kind ever found in Ireland. The floors of round huts, kitchen middens, and a burial cairn are all clearly visible.

1½M W Ballintoy (159 A8)

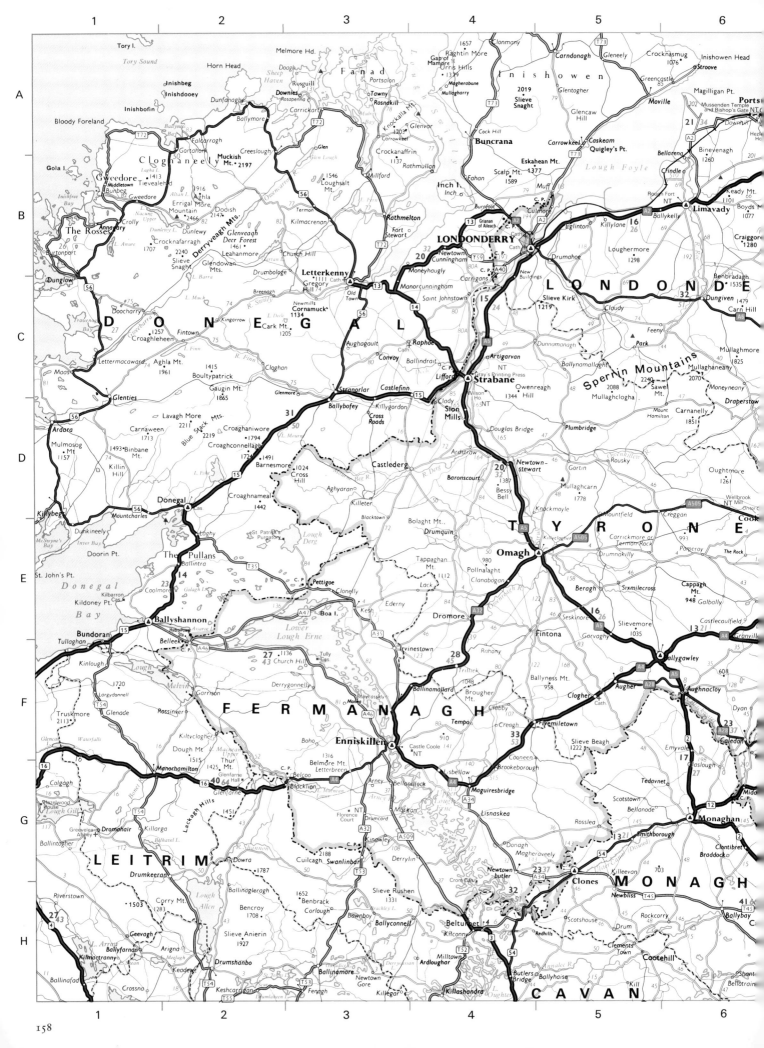

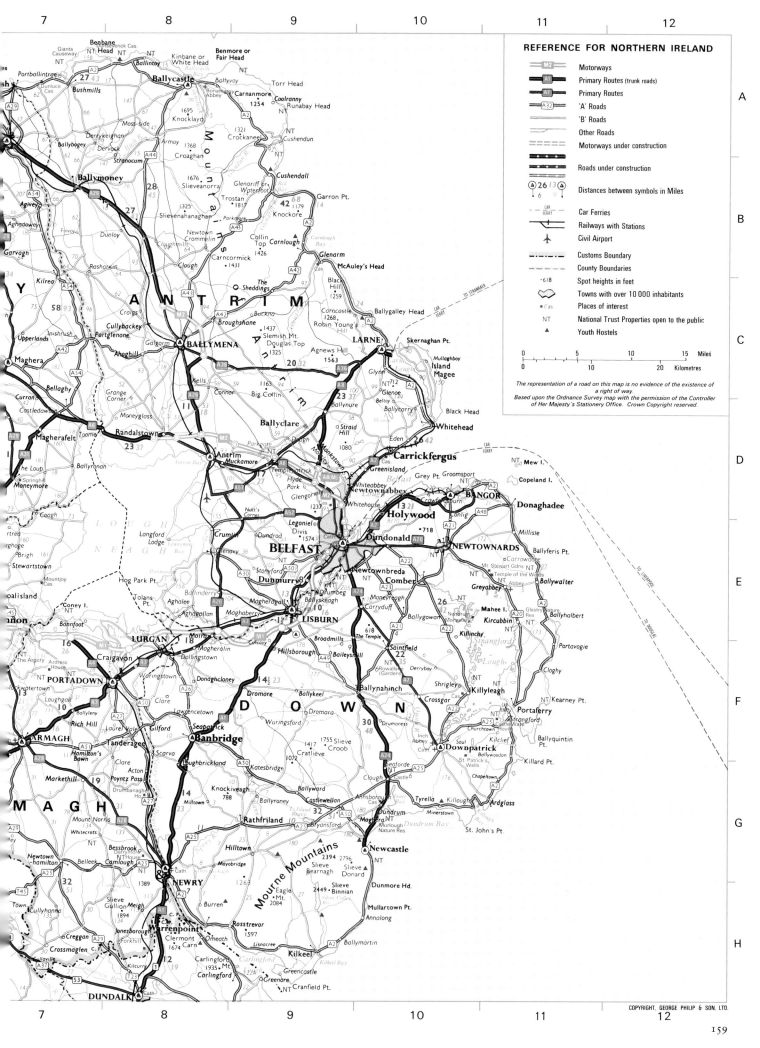

Glossary

	top projecting part of an *entablature* in classical architecture
cottage ornée	an intentionally rustic building that was a product of the picturesque cult of the late eighteenth and early nineteenth century
cove	a curved, concave junction of wall and ceiling
cruck	a simple but massive construction used in some forms of *half-timbering*. Two curved timbers form an inverted V and support the roof, and in some cases the walls also
cupola	a dome, especially a small dome crowning a roof or turret
curtain wall	the outer wall encircling a castle, usually punctuated with towers
dado	in *classical* architecture the cubic block forming the body of a pedestal; also a skirting along the lower part of the walls of a room
Decorated	the middle phase of *Gothic* architecture in England, c.1290–1370, characterized by *ogee* arches and abundant carvings
doocot	Scots form of English 'dovecote'
Doric	denoting one of the Greek orders of architecture, distinguished by simplicity of design
enceinte	in military architecture, the main enclosure of a fortress, surrounded by a wall or ditch
entablature	the structure supported by the column of *classical* architecture. It consists of an architrave, *frieze* and *cornice*
escutcheon	a shield on which a coat of arms is represented
foil	a lobe or leaf-shaped curve formed by the cusping of a circle or an arch. A prefix indicates the number of foils, e.g. trefoil, quatrefoil
frieze	a decorated band along the upper part of an internal wall, immediately below the *cornice*. In *classical* architecture, the middle division of an entablature
gable	the triangular upper part of a wall at the end of a pitched roof, corresponding to a *pediment* in *classical* architecture
Gothic	architecture of the medieval period featuring the pointed arch, stone vaults and huge traceried windows
Gothick	the conscious use in the eighteenth and early nineteenth century of what was thought to be medieval Gothic style
Gothic Revival	the nineteenth-century interpretation of Gothic architecture which developed from *Gothick*
ha-ha	a sunken ditch, intended to be invisible from the house, which kept park animals away from the lawn but allowed an uninterrupted view into the park

ambulatory	an enclosed space for walking
apse	a semi-circular or polygonal recess, with an arched or domed roof
bailey	the open space or court of a castle, also known as a *ward*. See *motte and bailey*
baluster	one of the posts or pillars supporting a rail and thus forming a balustrade
balustrade	*see baluster*
barbican	the outer defence of a castle that protects the entrance; often a double tower over a gate or bridge
Baroque	architecture of the seventeenth and early eighteenth century characterized by exuberant decoration, curvaceous forms and large-scale compositions
bressummer	a horizontal timber supporting a wall above it, such as the lintel of a fireplace. Also the principal horizontal beam in a timber-framed building
buttress	masonry or brickwork projecting from or built against a wall to give additional strength
cap house	the superstructure roofing a tower or stair-well
capital	the head or crowning feature of a column
classical	forms in architecture or decoration based on those developed in ancient Rome or Greece
collar-beam	a horizontal timber that lies across the pitch of the roof above the point where roof and walls meet (*see tie-beam*)
corbel	a projecting block or bracket, usually of stone, built into a wall to support a vault or beam
corbelling	brick or masonry courses, each built out beyond the one below like a series of *corbels* to support, for example, a projecting window
cornice	any projecting ornamental moulding on the top of a building, or wall of a room. Also the

half-timbering (*timber-framing*) a method of construction in which walls are built of interlocking vertical and horizontal timbers. The spaces are infilled with *wattle and daub*, lath and plaster or brick

hammer beam horizontal brackets of timber projecting at the level of the base of the rafts in a roof. The inner ends support hammer-posts and braces to a *collar beam*

hammer-pond an artificial pond providing water for a mill

hill-fort a prehistoric stronghold on a hill

hypocaust a space under a floor for heating by hot air or furnace gases, as characteristic of ancient Roman villas

inglenook a recess for a bench or seat built beside a fireplace

Ionic a style of Greek architecture characterized by *capitals* decorated with spiral scrolls

keep the principal central tower of a castle

king-post a vertical timber standing centrally on a *tie-* or *collar-beam* and rising to the apex of the roof where it supports a ridge

knot garden a garden of beds forming elaborate designs, planted with foliage and flowers in patterns. The beds are hedged in box or some other dwarf plant. The knot garden was at its height in the late sixteenth and early seventeenth centuries

linenfold Tudor panelling ornamented with a conventional representation of a piece of linen laid in vertical folds

loggia a gallery open on one or more sides, sometimes pillared; it may also be a separate structure, usually in a garden

loop a small, narrow and often unglazed window opening

louvre a series of overlapping boards or strips of glass (in a window) that can be opened or closed

machicolation a gallery or parapet built on the outside of castle towers or walls, with apertures through which missiles could be thrown

motte a steep mound, the main feature of many eleventh- and twelfth-century castles

motte and bailey a post-Roman and Norman defence system consisting of an earthen mound topped with a wooden tower, placed within a *bailey* encircled by a ditch and palisade

mullion a vertical post or other upright dividing a window or other opening

neo-classical the architectural style which developed after 1750 based upon the direct study of the buildings of ancient Greece and Rome

newel stair a spiral staircase with a continuous post supporting the narrow inner ends of the treads

ogee arch an arch formed of shallow S-shaped curves meeting in a point

oriel a bay window on an upper storey or storeys

Palladianism the architectural style influenced by the designs and buildings of Andrea Palladio, the sixteenth-century Italian architect, and introduced to England by Inigo Jones in the early seventeenth century. Palladio believed that architecture could be governed by certain universal rules reflected in the buildings of ancient Rome, notably symmetrical planning and the use of harmonic proportions. Palladianism was revived in England in the early eighteenth century

pargetting the exterior plastering of half-timbered buildings, usually decorated

parterre the elaborate, formal gardens, planted in intricate patterns and often to flowing designs, which developed from *knot gardens*

pediment in *classical* architecture, a low-pitched gable above a *portico*

pele tower a small or moderate-sized, easily defended tower or keep, usually built between the thirteenth and fifteenth centuries. Pele towers are peculiar to houses and castles on both sides of the Scottish border

piano nobile the main floor of a house, containing the reception rooms

pilaster a shallow rectangular column projecting slightly from a wall

portico a roofed space, open or partly enclosed, often forming the entrance and centre piece of the façade of a temple or house

potence in a dovecote, a vertical beam in the centre of the building to which several horizontal beams are attached at varying heights. The vertical beam pivots so that all nesting boxes can be reached from ladders fixed to the end of each horizontal beam

quatrefoil *see foil*

quoins the dressed stones at the corners of buildings, usually laid so that the exposed faces are alternately long and short (known as long-and-short work)

rococo the light-hearted sequel to *Baroque*. Formulated in France, it reached England after 1730 and remained for thirty years. The decoration is characterized by rocaille (shell-like and coral-like forms), C and S curves, and naturalistic scenes

rotunda a circular room or building, usually domed

screens passage the space or corridor at the service end of a

	medieval hall, dividing it from the buttery, pantry and kitchen
solar	the living room in an upper storey of a medieval house or castle
studs (studding)	in half-timbered buildings, the secondary vertical timbers in the walls
tie-beam	the horizontal transverse roof beam connecting the base of the rafters
timber-framing	*see half-timbering*
tower-house	a medieval type of fortified house exclusive to Scotland. The main hall is raised above the ground and has one or more storeys above
transept	the part of a building at right-angles to the main body, usually that part of a church at right-angles to the nave
transom	a horizontal bar of stone or wood across the opening of a window, or across a panel

trefoil	*see foil*
trompe l'oeil	in painting, the representation of an object with such exactitude as to deceive the eye into believing the object real
truss	a number of timbers framed together to bridge a space or form a bracket
vallum	a rampart, usually formed of material from the associated ditch
vault	an arched ceiling or roof of stone or brick. The simplest form is a tunnel vault or barrel vault, consisting of a continuous vault of semi-circular or pointed sections
ward	the court of a castle
wattle and daub	a method of simple wall construction in which branches or thin wooden laths (wattle) are roughly plastered over with mud or clay (daub) used as a filling between the uprights of a half-timbered house

Architects and Craftsmen

In the entries below, some examples of National Trust properties (where the architects etc worked) are mentioned in *italics*. These, for reasons of space, by no means comprise a complete list, nor are the architects, craftsmen and landscape gardeners necessarily always mentioned in the brief descriptions of the properties in the main text of this *Atlas*. The Trusts' guidebooks to individual properties will give the interested visitor full details.

Robert Adam (1728–92) Architect. A Scot by birth, working within a family firm, the Adam Brothers, he devised a neo-classical style lighter and more elegant than the prevailing Palladian. He enlivened the rather monumental Palladian style with ornament and decoration while retaining Palladian balance and proportion. Equally distinguished as an interior decorator; noted for his elegant fireplaces and furniture. (*Charlotte Square, Culzean Castle, Hatchlands, Nostell Priory, Osterley, Saltram*)

Thomas Archer (1668–1743) Successful English practitioner of the florid Baroque architecture of southern Europe.

Sir Herbert Baker (1862–1946) Worked with Lutyens in New Delhi. In general his style was a somewhat heavy imperial classicism. (*Owletts*)

Sir Charles Barry (1795–1860) Versatile early Victorian architect. His early work is neo-Gothic, but later he gracefully adapted Greek and Italian classical ideas, as in the rebuilding of *Cliveden*.

G. F. Bodley (1827–1907) Of Scottish descent, first pupil of George Gilbert Scott, he mainly worked on churches, always in the Gothic style. An early patron of William Morris. (*Clumber Chapel*)

Charles Bridgeman (d. 1738) Landscape gardener, credited with introducing the ha-ha into England from France (at Stowe in 1719). Little of his original work remains. (*Wimpole Hall*)

Lancelot ('Capability') Brown (1716–83) Most famous figure in English eighteenth-century landscape gardening. 'Improved' nature through informal, though carefully planned, parks, typically including wide sweeps of grass, clumped trees and serpentine lakes. (*Berrington Hall, Charlecote Park, Claremont Landscape Garden, Petworth Park, Wimpole Hall*)

William Burges (1827–81) Eclectic Victorian Gothic Revivalist. Created sumptuous interiors using a wide range of media from stained glass to fabrics, all of which he designed. Interesting and original architect. (*Knightshayes*)

William Burn (1789–1870) Initiator of 'Scottish Baronial' style for country houses *c.*1830. Richard Norman Shaw was a pupil. (*Brodie Castle, House of The Binns*)

Colen Campbell (1676–1729) One of the chief perpetrators of the large English Palladian country house. (*Stourhead*)

John Carr (1723–1807) Late exponent of Palladianism, working mainly in Yorkshire. Associated with Robert Adam in building Harewood House (begun 1759), and afterwards was responsible for many large country houses. (*Basildon Park*)

Sir William Chambers (1723–96) The leading official architect of his day in England, his reputation with public buildings (Somerset House, for instance) brought commissions for country houses – all in the Palladian style.

Thomas Chippendale (1718–79) Furniture maker, whose reputation was founded on his *Gentleman and Cabinet-Maker's Director* (in the 1750s), a catalogue of his firm's designs. Since others worked from Chippendale's designs, much that is called 'Chippendale' is in fact Chippendale-style, and not made by his firm. He worked in different styles, Chinese Chippendale being one of the most famous. (*Nostell Priory, Osterley*)

Thomas Cubitt (1788–1855) Speculative builder, who with his more architecturally gifted brother Lewis was largely responsible for Bloomsbury, Belgravia (not Belgrave Square) and Pimlico. (*Polesden Lacey*)

Henry Flitcroft (1697–1769) Protégé of Lord Burlington, and succeeded William Kent as Master Mason and Deputy Surveyor in the Office of Works. His work was in the Palladian style. (*Stourhead temples, Wimpole Hall*)

Grinling Gibbons (1648–1720) Of Dutch origin, he was the most gifted woodcarver to work in Britain. Using softwoods (pear, lime etc.) he created life-size and life-like festoons of flowers, fruits etc. (*Petworth House*)

James Gibbs (1682–1754) Influential early eighteenth-century London church architect. Influenced by Sir Christopher Wren and the Baroque, and also incorporating Palladian features in his work. St Martin-in-the-Fields in Trafalgar Square is his best-known work. (*Wimpole Hall*)

Henry Holland (1745–1806) Architect, once assistant to 'Capability' Brown, with a style owing something both to Chambers and Adam, his interior decoration approached French neo-classicism in elegance. (*Berrington Hall*)

Inigo Jones (1573–1652) Initially famous as a stage designer, he was the first to introduce classical Palladian architecture to England. (He encountered the designs of Andrea Palladio while journeying in Italy in 1613.) The Queen's House, Greenwich, was the first strictly classical building in England.

William Kent (1685–1748) Painter, furniture designer, landscape gardener and architect, starting life as a barely literate coach-painter. Protégé of Lord Burlington, he became Master Mason and Deputy Surveyor in the Office of Works in 1735. Major commissions were designed along Palladian lines. His interior decoration is rich with sumptuous carving and gilt. Historically most important as a landscape gardener – one of the first to revolt against the formal seventeenth-century garden and to harmonize landscape and country house. (*Claremont Landscape Garden*)

Giacomo Leoni (*c.*1686–1746) Born in Venice, he settled in England before 1715. An architect in the Palladian style. (*Clandon Park, Lyme Park*)

Sir Edwin Lutyens (1869–1944) Architect of some of the last spectacular English country houses, including *Castle Drogo* and *Lindisfarne*. Also responsible for a number of fine country houses in the Arts and Crafts style. The chief designer of New Delhi.

Sanderson Miller (1717–80) Gothic Revivalist and noted builder of sham castles in the 1740s. (*Lacock Abbey hall, Wimpole Hall Gothic tower*)

William Morris (1834–96) Vigorous opponent of Victorian industrialization and champion of traditional crafts. Designer of wallpapers, stained glass, fabrics, and carpets for the firm of Morris & Co. A profound influence on the arts and crafts of the time. (*Cragside, Standen, Wallington, Wightwick Manor*)

John Nash (1752–1835) Prolific architect in many styles, including the Picturesque. Greatest achievement was the layout of Regent's Park and its terraces and Regent Street. (*Attingham Park, Blaise Hamlet village*)

James Paine (1717–89) Architect in the Palladian tradition, working largely in the north of England. His interiors are noted for especially fine rococo ceilings. (*Felbrigg Hall, Nostell Priory, Wallington bridge*)

J. B. Papworth (1775–1847) Designed several country houses; also a landscape gardener. Much of his work was in Cheltenham. (*Claremont Landscape Garden*)

Augustus Welby Pugin (1812–52) A principal architect of the Victorian Gothic Revival and responsible for the decorative detail in Barry's Houses of Parliament. His work was chiefly ecclesiastical.

Humphry Repton (1752–1818) Leading landscape gardener of the generation after Brown. He introduced formal gardens with parterres and terraces close to the houses, contrasting with the landscaped parks beyond. (*Attingham Park, Tatton Park*)

Anthony Salvin (1799–1881) Medieval architecture expert and a central figure in the Victorian Gothic Revival, though using a wide range of styles. A pupil of Nash and an authority on the restoration and improvement of castles. (*Dunster Castle, Petworth House south front*)

Richard Norman Shaw (1831–1912) Influential domestic architect of the late Victorian era. His early work was Gothic in style but later he turned to the so-called 'Queen Anne style', influenced by Dutch examples and the architecture of the William and Mary period. (*Cragside*)

Sir Robert Smirke (1780–1867) The leading Greek Revival architect in England and designer of the British Museum.

Robert Smythson (*c.*1536–1614) Elizabethan architect, builder of spectacular houses for the magnates of the time. (*Gawthorpe Hall, Hardwick Hall*)

Sir John Soane (1753–1837) Notably individual architect and designer influenced by and of the generation after Robert Adam. (*Wimpole Hall*)

James 'Athenian' Stuart (1713–88) Important in the history of neo-Greek architecture for his temple at Hagley (1758). His best surviving works are his Doric Temple etc in the park at *Shugborough*.

William Talman (1650–1719) Leading country house architect until eclipsed by Vanbrugh. His large, lavish houses are Baroque in character. (*Dyrham Park*)

John Webb (1611–72) Pupil of Inigo Jones, with whom he worked closely. Little of his independent work survives. (*The Vyne portico*)

Philip Speakman Webb (1831–1915) With Norman Shaw, one of the most influential domestic architects of the late Victorian period. Designed furniture for William Morris's firm. (*Standen*)

William Winde (d. 1722) Starting in middle age, he became a leader of the Anglo-Dutch school of architects. None of his buildings definitely survive, though he may have been the architect of *Ashdown House*.

James Wyatt (1747–1813) Most successful architect of his day, willing to give his clients what they wanted. His classical houses include *Castle Coole* in Northern Ireland. He also designed neo-Gothic extravaganzas.

Sir Jeffry Wyatville (1766–1840) Nephew of James Wyatt, competent classical architect, but specialized in neo-Gothic and Tudor collegiate mansions. Knighted for his work on Windsor Castle. (*Philipps House*)

Index to text

County index to properties

NORTHERN IRELAND

Great Britain map index

ABBREVIATIONS

Beds. – Bedfordshire
Berks. – Berkshire
Bucks. – Buckinghamshire
Cambs. – Cambridgeshire
Cas. – Castle
Ches. – Cheshire
Co. – County
Com. – Common
Corn. – Cornwall
Cumb. – Cumbria

Derby. – Derbyshire
Dumf. & Gall. – Dumfries &
  Galloway
Dur. – Durham
E. – East
E. Sussex – East Sussex
Glos. – Gloucestershire
Gt. – Great
Grn. – Green
Hants. – Hampshire

Heref. & Worcs. – Hereford &
  Worcester
Hth. – Heath
Herts. – Hertfordshire
Ho. – House
Humber. – Humberside
I.o.M. – Isle of Man
I.o.W. – Isle of Wight
Junc. – Junction
Lancs. – Lancashire

Leics. – Leicestershire
Lincs. – Lincolnshire
Lo. – Lodge
London – Greater London
Manchester – Greater
  Manchester
Mid Glam. – Mid Glamorgan
Norf. – Norfolk
N. – North
N. Yorks. – North Yorkshire

Northants. – Northamptonshire
Northumb. – Northumberland
Notts. – Nottinghamshire
Oxon. – Oxfordshire
Salop. – Shropshire
Som. – Somerset
S. – South
S. Glam. – South Glamorgan
S. Yorks. – South Yorkshire
Staffs. – Staffordshire

Sta. – Station
Suff. – Suffolk
War. – Warwickshire
W. – West
W. Glam. – West Glamorgan
W. Mid. – West Midlands
W. Sussex – West Sussex
W. Yorks. – West Yorkshire
W. Isles – Western Isles
Wilts. – Wiltshire

AB

96 Ab Kettleby ....H 4	58 Abercegir ....B 4	56 Abertysswg ....D 5	148 Achiltibuie ....F 2	116 Acklam, Cleveland ...C 5	85 Adstock ....
39 Abbas Combe ......D 10	143 Aberchalder ....J 7	140 Aberuthven ....F 5	149 Achina ....B 7	112 Acklam, N. Yorks. ...A 5	89 Adstone ....
88 Abberley ....E 1	146 Aberchirder ....B 4	56 Aberyscir ....A 3	139 Achindarroch ....B 7	88 Ackleton ....B 1	41 Adversane ....
87 Abberton, Essex ....B 10	55 Abercraf ....F 11	58 Aberystwyth ....D 2	143 Achintee, Highland ..M 5	133 Acklington ....C 10	144 Advie ....
88 Abberton,	56 Abercrave ....C 2	84 Abingdon ....D 6	142 Achintee, Highland ..F 3	112 Ackton ....E 2	112 Adwick le Street ....
Heref. & Worcs ...G 3	56 Abercregan ....E 2	41 Abinger Common ...B 12	142 Achintraid ....F 2	112 Ackworth Moor Top .F 2	112 Adwick upon Dearne
133 Abberwick ....B 9	56 Abercwmboi ....D 3	41 Abinger Hammer ...A 12	143 Achlain ....H 6	92 Acle ....D 7	36 Adworthy ....
86 Abbess Roding ......C 6	54 Abercych ....C 6	136 Abington ....G 2	145 Achlean ....K 4	88 Acock's Green .....D 5	146 Adziel ....
38 Abbey ....E 5	56 Abercynafon ....C 4	91 Abington Pigotts ....L 4	138 Achleck ....C 1	43 Acol ....A 11	131 Ae Bridgend ....
57 Abbey Dore ....A 7	56 Abercynon ....E 4	84 Ablington, Glos, ...C 2	134 A'Chleit ....E 2	133 Acomb, Northumb. ..F 7	131 Ae Village ....
38 Abbey Hill ....D 6	56 Aberdare ....D 3	40 Ablington, Wilts. ....A 3	139 Achlian ....E 8	112 Acomb, N. Yorks. ...B 4	36 Affeton Barton .....
95 Abbey Hulton ......E 7	60 Aberdaron ....H 1	95 Abney ....B 10	143 Achluachrach ....L 7	57 Aconbury ....A 8	146 Affleck, Grampian ..
137 Abbey St. Bathans ..C 10	147 Aberdeen ....G 7	147 Aboyne ....H 3	148 Achlyness ....B 4	110 Acre ....E 6	146 Affleck, Grampian ..
96 Abbey Town ....F 12	60 Aberdesach ....E 4	110 Abram ....G 5	148 Achmelvich ....E 2	41 Acre Street ....F 9	39 Affpuddle ....
110 Abbey Village ......E 5	136 Aberdour ....A 5	144 Abriachan ....F 1	140 Achmore, Central ...D 1	61 Acrefair ....F 12	37 Afton, Devon ......
58 Abbeycwmhir ....E 6	58 Aberdovey ....C 2	86 Abridge ....D 5	142 Achmore, Highland ..F 2	94 Acton, Cheshire .....E 5	40 Afton, I.o.W. ......
114 Abbeylands, I.o.M. ..G 2	55 Aberdulais ....G 11	57 Abson ....G 10	151 Achmore, W. Isles ..D 4	40 Acton, Dorset ......H 1	135 Afton Bridgend .....
133 Abbeylands,	58 Aberedw ....H 6	89 Abthorpe ....G 10	139 Achnaba, Strathclyde .D 7	86 Acton, London .....F 2	116 Agglethorpe ....
Northumb. ....B 10	54 Abereiddy ....D 2	97 Aby ....B 11	134 Achnaba, Strathclyde .A 4	59 Acton, Salop ....D 8	114 Agneash ....
110 Abbeystead ....B 4	60 Abererch ....G 3	59 Acaster Malbis .....C 4	145 Achnabat ....G 2	93 Acton, Suffolk .....L 2	151 Aignish ....
36 Abbotsham ....E 3	56 Aberfan ....D 4	112 Acaster Selby ....C 3	148 Achnacarnin ....D 2	94 Acton Bridge ....C 4	113 Aike ....
95 Abbots Bromley ....H 9	140 Aberfeldy ....B 3	36 Accott ....C 5	143 Achnacarry ....L 5	59 Acton Beauchamp ..G 12	151 Aikerness ....
85 Abbots Langley ....D 11	60 Aberffraw ....C 3	110 Accrington ....D 6	150 Achnacloich ....G 5	59 Acton Burnell ......B 10	152 Aikers ....
57 Abbots Leigh ....G 8	58 Aberffrwd ....E 2	150 Achachork ....D 4	139 Achnacon ....B 8	59 Acton Green ......G 12	131 Aiket ....
88 Abbot's Morton .....G 4	112 Aberford ....C 2	138 Achadun ....D 5	138 Achnacraig ....C 2	94 Acton Park ....E 2	132 Aikton ....
91 Abbots Ripton ......G 3	139 Aberfoyle ....G 12	138 Achafolla ....F 5	138 Achnacroish ....C 6	59 Acton Pigott ....B 11	59 Ailey ....
88 Abbot's Salford ....G 4	55 Abergarwed ....G 11	134 Achagary ....B 7	138 Achnadrish ....B 2	59 Acton Round ....C 11	90 Ailsworth ....
39 Abbotsbury ....H 9	56 Abergavenny ....C 6	134 Achahoish ....B 3	139 Achnafalnich ....E 9	59 Acton Scott ....C 10	116 Ainderby Steeple ...
36 Abbotsham ....C 3	61 Abergele ....B 9	139 Achallader ....C 10	143 Achnafraschoille ....L 6	95 Acton Trussell ......H 8	87 Aingers Green .....
37 Abbotskerswell .....J 7	55 Abergiar ....C 8	138 Achamore Farm .....E 1	144 Achnagarron ....C 2	57 Acton Turville .....F 11	110 Ainsdale ....
91 Abbotsley ....K 3	56 Abergorlech ....D 9	142 Achanalt ....D 6	138 Achnaha ....A 2	94 Adbaston ....G 6	115 Ainstable ....
40 Abbotswood ....D 5	58 Abergwesyn ....G 4	134 Achanamara ....A 3	148 Achnahanat ....G 6	39 Adber ....D 9	110 Ainsworth ....
40 Abbots Ann ....B 5	55 Abergwili ....E 8	144 Achandunie ....C 2	138 Achnalea ....A 6	94 Adderley ....F 5	117 Ainthorpe ....
59 Abcott ....E 9	56 Abergwynfi ....E 2	148 Achany ....F 6	149 Achnaluachrach .....F 7	133 Adderstone ....C 12	110 Aintree ....
59 Abdon ....D 11	58 Abergynolwyn ......B 2	143 Achaphubuil ....M 5	143 Achnanellan ....L 5	136 Addiewell ....C 3	130 Aird, Dumf & Gall.
55 Aber, Dyfed ....B 8	58 Aberhosan ....C 4	138 Acharacle ....A 4	148 Achnanerain ....F 6	111 Addingham ....B 9	138 Aird, Strathclyde ..
60 Aber, Gwynedd .....C 6	56 Aberkenfig ....F 2	138 Acharn, Highland ...C 4	143 Achnangart ....H 3	85 Addington, Bucks. ..A 8	151 Aird, W. Isles .....
55 Aberarth ....A 8	137 Aberlady ....A 7	140 Acharn, Tayside ....C 2	143 Achnasaul ....K 5	42 Addington, Kent ....B 9	150 Aird of Sleat .....
58 Aber Gwydol ....B 3	141 Aberlemno ....B 10	46 Acharole ....C 11	142 Achnasheen ....D 5	86 Addington, London ..G 4	151 Aird of Tunga .....
60 Aber-Gwynant ......H 6	58 Aberllefenni ....A 3	134 Acharosson ....B 4	142 Achnashellach ....E 4	137 Addinston ....D 8	151 Aird Uig ....
56 Aber Village ....B 4	58 Abermeurig ....G 1	138 Achateny ....A 3	144 Achnastank ....F 8	85 Addlestone ....H 11	148 Airdachuilinn .....
55 Aberaeron ....A 8	59 Abermule ....C 7	146 Achath ....F 5	138 Achosnich ....A 2	97 Addlethorpe ....C 12	135 Airdrie ....
56 Aberaman ....D 3	55 Abernant, Dyfed ....E 7	149 Achavanich ....C 11	138 Achranich ....C 4	112 Adel ....C 1	135 Airdsgreen ....
58 Aberangell ....A 4	56 Aber-nant, Mid Glam. D 3	144 Achavraat ....E 5	149 Achreamie ....A 9	94 Adeney ....H 5	149 Airdtorrisdale .....
145 Aberarder, Highland .G 2	141 Abernethy ....E 7	144 Achavraie ....F 2	139 Achriabhach ....A 8	58 Adfa ....B 6	142 Airigh-drishaig ....
143 Aberarder, Highland .L 8	141 Abernyte ....D 7	55 Achddu ....G 8	148 Achriesgill ....B 4	59 Adforton ....E 9	112 Airmyn ....
140 Aberargie ....E 6	54 Aberporth ....B 6	148 Achentoul ....D 8	149 Achrimsdale ....F 9	43 Adisham ....C 11	140 Airntully ....
55 Aberavon ....H 11	60 Abersoch ....G 3	148 Achfary ....C 4	149 Achtoty ....B 7	84 Adlestrop ....A 3	143 Airor ....
55 Aber-banc ....C 7	56 Abersychan ....D 6	148 Achfrish ....F 6	91 Achurch ....G 1	112 Adlingfleet ....E 6	140 Airth ....
56 Aberbeeg ....D 5	56 Aberthin ....G 3	148 Achgarve ....G 1	148 Achuvoldrach ....B 6	95 Adlington, Ches. ....B 7	111 Airton ....
56 Aberbran ....A 3	56 Abertillery ....D 5	148 Achiemore, Kyle of	149 Achvaich ....G 7	110 Adlington, Lancs. ...F 5	130 Airyhassen ....
56 Abercanaid ....D 4	56 Abertridwr,		Durness, Highland .A 4	145 Achvraid, Highland ..G 2	59 Admaston, Salop. ...A 11	
56 Abercarn ....E 5		Mid Glam. ....E 4	149 Achiemore, Highland .B 9	144 Achvraid, Highland ..F 2	95 Admaston, Staffs. ...H 9	
54 Abercastle ....D 2	61 Abertridwr, Powys ...H 9	150 A'Chill ....H 2	149 Ackergill ....B 12	88 Admington ....G 5	

176

Bliss Gate E 1
Blissford E 3
Blisworth G 10
Blithbury H 9
Blithford H 9
Blitterlees F 11
Blo Norton G 3
Blockley A 3
Blofield E 6
Blofield Corner D 6
Bloomfield, Dumf. & Gall. D 10
Bloomfield, Borders G 8
Blore E 10
Blounts Green G 9
Bloxham A 5
Bloxholm E 8
Bloxwich B 3
Bloxworth G 12
Blubberhouses B 10
Blue Anchor, Corn. D 6
Blue Anchor, Somerset B 4
Blue Anchor, W. Glam. G 9
Bluebell Hill B 6
Blughasary F 3
Blundellsands G 2
Blundeston F 8
Blunham K 3
Blunsdon St. Andrew E 2
Bluntington E 2
Bluntisham H 5
Blunts C 10
Blyborough H 7
Blyford H 7
Blymhill A 2
Blyth, Northumb. E 11
Blyth, Notts. B 3
Blyth Bridge E 4
Blyth Marsh F 8
Blythburgh H 7
Blythe Bridge E 4
Blythe Marsh F 8
Blythebridge G 9
Blyton H 6
Boarhills F 10
Boarhunt E 7
Boars Hill D 6
Boarshead E 4
Boarstall C 7
Boasley Cross F 4
Boat of Garten H 5
Boath B 1
Bobbing B 7
Bobbington C 2
Bobbingworth C 5
Boblainy F 1
Bocking B 7
Bocking Churchstreet A 7
Boconnoc D 8
Boddam, Grampian C 8
Boddam, Shetland Is. F 7
Bodden B 10
Bodedern B 3
Bodelwyddan C 9
Bodenham, Heref. & Worcs. G 10
Bodenham, Wilts. D 3
Bodenham Moor G 11
Boderwryd A 3
Bodfari C 10
Bodffordd C 4
Bodfuan F 3
Bodham Street B 4
Bodiam E 6
Bodicote H 8
Bodieve B 7
Bodinnick D 8
Bodle Street Grn. G 5
Bodmin C 8
Bodnant C 7
Bodney E 1
Bodorgan C 3
Bodsham Green D 9
Boduan F 3
Bodwen D 7
Bogallan E 2
Bogbrae D 8
Bogend, Borders D 10
Bogend, Strathclyde F 9
Boghall, Lothian C 5
Boghall, Lothian C 3
Boghall, Strathclyde H 9
Boghead, Grampian E 7
Boghead, Strathclyde F 10
Boghead, Strathclyde E 12
Bogknowe F 10
Bogmarsh A 8
Bogmoor A 1
Bogmuire K 4
146 Bogniebrae C 3
41 Bognor Regis F 11
146 Bograxie F 4
136 Bogsbank D 4
136 Bogside D 1
146 Bogton C 4
131 Bogue C 7
34 Bohortha F 6
143 Bohuntine L 7
35 Bokiddick C 7
116 Bolam, Durham C 2
133 Bolam, Northumb. E 9
37 Bolberry M 6
94 Bold Heath A 4
133 Boldon Colliery G 11
40 Boldre F 5
138 Boldron D 1
96 Bole B 5
95 Bolehill E 11
34 Boleigh G 2
137 Boleside F 7
140 Bolfracks B 3
38 Bolham E 3
38 Bolham Water E 5
34 Bolingey D 5
95 Bollington, Ches. B 8
94 Bollington, Ches. B 6
95 Bollington Cross C 8
42 Bolney F 1
91 Bolnhurst J 2
141 Bolshan B 11
96 Bolsover C 2
111 Bolsterstone G 11
57 Bolstone A 8
116 Boltby F 5
85 Bolter End E 9
115 Bolton, Cumbria C 8
110 Bolton, Manchester F 6
112 Bolton, Humber. B 5
137 Bolton, Lothian B 7
133 Bolton, Northumb. B 9
111 Bolton Abbey B 9
111 Bolton Bridge B 9
110 Bolton by Bowland B 6
115 Bolton-le-Sands H 7
114 Bolton Low Houses A 5
112 Bolton-on-Dearne G 2
116 Bolton-on-Swale E 3
112 Bolton Percy C 3
115 Bolton Town End H 7
132 Boltonfellend F 3
35 Bolventor B 9
94 Bomere Heath H 3
148 Bonar Bridge G 6
139 Bonawe Quarries D 7
113 Bonby F 8
54 Boncath C 5
132 Bonchester Bridge B 4
41 Bonchurch H 7
36 Bondleigh E 5
110 Bonds C 4
88 Bonehill B 5
136 Bo'ness A 3
140 Bonhard D 6
135 Bonhill A 9
88 Boningdale B 2
137 Bonjedward G 9
136 Bonkle D 1
136 Bonnington B 4
141 Bonnybank G 8
136 Bonnybridge A 1
146 Bonnykelly B 6
136 Bonnyrigg and Lasswade C 6
135 Bonnyton F 9
95 Bonsall D 11
57 Bont B 7
60 Bont Newydd F 6
60 Bontddu H 6
58 Bont-dolgadfan B 4
58 Bontnewydd, Dyfed F 2
60 Bont-newydd, Gwynedd D 4
58 Bontrhydgaled D 4
61 Bontuchel D 10
56 Bonvilston G 4
55 Bon-y-maen G 10
36 Boode B 4
94 Booley H 4
115 Boon E 8
117 Boosbeck C 7
36 Boot F 1
112 Booth D 5
111 Booth Wood E 9
97 Boothby Graffoe D 7
97 Boothby Pagnell G 7
110 Boothtown G 6
114 Bootle, Cumbria F 4
110 Bootle, Merseyside H 2
135 Boquhan A 10
59 Boraston E 11
41 Borden D 9
111 Bordley A 8
41 Bordon C 9
87 Boreham C 7
42 Boreham Street G 5
86 Borhamwood D 2
140 Boreland, Central D 1
131 Boreland, Dumf. & Gall. B 12
131 Boreland of Girthon F 7
150 Boreraig C 1
137 Borewell D 12
149 Borgie B 7
131 Borgue, Dumf. & Gall. G 7
149 Borgue, Highland E 10
93 Borley L 1
150 Bornaskitaig A 3
131 Borness G 7
42 Borough Green B 5
116 Boroughbridge H 4
94 Borras Head E 2
149 Borrobol Lodge E 8
96 Borrowash G 1
116 Borrowby F 4
114 Borrowdale D 5
147 Borrowfield H 6
58 Borth C 2
132 Borthwickbrae B 2
132 Borthwickshiels B 3
60 Borth-y-gest F 5
150 Borve C 4
151 Borve Lodge G 1
151 Borvemore G 1
115 Borwick H 7
59 Bosbury H 12
35 Boscastle A 8
40 Boscombe, Dorset G 3
40 Boscombe, Wilts. B 3
35 Boscoppa D 7
41 Bosham F 9
54 Bosherston G 3
34 Boskenna G 1
95 Bosley D 7
95 Bossall A 5
147 Bossholes H 6
35 Bossiney A 8
43 Bossingham C 10
38 Bossington A 3
94 Bostock Green C 5
90 Boston A 4
97 Boston Long Hedges E 10
112 Boston Spa C 2
35 Boswinger F 7
34 Botallack F 1
86 Botany Bay D 3
146 Botary Mains C 2
89 Botcheston B 8
93 Botesdale H 3
133 Bothal D 10
96 Bothamsall C 4
131 Bothel H 12
39 Bothenhampton G 8
135 Bothwell D 12
85 Botley, Bucks. D 10
40 Botley, Hants. E 6
84 Botley, Oxon. C 6
85 Botolph Claydon B 8
42 Botolphs G 1
142 Bottacks D 8
113 Bottesford, Humber. F 7
96 Bottesford, Leics. F 5
91 Bottisham J 6
84 Bottlesford H 2
90 Bottom House E 9
110 Bottom O'th'Moor F 5
141 Bottomcraig E 8
111 Bottoms E 8
114 Bottongate A 5
36 Bottreaux Mill C 7
35 Botusfleming D 11
60 Botwnnog G 2
42 Bough Beech C 4
59 Boughrood H 7
59 Boughrood Brest H 7
57 Boughspring E 9
90 Boughton, Norfolk E 8
96 Boughton, Notts. C 4
43 Boughton Aluph C 9
89 Boughton E 11
43 Boughton Lees C 9
43 Boughton Malherbe C 7
42 Boughton Monchelsea C 6
43 Boughton Street B 9
117 Boulby C 8
59 Bouldon D 11
133 Boulmer B 11
54 Boulston F 3
146 Boultenstone F 2
96 Boultham C 6
91 Bourn K 4
90 Bourne D 2
91 Bourne End, Beds. L 1
85 Bourne End, Bucks. E 10
85 Bourne End, Herts. D 11
85 Bournebridge D 5
40 Bournemouth G 3
87 Bournes Green, Essex E 9
57 Bournes Green, Gloucestershire D 12
88 Bournheath E 3
133 Bournmoor H 11
88 Bournville D 4
84 Bourton, Oxon. E 3
39 Bourton, Dorset C 11
59 Bourton, Salop. C 11
89 Bourton on Dunsmore E 8
84 Bourton-on-the-Hill A 3
84 Bourton-on-the-Water A 3
132 Boustead Hill G 1
114 Bouth G 6
116 Bouthwaite H 2
85 Boveney F 10
56 Boverton G 3
37 Bovey Tracey H 7
85 Bovingdon D 11
85 Bovingdon Green E 9
86 Bovinger C 5
137 Bow, Borders E 7
36 Bow, Devon F 6
152 Bow, Orkney Is E 2
85 Bow Brickhill A 10
141 Bow of Fife F 8
58 Bow Street D 2
115 Bowbank C 11
116 Bowburn A 3
40 Bowcombe G 6
38 Bowd G 4
137 Bowden, Borders F 8
37 Bowden, Devon L 7
57 Bowden Hill H 12
115 Bowerdale E 9
94 Bowdon B 6
132 Bower E 6
39 Bower Hinton D 8
40 Bowerchalke D 2
57 Bowerhill H 12
149 Bowermadden B 11
95 Bowers G 7
87 Bowers Gifford E 7
140 Bowershall H 6
149 Bowertower B 11
115 Bowers D 12
110 Bowgreave C 4
137 Bowhill G 7
131 Bowhouse E 11
35 Bowithick A 9
110 Bowker's Green G 3
114 Bowland Bridge F 6
59 Bowley G 11
41 Bowlhead Green B 10
135 Bowling B 9
88 Bowling Green G 2
114 Bowmanstead F 5
132 Bowness-on-Solway G 1
114 Bowness-on-Windermere E 6
137 Bowsden E 12
149 Bowside Lodge B 8
136 Bowtrees A 2
57 Box, Glos. D 11
57 Box, Wilts. G 11
57 Boxbush C 10
84 Boxford, Berks. G 5
93 Boxford, Suffolk L 3
41 Boxgrove E 10
42 Boxley B 6
36 Box's Shop F 1
93 Boxted, Essex M 3
93 Boxted, Suffolk K 1
93 Boxted Cross M 3
91 Boxworth J 4
91 Boxworth End H 5
43 Boyden Gate B 11
95 Boylestone G 10
146 Boyndie A 4
117 Boynton H 11
39 Boys Hill E 10
37 Boyton, Cornwall G 2
93 Boyton, Suffolk K 7
40 Boyton, Wilts. B 1
86 Boyton Cross C 6
89 Bozeat F 12
114 Braaid H 2
93 Brabling Green J 6
43 Brabourne D 9
43 Brabourne Lees D 9
149 Brabstermire A 12
150 Bracadale D 3
90 Braceborough D 2
97 Bracebridge Heath C 7
97 Braceby G 7
111 Bracewell B 7
96 Brackenfield D 1
147 Brackenrigg K 5
114 Brackenthwaite, Cumbria C 4
132 Brackenthwaite, Cumbria H 1
41 Bracklesham F 9
143 Brackletter L 6
89 Brackley, Northants. H 9
134 Brackley, Strathclyde E 3
148 Brackloch E 3
85 Bracknell G 9
140 Braco F 3
146 Bracobrae B 3
92 Bracon Ash E 5
143 Bracora K 1
143 Bracorina K 1
95 Bradbourne E 10
116 Bradbury B 3
114 Bradda H 1
89 Bradden G 10
85 Bradenham D 9
84 Bradenstoke F 1
85 Bradfield, Berks. G 7
38 Bradfield, Devon E 4
93 Bradfield, Essex M 4
111 Bradfield, S. Yorks. H 11
93 Bradfield Combust J 2
94 Bradfield Green D 5
93 Bradfield Heath M 4
93 Bradfield St. Clair J 2
93 Bradfield St. George J 2
36 Bradford, Devon E 3
133 Bradford, Northumb. D 11
111 Bradford, W. Yorks. D 10
39 Bradford Abbas E 9
57 Bradford Leigh H 11
36 Bradford Mill D 7
57 Bradford-on-Avon H 11
38 Bradford-on-Tone D 5
41 Brading G 7
94 Bradley, Clwyd E 2
95 Bradley, Derby. F 10
41 Bradley, Hants. B 7
113 Bradley, Humber. F 10
115 Bradley, N. Yorks. G 12
95 Bradley, Staffs. H 7
88 Bradley, W. Midlands C 3
94 Bradley Common F 4
88 Bradley Green F 3
95 Bradley in the Moors F 9
96 Bradmore G 3
39 Bradney B 7
38 Bradninch F 3
95 Bradnop E 8
39 Bradpole G 8
110 Bradshaw F 6
37 Bradstone H 3
94 Bradwall Green D 6
95 Bradwell, Derby. B 10
87 Bradwell, Essex B 8
92 Bradwell, Suffolk E 8
89 Bradwell, Bucks. H 11
84 Bradwell Grove C 3
87 Bradwell-on-Sea C 10
87 Bradwell Waterside C 10
36 Bradworthy E 2
36 Bradworthy Cross E 2
152 Brae C 7
148 Brae Doune G 5
148 Brae of Achnahaird E 2
143 Brae Roy Lodge K 7
144 Braeantra B 1
145 Braedownie M 8
131 Braefoot A 9
146 Braehead, Grampian F 7
130 Braehead, Dumf. & Gall. F 5
152 Braehead, Orkney Is. D 3
136 Braehead, Strathclyde D 2
136 Braehead, Strathclyde F 1
141 Braehead, Tayside B 11
149 Braehungie D 11
142 Braeintra F 2
148 Braelangwell Lodge G 6
145 Braemar K 7
149 Braemore, Highland D 10
142 Braemore, Highland B 6
135 Braeside B 7
139 Braeval E 12
116 Brafferton, Dur. C 3
116 Brafferton, N. Yorks. H 4
89 Brafield-on-the-Green F 11
151 Bragar B 4
86 Bragbury End B 3
138 Braglenbeg E 6
110 Braides B 3
137 Braidshawrig D 8
136 Braidwood E 1
95 Brailsford F 11
133 Brainshaugh C 10
87 Braintree B 7
93 Braiseworth H 4
40 Braishfield D 5
114 Braithwaite, Cumb. C 5
112 Braithwaite, S. Yorks. F 4
96 Braithwell A 3
42 Bramber G 1
96 Bramcote F 2
41 Bramdean C 7
92 Bramerton E 6
86 Bramfield, Herts. B 3
93 Bramfield, Suffolk H 7
93 Bramford K 4
95 Bramhall B 7
112 Bramham C 2
112 Bramham Crossroads C 2
111 Bramhope C 11
41 Bramley, Surrey B 11
96 Bramley, S. Yorks. A 2
85 Bramley Green H 7
38 Brampford Speke F 3
91 Brampton, Cambs. H 3
132 Brampton, Cumb. G 4
115 Brampton, Cumb. C 9
57 Brampton, Heref. & Worc. A 7
96 Brampton, Lincs. B 6
112 Brampton, S. Yorks. G 2
93 Brampton, Suffolk G 7
57 Brampton Abbots B 9
89 Brampton Ash C 11
59 Brampton Bryan E 9
96 Brampton en le Morthen A 2
95 Bramshall G 9
40 Bramshaw E 4
41 Bramshott C 9
86 Bran End A 6
92 Brancaster A 1
92 Brancaster Staithe A 1
116 Brancepeth A 2
144 Branchill D 6
57 Brand Green B 10
144 Branderburgh C 8
113 Brandesburton B 9
93 Brandeston J 5
36 Brandis Corner E 3
92 Brandiston C 4
114 Brandingill C 4
116 Brandon, Durham A 3
96 Brandon, Lincs. E 6
133 Brandon, Northumb. A 8
93 Brandon, Suffolk G 1
89 Brandon, War. D 7
90 Brandon Creek F 7
92 Brandon Parva E 4
116 Brandsby H 6
113 Brandy Wharf G 8
34 Brane G 1
40 Branksome G 2
40 Branksome Park G 2
40 Bransbury B 6
96 Bransby C 6
38 Branscombe G 5
88 Bransford G 1
40 Bransgore F 3
88 Branson's Cross E 4
96 Branston, Leics. G 5
97 Branston, Lincs. C 7
95 Branston, Staffs. H 10
97 Branston Booths C 8
41 Branstone H 7
96 Brant Broughton E 6
132 Branteth E 1
93 Brantham M 4
114 Branthwaite, Cumb. C 3
114 Branthwaite, Cumb. B 5
113 Brantingham D 7
133 Branton, Northumb. A 8
112 Branton, S. Yorks. G 4
132 Branxholme B 3
137 Branxton F 11
137 Branxtonmoor F 11
95 Brassington E 11
42 Brasted C 3
42 Brasted Chart C 3
147 Brathens H 4
97 Bratoft D 11
96 Brattleby B 6
38 Bratton, Somerset B 3
40 Bratton, Wilts. A 1
37 Bratton Clovelly G 3
36 Bratton Fleming B 5
39 Bratton Seymour C 10

86 Braughing A 4
89 Braunston, Leics. A 11
89 Braunston, Northants. E 9
89 Braunstone B 9
36 Braunton B 4
54 Brawby, Dyfed E 2
117 Brawby, N. Yorks. G 7
149 Brawlbin B 10
85 Bray F 10
35 Bray Shop B 10
85 Bray Wick F 9
89 Braybrooke D 11
36 Brayford C 6
112 Brayton D 4
35 Brazacott A 9
150 Breabost C 3
43 Breach B 7
86 Breachwood Green B 2
151 Breaclete C 2
95 Breadsall F 12
57 Breadstone D 10
142 Breafield F 8
34 Breage G 3
142 Breakachy E 8
57 Bream D 9
40 Breamore D 3
57 Bream's Eaves D 9
38 Brean A 6
111 Brearton A 11
151 Breasclete C 3
96 Breaston G 2
55 Brechfa D 8
147 Brechin L 4
131 Breckonside A 9
150 Breckrey B 4
56 Brecon A 4
111 Bredbury H 8
43 Brede F 7
59 Bredenbury G 11
93 Bredfield K 6
43 Bredger B 7
43 Bredhurst B 7
88 Bredicot G 3
57 Bredon A 12
88 Bredon's Norton H 3
59 Bredwardine H 9
96 Breedon on the Hill H 1
136 Breich C 2
112 Breighton D 5
59 Breinton H 10
59 Breinton Com. H 10
84 Bremhill G 1
139 Brenachoille G 7
42 Brenchley D 5
36 Brendon A 6
134 Brenfield A 3
151 Brenish D 1
133 Brenkley F 10
86 Brent E 2
93 Brent Eleigh K 2
38 Brent Knoll A 6
91 Brent Pelham M 5
86 Brentford F 2
86 Brentwood E 6
43 Brenzett E 8
88 Brereton A 4
94 Brereton Green D 6
94 Brereton Heath D 6
152 Bressay E 7
93 Bressingham G 4
95 Bretby H 11
89 Bretford D 7
88 Bretforton H 4
115 Bretherdale Head E 8
110 Bretherton E 4
38 Brett B 4
152 Brettabister D 7
93 Brettenham, Suff. K 3
93 Brettenhm, Norf. G 2
94 Bretton D 2
42 Brewer Street C 2
141 Brewlands Bridge A 7
88 Brewood A 2
144 Briach D 6
39 Briantspuddle G 11
86 Bricket Wood D 1
88 Bricklehampton H 3
114 Bride F 2
114 Bridekirk B 4
54 Bridell C 5
37 Bridestowe G 4
146 Brideswell D 3
37 Bridford G 7
43 Bridge, Kent C 10
34 Bridge, Cornwall E 4
91 Bridge End, Beds. K 1
90 Bridge End, Lincs. B 2
133 Bridge End, Northumb. B 9
116 Bridge Hewick H 4
146 Bridge of Alford F 3
140 Bridge of Allan G 3
144 Bridge of Avon F 7
139 Bridge of Awe E 7
139 Bridge of Balgie, Perth C 12
145 Bridge of Brown G 7
140 Bridge of Cally B 6
147 Bridge of Canny H 4
141 Bridge of Craigisla B 7
131 Bridge of Dee F 8
144 Bridge of Derrybeg F 8
146 Bridge of Don F 7
147 Bridge of Dun L 4
147 Bridge of Dye J 4
140 Bridge of Earn E 6
139 Bridge of Ericht B 12
147 Bridge of Feugh H 4
149 Bridge of Forss A 10
147 Bridge of Gairn H 1
139 Bridge of Gaur B 12
141 Bridge of Lintrathen B 7
147 Bridge of Murchalls H 6
143 Bridge of Oich J 7
139 Bridge of Orchy D 10
140 Bridge of Tilt A 4
152 Bridge of Waith D 1
152 Bridge of Walls D 6
135 Bridge of Weir C 9
36 Bridge Reeve E 5
59 Bridge Sollars H 9
93 Bridge Street K 2
94 Bridge Trafford C 3
91 Bridgefoot, Cambs. L 5
114 Bridgefoot, Cumb. B 3
39 Bridgehampton D 9
137 Bridgelands F 7
41 Bridgemary F 7
35 Bridgend, Corn. D 8
114 Bridgend, Cumbria D 6
131 Bridgend, Dumf. & Gall. A 11
54 Bridgend, Dyfed B 5
141 Bridgend, Fife F 8
146 Bridgend, Grampian C 5
146 Bridgend, Grampian D 3
146 Bridgend, Grampian E 6
146 Bridgend, Grampian D 1
142 Bridgend, Highland D 7
136 Bridgend, Lothian B 3
56 Bridgend, Mid Glam. F 2
138 Bridgend, Strathclyde H 6
147 Bridgend, Tayside K 3
140 Bridgend, Tayside E 6
36 Bridgerule F 1
59 Bridges C 9
35 Bridgetown, Corn. A 10
38 Bridgetown, Som. C 3
88 Bridgetown, Staffs. A 3
93 Bridgham G 3
59 Bridgnorth C 12
39 Bridgwater B 6
117 Bridlington H 12
39 Bridport G 8
57 Bridstow B 9
111 Brierfield D 7
57 Brierley, Glos. C 9
59 Brierley, Heref. & Worc. G 10
112 Brierley, S. Yorks. F 2
88 Brierley Hill C 3
116 Brierton B 5
56 Briery Hill C 5
139 Brig o' Turk G 12
113 Brigg F 8
147 Briggs of Criggie J 6
117 Briggswath D 9
114 Brigham, Cumb. B 3
113 Brigham, Humber. B 8
111 Brighouse E 10
40 Brighstone H 6
84 Brighthampton D 5
95 Brightgate D 11
42 Brightling F 5
87 Brightlingsea B 10
34 Brighton, Corn. D 6
42 Brighton, E. Sussex H 2
136 Brightons B 2
84 Brightwalton F 5
85 Brightwell, Oxon. E 7
93 Brightwell, Suffolk L 5
85 Brightwell Baldwin E 7
116 Brignall D 1
113 Brigsley G 10
115 Brigsteer F 7
89 Brigstock D 12
85 Brill, Bucks. C 7
34 Brill, Cornwall G 4
59 Brilley G 8
54 Brimaston D 3
59 Brimfield F 10
96 Brimington C 1
57 Brimpsfield C 12
84 Brimpton H 6
152 Brims E 1
57 Brimscombe D 11
94 Brimstage B 2
145 Brin G 2
143 Brinacory K 1
112 Brind D 5
152 Brindister, Shetland Is. D 6
152 Brindister, Shetland Is. E 7
110 Brindle E 5
95 Brindley Ford E 7
88 Brineton A 2
89 Bringhurst C 11
91 Brington H 2
92 Briningham B 3
93 Brinkhill C 10
91 Brinkley K 7
89 Brinklow D 8
84 Brinkworth F 1
110 Brinscall E 5
57 Brinsea H 7
96 Brinsley E 2
59 Brinsop H 10
96 Brinsworth A 1
92 Brinton B 3
152 Brinyan B 2
92 Brisley C 3
57 Brislington G 9
43 Brissenden Green D 8
57 Bristol G 9
92 Briston B 4
93 Britannia E 7
40 Britford C 3
61 Brithdir, Gwynedd H 7
56 Brithdir, Mid Glam. D 5
42 British Legion Village B 6
55 Briton Ferry G 10
85 Britwell Salome E 7
37 Brixham K 8
37 Brixton K 4
39 Brixton Deverill B 11
89 Brixworth E 10
84 Brize Norton C 4
84 Broad Blunsdon E 3
88 Broad Campden H 5
40 Broad Chalke C 2
38 Broad Clyst F 3
91 Broad Green, Beds. L 1
87 Broad Green, Essex B 8
88 Broad Green, Heref. & Worc. F 1
54 Broad Haven F 2
91 Broad Hill H 7
84 Broad Hinton F 2
84 Broad Laying H 5
88 Broad Marston G 5
114 Broad Oak, Cumb. F 4
55 Broad Oak, Dyfed E 9
43 Broad Oak, E. Sussex F 7
57 Broad Oak, Heref. & Worc. B 8
112 Broad Oak, N. Yorks. B 4
43 Broad Street B 7
87 Broad Street Green C 8
84 Broad Town F 2
111 Broadbottom H 8
41 Broadbridge E 9
41 Broadbridge Hth. C 12
54 Broadfield G 5
150 Broadford F 5
40 Broadford Bri. D 12
136 Broadgairhill H 5
132 Broadhaugh B 3
149 Broadhaven C 12
94 Broadheath A 6
39 Broadhembury F 5
37 Broadhempston J 7
43 Broadland Row F 7
55 Broadlay F 7
146 Broadley B 1
86 Broadley Com. C 4
137 Broadmeadows F 7
41 Broadmere A 7
54 Broadmoor F 4
42 Broadoak, E. Sussex F 5
43 Broadoak, Kent B 10
146 Broadrashes B 2
146 Broadsea E 5
43 Broadstairs A 12
40 Broadstone, Dorset F 2
59 Broadstone, Salop. C 11
84 Broadtown Lane F 2
88 Broadwas G 1
86 Broadwater, Herts. B 2
41 Broadwater, W. Sussex F 12
54 Broadway, Dyfed F 6
54 Broadway, Dyfed F 2
88 Broadway, Heref. & Worc. H 4
38 Broadway, Som. E 6
84 Broadwell, Glos. A 3
84 Broadwell, Oxon D 3
89 Broadwell, War. F 8
133 Broadwell House H 7
57 Broadwell Lane End C 9
39 Broadwey H 10
39 Broadwindsor F 8
36 Broadwood-Kelly E 5
37 Broadwoodwidger G 3
59 Brobury H 9
150 Brochel D 5
41 Brockbridge D 7
133 Brockdam A 9
93 Brockdish G 5
40 Brockenhurst F 4
136 Brocketsbrae E 1
93 Brockford Street J 4
89 Brockhall F 9
42 Brockham C 1
84 Brockhampton, Glos. B 1
57 Brockhampton, Heref. & Worc. A 9
39 Brockhampton Green F 10
111 Brockholes F 10
41 Brockhurst F 7
114 Brocklebank A 5
113 Brocklesby F 9
57 Brockley H 8
93 Brockley Green K 1
88 Brockton, Salop. B 1
59 Brockton, Salop. B 8
59 Brockton, Salop. C 11
57 Brockweir D 8
41 Brockwood D 7
57 Brockworth C 12
95 Brocton H 8
134 Brodick F 5
146 Brodiesord B 3
112 Brodsworth F 3
150 Brogaig A 4
91 Brogborough L 1
94 Broken Cross, Cheshire C 6
95 Broken Cross, Cheshire C 7
57 Brokenborough E 12
94 Bromborough B 2
93 Brome H 4
93 Brome Street H 5
93 Bromeswell K 6
131 Bromfield, Cumb. G 12
59 Bromfield, Salop. E 10
91 Bromham, Beds. K 1
84 Bromham, Wilts. H 1
86 Bromley G 4
43 Bromley Green D 8
42 Brompton, Kent A 6
117 Brompton, N. Yorks. G 9
116 Brompton, N. Yorks. E 4
59 Brompton Hall C 8
116 Brompton-on-Swale E 2
38 Brompton Ralph C 4
38 Brompton Regis C 3
57 Bromsash B 9
57 Bromsberrow A 10
88 Bromsgrove E 3
59 Bromyard G 12
59 Bromyard Downs G 12
60 Bronaber G 6
58 Bronant F 2
54 Brongest C 6
94 Bronington F 4
56 Bronllys A 5
55 Bronwydd Arms E 7
59 Bronydd H 8
54 Brook, Dyfed F 6
40 Brook, Hants. C 5
40 Brook, Hants. E 4
40 Brook, I.o.W. H 5
43 Brook, Kent D 9
41 Brook, Surrey B 12
41 Brook, Surrey B 10
91 Brook End J 2
40 Brook Hill E 4
86 Brook Street, Essex E 6
42 Brook Street, W. Sussex E 2
89 Brooke, Leics. B 12
92 Brooke, Norfolk E 6
57 Brookend D 9
135 Brookfield C 9
95 Brookhouse, Ches. C 8
110 Brookhouse, Lancs. A 4
95 Brookhouse Green D 7
43 Brookland E 8
131 Brooklands D 9
86 Brookmans Park D 2
59 Brooks C 7
85 Brookwood H 10
91 Broom, Beds. L 3
116 Broom, Durham A 3
88 Broom, War. G 4
40 Broom Hill F 2
140 Broom of Dalreoch E 5
137 Broomdykes D 11
88 Broome, Heref. & Worcs. D 3
92 Broome, Norfolk F 6
59 Broome, Salop. D 9
42 Broome Park C 1
94 Broomedge B 5
41 Broomer's Crn. D 12
87 Broomfield, Essex C 7
146 Broomfield, Grampian D 7
43 Broomfield, Kent A 10
43 Broomfield, Kent C 7
38 Broomfield, Som. C 6
136 Broomfield, Strathclyde E 1
112 Broomfleet D 6
85 Broomhall G 10
133 Broomhaugh G 8
133 Broomhill, Northumb. C 10
144 Broomhill, Highland C 3
145 Broomhill House G 6
92 Broomholm B 6
133 Broomhouse C 11
131 Broomhouses C 12
133 Broomley G 8
57 Brooms Green A 10
57 Broomsberrow Heath A 10
149 Brora F 9
59 Broseley B 12
88 Brotheridge Green H 2
137 Brotherstone F 9
97 Brothertoft F 10
112 Brotherton E 3
133 Brotherwick C 10
117 Brotton C 7
149 Broubster B 10
115 Brough, Cumbria D 10
95 Brough, Derby. B 10
149 Brough, Highland A 11
113 Brough, Humberside D 7
96 Brough, Notts. D 5
152 Brough, Orkney Is. C 2
152 Brough, Whalasay, Shetland Is. C 8
152 Brough, Yell, Shetland Is. C 7
152 Brough, Zetland, Shetland Is. C 7
152 Brough Lodge B 8
115 Brough Sowerby D 10
94 Broughall F 4
89 Broughton, Bucks. H 12
136 Broughton, Borders F 4
91 Broughton, Cambs. G 4
94 Broughton, Clwyd D 2
114 Broughton, Cumb. B 3
40 Broughton, Hants. C 4
113 Broughton, Humber. F 7
110 Broughton, Lancs. D 4
56 Broughton, Mid Glam. G 2
89 Broughton, Northants. E 11
117 Broughton, N. Yorks. H 8
111 Broughton, N. Yorks. B 8
152 Broughton, Orkney Is. A 2
89 Broughton, Oxon H 7
89 Broughton Astley C 8
114 Broughton Beck G 5
57 Broughton Com. H 12
84 Broughton Foggs D 3
57 Broughton Gifford H 12
88 Broughton Hackett G 3
114 Broughton in Furness F 5
114 Broughton Mills F 4
114 Broughton Moor B 3
152 Broughtown B 4
141 Broughty Ferry D 9
132 Browhouses G 1
41 Brown Candover B 7
95 Brown Edge E 7
146 Brownhill, Grampian D 6
94 Brownhill, Salop. H 3
141 Brownhills, Fife F 10
88 Brownhills, W. Midlands B 4
95 Brownlow Heath D 7
147 Brownmuir K 5
133 Brownridge B 11
57 Brown's Hill D 12
89 Brownsover D 8
37 Brownston K 6
133 Brownyside
85 Brox
117 Broxa
86 Broxborune
137 Broxburn, Lothian
136 Broxburn, Lothian
86 Broxted
94 Broxton
59 Broxwood
42 Broyle Side
149 Bruan
145 Bruar Lodge
151 Brue
94 Bruera
84 Bruern Abbey
93 Bruisyard
93 Bruisyard Street
112 Brumby
95 Brund
92 Brundhall
93 Brundish
93 Brundish Street
143 Brunery
133 Brunswick Village
89 Bruntingthorpe
141 Brunton, Fife
133 Brunton, Northumb.
84 Brunton, Wilts.
38 Brushford
36 Brushford Barton
39 Bruton
39 Bryanston
131 Brydekirk
61 Brymbo
39 Brympton
61 Bryn, Clwyd
55 Bryn, Dyfed
110 Bryn, Manchester
55 Bryn, W. Glam
59 Bryn, Salop.
56 Bryn Golau
60 Bryn-Siencyn
55 Brynamman
54 Brynberian
55 Brynbryddan
56 Bryncethin
60 Bryncir
55 Bryn-coch
60 Bryncroes
58 Bryncrug
61 Bryneglwys
61 Brynford
60 Bryngwran
57 Bryngwyn, Gwent
59 Bryngwyn, Powys
54 Bryn-henllan
55 Brynhoffnant
110 Bryning
56 Brynmawr
56 Brynmenyn
60 Bryn'refail
56 Brynsadler
61 Bryn-teg
56 Bryn-y-Cae
56 Bryn-y-gwenin
61 Bryn-y-maen
150 Bualintur
89 Bubbenhall
112 Bubwith
136 Buccleuch
130 Buchan
135 Buchanan Castle
139 Buchanan Smithy
146 Buchanhaven
140 Buchanty
140 Buchlyvie
146 Buchts
132 Buckabank
91 Buckden, Cambs.
115 Buckden, N. Yorks.
92 Buckenham
38 Buckerell
37 Buckfast
37 Buckfastleigh
141 Buckhaven
137 Buckholm
86 Buckhurst Hill
146 Buckie
85 Buckingham
85 Buckinghamshire, Co
85 Buckland, Bucks.
37 Buckland, Devon
84 Buckland, Glos.
91 Buckland, Herts.
43 Buckland, Kent
84 Buckland, Oxon
42 Buckland, Surrey
36 Buckland Brewer
85 Buckland Com.
39 Buckland Dinham

91 Clopton G 2
93 Clopton Green K 1
114 Close Clark H 1
131 Closeburn B 9
131 Closeburnmill B 10
39 Closworth E 9
91 Clothall M 4
116 Clotherholme H 3
94 Clotton D 4
111 Clough F 9
111 Clough Foot E 8
117 Cloughton F 10
117 Cloughton Newlands F 10
152 Clousta D 6
146 Colva, Grampian E 2
147 Clova, Tayside K 1
115 Clove Lodge C 11
36 Clovelly D 2
137 Clovenfords F 7
146 Clovenstone F 5
144 Cloves D 7
139 Clovulin A 7
111 Clow Bridge D 7
96 Clowne C 2
143 Cluanie Inn H 4
143 Cluanie Lodge H 5
59 Cluddley A 11
151 Cluer H 2
59 Clun D 8
59 Clunbury D 9
144 Clune E 7
143 Clunes K 6
59 Clungunford E 9
146 Clunie, Grampian C 4
140 Clunie, Tayside C 6
59 Clunton D 9
141 Cluny H 7
145 Cluny Castle K 2
57 Clutton, Avon H 9
94 Clutton, Cheshire E 3
61 Clwyd, Co. E 10
56 Clydach, Gwent C 5
55 Clydach, W. Glam. G 10
56 Clydach Vale E 3
135 Clydebank B 10
54 Clydey C 6
84 Clyffe Pypard F 2
135 Clynder A 7
54 Clynderwen E 5
55 Clyne G 11
149 Clynelish F 8
60 Clynnog-fawr E 4
59 Clyro H 7
38 Clyst Honiton G 3
38 Clyst Hydon F 4
38 Clyst St. George G 3
38 Clyst St. Lawrence F 4
38 Clyst St. Mary G 3
60 Clywt-y-bont D 5
58 Cnwch Coch E 2
146 Coachford C 2
35 Coad's Green B 10
96 Coal Ashton B 1
59 Coalbrookdale B 12
56 Coalbrookvale C 5
136 Coalburn F 1
133 Coalburns G 9
115 Coalcleugh A 10
57 Coaley D 11
147 Coalford G 6
135 Coalhall G 9
87 Coalhill D 7
57 Coalpit Heath F 10
95 Coalpit Hill E 7
59 Coalport B 12
140 Coalsnaughton H 4
141 Coaltown of Balgonie G 8
141 Coaltown of Wemyss H 8
89 Coalville A 8
57 Coalway Lane End C 9
39 Coat D 8
135 Coatbridge C 12
135 Coatdyke C 12
84 Coate, Wilts. H 2
84 Coate, Wilts. F 3
90 Coates, Cambs. F 4
84 Coates, Glos. D 1
41 Coates, W. Sussex D 11
116 Coatham C 6
116 Coatham Mundeville C 3
131 Coatsgate A 11
36 Cobbaton C 5
57 Coberley C 12
42 Cobham, Kent A 5
85 Cobham, Surrey H 11
139 Cobleland H 12
59 Cobnash F 10
146 Coburty A 7
145 Cock Bridge H 8
87 Cock Clarks D 8
59 Cock Gate F 10
116 Cockayne E 6
91 Cockayne Hatley K 4
137 Cockburnspath B 10
137 Cockenzie and
Port Seton B 7
110 Cockerham B 3
114 Cockermouth B 4
86 Cockernhoe B 1
116 Cockfield, Durham C 2
93 Cockfield, Suffolk K 2
41 Cocking D 10
37 Cockington J 8
39 Cocklake A 8
133 Cocklaw F 7
137 Cocklawfoot G 11
137 Cockles B 8
92 Cockley Clet E 1
146 Cockmuir D 4
85 Cockpole Green F 9
94 Cockshutt G 3
92 Cockthorpe A 3
38 Cockwood H 3
57 Cockyard A 7
35 Codda B 9
93 Coddenham K 4
94 Coddington, Ches. E 3
59 Coddington,
Heref. & Worc. H 12
96 Coddington, Notts. E 5
40 Codford St. Mary B 1
40 Codford St. Peter B 1
86 Codicote B 2
41 Codmore Hill D 12
96 Codnor E 1
57 Codrington F 10
88 Codsall B 2
88 Codsall Wood B 2
56 Coedely F 4
57 Coed Morgan C 7
60 Coed Ystumgwern H 5
60 Coedana B 4
56 Coedkernew F 6
61 Coedpoeth E 12
59 Coedway A 9
55 Coed-y-bryn C 7
57 Coed-y-fedw C 7
56 Coed-yr-ynys B 5
56 Coelbren C 2
37 Coffinswell J 8
38 Cofton H 3
88 Cofton Hacket E 3
56 Cogan G 5
89 Cogenhoe F 11
87 Coggeshall B 8
87 Coggeshall Hamlet B 8
145 Coignafearn Lo. H 2
145 Coignafeuinternich H 3
145 Coignascallan H 3
147 Coilacreich H 1
145 Coilintuie J 6
139 Coillaig E 7
143 Coille Mhorgil J 5
150 Coillore D 3
145 Coire Bhachdaidh
Lodge M 1
56 Coity F 3
148 Colaboll F 6
34 Colan D 6
38 Colaton Raleigh G 4
150 Colbost C 1
116 Colburn E 2
40 Colbury E 5
115 Colby, Cumbria C 9
114 Colby, I.o.M. H 1
92 Colby, Norfolk B 5
87 Colchester A 10
84 Cold Ash G 6
89 Cold Ashby D 10
57 Cold Ashton G 10
84 Cold Aston B 2
54 Cold Blow F 5
89 Cold Brayfield G 12
97 Cold Hanworth B 7
94 Cold Hatton H 5
133 Cold Hesleden H 12
111 Cold Hiendly F 12
89 Cold Higham G 10
116 Cold Kirby G 5
35 Cold Northcott A 9
87 Cold Norton D 8
89 Cold Overton A 11
115 Coldbeck E 9
148 Coldbackie B 6
42 Coldean G 2
37 Coldeast H 7
40 Colden Common D 6
93 Coldfair Green J 7
90 Coldham E 5
57 Coldharbour, Glos. D 8
42 Coldharbour, Kent C 4
146 Coldhome C 3
137 Coldingham C 11
140 Coldrain G 6
43 Coldred C 11
36 Coldridge E 6
137 Coldstream E 11
41 Coldwaltham D 11
146 Coldwells D 8
146 Coldwells Croft E 3
39 Cole C 10
86 Cole Green C 3
40 Cole Henley A 6
59 Colebatch D 8
38 Colebrook F 3
36 Colebrooke F 6
144 Coleburn D 8
113 Coleby, Humber. E 7
97 Coleby, Lincs. D 7
36 Coleford, Devon F 6
57 Coleford, Glos. C 9
39 Coleford, Som. A 10
40 Colehill F 2
42 Coleman's Hatch E 3
94 Colemere G 3
41 Colemore C 8
96 Coleorton H 1
57 Colerne G 11
84 Colesbourne C 1
91 Colesden K 2
85 Coleshill, Bucks. E 10
84 Coleshill, Oxon E 3
88 Coleshill, War. C 5
38 Colestocks F 4
42 Colgate E 1
135 Colgrain A 8
141 Colinsburhg G 9
136 Colinton C 5
134 Colintraive B 5
92 Colkirk C 2
151 Coll C 6
141 Collace D 7
152 Collafirth C 7
34 Collamoor Head B 2
37 Collaton L 4
37 Collaton St. Mary K 7
135 Collenan F 8
141 Collessie F 7
36 Colleton Mills D 5
86 Collier Row E 5
42 Collier Street C 6
86 Collier's End B 4
146 Collieston E 8
131 Collin D 11
40 Collingbourne Ducis A 4
40 Collingbourne
Kingston A 4
111 Collingham C 12
59 Collington F 12
89 Collingtree G 11
110 Collins Green H 4
141 Colliston C 10
38 Colliton F 4
147 Collmuir G 3
146 Collynie D 6
90 Collyweston E 1
130 Colmonell C 3
91 Colmworth J 2
84 Coln Rogers C 2
84 Coln St. Aldwyn D 2
84 Coln St. Dennis C 2
145 Colnabaichin H 8
85 Colnbrook F 11
91 Colne, Cambs. H 5
111 Colne, Lancs. C 7
93 Colne Engaine M 2
92 Colney E 5
86 Colney Heath C 2
86 Colney Street D 2
133 Colpitts Grange G 8
146 Colpy D 4
136 Colquhar E 6
36 Colscott D 2
116 Colsterdale G 2
96 Colsterworth H 6
96 Colston Bassett G 4
144 Coltfield C 7
92 Coltishall D 6
114 Colton, Cumbria G 5
92 Colton, Norfolk D 4
112 Colton, N. Yorks. C 3
95 Colton, Staffs. H 9
111 Colton, W. Yorks. D 12
59 Colva G 7
88 Colwall Green H 1
88 Colwall Stone H 1
133 Colwell E 8
95 Colwich H 8
56 Colwinston G 3
114 Colwith E 5
41 Colworth F 10
61 Colwyn Bay B 8
38 Colyford G 6
38 Colyton G 6
132 Comb D 6
84 Combe, Berks. H 5
59 Combe,
Heref. & Worc. F 9
84 Combe, Oxon C 5
41 Combe Common B 10
59 Combe Moor F 9
38 Combe Florey C 5
36 Combe Martin A 5
38 Combe Raleigh F 5
38 Combe St. Nicholas E 6
37 Combebow G 4
37 Combeinteignhead J 8
94 Comberbach C 5
91 Comberton, Cambs. K 5
59 Comberton,
Heref. & Worc. F 10
38 Combpyne G 6
95 Combridge F 9
88 Combrook G 6
95 Combs, Derby B 9
93 Combs, Suffolk K 3
38 Combwich B 6
147 Comers G 4
58 Comin Capel Betws G 2
58 Comins-coch Dyfed D 2
58 Comins-coch Powys B 4
146 Comisty C 3
56 Common Coed-y-paen D 6
35 Common Moor C 9
96 Common Side C 1
117 Commondale D 7
95 Compstall A 8
131 Compstonend F 7
84 Compton, Berks. F 6
37 Compton, Devon J 7
40 Compton, Hants. C 6
41 Compton, Surrey A 11
41 Compton, W. Sussex E 9
40 Compton, Wilts. A 3
39 Compton Abbas D 12
84 Compton Abdale C 2
84 Compton Bassett G 1
84 Compton Beauchamp E 4
39 Compton Bishop A 7
40 Compton
Chamberlayne C 2
57 Compton Dando H 9
39 Compton Dundon C 8
57 Compton Greenfield F 9
39 Compton Martin A 8
39 Compton Pauncefoot D 10
39 Compton Valence G 9
140 Comrie, Fife H 5
140 Comrie, Tayside E 3
139 Conaglen House A 7
134 Conchra A 5
110 Conder Green B 3
84 Condicote A 3
135 Condorrat B 12
59 Condover B 10
93 Coney Weston G 3
41 Coneyhurst Com. D 12
117 Coneysthorpe H 7
111 Coneythorpe A 12
146 Confunderland F 3
35 Congdon's Shop B 10
131 Congeith E 9
89 Congerstone B 7
90 Congham C 8
95 Congleton D 7
60 Congl-y-wal F 6
57 Congresbury H 7
144 Conicavel D 5
97 Coningsby D 9
91 Conington, Cambs. J 4
91 Conington, Cambs. G 3
112 Conisbrough G 3
113 Conisholme H 11
114 Coniston, Cumbria E 5
113 Coniston, Humber. D 9
111 Coniston Cold B 7
115 Conistone H 12
61 Connah's Quay C 12
138 Connel D 6
135 Connel Park H 11
135 Connelbush H 12
34 Connor Downs F 3
144 Cononbridge D 1
111 Cononley B 8
141 Cononsyth C 10
95 Consall E 8
133 Consett H 9
116 Constable Burton F 2
34 Constantine G 4
34 Constantine Bay B 6
142 Contin D 8
137 Conundrum D 12
147 Conveth Mains K 5
144 Convinth F 1
61 Conwy B 7
43 Conyer B 8
93 Conyer's Green H 2
42 Cooden G 6
36 Cookbury E 3
85 Cookham F 10
85 Cookham Dean F 9
85 Cookham Rise F 9
88 Cookhill F 4
88 Cookley,
Heref. & Worc. D 2
93 Cookley, Suffolk H 6
85 Cookley Green E 8
147 Cookney H 6
42 Cooksbridge G 3
86 Cooksmill Green C 6
41 Coolham D 12
42 Cooling, Kent A 6
87 Cooling, Kent F 7
42 Cooling Street A 6
34 Coombe, Cornwall D 6
36 Coombe, Cornwall E 1
38 Coombe, Devon D 4
40 Coombe, Wilts. A 3
40 Coombe Bissett C 3
57 Coombe Down H 11
57 Coombe Hay H 10
57 Coombe Hill B 12
39 Coombe Keynes H 11
42 Coombes G 1
54 Coombs F 4
144 Cooperhill D 6
42 Cooper's Corner C 4
42 Cooper's Green F 4
86 Coopersale Com. D 5
41 Cootham E 12
93 Copdock L 4
87 Copford Green B 9
152 Copister C 7
91 Cople K 2
116 Copley C 1
112 Copmanthorpe B 3
34 Coppathorne A 2
95 Coppenhall H 7
34 Copperhouse F 3
91 Coppingford G 3
39 Coppleridge D 11
36 Copplestone F 6
110 Coppull F 4
110 Coppull Moor F 4
42 Copsale F 1
110 Copster Green D 5
88 Copt Heath D 5
116 Copt Hewick H 4
89 Copt Oak A 8
42 Copthorne D 2
92 Copy's Green B 2
40 Copythorne E 5
133 Corbridge G 8
89 Corby C 12
97 Corby Glen H 7
59 Coreley E 11
85 Cores End E 10
38 Corfe D 6
40 Corfe Castle H 1
40 Corfe Mullen F 1
59 Corfton D 10
145 Corgarff J 8
41 Corhampton D 7
42 Cork's Pond D 5
88 Corley D 6
88 Corley Ash C 6
88 Corley Moor D 6
136 Cormiston F 3
139 Cormonachan H 9
141 Cormuir A 8
145 Corndavon Lodge J 8
116 Cornforth B 3
146 Cornhill B 3
137 Cornhill-on-Tweed E 11
133 Cornhills E 8
111 Cornholme D 8
91 Cornish Hall End L 8
116 Cornsay A 2
116 Cornsay Colliery A 2
144 Corntown, Mid Glam. G 3
144 Corntown, Highland D 1
147 Corntulloch H 2
35 Cornwall, County C 8
84 Cornwell A 4
37 Cornwood K 5
37 Cornworthy K 7
143 Corpach M 5
92 Corpusty C 4
139 Corran, Highland A 7
143 Corran, Highland J 2
134 Corranbuie
114 Corrany
143 Corribeg
134 Corrie
131 Corrie Common C
134 Corriecravie
142 Corriefeol
143 Corriegour
142 Corriemoillie
148 Corriemulzie Lo
145 Corrievorrie
142 Corrieviuc
143 Corrimony
87 Corringham, Essex
96 Corringham, Lincs.
58 Corris
139 Corrour Shooting
Lodge A
139 Corrow
150 Corry
144 Corry of
Ardnagrask
134 Corrygills
143 Corryhully
148 Corrykinloch
140 Corrymuckloch
138 Corrynachenchy
137 Corsbie
39 Corscombe
146 Corse, Grampian
146 Corse, Grampian
147 Corse House
146 Corse of Kinnoir
147 Corsebauld
146 Corsehill
130 Corsemalzie
57 Corhsam G
147 Corsindae
39 Corsley B
39 Corsley Heath B
135 Corsliehill
131 Corsock
57 Corston, Avon H
57 Corston, Wilts.
136 Corstorphine
147 Cortachy Castle
92 Corton, Suffolk
40 Corton, Wilts.
39 Corton Denham
139 Coruanan Lodge
61 Corwen
39 Coryates
37 Coryton, Devon
87 Coryton, Essex
89 Cosby
88 Coseley
89 Cosgrove H
41 Cosham
54 Cosheston
140 Coshieville
96 Cossall
89 Cossington
152 Costa
92 Costessey
96 Costock
96 Coston, Leics.
92 Coston, Norfolk
132 Cote
94 Cotebrook
132 Cotehill
95 Cotes, Cumbria
95 Cotes, Staffs.
89 Cotesbach
96 Cotgrave
146 Cothall
96 Cotham
38 Cothelstone
115 Cotherstone
137 Cothill, Borders
84 Cothill, Oxon
38 Cotleigh
96 Cotmanhay
91 Coton, Cambs.
89 Coton, Northants.
95 Coton, Staffs.
95 Coton, Staffs.
95 Coton Clanford
95 Coton in the Clay
88 Coton in the Elms
37 Cott
110 Cottam, Lancs.
96 Cottam, Notts.
144 Cottartown
91 Cottenham
115 Cotterdale
86 Cottered
90 Cotterstock
89 Cottesbrooke
89 Cottesmore
38 Cotteylands

135 Earlston, Strathclyde F 9
88 Earlswood E 5
57 Earlswood Com. E 8
41 Earnley F 9
133 Earsdon, Northumb. D 10
133 Earsdon, Tyne & Wear F 11
92 Earsham F 6
112 Earswick A 4
41 Eartham E 10
114 Earystane H 1
116 Easby, N. Yorks. D 6
116 Easby, N. Yorks. E 2
138 Easdale F 5
41 Easebourne D 10
89 Easenhall D 8
41 Eashing B 11
85 Easington, Bucks. C 8
117 Easington, Cleveland C 7
116 Easington, Dur. A 4
113 Easington, Humberside E 11
133 Easington, Northumb. C 12
85 Easington, Oxon. D 7
116 Easington Colliery A 4
133 Easington Grange B 12
133 Easington Lane H 12
116 Easingwold H 5
43 Easole Street C 11
141 Eassie & Nevay C 8
56 East Aberthaw H 4
84 East Adderbury A 6
37 East Allington L 6
133 East Ancroft A 11
116 East Appleton E 3
36 East Anstey C 7
41 East Ashling E 9
146 East Auchronie F 6
117 East Ayton G 10
56 East Bank D 5
97 East Barkwith B 9
42 East Barming C 6
117 East Barnby D 8
86 East Barnet D 3
137 East Barns B 9
92 East Barsham B 2
92 East Beckham B 5
86 East Bedfont F 1
93 East Bergholt M 4
92 East Bilney D 3
137 East Blanerne D 11
42 East Blatchington H 4
39 East Bloxworth G 12
133 East Boldon G 11
40 East Boldre F 5
133 East Bolton A 9
135 East Brackenridge E 11
92 East Bradenham E 2
39 East Brent A 7
93 East Bridge J 7
96 East Bridgford F 4
133 East Brunton F 10
36 East Buckland C 5
38 East Budleigh H 4
152 East Burra E 7
152 East Burrafirth D 7
39 East Burton G 11
116 East Butsfield A 1
112 East Butterwick G 6
147 East Cairnbeg K 5
136 East Calder C 4
92 East Carleton E 5
89 East Carlton C 11
84 East Challow E 5
39 East Chelborough F 9
42 East Chiltington G 3
39 East Chinnock E 8
40 East Chisenbury A 3
41 East Clandon A 12
85 East Claydon B 8
57 East Clevedon G 7
149 East Clyne F 9
39 East Coker E 9
38 East Combe C 5
39 East Compton B 9
112 East Cottingwith C 5
40 East Cowes F 6
112 East Cowick E 4
116 East Cowton E 3
133 East Cramlington E 11
39 East Cranmore B 10
40 East Creech H 1
145 East Croachy G 2
134 East Darlochan G 2
40 East Dean, Hants C 4
41 East Dean, W. Sussex E 10
92 East Dereham D 3
133 East Ditchburn A 9
36 East Down B 5
96 East Drayton C 5
57 East Dundry H 9
133 East Edington E 10
57 East End, Avon G 8
40 East End, Dorset F 2
84 East End, Hants. H 5
41 East End, Hants. D 8
40 East End, Hants. F 5
86 East End, Herts A 4
113 East End, Humber. D 10
43 East End, Kent E 7
92 East End, Norfolk D 8
84 East End, Oxon C 5
40 East Erlestoke A 1
42 East Farleigh C 6
89 East Farndon D 10
112 East Ferry G 6
133 East Fleetham D 12
141 East Flisk E 8
137 East Fortune A 8
112 East Garforth D 2
84 East Garston F 5
84 East Ginge E 5
137 East Gordon E 9
84 East Grafton H 4
40 East Grimstead C 4
42 East Grinstead D 3
43 East Guldeford F 8
89 East Haddon E 10
84 East Hagbourne E 6
113 East Halton E 9
113 East Halton Skitter E 9
86 East Ham F 4
84 East Hanney E 5
87 East Hanningfield D 7
112 East Hardwick E 2
93 East Harling G 3
116 East Harlsey E 4
40 East Harnham C 3
39 East Harptree A 9
133 East Hartford E 11
41 East Harting D 9
39 East Hatch C 12
91 East Hatley K 4
140 East Haugh B 4
116 East Hauxwell F 2
141 East Haven D 10
90 East Heckington A 3
116 East Hedleyhope A 2
84 East Hendred E 5
117 East Heslerton G 9
42 East Hoathly F 4
39 East Horrington B 9
41 East Horsley A 12
133 East Horton C 11
39 East Huntspill B 7
85 East Hyde B 12
36 East Ilkerton A 6
84 East Ilsley F 6
97 East Keal D 11
84 East Kennett G 2
111 East Keswick C 12
135 East Kilbride D 11
146 East Kinharrachie D 7
97 East Kirkley D 10
117 East Knapton G 9
39 East Knighton H 11
36 East Knowstone D 7
39 East Knoyle C 12
39 East Lambrook D 7
43 East Langdon C 12
89 East Langton C 10
149 East Langwell F 7
41 East Lavant E 10
116 East Layton D 2
96 East Leake H 3
36 East Leigh E 6
137 East Learmouth F 11
92 East Lexham D 2
133 East Lilburn A 8
137 East Linton B 8
41 East Liss C 9
135 East Lockhead D 8
35 East Looe D 9
112 East Lound G 6
41 East Lovington E10
39 East Lulworth H 12
117 East Lutton H 9
39 East Lydford C 9
147 East Mains H 4
42 East Malling B 6
41 East Marden E 9
96 East Markham C 5
111 East Marton B 8
41 East Meon D 8
38 East Mere E 3
87 East Mersea C 10
85 East Molesey G 12
39 East Mordon G 12
131 East Morton, Dumf. & Gall. B 9
111 East Morton, W. Yorks. C 9
130 East Muntloch H 2
117 East Ness G 7
89 East Norton B 11
38 East Nynehead D 5
41 East Oakley A 7
37 East Ogwell J 7
39 East Orchard D 11
137 East Ord D 12
37 East Panson G 2
42 East Peckham C 5
39 East Pennard C 9
92 East Poringland E 6
37 East Portlemouth M 6
37 East Prawle M 6
41 East Preston F 12
38 East Quantoxhead B 5
133 East Rainton H 11
113 East Ravendale G 10
92 East Raynham C 2
96 East Retford B 4
111 East Rigton C 12
116 East Rounton E 4
92 East Rudham C 1
92 East Runton A 5
92 East Ruston C 6
137 East Saltoun C 7
132 East Scales F 1
84 East Shefford G 5
133 East Sleekburn E 11
92 East Somerton D 8
112 East Stockwith H 6
39 East Stoke, Dorset H 12
96 East Stoke, Notts. E 5
39 East Stour D 11
43 East Stourmouth B 11
36 East Stowford C 5
41 East Stratton B 7
43 East Studdal C 11
42 East Sussex, Co F 5
35 East Taphouse C 9
87 East Tilbury F 7
131 East Tinwald C 11
41 East Tistead C 8
97 East Torrington B 8
147 East Town J 5
92 East Tuddenham D 4
40 East Tytherley C 4
84 East Tytherton G 1
36 East Village E 7
90 East Walton D 8
36 East Warlington E 6
37 East Week G 5
40 East Wellow D 5
141 East Wemyss G 8
136 East Whitburn C 2
87 East Wick D 10
54 East Williamston F 4
90 East Winch D 8
41 East Wittering F 9
116 East Witton G 2
133 East Woodburn D 7
84 East Woodhay H 5
41 East Worldham B 9
92 East Wretham F 2
36 East Youlstone D 1
42 Eastbourne H 5
113 Eastburn B 7
86 Eastbury, Herts E 1
84 Eastbury, Berks F 4
43 Eastchurch A 8
57 Eastcombe D 12
86 Eastcote, London E 1
89 Eastcote, Northants G 10
88 Eastcote, W. Midlands D 5
36 Eastcott, Devon D 1
40 Eastcott, Wilts A 2
84 Eastcourt, Wilts. H 3
84 Eastcourt, Wilts. E 1
42 Eastdean H 4
87 Eastend E 9
145 Easter Aberchalder G 1
144 Easter Ardross B 2
144 Easter Balcroy E 4
145 Easter Balmoral K 8
145 Easter Boleskine G 1
144 Easter Brae C 2
57 Easter Compton F 9
142 Easter Crochail F 8
144 Easter Culbo D 2
147 Easter Davoch G 2
143 Easter Drummond H 8
140 Easter Dullater F 1
131 Easter Earshaig A 11
149 Easter Fearn H 7
132 Easter Fodderlee B 4
144 Easter Galcantray E 4
88 Easter Green D 6
136 Easter Happrew E 4
136 Easter Howgate C 5
137 Easter Howlaws E 10
144 Easter Kinkell D 1
137 Easter Langlee F 8
141 Easter Lednathie A 8
144 Easter Milton D 5
144 Easter Moniack E 1
144 Easter Muckovie E 3
141 Easter Ogil A 9
147 Easter Ord G 6
135 Easter Pencaitland B 7
152 Easter Quarff E 7
146 Easter Silverford A 5
152 Easter Skeld D 6
137 Easter Softlaw F 10
147 Easter Tillygarmond H 4
147 Easter Tulloch K 5
144 Easterfield E 3
41 Eastergate F 11
135 Easterhouse, Strathclyde C 11
136 Easterhouse, Strathclyde D 3
40 Easterton A 2
146 Eastertown, Grampian D 1
136 Eastertown, Strathclyde F 2
136 Eastertown, Strathclyde E 3
39 Eastertown, Som. A 7
146 Eastertown of Auchleuchries D 8
147 Eastfield, Grampian H 1
117 Eastfield, N. Yorks G 10
136 Eastfield, Strathclyde C 2
136 Eastfield, Strathclyde E 2
133 Eastfield Hall B 10
137 Eastfield of Lempitlaw F 10
115 Eastgate, Dur. A 11
92 Eastgate, Norfolk C 4
94 Eastham B 2
85 Easthampstead G 9
85 Eastheath G 9
36 East-the-Water C 3
59 Easthope C 11
87 Easthorpe, Essex B 9
96 Easthorpe, Notts. E 4
136 Easthouses C 6
36 Eastington, Devon E 6
57 Eastington, Glos. D 11
84 Eastington, Glos. C 2
84 Eastleach Martin D 3
84 Eastleach Turville D 3
36 Eastleigh, Devon C 4
40 Eastleigh, Hants D 6
43 Eastling B 8
133 Eastnook D 8
57 Eastnor A 10
112 Eastoft E 6
41 Eastoke F 8
91 Easton, Cambs H 2
132 Easton, Cumb. G 1
132 Easton, Cumb. F 3
37 Easton, Devon G 6
39 Easton, Dorset H 7
40 Easton, Hants. C 6
40 Easton, I.o.W. G 5
96 Easton, Leics. G 6
92 Easton, Norfolk D 4
39 Easton, Somerset A 8
93 Easton, Suffolk J 6
57 Easton, Wilts. G 12
57 Easton Grey E 12
57 Easton-in-Gordano G 8
89 Easton Maudit F 12
90 Easton-on-the-Hill E 1
84 Easton Royal H 3
90 Eastrea F 4
132 Eastriggs F 1
112 Eastrington D 5
43 Eastry C 11
57 Eastville E 11
96 Eastwell G 5
86 Eastwick C 4
87 Eastwood, Essex E 8
96 Eastwood, Notts F 2
89 Eathorpe E 7
94 Eaton, Cheshire D 4
95 Eaton, Cheshire D 7
96 Eaton, Leics B 4
96 Eaton, Leics G 5
92 Eaton, Norfolk E 5
84 Eaton, Oxon. D 5
59 Eaton, Salop C 9
59 Eaton, Salop. C 10
59 Eaton Bishop H 10
85 Eaton Bray B 10
59 Eaton Constantine B 11
85 Eaton Green B 10
91 Eaton Socon J 3
94 Eaton upon Tern H 5
117 Ebberston G 9
40 Ebbesbourne Wake D 2
56 Ebbw Vale C 5
133 Ebchester G 9
57 Ebdon H 7
38 Ebford G 3
57 Ebley D 11
88 Ebrington H 5
37 Ebsworthy Town G 4
84 Ecchinswell H 6
137 Ecclaw C 10
131 Ecclefechan D12
137 Eccles, Borders E 10
42 Eccles, Kent B 6
110 Eccles, Manchester G 6
59 Eccles Green H 9
92 Eccles Road F 3
137 Eccles Tofts E 10
96 Ecclesall B 1
111 Ecclesfield H 12
147 Ecclesgreig L 5
95 Eccleshall G 7
111 Eccleshill D 10
136 Ecclesmachan B 3
94 Eccleston, Ches. D 3
110 Eccleston, Lancs. E 4
110 Eccleston, Merseyside H 4
111 Eccup C 11
147 Echt G 5
137 Eckford G 9
88 Eckington H 3
89 Ecton F 11
95 Edale B 9
42 Edburton G 1
131 Edderside G 11
149 Edderton H 7
84 Eddington, Berks. G 4
43 Eddington, Kent A 10
36 Eddistone D 1
136 Eddleston E 5
135 Eddlewood D 12
137 Eden Hall F 10
42 Edenbridge C 3
111 Edenfield E 7
115 Edenhall B 8
90 Edenham C 2
95 Edensor C 11
139 Edentaggart H 10
112 Edenthorpe F 4
132 Edentown G 2
60 Edern F 2
39 Edgarley C 8
88 Edgbaston D 4
85 Edgcott, Bucks. B 8
38 Edgcott, Som. B 2
59 Edge B 9
57 Edge End C 9
94 Edge Green, Ches. E 3
93 Edge Green, Norf. G 3
94 Edge Hill A 2
94 Edgebolton H 4
92 Edgefield B 4
92 Edgefield Green B 6
94 Edgemond H 6
132 Edgerston B 5
132 Edges Green F 5
111 Edgeside E 7
57 Edgeworth D 12
36 Edgeworthy E 7
94 Edgmond H 6
94 Edgmond Marsh H 6
59 Edgton D 9
86 Edgware E 2
110 Edgworth E 6
140 Edinample E 1
150 Edinbain C 3
136 Edinburgh B 5
88 Edingale A 6
96 Edingley E 4
92 Edingthorpe B 6
137 Edington, Borders D 11
39 Edington, Som. B 7
40 Edington, Wilts. A 1
39 Edington Burtle B 7
39 Edingworth A 7
146 Edintore C 2
89 Edith Weston B 12
38 Edithmead A 6
85 Edlesborough B 10
133 Edlingham B 9
97 Edlington C 9
40 Edmondsham E 2
133 Edmondsley H 10
96 Edmondthorpe H 6
152 Edmonstone C 3
86 Edmonton E 3
133 Edmundbyers H
137 Ednam F
139 Edra F
137 Edrom D
94 Edstaston G
88 Edstone
59 Edvin Loach G
96 Edwalton G
93 Edwardstone
55 Edwinsford D
96 Edwinstowe D
91 Edworth
59 Edwyn Ralph G
147 Edzell K
56 Efail Isaf
60 Efailnewydd
61 Efail-rhyd H
54 Efailwen
61 Efenechtyd E
41 Effingham A
152 Effirth
36 Efford
43 Egerton, Kent
110 Egerton, Manchester
37 Eggbuckland K
85 Eggington B
116 Egglescliffe
115 Eggleston C
85 Egham G
89 Egleton A
133 Eglingham
35 Egloshayle
35 Egloskerry
56 Eglwys-Brewis
61 Eglwysbach
58 Eglwysfach
54 Eglwyswrw
96 Egmanton
114 Egremont, Cumb
94 Egremont, Merseyside
117 Egton
117 Egton Bridge
85 Egypt F
87 Eight Ash Green
138 Eignaig
143 Eilanreach
137 Eildon
148 Eilean Darach
144 Eileanach Lodge
151 Eishken
58 Elan Village
57 Elberton
37 Elburton
140 Elcho
84 Elcombe
90 Eldernell
57 Eldersfield A
116 Eldon
130 Eldrick
110 Eldroth
111 Eldwick C
58 Elerch
147 Elfhill
133 Elford, Northumb. D
88 Elford, Staffs
144 Elgin
150 Elgol
43 Elham D
141 Elie
133 Elilaw
60 Elim
40 Eling
150 Elishader
133 Elishaw
96 Elkesley
84 Elkstone
145 Ellan
111 Elland
134 Ellary
95 Ellastone
110 Ellel
137 Ellemford
95 Ellenhall
41 Ellen's Green
116 Ellerbeck
117 Ellerby
94 Ellerdine Heath
38 Ellerhayes
139 Elleric
113 Ellerker
112 Ellerton, Humber.
116 Ellerton, N. Yorks.
94 Ellerton, Salop
85 Ellesborough
94 Ellesmere
94 Ellesmere Port
40 Ellingham, Hants
92 Ellingham, Norf.
133 Ellingham, Northumb.

96 Haughton, Notts. ....C 4
59 Haughton, Salop. ...A 11
59 Haughton, Salop. ...C 12
94 Haughton, Salop. ....G 2
95 Haughton, Staffs. ....H 7
133 Haughton Castle .....F 7
111 Haughton Green ....H 8
94 Haughton Moss .....E 4
88 Haunton ....A 6
133 Hauxley ....C 11
41 Havant ....F 8
59 Haven ....G 9
112 Havercroft ....F 2
54 Haverfordwest ......E 3
91 Haverhill ....L 8
114 Haverigg ....G 4
86 Havering ....E 5
86 Havering-atte-Bower .E 5
89 Haversham ....H 11
114 Haverthwaite ....G 6
116 Haverton Hill ....C 5
61 Hawarden ....D 12
87 Hawbush Green .....B 8
55 Hawen ....B 7
115 Hawes ....F 11
88 Hawford ....F 2
132 Hawick ....B 3
95 Hawk Green ....B 8
39 Hawkchurch ....F 7
93 Hawkedon ....K 1
42 Hawkenbury ....D 5
39 Hawkeridge ....A 11
88 Hawkes End ....D 6
57 Hawkesbury ....F 10
57 Hawkesbury Upton .F 11
133 Hawkhill ....B 10
42 Hawkhurst ....E 6
41 Hawkley ....C 8
38 Hawkridge ....C 2
110 Hawkshaw ....F 6
114 Hawkshead ....E 6
114 Hawkshead Hill .....E 6
136 Hawksland ....E 1
115 Hawkswick ....H 12
96 Hawksworth, Notts...E 5
111 Hawksworth,
W. Yorks.........C 10
86 Hawkwell ....E 8
42 Hawley ....A 4
85 Hawley ....H 9
84 Hawling ....B 2
116 Hawnby ....F 5
111 Haworth ....D 9
93 Hawstead ....J 1
116 Hawthorn, Dur. .....A 4
57 Hawthorn, Wilts. ...G 11
132 Hawthornside ....B 4
90 Hawthorpe ....C 2
96 Hawton ....E 5
112 Haxby ....A 4
112 Haxey ....G 5
42 Haxted ....D 3
59 Hay-on-Wye ....H 8
86 Hay Street ....A 4
54 Haycastle ....D 2
54 Haycastle Cross .....D 3
110 Haydock ....G 4
39 Haydon, Dorset ....E 10
133 Haydon, Northumb...F 7
133 Haydon Bridge ......G 7
84 Haydon Wick ....E 2
35 Haye ....C 10
86 Hayes, Kent ....G 4
86 Hayes, London ......F 1
95 Hayfield, Derby .....B 9
141 Hayfield, Fife ....H 7
135 Hayhill ....H 9
34 Hayle ....F 3
41 Hayling Island ....F 8
137 Haymount ....F 9
38 Hayne ....F 2
91 Haynes ....L 2
91 Haynes West End ....L 2
42 Haysden ....D 4
141 Hayshead ....C 11
131 Hayton, Cumb. ....G 11
132 Hayton, Cumb. ......G 3
147 Hayton, Grampian ...G 7
112 Hayton, Humber. ....C 6
96 Hayton, Notts. ....B 4
59 Hayton's Bent ......D 10
37 Haytor Vale ....H 6
42 Hayward's Heath ....F 2
96 Haywood Oaks ......E 3
95 Hazel Grove ....B 8
136 Hazelbank ....E 1
39 Hazelbury Bryan ....E 11
85 Hazeley ....H 8
88 Hazelslade ....A 4
141 Hazelton Walls ......E 8
95 Hazelwood ....F 11
85 Hazlemere ....E 10
133 Hazlerigg ....F 10
84 Hazleton ....B 2
133 Hazon ....C 10
90 Heacham ....B 8
40 Headbourne Worthy .C 6
59 Headbrook ....G 8
43 Headcorn ....D 7
111 Headingley ....D 11
84 Headington ....C 6
116 Headlam ....C 2
88 Headless Cross .....F 4
41 Headley, Hants. .....C 9
84 Headley, Hants. .....H 6
42 Headley, Surrey ....C 1
41 Headley Down .....B 10
96 Headon ....C 5
135 Heads ....E 12
132 Heads Nook ....G 3
96 Heage ....E 1
115 Healaugh, N. Yorks. E 12
112 Healaugh, N. Yorks. .B 3
36 Heale, Devon ....A 5
39 Heale, Somerset ....B 10
111 Healey, Lancs. ....E 7
133 Healey, Nothumb. ...G 8
116 Healey, N. Yorks. ...G 2
133 Healey Cote ....C 9
133 Healeyfield ....H 9
113 Healing ....F 10
34 Heamor ....G 2
96 Heanor ....F 2
36 Heanton Punchardon .B 4
96 Heapham ....A 6
136 Hearthstane ....G 4
36 Heasley Mill ....C 6
150 Heast ....F 6
96 Heath ....C 2
85 Heath and Reach ...A 10
36 Heath Cross ....F 7
85 Heath End, Berks. ...H 7
41 Heath End, Surrey ..A 10
88 Heath End,
W. Midlands ......B 4
88 Heath Hayes ....A 4
88 Heath Hill ....A 1
39 Heath House ....B 7
38 Heath Pault Cross ...C 3
88 Heath Town ....B 3
95 Heathcote ....D 10
89 Heather ....A 7
150 Heatherfield ....D 4
149 Heatherwood Park ...G 8
140 Heatheryhaugh ......B 6
131 Heathfield, Cumb. ..G 12
37 Heathfield, Devon ...H 7
42 Heathfield, East Sussex F 4
38 Heathfield, Som. ....D 5
135 Heathfield, Strathclyde C 8
131 Heathhall ....D 10
88 Heathton ....C 2
94 Heatley ....A 5
110 Heaton, Lancs. ......A 3
111 Heaton, Manchester .H 7
95 Heaton, Staffs. ......D 8
111 Heaton, W. Yorks...D 10
110 Heaton's Bridge ......F 3
42 Heaverham ....B 4
38 Heavitree ....G 3
133 Hebburn ....G 11
111 Hebden ....A 9
111 Hebden Bridge ......D 8
94 Hebden Green ....D 5
54 Hebron, Dyfed ......D 5
133 Hebron, Northumb. D 10
131 Heck ....D 11
85 Heckfield ....H 8
93 Heckfield Green .....H 5
90 Heckington ....A 2
136 Hecklebirnie ....F 2
111 Heckmondwike .....E 10
84 Heddington ....G 1
84 Heddington Wick ....G 1
36 Heddon ....C 5
133 Heddon on the Wall ..F 9
92 Hedenham ....F 6
37 Hedge Cross ....G 4
40 Hedge End ....E 6
85 Hedgerley ....E 10
38 Hedging ....C 6
133 Hedley on the Hill ..G 9
88 Hednesford ....A 3
113 Hedon ....D 9
85 Hedsor ....E 10
59 Hedgon Hill ....G 11
133 Heiferlaw Bank .....A 10
116 Heighington, Dur. ...C 3
97 Heighington, Lincs. ..C 7
144 Heights of Brae ......D 1
142 Heights of Kinlochewe C 4
148 Heilam ....B 5
137 Heiton ....F 9
38 Hele, Devon ....F 3
36 Hele, Devon ....A 4
37 Hele, Devon ....G 2
38 Hele, Somerset ......D 5
135 Helensburgh ....A 8
135 Helentongate ....F 9
34 Helford ....G 5
34 Helford Passage ....G 5
92 Helhoughton ....C 2
91 Helions Bumpstead ...L 7
35 Helland ....C 8
35 Hellandbridge ....C 8
92 Hellesdon ....D 5
89 Hellidon ....F 8
111 Hellifield ....B 7
42 Helling ....G 4
92 Hellington ....E 6
133 Helm ....C 10
89 Helmdon ....H 9
93 Helmingham ....J 5
116 Helmington Row ....B 2
149 Helmsdale ....E 10
110 Helmshore ....E 6
116 Helmsley ....G 6
116 Helperby ....H 5
117 Helperthorpe ....H 9
90 Helpringham ....B 2
90 Helpston ....E 2
94 Helsby ....C 3
34 Helston ....G 4
35 Helstone ....B 8
115 Helton ....C 7
115 Helwith Bridge .....H 10
85 Hemel Hempstead ..D 11
112 Hemingbrough ......D 4
97 Hemingby ....C 9
112 Hemongfield ....G 2
91 Hemingford Abbots ..H 4
91 Hemingford Grey ....H 4
93 Hemingstone ....K 5
96 Hemington, Leics. ...G 2
91 Hemington,
Northants. ....G 2
39 Hemington, Som. ...A 10
93 Hemley ....L 6
116 Hemlington ....D 5
88 Hempholme ....B 8
92 Hempnall ....F 5
92 Hempnall Green .....F 5
91 Hempstead, Essex ....L 7
42 Hempstead, Kent ....B 6
92 Hempstead, Norf. ....B 6
57 Hempsted ....C 11
92 Hempton, Norfolk ...C 2
84 Hempton, Oxon. ....A 5
92 Hemsby ....D 8
96 Hemswell ....A 6
112 Hemsworth ....F 2
38 Hemyock ....E 5
57 Henbury, Avon ......F 9
95 Henbury, Ches. ......C 7
36 Henderbarrow Corner F 3
86 Hendon, London .....E 2
133 Hendon,
Tyne & Wear ....G 12
57 Hendre ....C 8
56 Hendreforgan ....E 3
54 Hendre-wen ....D 3
55 Hendy ....G 9
60 Heneglwys ....C 4
54 Hen-feddau ....D 6
57 Henfield, Avon .....F 10
42 Henfield, W. Sussex ..F 1
43 Hengherst ....D 8
56 Hengoed, Mid Glam. .E 5
59 Hengoed, Powys .....G 8
94 Hengoed, Salop. .....G 2
93 Hengrave ....H 1
86 Henham ....A 5
133 Henhill ....E 12
59 Heniarth ....B 7
38 Henlade ....D 6
133 Henlaw ....C 11
39 Henley, Dorset .....F 10
59 Henley, Salop. .....D 10
39 Henley, Somerset ....C 8
93 Henley, Suffolk .....K 5
41 Henley, W. Sussex ..D 10
88 Henley-in-Arden ....E 5
85 Henley-on-Thames ...F 8
42 Henley Street ....A 5
61 Henllan, Clwyd ......C 9
55 Henllan, Dyfed ......C 7
54 Henllan Amgoed .....E 5
56 Henllys ....E 6
91 Henlow ....L 3
37 Hennock ....H 7
93 Henny Street ....L 2
61 Henryd ....C 7
54 Henry's Moat ....D 4
112 Hensall ....E 4
132 Henshaw ....G 6
114 Hensingham ....D 2
93 Henstead ....G 8
39 Henstridge ....D 10
39 Henstridge Ash .....D 10
39 Henstridge Bowden .D 10
85 Henton, Oxon. ......D 8
39 Henton, Som. ....B 8
39 Henstridge Marsh ..D 11
88 Henwick ....G 2
35 Henwood ....B 9
152 Heogan ....D 7
56 Heol Senni ....B 3
55 Heol-las ....G 10
56 Heol-y-Cyw ....F 3
133 Hepburn ....A 9
133 Hepple ....C 8
133 Hepple Whitefield ...C 8
133 Hepscott ....E 10
111 Hepstonstall ....D 8
93 Hepworth, Suff. .....H 3
111 Hepworth, W. Yorks. F 10
54 Herbrandston ....F 2
59 Hereford ....H 10
88 Hereford & Worcester,
Co. ....F 2
136 Heriot ....D 6
137 Hermiston ....G 8
84 Hermitage, Berks. ....G 6
132 Hermitage, Borders ..C 3
39 Hermitage, Dorset ..F 10
132 Hermitage,
Dumf. & Gall. .....E 9
41 Hermitage, W. Sussex .F 9
55 Hermon, Dyfed ....D 10
54 Hermon, Dyfed ......D 5
60 Hermon, Gwynedd ...C 3
43 Herne ....B 10
43 Herne Bay ....A 10
36 Herner ....C 5
43 Hernhill ....B 9
35 Herodsfoot ....D 9
43 Heronden ....C 11
86 Herongate ....E 6
130 Heronsford ....C 2
85 Heronsgate ....E 11
41 Herriard ....B 8
92 Herringfleet ....F 8
91 Herring's Green .....L 2
91 Herringswell ....H 8
133 Herrington ....H 11
43 Hersden ....B 10
85 Hersham ....H 12
42 Herstmonceux ......G 5
40 Herston, Dorset .....H 2
152 Herston, Orkney Is. ..E 2
86 Hertford ....C 3
86 Hertford Heath ......C 3
86 Hertfordshire, Co. ...B 2
86 Hertingfordbury .....C 3
114 Hesket Newmarket ..A 6
110 Hesketh Bank ....E 3
110 Hesketh Lane ....C 5
110 Heskin Green ....F 4
116 Hesleden ....A 4
132 Hesleyside ....E 6
112 Heslington ....B 4
112 Hessay ....B 3
35 Hessenford ....D 10
93 Hessett ....J 2
135 Hessilhead ....D 9
113 Hessle ....E 8
110 Hest Bank ....A 3
86 Heston ....F 1
94 Heswall ....B 1
85 Hethe ....A 7
92 Hethersett ....E 5
132 Hethersgill ....F 3
137 Hethpool ....G 11
116 Hett ....B 3
111 Hetton ....A 8
133 Hetton Downs .....H 11
133 Hetton Law ....C 11
133 Hetton Steads .....B 11
133 Hetton-le-Hole .....H 11
133 Heugh ....F 9
146 Heugh-head ....F 1
93 Heveningham ......H 6
42 Hever ....D 4
115 Heversham ....G 7
92 Hevingham ....C 5
57 Hewelsfield ....D 9
57 Hewish, Avon ....H 7
39 Hewish, Somerset ....E 7
112 Heworth ....B 4
133 Hexham ....G 7
137 Hexpath ....E 9
42 Hextable ....A 4
37 Hexworthy ....H 5
87 Heybridge, Essex ....C 8
86 Heybridge, Essex ....D 6
87 Heydridge Basin .....C 8
37 Heybrook Bay ....L 4
91 Heydon, Cambs. .....L 5
92 Heydon, Norfolk ....C 4
97 Heydour ....F 7
110 Heysham ....A 3
111 Heyshaw ....A 10
41 Heyshott ....D 10
40 Heytesbury ....B 1
84 Heythrop ....A 4
111 Heywood, Manchester F 7
39 Heywood, Wilts. ...A 12
113 Hibaldstow ....G 7
112 Hickleton ....G 3
92 Hickling, Norfolk ...C 7
96 Hickling, Notts. ....G 4
92 Hickling Green ......C 7
88 Hidcote Bartrim .....H 5
112 High Ackworth ......E 2
133 High Angerton ......E 9
115 High Bankhill ....A 8
86 High Beach ....D 4
115 High Bentham ......H 9
36 High Bickington .....D 5
115 High Birkwith ......G 10
135 High Blantyre ......D 11
136 High Bonnybridge ...B 1
131 High Borgue ....F 7
111 High Bradley ....B 9
36 High Bray ....C 6
42 High Brooms ....D 5
36 High Bullen ....D 4
116 High Burton ....G 2
133 High Buston ....B 10
133 High Callerton .....F 10
112 High Catton ....B 5
133 High Church ....E 10
135 High Cleughearn ....E 11
84 High Cogges ....C 5
116 High Conniscliffe ....D 3
137 High Cross, Borders ..E 8
41 High Cross, Hants. ...C 8
86 High Cross, Herts. ....B 4
95 High Cross Bank ...H 11
135 High Duncryne ......A 9
86 High Easter ....B 6
116 High Ellington ......G 2
116 High Entercommon ..E 4
59 High Ercall ....A 11
116 High Etherley ....B 2
87 High Garrett ....A 7
116 High Grange ....B 2
88 High Green,
Heref. & Worcs. ...H 2
92 High Green, Norf. ....E 4
111 High Green,
S. Yorks. ....G 12
43 High Halden ....D 8
42 High Halstow ....A 6
39 High Ham ....C 8
114 High Harrington .....C 3
116 High Haswell ....A 4
94 High Hatton ....H 5
117 High Hawsker ......D 9
115 High Hesket ....A 7
116 High Hesleden ......A 5
111 High Hoyland ......F 11
113 High Hursley ....D 7
42 High Hurstwood .....E 4
117 High Hutton ....H 8
114 High Ireby ....B 5
116 High Kilburn ....G 5
95 High Lane, Manchester B 8
59 High Lane,
Heref. & Worcs. ..F 12
86 High Laver ....C 5
94 High Legh ....B 5
116 High Leven ....D 5
57 High Littleton ....H 9
114 High Lorton ....C 4
117 High Marishes ......G 8
96 High Marnham ......C 5
112 High Melton ....G 3
133 High Mickley ....G 9
130 High Mindork ....F 4
117 High Mowthorpe ....H 8
114 High Newton ....G 6
133 High Newton by-the-
Sea ....E 12
114 High Nibthwaite .....F 5
94 High Offley ....H 6
86 High Ongar ....D 5
88 High Onn ....A 2
130 High Pennyvenie .....A 6
86 High Roding ....B 6
114 High Row ....
115 High Shaw ....
116 High Skelding ......
133 High Spen ....
116 High Stoop ....
35 High Street, Corn. ...
93 High Street, Suff. ....
93 High Street, Suff. ....
93 High Street Green ....
116 High Throston .....
97 High Toynton .....
133 High Trewhitt ......
136 High Valleyfield ....
133 High Warden ......
114 High Wray ....
86 High Wych ....
85 High Wycombe .....
96 Higham, Derby .....
42 Higham, Kent ......
111 Higham, Lancs. .....
91 Higham, Suffolk .....
93 Higham, Suffolk ....
133 Higham Dykes ......
91 Higham Ferrers .....
91 Higham Gobion .....
89 Higham on the Hill ...
42 Higham Wood ......
36 Highampton ....
143 Highbridge, Highland
38 Highbridge, Som. ....
42 Highbrook ....
111 Highburton ....
39 Highbury ....
132 Highchesters ......
84 Highclere ....
40 Highcliffe ....
39 Higher Alham ......
39 Higher Ansty ......
38 Higher Ashton ......
110 Higher Ballam ......
34 Higher Boscaswell ...
38 Higher Combe .....
34 Higher Crackington .
110 Higher End ....
94 Higher Heath .....
61 Higher Kinnerton ...
39 Higher Nyland .....
110 Higher Penwortham .
95 Higher Poynton .....
34 Higher Town ....
94 Higher Walton, Ches.
110 Higher Walton, Lancs.
39 Higher Whatcombe .
94 Higher Whitley .....
94 Higher Wych ......
96 Highfield, S. Yorks. .
135 Highfield, Strathclyde
133 Highfield,
Tyne & Wear ....
91 Highfields, Cambs. ..
137 Highfields,
Northumb. ....
86 Highgate, London ...
112 Highgate, N. Yorks. .
132 Highgreen Manor ...
116 Highlands, Dur. ....
146 Highlands, Grampian
96 Highlane ....
57 Highleadon ....
41 Highleigh ....
88 Highley ....
85 Highmoor Cross ....
57 Highmoor Hill .....
57 Highnam Green ....
36 Highridge ....
43 Highsted ....
93 Highstreet Green ...
93 Hightae ....
95 Hightown, Ches. ...
131 Hightown,
Dumf. & Gall. ....
110 Hightown, Merseysid
131 Hightown of Craigs .
34 Highway, Corn. ....
84 Highway, Wilts. ....
37 Highweek ....
84 Highworth ....
92 Hilborough ....
96 Hilcote ....
84 Hilcott ....
42 Hilden Park ......
42 Hildenborough .....
91 Hildersham ....
95 Hilderstone ....
113 Hilderthorpe ......
39 Hilfield ....
90 Hilgay ....
57 Hill, Avon ....
36 Hill, Devon ....
88 Hill, W. Midlands ...

Lealholm D 8
Leatt B 4
Leamington E 7
Leamington Hastings E 8
Leamonsley A 4
Leamside H 11
Leanach H 7
Leanachan L 6
Leanaig D 1
Leargybreck B 1
Leasgill G 7
Leasingham E 7
Leasingthorne B 3
Leatherhead H 12
Leathley B 11
Leaths E 8
Leaton H 3
Leaveland C 8
Leavening A 5
Leaves Green H 4
Leavesden Green D 1
Leazes G 10
Lebberston G 10
Lechlade D 3
Leck G 9
Leckford B 5
Leckfurin B 7
Leckhampstead, Berks. G 5
Leckhampstead, Bucks. H 10
Leckhampstead Street F 5
Leckhampstead Thicket F 5
Leckhampton B 12
Leckie C 5
Leckmelm G 3
Leckroy K 7
Leckwith G 5
Leconfield C 8
Ledaig D 6
Ledburn B 10
Ledbury A 10
Ledcharrie E 12
Ledgemoor G 9
Ledgowan D 5
Ledicot F 9
Ledmore F 4
Lednagullin B 8
Ledsham, Ches. C 2
Ledsham, W. Yorks. D 2
Ledston D 2
Ledwell A 5
Lee, Devon A 4
Lee, Hampshire D 5
Lee, Lancashire B 4
Lee, Shropshire G 3
Lee Brockenhurst G 4
Lee Clump D 10
Lee Mill Bridge K 5
Lee Mill Estate K 5
Lee Moor J 4
Lee-on-the-Solent F 7
Leebotwood C 10
Leece H 5
Leeds, Kent C 7
Leeds, W. Yorks. D 11
Leedstown F 3
Leek E 8
Leek Wootton E 6
Leeming F 3
Leeming Bar F 3
Lees, Derby F 11
Lees, Manchester G 8
Lees Hill F 4
Leeswood D 12
Leftwich C 5
Legbourne B 10
Legerwood E 8
Legsby B 8
Leicester B 9
Leicestershire, Co. B 9
Leicester For. East. B 8
Leigh, Dorset E 9
Leigh, Glos. B 11
Leigh, Kent C 4
Leigh, Manchester G 5
Leigh, Shropshire B 9
Leigh, Surrey C 1
Leigh, Wiltshire E 2
Leigh, Heref. & Worc. G 1
Leigh Beck F 8
Leigh Delamere F 12
Leigh Green E 8
Leigh-on-Sea E 8
Leigh Park E 8
Leigh Sinton G 1
Leigh upon Mendip B 10
Leighland Chapel C 4
Leighterton E 11
116 Leighton, N. Yorks. G 2
59 Leighton, Powys B 8
59 Leighton, Salop B 11
39 Leighton, Som. B 10
91 Leighton Bromswold H 2
85 Leighton Buzzard B 10
147 Leightonhill L 4
57 Leighwoods G 9
59 Leinthall Earls F 10
59 Leinthall Starkes E 10
59 Leintwardine E 9
89 Leire C 8
148 Leirinmore A 5
93 Leiston J 7
141 Leitfie C 7
136 Leith B 5
137 Leitholm E 10
34 Lelant F 3
113 Lelley D 10
144 Lemlair D 1
133 Lemmington Hall B 9
137 Lempitlaw F 10
151 Lemreway F 5
86 Lemsford C 2
146 Lenabo C 8
88 Lenchwick G 4
130 Lendalfoot C 2
139 Lendrick G 12
43 Lenham C 7
43 Lenham Heath C 8
137 Lennel E 11
130 Lennies F 5
135 Lennoxtown B 11
85 Lent Rise F 10
90 Lenton C 1
92 Lenwade D 4
135 Lenzie B 11
146 Leochel-Cushnie F 3
59 Leominster F 10
57 Leonard Stanley D 11
40 Lepe F 6
150 Lephin C 1
139 Lephinchapel H 7
139 Lephinmore H 7
112 Leppington A 5
111 Lepton F 10
138 Lerags E 6
35 Lerryn D 8
152 Lerwick E 7
133 Lesbury B 10
141 Leslie, Fife G 7
146 Leslie, Grampian E 3
136 Lesmahagow E 1
34 Lesnewth B 2
92 Lessingham C 7
132 Lessonhall H 1
130 Leswalt E 1
86 Letchmore Heath D 2
91 Letchworth M 3
84 Letcombe Bassett F 5
84 Letcombe Regis E 5
141 Letham, Fife F 8
141 Letham, Tayside B 10
140 Letham, Tayside E 6
141 Letham Grange C 11
144 Lethen House D 5
145 Lethendryveole H 5
146 Lethenty D 5
93 Letheringham J 6
92 Letheringsett B 4
37 Lettaford G 6
152 Lettan A 4
142 Letterewe C 3
143 Letterfearn G 3
143 Letterfinlay K 6
143 Lettermorar K 1
138 Lettermore C 2
148 Letters H 3
136 Lettershaws G 2
54 Letterston D 3
145 Lettoch, Highland H 6
144 Lettoch, Highland F 6
59 Letton, Heref. & Worc. E 9
59 Letton, Heref. & Worc. H 9
86 Letty Green C 3
96 Letwell B 3
141 Leuchars E 9
144 Leuchars House C 8
151 Leurbost D 5
88 Levedale A 3
113 Leven, Humberside C 8
141 Leven, Fife G 8
134 Levencorroch G 5
115 Levens G 7
111 Levenshulme H 7
152 Levenwick F 7
151 Leverburgh H 1
90 Leverington D 5
84 Leverton, Berks. G 4
97 Leverton, Lincs. E 11
97 Leverton Outgate E 11
93 Levington L 5
117 Levisham F 8
143 Levishie H 8
84 Lew D 4
35 Lewannick B 9
37 Lewdown G 3
42 Lewes G 3
54 Leweston E 3
86 Lewisham G 3
145 Lewiston G 1
56 Lewistown E 3
85 Lewknor D 8
36 Leworthy B 5
151 Lews Castle D 5
43 Lewson Street B 8
37 Lewtrenchard G 3
35 Ley, Cornwall C 9
146 Ley, Grampian F 3
42 Leybourne B 5
116 Leyburn F 1
94 Leycett E 6
86 Leygreen B 2
85 Leyhill D 10
110 Leyland E 4
146 Leylodge F 5
146 Leys B 7
144 Leys Castle F 2
141 Leys of Cossans B 8
146 Leys of Dummuies D 3
43 Leysdown-on-Sea A 9
141 Leysmill B 10
86 Leyton E 4
86 Leytonstone E 4
35 Lezant B 10
142 Liatrie F 6
56 Libanus B 3
136 Liberton, Lothian B 5
136 Libberton, Strathclyde E 3
88 Lichfield A 5
88 Lickey E 3
88 Lickey End E 3
41 Lickfold D 10
138 Liddesdale B 5
84 Liddington F 3
91 Lidgate J 8
91 Lidlington L 1
84 Lidstone B 4
143 Lienassie G 3
141 Liff D 8
37 Lifton G 3
37 Liftondown G 2
89 Lighthorne G 7
85 Lightwater H 10
95 Lightwood F 7
89 Lilbourne D 9
137 Lilburn Hill G 12
133 Lilburn Tower A 8
88 Lilleshall A 1
84 Lilley, Berks. F 5
86 Lilley, Herts. A 1
137 Lilliesleaf G 8
89 Lillingstone Dayrell H 10
89 Lillingstone Lovell H 10
39 Lillington, Dorest E 9
89 Lillington, War. E 7
40 Lilliput G 2
38 Lilstock B 5
135 Lilybank B 8
110 Limbrick F 5
111 Limefield F 7
135 Limekilnburn D 12
136 Limekilns A 3
136 Limerigg B 1
40 Limestone H 6
132 Limestone Brae H 6
39 Limington D 8
92 Limpenhoe E 7
57 Limpley Stoke H 11
42 Limpsfield C 3
136 Linburn C 4
96 Linby E 3
41 Linchmere C 10
131 Lincluden D 10
97 Lincoln C 7
97 Lincolnshire, Co. D 8
88 Lincomb E 2
114 Lindal in Furness H 5
114 Lindale G 6
137 Lindean F 7
42 Lindfield E 2
41 Lindford C 9
141 Lindifferon E 8
111 Lindley E 10
111 Lindley Green B 11
141 Lindores E 7
59 Lindridge E 12
86 Lindsell A 6
93 Lindsey L 3
114 Linefoot B 3
87 Linford, Essex F 7
40 Linford, Hants. E 3
114 Lingague H 1
117 Lingdale D 7
59 Lingen F 9
42 Lingfield D 3
42 Lingfield Com. D 3
94 Lingley Green A 4
92 Lingwood E 7
132 Linhope, Borders C 2
133 Linhope, N'thumb. A 8
84 Linkenholt H 5
35 Linkinhorne B 10
152 Linklater E 2
141 Linktown H 7
59 Linley Green G 12
136 Linlithgow B 3
136 Linlithgow Bridge B 3
148 Linneraineach F 3
54 Linney G 2
131 Linns D 11
151 Linshader D 3
133 Linshiels B 7
148 Linsidemore G 6
85 Linslade B 10
93 Linstead Parva G 6
132 Linstock G 3
137 Linthaugh F 12
111 Linthwaite F 9
137 Lintlaw D 11
146 Lintmill A 3
137 Linton, Borders G 10
91 Linton, Cambs. K 7
88 Linton, Derby A 6
57 Linton, Heref. & Worc. B 9
42 Linton, Kent C 6
111 Linton, N. Yorks. A 8
111 Linton, W. Yorks. B 12
112 Linton-on-Ouse A 3
40 Linwood, Hants. E 3
97 Linwood, Lincs. B 8
135 Linwood, Strathclyde C 9
61 Lioc C 10
151 Lionel A 6
41 Liphook C 9
38 Liscombe C 2
35 Liskeard C 9
41 Liss C 9
41 Liss Forest C 9
113 Lisset A 9
97 Lissington B 8
56 Lisvane F 5
57 Liswerry F 7
92 Litcham D 2
89 Litchborough G 9
40 Litchfield A 6
110 Litherland G 2
91 Litlington, Camb. L 4
42 Litlington, E. Sussex H 4
91 Little Abington K 6
91 Little Addington H 1
88 Little Alne F 5
148 Little Assynt E 3
88 Little Aston B 4
40 Little Atherfield H 6
152 Little Ayre E 1
116 Little Ayton D 6
87 Little Baddow C 7
57 Little Badminton F 11
140 Little Ballinluig B 4
132 Little Bampton G 1
91 Little Bardfield M 8
91 Little Barford J 3
92 Little Barningham B 4
84 Little Barrington C 3
94 Little Barrow C 3
117 Little Barugh G 8
133 Little Bavington E 8
93 Little Bealings K 5
84 Little Bedwyn G 4
87 Little Bentley A 11
86 Little Berkhampsted C 3
89 Little Billing F 11
57 Little Birch A 8
93 Little Blakenham K 4
115 Little Blencow B 7
41 Little Bookham A 12
89 Little Bowden C 11
91 Little Bradley K 8
59 Little Brampton D 9
87 Little Braxted B 8
147 Little Brechin L 3
85 Little Brickhill A 10
89 Little Brington F 10
87 Little Bromley A 10
94 Little Budworth D 5
86 Little Burstead E 6
90 Little Bytham D 1
130 Little Cairnbrock E 1
97 Little Carlton, Lincs. B 11
96 Little Carlton, Notts. D 5
90 Little Casterton E 1
97 Little Cawthorpe B 10
85 Little Chalfont D 11
43 Little Chart D 8
39 Little Cheney G 9
91 Little Chesterford L 6
40 Little Cheverell A 2
91 Little Chishill L 5
87 Little Clacton B 11
114 Little Clifton B 3
146 Little Colp C 5
88 Little Comberton H 3
84 Little Compton A 4
93 Little Cornard L 2
59 Little Cowarne G 11
84 Little Coxwell E 4
116 Little Crakehall F 3
92 Little Cressingham E 2
110 Little Crosby G 2
89 Little Dalby A 11
59 Little Dawley B 12
146 Little Dens C 8
57 Little Dewchurch A 8
113 Little Driffield A 8
92 Little Dunham D 2
140 Little Dunkeld C 5
86 Little Dunmow B 6
86 Little Easton B 6
95 Little Eaton F 12
92 Little Ellingham E 3
39 Little Elm B 10
86 Little End D 5
91 Little Eversden K 5
93 Little Fakenham H 2
84 Little Faringdon D 3
116 Little Fencote F 3
112 Little Fenton D 3
92 Little Fransham D 2
85 Little Gaddesden C 11
57 Little Garway B 8
91 Little Gidding G 2
93 Little Glemham J 6
91 Little Gransden K 4
39 Little Green A 10
97 Little Grimsby A 10
148 Little Gruinard G 1
86 Little Hadham B 4
90 Little Hale B 2
86 Little Hallingbury B 5
85 Little Hampden D 9
89 Little Harrowden E 12
85 Little Haseley D 7
113 Little Hatfield C 9
54 Little Haven F 2
88 Little Hay B 5
95 Little Hayfield A 9
95 Little Haywood H 8
59 Little Hereford F 11
93 Little Horkesley M 2
86 Little Hormead A 4
42 Little Horsted F 3
111 Little Horton D 10
85 Little Horwood A 9
89 Little Houghton F 11
95 Little Hucklow B 10
110 Little Hulton G 6
89 Little Irchester E 12
113 Little Kelk A 8
85 Little Kimble C 9
85 Little Kingshill D 10
114 Little Langdale E 5
40 Little Langford C 2
146 Little Ledikin E 4
94 Little Leigh C 5
87 Little Leighs B 7
110 Little Lever F 6
89 Little Linford H 11
42 Little Londond, E. Sussex F 4
40 Little London, Hants. A 5
85 Little London, Hants. H 7
90 Little London, Lincs. C 5
111 Little London, W. Yorks. C 10
95 Little Longstone C 10
146 Little Lynturk F 3
88 Little Malvern H 1
93 Little Maplestead M 1
57 Little Marcle A 10
85 Little Marlow E 9
92 Little Massingham C 1
92 Little Melton E 5
54 Little Milford F 3
56 Little Mill D 6
85 Little Milton D 7
85 Little Missenden D 10
94 Little Ness H 3
94 Little Neston C 2
54 Little Newcastle D 3
116 Little Newsham C 1
87 Little Oakley, Essex A 12
89 Little Oakley, Northants. D 12
132 Little Orton G 2
112 Little Ouseburn A 2
91 Little Paxton J 3
34 Little Petherick B 6
130 Little Pinmore C 3
92 Little Plumstead D 6
96 Little Ponton G 6
36 Little Potheridge E 4
91 Little Raveley G 4
111 Little Ribson B 12
84 Little Rissington B 3
92 Little Ryburgh C 3
133 Little Ryle B 8
115 Little Salkeld B 8
40 Little Samborne C 5
91 Little Sampford M 7
85 Little Sandhurst H 9
93 Little Saxham J 1
142 Little Scatwell D 7
91 Little Shelford K 5
36 Little Silver, Devon F 7
38 Little Silver, Devon E 3
110 Little Singleton C 3
112 Little Smeaton E 3
92 Little Snoring B 2
57 Little Sodbury F 10
84 Little Somerford F 1
116 Little Stainton C 4
94 Little Stanney C 3
91 Little Staughton J 2
97 Little Steeping D 11
93 Little Stonham J 4
89 Little Stretton, Leics. B 10
59 Little Stretton, Shropshire C 10
115 Little Strickland C 8
91 Little Stukeley H 3
133 Little Swinburne E 8
137 Little Swinton E 11
84 Little Tew A 5
91 Little Thetford H 6
91 Little Thurlow K 8
86 Little Thurrock F 6
130 Little Torhouse F 5
36 Little Torrington D 4
133 Little Tosson C 8
87 Little Totham C 9
114 Little Town C 5
144 Little Urchany E 4
114 Little Urswick H 5
87 Little Wakering E 9
93 Little Waldingfield L 2
92 Little Walsingham B 2
87 Little Waltham C 7
86 Little Warley E 6
113 Little Weighton D 7
93 Little Welnetham J 2
59 Little Wenlock B 12
93 Little Whittingham Green H 6
133 Little Whittington F 8
91 Little Wilbraham J 6
40 Little Wishford B 2
88 Little Witley F 1
84 Little Wittenham E 6
84 Little Wolford A 3
89 Little Woolstone H 12
91 Little Wymington J 1
86 Little Wymondley A 2
88 Little Wyrley B 4
93 Little Yeldam L 1
152 Little-ayre C 6
117 Littlebeck E 9
111 Littleborough, Manchester F 8
96 Littleborough, Notts. B 5
43 Littlebourne B 10
39 Littlebredy G 9
91 Littlebury L 6
110 Littledale A 4
57 Littledean C 10
149 Littleferry G 8
36 Littleham, Devon D 3
38 Littleham, Devon H 4
41 Littlehampton F 11
37 Littlehempston J 7
133 Littlehoughton A 10
147 Littlemill, Grampian H 1
144 Littlemill, Highland E 5
133 Littlemill, Northumb. A 10
135 Littlemill, Strathclyde H 9
84 Littlemore D 6
95 Littleover G 11

Newby, N. Yorks. ... H 9
Newby Bridge ... G 6
Newby East ... G 3
Newby West ... H 2
Newby Wiske ... F 4
Newcastle, Gwent ... C 7
Newcastle, Salop ... D 8
Newcastle Emlyn ... C 6
Newcastle-under-Lyme F 7
Newcastle upon Tyne F 10
Newcastleton ... D 3
Newchapel, Dyfed ... C 6
Newchapel, Staffs. ... E 7
Newchapel, Surrey ... D 2
Newchurch, Dyfed ... E 7
Newchurch, Gwent ... E 8
Newchurch, I.o.W. ... H 7
Newchurch, Kent ... E 9
Newchurch, Lancs. ... C 7
Newchurch, Lancs. ... E 7
Newchurch, Powys ... G 7
Newchurch, Staffs. . H 10
Newcott ... E 6
Newdigate ... D 1
Newell Green ... G 9
Newenden ... E 7
Newent ... B 10
Newerne ... D 9
Newfield, Dumf. & Gall. ... E 12
Newfield, Dumf. & Gall. ... E 9
Newfield, Dur. ... B 2
Newfield, Dur. ... H 10
Newfield, Highland ... B 3
Newfound ... A 7
Newglae ... E 2
Newgate ... A 3
Newgate Street ... C 3
Newgord ... A 8
Newhall, Borders ... F 6
Newhall, Ches. ... F 5
Newhall, Derby ... H 11
Newhallpoint ... C 3
Newham, London ... F 4
Newham, Northumb. E 12
Newham Hall ... D 12
Newhaven ... H 3
Newhaven House ... D 10
Newholm ... D 8
Newhouse ... C 1
Newhouses ... E 8
Newick ... F 3
Newingreen ... D 10
Newington, Kent ... B 7
Newington, Kent ... D 10
Newington, Notts. ... A 4
Newington, Oxen ... D 7
Newington, Salop ... D 9
Newland, Glos. ... C 9
Newland, Heref. & Worc. ... G 2
Newland, Humber. ... D 8
Newland, N. Yorks. ... E 5
Newland, Som. ... B 2
Newlandhead ... C 9
Newlands, Borders ... D 3
Newlands, Dumf. & Gall. ... C 10
Newlands, Grampian . E 8
Newlands, Northumb. G 9
Newlands of Geise ... A 10
Newlyn ... G 2
Newmachar ... F 6
Newmains ... D 1
Newmarket, Suff. ... J 7
Newmarket, W. Isles . C 5
Newmill, Borders ... B 3
Newmill, Corn. ... F 2
Newmill, Grampian ... B 2
Newmill of Inshewan . L 2
Newmillerdam ... F 12
Newmills, Fife ... A 3
Newmills, Gwent ... D 8
Newmills, Highland ... C 2
Newmills, Lothian ... C 4
Newmills of Boyne ... B 3
Newmiln ... D 6
Newmilns ... F 10
Newnham, Glos. ... C 10
Newnham, Hants. ... A 8
Newnham, Herts. ... L 3
Newnham, Kent ... B 8
Newnham, Northants . F 9
Newnham Bridge ... E 11
Newpark ... F 9
Newport, Devon ... C 4
Newport, Dyfed ... C 4
Newport, Essex ... M 6
Newport, Glos. ... E 10
56 Newport, Gwent ... F 6
149 Newport, Highland . E 10
112 Newport, Humber. ... D 6
40 Newport, I.o.W. ... G 6
92 Newport, Norfolk ... D 8
94 Newport, Salop ... H 6
141 Newport-on-Tay ... D 9
89 Newport Pagnell ... H 12
54 Newport Sands ... C 4
41 Newpound Com. ... C 11
34 Newquay ... D 5
140 Newrow ... H 4
146 Newseat ... D 4
110 Newsham, Lancs. ... D 4
116 Newsham, N. Yorks. . D 1
116 Newsham, N. Yorks. . G 4
112 Newsholme, Humberside ... D 5
111 Newsholme, Lancs. ... B 7
111 Newsholme, W. Yorks. ... C 9
137 Newstead, Borders ... F 8
133 Newstead, Northumb. ... E 12
96 Newstead, Notts. ... E 2
112 Newthorpe ... D 3
137 Newton, Borders ... G 8
91 Newton, Cambs. ... K 5
94 Newton, Ches. ... C 3
94 Newton, Ches. ... C 4
94 Newton, Ches. ... D 4
111 Newton, Ches. ... G 8
116 Newton, Cleveland ... D 6
114 Newton, Cumbria ... H 5
96 Newton, Derby ... D 2
39 Newton, Dorset ... E 11
131 Newton, Dumf. & Gall. ... B 12
146 Newton, Grampian ... C 8
144 Newton, Grampian ... C 7
57 Newton, Heref. & Worc. ... A 7
59 Newton, Heref. & Worc. ... G 10
149 Newton, Highland ... C 12
144 Newton, Highland ... E 3
144 Newton, Highland ... C 3
144 Newton, Highland ... E 1
148 Newton, Highland ... D 4
110 Newton, Lancs. ... D 2
110 Newton, Lancs. ... D 3
115 Newton, Lancs. ... H 8
110 Newton, Lancs. ... B 6
90 Newton, Lincs. ... B 1
136 Newton, Lothian ... B 4
56 Newton, Mid Glam. . G 2
90 Newton, Norfolk ... D 5
92 Newton, Norfolk ... D 1
89 Newton, Northants. D 12
133 Newton, Northumb. . B 8
133 Newton, Northumb. . G 8
96 Newton, Notts. ... F 4
38 Newton, Som. ... B 5
95 Newton, Staffs. ... H 9
136 Newton, Strathclyde . F 2
93 Newton, Suffolk ... L 2
140 Newton, Tayside ... D 4
89 Newton, War. ... D 8
55 Newton, W. Glam. ... H 9
112 Newton, W. Yorks. ... D 2
40 Newton, Wilts. ... D 4
37 Newton Abbot ... J 7
131 Newton Arlosh ... F 12
116 Newton Aycliffe ... C 3
116 Newton Bewley ... C 5
89 Newton Blossomville G 12
91 Newton Bromswold ... J 1
89 Newton Burgoland ... A 7
97 Newton by Toft ... B 7
37 Newton Ferrers ... L 4
92 Newton Flotman ... F 5
89 Newton Harcourt ... B 9
146 Newton House ... E 4
110 Newton-le-Willows, Lancashire ... H 4
116 Newton-le-Willows, N. Yorkshire ... F 2
112 Newton Kyme ... C 2
85 Newton Longville ... A 9
135 Newton Mearns ... D 10
116 Newton Morrell ... D 3
117 Newton Mulgrave ... D 8
54 Newton Mountain ... F 3
138 Newton of Ardtoe ... A 4
140 Newton of Balcanquhal F 6
141 Newton of Falkland ... F 7
146 Newton of Murcar ... F 7
148 Newton of Ochtow ... G 5
140 Newton of Pitcairns ... F 5
112 Newton-on-Ouse ... A 3
117 Newton-on-Rawcliffe . F 8
133 Newton-on-the-Moor C 10
96 Newton on Trent ... C 5
38 Newton Poppleford ... G 4
85 Newton Purcell ... A 7
88 Newton Regis ... A 6
115 Newton Reigny ... B 7
137 Newton St. Boswells ... F 8
36 Newton St. Cyres ... F 7
92 Newton St. Faith ... D 5
57 Newton St. Loe ... H 10
36 Newton St. Petrock ... E 3
95 Newton Solney ... H 11
40 Newton Stacey ... B 6
130 Newton Stewart ... E 5
40 Newton Toney ... B 4
36 Newton Tracey ... C 4
135 Newton upon Ayr ... G 8
112 Newton upon Derwent B 5
41 Newton Valence ... C 8
131 Newtonairds ... D 9
146 Newtongarry Croft ... D 3
136 Newtongrange ... C 6
147 Newtonmill ... L 3
145 Newtonmore ... J 3
95 Newtown, Ches. ... B 8
94 Newtown, Ches. ... E 5
34 Newtown, Corn. ... G 4
132 Newtown, Cumb. ... G 2
132 Newtown, Cumb. ... G 3
115 Newtown, Cumbria ... C 7
36 Newtown, Devon ... C 6
40 Newtown, Dorset ... G 2
57 Newtown, Glos. ... A 12
57 Newtown, Glos. ... D 10
144 Newtown, Grampian . C 7
40 Newtown, Hants. ... D 4
41 Newtown, Hants. ... D 7
40 Newtown, Hants. ... E 4
41 Newtown, Hants. ... E 7
84 Newtown, Hants. ... H 6
59 Newtown, Heref. & Worc. ... G 10
59 Newtown, Heref. & Worc. ... H 11
143 Newtown, Highland ... J 7
114 Newtown, I.o.M. ... H 2
40 Newtown, I.o.W. ... G 5
110 Newtown, Lancs. ... E 4
133 Newtown, Northumb. A 8
133 Newtown, Northumb. C 8
137 Newtown, Northumb. ... F 12
58 Newtown, Powys ... C 6
94 Newtown, Salop ... G 3
95 Newtown, Staffs. ... D 7
95 Newtown, Staffs. ... D 9
39 Newtown, Wilts. ... C 12
89 Newtown Linford ... A 8
136 Newtown of Covington ... E 3
146 Newtown of Melrose . A 5
141 Newtyle ... C 8
54 Neyland ... F 3
57 Nibley ... F 10
152 Nibon ... C 6
38 Nicholashayne ... E 5
55 Nicholaston ... H 8
132 Nickie's Hill ... F 4
111 Nidd ... A 11
147 Nigg, Grampian ... G 7
144 Nigg, Highland ... C 4
144 Nigg Station ... B 4
38 Nightcott ... D 2
86 Nine Ashes ... D 6
136 Nine Mile Burn ... D 4
132 Ninebanks ... H 6
42 Ninfield ... G 6
40 Ningwood ... G 5
137 Nisbet ... G 9
131 Nithside ... D 10
40 Niton ... H 6
94 No Man's Heath, Cheshire ... E 4
88 No Man's Heath, Warwickshire ... A 6
34 No Man's Land, Cornwall ... C 6
36 No Man's Land, Devon E 7
86 Noak Hill ... E 5
136 Noblehouse ... D 5
59 Nobold ... A 10
89 Nobottle ... F 10
97 Nocton ... D 8
84 Noke ... C 6
54 Nolton ... E 2
54 Nolton Haven ... E 2
94 Noneley ... G 3
43 Nonington ... C 11
115 Nook ... G 8
94 Norbury, Ches. ... E 4
95 Norbury, Derby ... F 9
59 Norbury, Salop ... C 9
94 Norbury, Staffs. ... H 6
152 Norby ... D 6
90 Nordelph ... E 7
111 Norden ... F 7
40 Norden ... H 1
59 Nordley ... C 12
84 Nore Marsh ... F 2
92 Norfolk, Co. ... D 4
137 Norham ... E 11
94 Norley ... C 4
40 Norley Wood ... F 5
90 Norman Cross ... F 3
112 Normanby, Humber. . E 6
117 Normanby, N. Yorks. G 7
97 Normanby-by-Spital . A 7
113 Normanby le Wold ... H 9
41 Normandy ... A 10
42 Norman's Bay ... G 6
38 Norman's Green ... F 4
40 Normansland ... D 4
95 Normanton, Derbyshire ... G 11
96 Normanton, Leics. ... F 5
96 Normanton, Lincs. ... F 6
96 Normanton, Notts. ... E 4
112 Normanton, W. Yorks. ... E 2
89 Normanton le Heath . A 7
96 Normanton on Soar . H 2
96 Normanton on the Wolds ... G 3
96 Normanton on Trent . C 5
110 Normoss ... C 2
41 Norney ... B 10
57 Norrington Com. ... H 12
95 Norris Hill ... H 11
96 North Anston ... B 2
84 North Aston ... A 6
146 North Atrochie ... D 7
40 North Baddesley ... D 5
139 North Ballachulish ... B 8
39 North Barrow ... C 9
92 North Barsham ... B 2
87 North Benfleet ... E 7
41 North Bersted ... F 10
137 North Berwick ... A 8
41 North Boarhunt ... E 7
37 North Bovey ... G 6
135 North Brackenridge . E 12
39 North Bradley ... A 12
37 North Brentor ... H 4
39 North Brewham ... C 10
36 North Buckland ... B 4
92 North Burlingham ... D 7
39 North Cadbury ... D 9
96 North Carlton, Lincolnshire ... B 6
96 North Carlton, Notts. B 3
134 North Carrine ... H 2
112 North Cave ... D 6
84 North Cerney ... C 1
41 North Chapel ... C 11
40 North Charford ... D 3
133 North Charlton ... A 10
39 North Cheriton ... D 10
39 North Chideock ... G 8
112 North Cliffe ... C 6
96 North Clifton ... C 5
113 North Coates ... G 11
97 North Cockerington A 10
39 North Coker ... E 9
96 North Collingham ... D 5
42 North Common ... F 3
56 North Cornelly ... F 2
138 North Corry ... B 5
146 North Cottown ... F 5
92 North Cove ... F 8
131 North Cowshaw ... C 11
116 North Cowton ... E 3
89 North Crawley ... H 12
86 North Cray ... G 5
92 North Creake ... B 2
39 North Curry ... D 7
113 North Dalton ... B 7
35 North Darley ... B 10
111 North Deighton ... B 12
135 North Drumboy ... D 10
112 North Duffield ... C 5
97 North Elkington ... A 10
92 North Elmham ... C 3
112 North Elmsall ... F 3
57 North End, Avon ... G 11
57 North End, Avon ... H 7
85 North End, Bucks. ... A 9
85 North End, Bucks. ... E 8
39 North End, Dorset . D 11
86 North End, Essex ... B 6
41 North End, Hants. ... F 8
84 North End, Hants. ... H 5
113 North End, Humberside ... D 10
90 North End, Lincs. ... B 3
133 North End, Northumb. C 9
38 North End, Som. ... D 6
41 North End, W. Sussex E 12
142 North Erradale ... B 1
38 North Esworthy ... D 2
87 North Fambridge ... D 8
150 North Fearns ... D 5
134 North Feorline ... F 4
113 North Ferriby ... E 7
113 North Frodingham ... B 8
151 North Galson ... A 5
152 North Gluss ... C 7
40 North Gorley ... E 3
146 North Gorrachie ... B 5
92 North Green ... F 5
132 North Greenhill ... F 4
117 North Grimston ... H 8
42 North Halling ... B 6
135 North Halls ... F 11
41 North Hayling ... F 9
133 North Hazelrigg ... C 12
41 North Heath ... D 12
35 North Hill ... B 9
84 North Hinksey ... D 6
42 North Holmwood ... C 1
135 North Hourat ... D 8
37 North Huish ... K 6
96 North Hykeham ... D 6
54 North Johnston ... F 3
113 North Kelsey ... G 8
144 North Kessock ... E 2
113 North Killingholme . E 9
116 North Kilvington ... G 4
89 North Kilworth ... D 9
146 North Kinmundy ... F 6
146 North Kirkton ... C 8
97 North Kyme ... E 8
42 North Lancing ... G 1
85 North Lee ... C 9
116 North Lees ... H 3
89 North Luffenham ... B 12
84 North Leigh ... C 5
96 North Leverton with Habblesthorpe ... B 5
88 North Littleton ... G 4
93 North Lopham ... G 3
133 North Lyham ... C 12
41 North Marden ... D 9
85 North Marston ... B 8
136 North Middleton, Lothian ... C 6
137 North Middleton, Northumb. ... G 12
36 North Molton ... C 6
146 North Monkshill ... C 5
117 North Moor ... H 12
84 North Moreton ... E 6
41 North Mundham ... F 10
96 North Muskham ... D 5
113 North Newbald ... C 7
89 North Newington ... H 7
84 North Newnton ... H 2
38 North Newton ... C 6
57 North Nibley ... E 10
41 North Oakley ... A 7
86 North Ockendon ... E 6
116 North Ormesby ... C 5
97 North Ormsby ... A 10
116 North Otterington ... F 4
113 North Owersby ... H 8
39 North Perrott ... E 8
38 North Petherton ... C 6
35 North Petherwin ... A 10
92 North Pickenham ... E 1
88 North Piddle ... G 3
39 North Poorton ... F 8
38 North Quarme ... C 3
136 North Queensferry ... A 4
36 North Radworthy ... C 6
97 North Rauceby ... F 7
111 North Rigton ... B 11
95 North Rode ... D 7
152 North Roe ... B 7
90 North Runcton ... D 7
152 North Sandwick ... B 8
114 North Scale ... H 4
96 North Scarle ... D 6
133 N. Seaton Colliery . D 11
151 North Shawbost ... B 4
138 North Shian ... C 6
133 North Shields ... F 11
87 North Shoebury ... E 9
110 North Shore ... D 2
136 North Shortcleugh ... H 2
114 North Side, Cumb. ... B 2
90 North Side, Cambs. . E 4
117 North Skelton ... C 7
113 North Somercotes . G 12
116 North Stainley ... G 3
115 North Stainmore ... D 10
57 North Stoke, Avon . G 10
85 North Stoke, Oxon ... F 7
41 North Stoke, W. Sussex ... E 11
85 North Street, Berks. . G 7
41 North Street, Hants. . C 8
133 North Sunderland . D 12
36 North Tamerton ... F 2
36 North Tawton ... F 5
113 North Thoresby ... G 10
40 North Tidworth ... A 4
133 North Togston ... C 10
151 North Tolsta ... B 6
92 North Tuddenham ... D 3
133 North Walbottle ... F 10
92 North Walsham ... C 6
41 North Waltham ... B 7
41 North Warnborough . A 9
147 North Water Bri. ... L 4
149 North Watten ... B 11
86 North Weald Bassett . D 5
96 North Wheatley ... B 5
57 North Wick ... H 9
37 North Whilborough . J 7
97 North Willingham ... A 8
96 North Wingfield ... D 1
96 North Witham ... H 6
39 North Wootton, Dorset ... E 10
90 North Wootton, Norfolk ... C 7
39 North Wootton, Somerset ... B 9
57 North Wraxall ... G 11
84 North Wroughton ... F 3
133 North Yardhope ... C 7
116 North Yorkshire, Co. . F 5
116 Northallerton ... F 4
36 Northam, Devon ... C 3
40 Northam, Hants. ... E 6
89 Northampton ... F 11
89 Northamptonshire, County ... E 11
86 Northaw ... D 3
90 Northborough Peakirk E 3
43 Northbourne ... C 12
40 Northbrook ... B 6
85 Northchurch ... C 10
37 Northcott ... G 2
89 Northend ... G 7
137 Northfield, Borders . C 11
147 Northfield, Grampian G 6
88 Northfield, W. Midlands ... D 4
42 Northfleet ... A 5
43 Northiam ... F 7
91 Northill ... K 3
41 Northington ... B 7
97 Northlands ... E 10
84 Northleach ... C 2
38 Northleigh ... G 5
36 Northlew ... F 4
84 Northmoor ... D 5
38 Northmoor Green or Moorland ... C 6
141 Northmuir ... B 8
41 Northney ... F 9
86 Northolt ... E 1
61 Northop ... C 11
61 Northophall ... C 12
90 Northorpe, Lincs. ... B 3
90 Northorpe, Lincs. ... D 2
113 Northorpe, Lincs. ... G 7
39 Northover, Som. ... B 8
39 Northover, Som. ... D 8
111 Northowram ... D 10
40 Northport ... G 1
92 Northrepps ... B 5
151 Northton ... H 1
152 Northtown ... D 3
133 Northumberland, County ... D 8
57 Northway, Glos. ... A 12
38 Northway, Som. ... C 5
94 Northwich ... C 5
57 Northwick ... F 9
90 Northwold ... F 8
40 Northwood, I.o.W. . G 6
86 Northwood, Lond. ... E 1
94 Northwood, Salop ... G 3
91 Northwood End ... L 2
57 Northwood Green . C 10
94 Northwood, Ches. ... B 4
116 Norton, Cleveland ... C 5
57 Norton, Glos. ... B 11

South Ockendon ..... F 6
South Ormsby ...... C 10
South Otterington .... F 4
South Owersby ...... A 8
South Oxhey .... E 1
South Perrott .... F 8
South Petherton ..... D 8
South Petherwin .... B 10
South Pickenham .... E 1
South Pool .... M 6
South Radworthy .... C 6
South Rauceby .... F 7
South Raynham ..... C 2
South Reston .... B 11
South Runcton ...... E 7
South Scarle .... D 6
South Shawbost ..... B 3
South Shields .... F 12
South Shore .... D 2
South Skirlaugh ..... C 9
South Somercotes ... A 11
South Stainley .... A 1
South Stifford .... F 6
South Stoke, Avon .. H 10
South Stoke, Oxon. ... F 7
South Stoke,
W. Sussex .... E 11
South Street, Kent .... B 9
South Street, London . H 4
South Street E. Sussex . F 3
South Tawton .... F 5
South Thoresby .... C 11
South Tidworth ..... A 4
South Town .... B 8
South Walsham ..... D 7
S. Warnborough ..... A 8
South Weald E6
South Weston .... D 8
South Wheatley, Corn. G 1
South Wheatley, Notts. B 5
South Widcombe A9
South Wigston .... B 9
South Willingham .... B 9
South Wingfield ..... E 1
South Witham ...... H 6
South Wonston ...... B 6
South Woodham
Ferrers .... D 6
South Wootton ...... C 7
South Wraxall ..... H 11
South Yorkshire, Co. . G 2
South Zeal .... F 5
Southall F1
Southam, Glos B1
Southam, War .... F 7
Southampton .... E 5
Southborough .... E 5
Southbourne, Dorset . G 3
Southbourne,
W. Sussex .... E 9
Southburgh .... E 3
Southburn .... B 7
Southchurch .... E 9
Southcott, Devon .... D 3
Southcott, Wilts ..... H 3
Southdean .... B 5
Southease .... G 5
Southend, Strathclyde H 2
Southend, Wilts ..... G 3
Southend on Sea ..... E 8
Southerndown ...... G 2
Southerness .... F 10
Southernknowe .... G 11
Southery .... F 7
Southfield .... G 7
Southfleet .... A 5
Southgate, London ... E 3
Southgate, Norfolk ... B 8
Southgate, Norfolk ... C 4
Southgate, W. Glam . H 9
Southill .... L 3
Southleigh .... G 5
Southminister .... D 9
Southmoor .... B 10
Southoe .... J 3
Southolt .... H 5
Southorpe .... E 2
Southowram .... E 10
Southport .... E 2
Southrepps .... B 6
Southrey D8
Southrop .... D 3
Southrope .... D 8
Southsea .... F 8
Southtown .... E 3
Southwark .... E 3
Southwater .... D 12
Southway .... B 8
Southwell, Dorset .... H 7
Southwell, Notts ..... E 4
133 Southwick,
Tyne & Wear .... G 12
41 Southwick, Hants .... E 8
90 Southwick, Northants F 1
42 Southwick, W. Sussex G 1
39 Southwick, Wilts ... A 11
93 Southwold .... H 8
92 Southwood, Norf .... E 7
39 Southwood, Som. .... C 9
137 Soutra Mains .... C 7
151 Soval Lodge .... D 4
116 Sowerby, N. Yorks. .. G 4
111 Sowerby, W. Yorks. .. E 9
111 Sowerby Bridge ...... E 9
114 Sowerby Row .... A 6
38 Sowton .... G 3
132 Spadeadam Farm ..... F 4
90 Spalding .... C 3
112 Spaldington .... D 5
91 Spaldwick .... H 2
141 Spalefield .... F 10
96 Spalford .... C 5
90 Spanby .... B 2
92 Sparham .... D 4
114 Spark Bridge .... G 5
39 Sparkford .... D 9
95 Sparklow .... D 9
37 Sparkwell .... K 4
95 Sparrowpit .... B 9
40 Sparsholt, Hants, ... C 6
84 Sparsholt, Oxon ..... E 4
133 Spartylea .... H 7
117 Spaunton .... F 7
38 Spaxton .... C 6
143 Spean Bridge .... L 6
40 Spearywell .... C 4
131 Speddoch .... C 9
84 Speen, Berks. .... G 5
85 Speen, Bucks. .... D 9
117 Speeton .... H 11
94 Speke .... B 3
42 Speldhurst .... D 4
86 Spellbrook .... B 5
84 Spelsbury .... B 4
56 Spelter .... E 2
85 Spencers Wood ...... G 8
116 Spennithorne .... F 2
116 Spennymoor .... B 3
88 Spetchley .... G 2
39 Spetisbury .... F 12
93 Spexhall .... G 7
146 Spey Bay .... A 1
145 Spey Bridge .... J 4
145 Speybridge .... G 6
144 Speyview .... E 8
97 Spilsby .... D 11
133 Spindlestone .... D 11
96 Spinkhill .... B 2
89 Spinney Hills .... B 9
149 Spinningdale .... G 7
97 Spital in the Street .... A 7
133 Spitalford .... A 10
42 Spithursthurst .... F 3
137 Spittal, Dumf. & Gall. E 5
130 Spittal, Dumf. & Gall. F 4
54 Spittal, Dyfed .... E 3
149 Spittal, Highland ... B 10
137 Spittal, Lothian ...... B 7
137 Spittal, Northumb. .. D 12
112 Spittal, Humberside .. B 5
147 Spittal of Glenmuick .. J 1
145 Spittal of Glenshee ... M 7
147 Spittalburn .... J 4
140 Spittalfield .... C 6
92 Spixworth .... D 5
35 Splatt .... A 9
42 Splayne's Green ...... F 3
111 Spofforth .... B 12
61 Spon Green .... D 12
96 Spondon .... G 1
92 Spooner Row .... F 4
92 Sporle .... D 2
137 Spott .... B 9
137 Spottiswoode .... D 8
89 Spratton .... E 10
41 Spreakley .... B 9
36 Spreyton .... F 6
97 Spridlington .... B 7
114 Spring Valley .... H 2
135 Springburn .... C 10
151 Springcotrie .... D 3
132 Springfield,
Dumf. & Gall. ..... F 2
141 Springfield, Fife ..... F 8
144 Springfield, Grampiam D 6
88 Springfield,
W. Midlands ...... D 4
88 Springhill .... B 3
131 Springholm .... E 9
132 Springkell .... E 1
135 Springside .... E 8
96 Springthorpe .... A 6
133 Springwell .... G 11
96 Springthorpe .... A 6
133 Springwell .... G 11
113 Sproatley .... D 9
94 Sproston Green ...... C 6
112 Spotbrough .... G 3
93 Sproughton .... L 4
137 Sprouston .... F 10
92 Sprowston .... D 6
96 Sproxton, Leics. ..... H 6
116 Sproxton, N. Yorks .. G 6
94 Spurstow .... E 4
145 Sronlairig Lodge ...... J 1
145 Sronpadruig .... L 3
111 Stackhouse .... A 7
54 Stackpole .... G 3
111 Stacksteads .... E 7
37 Staddiscombe .... K 4
112 Staddlethorpe .... E 6
85 Stadhampton .... D 7
115 Staffield .... A 8
150 Staffin .... A 4
95 Stafford .... H 8
95 Staffordshire, Co .... H 8
137 Stagehall .... E 7
90 Stag's Holt .... E 5
91 Stagsden .... K 1
91 Stagsden W. End ..... K 1
111 Stainburn .... B 11
96 Stainby .... H 6
111 Staincross .... F 12
85 Staines .... G 11
97 Stainfield, Lincs. ..... C 8
90 Stainfield, Lincs. ..... C 2
115 Stainforth, N. Yorks. H 10
112 Stainforth, S. Yorks. .. F 4
110 Staining .... D 2
111 Stainland .... E 9
117 Stainsacre .... D 9
116 Stainton, Cleveland .. D 5
115 Stainton, Cumb. ..... B 7
115 Stainton, Cumbria ... G 7
116 Stainton, Dur .... C 1
116 Stainton, N. Yorks. ... F 1
96 Stainton, S. Yorks. ... A 3
97 Stainton by Langworth B 8
113 Stainton le Vale ..... H 9
114 Stainton with Adgarley H 5
117 Staintondale .... E 10
114 Stair, Cumb. .... C 5
135 Stair, Strathclyde .... G 9
117 Staithes .... C 8
110 Stake Pool .... B 3
133 Stakeford .... D 11
39 Stalbridge .... D 10
39 Stalbridge Weston ... E 10
92 Stalham .... C 7
92 Stalham Green ...... C 7
43 Stalisfield Green ..... C 8
115 Stalling Busk .... G 11
113 Stallingborough ...... F 9
110 Stalmine .... C 3
111 Stalybridge .... G 8
91 Stambourne .... L 8
90 Stamford, Lincs ...... E 1
133 Stamford,
Northumb. .... A 10
112 Stamford Bridge ..... B 5
133 Stamfordham .... F 9
114 Stanah .... C 6
86 Stanborough .... C 2
85 Stanbridge, Beds. ... B 10
40 Stanbridge, Dorset ... F 2
111 Stanbury .... C 9
135 Stand .... C 12
136 Standburn .... B 2
88 Standeford .... A 3
43 Standen .... D 7
39 Standerwick .... A 11
41 Standford .... C 9
110 Standish .... F 4
84 Standlake .... D 5
40 Standon, Hants. ..... C 6
86 Standon, Herts ...... B 4
94 Standon, Staffs. ..... G 6
86 Standon Massey ..... D 6
93 Standwell Green ..... H 4
136 Stane .... C 2
92 Stanfield .... C 2
91 Stanford, Beds. ...... L 3
43 Stanford, Kent ..... D 10
59 Stanford Bishop .... G 12
88 Stanford Bridge ...... F 1
84 Stanford Dingley .... G 6
87 Stanford le Hope .... F 7
89 Stanford on Avon .... D 9
96 Stanford on Soar .... H 3
59 Stanford on Teme ... F 12
86 Stanford Rivers ...... D 5
84 Stanford the Vale .... E 4
42 Stanford's End ...... D 3
90 Stanground .... F 3
92 Stanhoe .... B 1
115 Stanhope .... A 12
89 Stanion .... C 12
140 Stank .... F 1
96 Stanley, Derby .... F 1
133 Stanley, Dur. .... H 10
95 Stanley, Staffs. ...... E 8
96 Stanley, Tayside ..... D 6
84 Stanley, Wilts .... G 1
111 Stanley, W. Yorks. .. E 12
96 Stanley Common ..... F 1
59 Stanley Hill .... H 12
42 Stanmer .... G 2
84 Stanmore, Berks. ..... F 6
40 Stanmore, Hants. .... C 6
86 Stanmore, London ... E 2
132 Stannersburn .... D 5
133 Stannington,
Northumb. .... E 10
95 Stannington,
S. Yorks .... A 11
59 Stansbatch .... F 9
93 Stansfield .... K 1
95 Stanshope .... E 9
93 Stanstead .... K 1
86 Stanstead Abbots .... C 4
93 Stanstead Street ...... K 1
42 Stansted .... B 5
86 Stansted Mountfitchet A 5
95 Stanton, Derby ..... H 11
84 Stanton, Glos .... A 2
56 Stanton, Gwent ...... B 6
133 Stanton, Northumb. .. D 9
95 Stanton, Staffs. ...... F 9
93 Stanton, Suffolk ..... H 3
95 Stanton by Bridge ... G 12
57 Stanton by Dale ...... F 2
57 Stanton Drew .... H 9
84 Stanton Fitzwarren ... E 3
84 Stanton Harcourt .... D 5
96 Stanton Hill .... D 2
95 Stanton in Peak ..... D 11
59 Stanton Lacy .... E 10
59 Stanton Long ...... C 11
96 Stanton on the Wolds . G 3
57 Stanton Prior ...... H 10
84 Stanton St. Bernard .. H 2
85 Stanton St. John ..... C 7
57 Stanton St. Quintin .. F 12
93 Stanton Street .... J 3
89 Stanton under Bardon A 8
94 Stanton upon Hine
Heath .... H 4
57 Stanton Wick .... H 9
94 Stanwardine in the
Fields .... H 3
87 Stanway, Essex ...... B 9
84 Stanway, Glos. ...... A 2
85 Stanwell .... G 11
85 Stanwell Moor ..... G 11
91 Stanwick .... H 1
117 Stape .... F 8
40 Stapehill .... F 2
94 Stapeley .... E 5
95 Stapenhill .... H 11
43 Staple, Kent .... B 11
38 Staple, Somerset ..... B 4
38 Staple Cross, Devon .. D 4
42 Staple Cross, E. Sussex F 6
38 Staple Fitzpaine ..... D 6
57 Staple Hill .... G 9
42 Staplefield .... E 2
91 Stapleford, Cambs. ... K 6
86 Stapleford,
Heref. & Worc. B3
96 Stapleford, Leics. .... H 5
96 Stapleford, Lincs ..... D 6
96 Stapleford, Notts. .... F 2
40 Stapleford, Wilts. .... B 2
86 Stapleford Abbotts ... D 5
86 Stapleford Tawney ... D 5
38 Staplegrove .... D 6
38 Staplehay .... D 5
42 Staplehurst .... D 6
40 Staplers .... G 6
132 Stapleton, Cumb. .... F 3
59 Stapleton,
Heref. & Worc. ... F 9
89 Stapleton, Leics. ..... B 8
116 Stapleton, N. Yorks. . D 3
59 Stapleton, Salop .... B 10
39 Stapleton, Som ...... D 8
132 Stapleton Grange ..... F 1
38 Stapley .... E 5
91 Staploe .... J 2
54 Star, Dyfed .... C 6
141 Star, Fife .... G 8
57 Star, Somerset .... H 7
115 Starbottom .... H 11
38 Starcross .... H 3
152 Starkigarth .... E 7
91 Starlings Green ..... M 6
93 Starston .... G 5
115 Starforth .... D 12
57 Startley .... F 12
39 Stathe .... C 7
96 Stathern .... G 5
116 Station Town .... B 4
91 Staughton Green ..... J 2
91 Staughton Highway ... J 2
57 Staunton, Glos. ...... C 9
57 Staunton, Glos. ..... A 11
95 Staunton Harold Hall H 12
96 Staunton in the Vale . F 5
59 Staunton on Arrow ... F 9
59 Staunton on Wye .... H 9
114 Staveley, Cumbria ... G 6
115 Staveley, Cumbria .... E 7
96 Stavely, Derby .... C 2
111 Staveley, N. Yorks. . A 12
37 Staverton, Devon ..... J 7
57 Staverton, Glos. .... B 12
89 Staverton, Northants. . F 9
57 Staverton, Wilts .... H 11
57 Staverton Bridge .... B 12
39 Stawell .... B 7
37 Stawford .... G 3
38 Stawley .... D 4
149 Staxigoe .... B 12
117 Staxton .... G 10
58 Staylittle .... C 4
110 Staynall .... C 2
96 Staythorpe .... E 5
116 Stean .... H 1
116 Stearsby .... H 6
38 Steart .... B 6
86 Stebbing .... B 6
152 Stebbligrind .... D 7
41 Stedham .... D 10
133 Steel Rigg .... E 8
132 Steele Road .... D 4
59 Steen's Bridge ...... G 11
41 Steep .... D 9
39 Steeple, Dorset ..... H 12
87 Steeple, Essex .... D 9
39 Steeple Ashton ..... A 12
84 Steeple Aston .... B 6
84 Steeple Barton .... B 5
91 Steeple Bumpstead ... L 8
85 Steeple Claydon ..... A 8
91 Steeple Gidding ...... G 2
40 Steeple Langford ..... B 2
91 Steeple Morden ...... L 4
111 Steeton .... C 9
150 Stein .... C 2
146 Steinmanhill .... C 5
133 Stelling Hall .... F 8
43 Stelling Minnis ..... C 10
35 Stenalees .... D 7
136 Stenhousemuir ...... A 2
152 Stenness .... C 6
150 Stenscholl .... A 4
95 Stenson .... G 11
152 Stenswall .... D 7
137 Stenton .... B 9
54 Stepaside .... F 5
131 Stepends .... C 9
86 Stepney .... F 4
91 Steppingley .... M 1
135 Stepps .... C 11
93 Sternfield .... J 7
84 Stert .... H 1
91 Stetchworth .... J 7
86 Stevenage .... B 2
135 Stevenston .... E 7
41 Steventon, Hants. .... A 7
84 Steventon, Oxon. .... E 5
91 Stevington .... K 1
91 Stewarby .... L 1
134 Stewarton, Strathclyde G 2
135 Stewarton, Strathclyde E 9
85 Stewkley .... B 9
97 Stewton .... B 10
54 Steynton .... F 4
36 Stibb .... E 1
36 Stibb Cross .... D 3
84 Stibb Green .... H 3
92 Stibbard .... C 3
90 Stibbington .... F 2
137 Stichill .... F 9
35 Sticker .... E 7
97 Stickford .... D 10
36 Sticklepath, Devon ... F 5
38 Sticklepath, Som. .... E 6
97 Stickney .... D 10
92 Stiffkey .... A 3
86 Stifford .... F 6
88 Stifford's Bridge ..... G 1
42 Stile Bridge .... C 6
112 Stillingfleet .... C 4
116 Stillington, Cleveland . C 4
116 Stillington, N. Yorks. H 6
90 Stilton .... F 3
57 Stinchcombe .... D 10
39 Stinsford .... G 10
59 Stirchley .... B 12
149 Stirkoke House ..... C 12
140 Stirling, Central ..... H 3
114 Stirling, Grampian ... C 8
87 Stisted .... A 8
84 Stitchcombe .... G 3
34 Stithians .... F 4
144 Stittenham .... B 2
89 Stivichall .... D 7
97 Stixwould .... D 9
136 Stobo .... F 4
39 Stoborough .... H 12
39 Stoborough Grn. .... H 12
132 Stobs Castle B3
137 Stobswood, Borders .. D 9
133 Stobswood,
Northumb. .... D 10
136 Stobwood .... D 2
87 Stock .... D 7
88 Stock Wood .... F 3
146 Stockbridge,
Grampian .... C 8
40 Stockbridge, Hants. .. C 5
131 Stockbridgehill ..... D 12
135 Stockbriggs .... F 12
43 Stockbury .... B 7
84 Stockcross .... G 5
114 Stockdale Wath ...... A 6
89 Stockerston .... B 11
41 Stockholm .... B 11
135 Stockiemuir .... A 10
86 Stocking Pelham ..... A 4
89 Stockingford .... C 7
38 Stockland .... F 6
38 Stockland Bristol ..... B 6
36 Stockleigh English .... E 7
36 Stockleigh Pomeroy .. F 7
84 Stockley .... G 1
39 Stocklinch .... E 7
95 Stockport .... A 7
111 Stocksbridge .... G 11
133 Stocksfield .... G 9
59 Stockton,
Heref. & Worcs. .. F 10
92 Stockton, Norfolk .... F 7
59 Stockton, Salop ...... B 8
88 Stockton, Salop ...... B 1
89 Stockton, War. ...... F 8
40 Stockton, Wilts. ..... B 1
94 Stockton Heath ...... B 5
116 Stocktonon-Tees ..... C 4
88 Stockton on Teme .... E 1
112 Stockton-on-the-
Forest .... B 4
43 Stodmarsh .... B 11
92 Stody .... B 4
148 Stoer .... D 2
39 Stoford, Som. .... E 9
40 Stoford, Wilts. .... C 2
38 Stogumber .... C 4
38 Stogursey .... B 5
36 Stoke, Devon .... D 1
40 Stoke, Hants. .... A 5
41 Stoke, Hants .... F 8
43 Stoke, Kent .... A 7
93 Stoke, Suffolk .... L 5
39 Stoke Abbott .... F 8
89 Stoke Albany .... C 11
93 Stoke Ash .... H 4
96 Stoke Bardolph ...... F 4
59 Stoke Bliss .... F 12
89 Stoke Bruerne ...... G 10
91 Stoke-by-Clare ...... L 8
93 Stoke-by-Nayland .... L 3
38 Stoke Canon .... F 3
40 Stoke Charity .... B 6
40 Stoke Climsland .... B 10
59 Stoke Cross .... G 11
85 Stoke D'Abernon ... H 12
91 Stoke Doyle .... G 1
89 Stoke Dry .... B 12
59 Stoke Edith .... H 11
40 Stoke Farthing ...... D 2
90 Stoke Ferry .... E 8
37 Stoke Fleming .... L 7
37 Stoke Gabriel .... K 7
57 Stoke Gifford .... F 9
89 Stoke Golding .... B 7
89 Stoke Goldington ... G 11
85 Stoke Green .... F 10
85 Stoke Hammond ..... A 9

Tullich Muir .... B 3
Tulliemet .... B 5
Tullo' of Benholm .... K 5
Tulloch House .... D 5
Tulloch .... L 7
Tullochan .... D 1
Tullochgorm .... H 7
Tullochmacarrick .... J 8
Tullochs .... C 2
Tullochvenus .... G 3
Tullybannocher .... E 2
Tullyfergus .... B 7
Tullymurdoch .... B 7
Tullynessle .... F 3
Tumble .... F 9
Tumby .... D 9
Tumby Woodside .... D 9
Tumford .... C 4
Tummel Bridge .... A 3
Tunbridge Wells .... D 5
Tunley .... H 10
Tunstall, Humber. .... D 10
Tunstall, Kent .... B 7
Tunstall, Lancs. .... H 8
Tunstall, N. Yorks. .... F 2
Tunstall, Staffs. .... E 7
Tunstall, Suffolk .... K 6
Tunstall,
Tyne & Wear .... H 12
Tunstall St. Mary .... E 7
Tunworth .... A 8
Tupsley .... H 10
Tupton .... D 12
Tur Langton .... C 10
Turgis Green .... H 8
Turin .... B 10
Turkdean .... B 2
Turleigh Freshford .... H 11
Turnastone .... A 7
Turnberry .... A 3
Turnditch .... F 11
Turner's Hill .... E 2
Turners Puddle .... G 11
Turnhouse .... B 4
Turnworth .... E 11
Turriff .... C 5
Turton Bottoms .... F 6
Turvelaws .... F 12
Turvey .... G 12
Turville .... E 8
Turville Heath .... E 8
Turweston .... H 9
Tushielaw .... G 6
Tutbury .... G 10
Tutnall .... E 3
Tutshill .... E 8
Tuttington .... C 5
Tutts Clump .... G 7
Tutwell .... B 11
Tuxford .... C 4
Twatt, Orkney Is. .... C 1
Twatt, Shetland Is. .... D 7
Twechar .... B 11
Tweeddaleburn .... D 5
Tweedmouth .... D 12
Tweedshaws .... H 3
Tweedsmuir .... G 4
Twelveheads .... E 5
Twemlow Green .... C 6
Twenty .... C 3
Twerton .... H 10
Twickenham .... G 2
Twigworth .... B 11
Twineham .... F 1
Twinhoe .... H 10
Twinstead .... L 2
Twinstead Green .... L 2
Twitchen, Devon .... B 4
Twitchen, Devon .... C 7
Twitchen, Salop .... D 9
Two Bridges .... H 5
Two Dales .... D 11
Two Gates .... B 5
Two Pots .... B 4
Twycross .... B 7
Twyford, Berks .... G 9
Twyford, Bucks .... B 7
Twyford, Derby .... G 11
Twyford, Hants .... D 6
Twyford, Leics. .... A 10
Twyford, Norf. .... C 3
Twyford Com .... A 8
Twyn Llanan .... E 11
Twyncarno .... C 4
Twynholm .... F 7
Twyning .... A 12
Twyning Green .... H 3
Twyn-mynydd .... F 10
Twyn-y-Sheriff .... D 7
Twywell .... D 12

60 Ty-Hen .... G 1
59 Tyberton .... H 9
55 Tycroes, Dyfed .... F 9
60 Ty-croes, Gwynedd .... C 3
61 Tycrwyn .... H 10
90 Tydd Gote .... D 5
90 Tydd St. Giles .... D 5
90 Tydd St. Mary .... D 5
61 Tyddyninco .... G 9
87 Tye Green, Essex .... B 7
91 Tye Green, Essex .... L 7
54 Ty-hen .... E 6
110 Tyldesley .... G 6
43 Tyler Hill .... B 10
85 Tylers Green, Bucks. .... E 10
42 Tyler's Grn., Surrey .... C 2
56 Tylorstown .... E 3
58 Tylwch .... D 5
61 Ty-nant, Clwyd .... F 9
61 Ty-nant, Gwynedd .... H 8
58 Tyncwm .... D 4
139 Tyndrum .... E 10
39 Tyneham .... H 12
133 Tyne & Wear, Co. .... F 10
136 Tynehead .... C 6
133 Tynemouth .... F 11
56 Tynewydd .... D 3
137 Tyninghame .... B 8
138 Tynribbie .... C 6
131 Tynron .... B 9
58 Tynswydd .... F 2
61 Ty'n-y-ffridd .... G 10
60 Ty'n-y-gongl .... B 4
61 Ty'n-y-groes .... C 7
60 Tyn-y-pwll .... B 4
61 Tyn-y-Wern .... G 10
89 Tyringham .... G 12
36 Tythecott .... D 3
56 Tythegston .... F 2
57 Tytherington, Avon .... E 10
95 Tytherington, Ches .... C 7
40 Tytherington, Wilts. .... B 1
39 Tytherington, Wilts. .... B 11
39 Tytherleigh .... F 7
35 Tywardreath .... D 8
35 Tywardreath Highway .... D 8
61 Tywyn .... B 7
58 Tywyn Mer .... B 2
142 Uags .... F 1
93 Ubbeston Green .... H 6
57 Ubley .... H 8
116 Uckerby .... E 3
42 Uckfield .... F 4
57 Uckington .... B 12
135 Uddingston .... C 11
136 Uddington .... F 1
43 Udimore .... F 7
146 Udny Green .... E 6
135 Udston .... E 12
135 Udstonhead .... E 12
84 Uffcott .... F 2
38 Uffculme .... E 4
90 Uffington, Lincs. .... E 2
84 Uffington, Oxon .... E 4
59 Uffington, Salop .... A 10
90 Ufford, Cambs. .... E 2
93 Ufford, Suffolk .... K 6
89 Ufton .... F 7
85 Ufton Green .... G 7
85 Ufton Nervet .... G 7
134 Ugadale .... F 3
37 Ugborough .... K 5
93 Uggeshall .... G 7
117 Ugglebarnby .... D 9
86 Ugley .... A 5
117 Ugthorpe .... D 8
150 Uig, Skye .... C 1
150 Uig, Skye .... B 3
134 Uig, Strathclyde .... A 6
150 Uigshader .... D 4
138 Uisken .... F 1
149 Ulbster .... C 12
97 Ulceby, Humberside .... F 8
97 Ulceby, Lincs. .... C 11
97 Ulceby Cross .... C 11
113 Ulceby Skitter .... F 9
43 Ulcombe .... C 7
114 Uldale .... B 5
57 Uley .... D 11
133 Ulgham .... D 10
148 Ullapool .... G 3
88 Ullenhall .... E 5
57 Ullenwood .... C 12
112 Ulleskelf .... C 3
89 Ullesthorpe .... C 8
96 Ulley .... B 2
59 Ullingswick .... G 11
150 Ullinish .... D 2
114 Ullock .... C 3
40 Ullwell .... H 2

114 Ulpha .... F 4
113 Ulrome .... B 9
152 Ulsta .... C 7
137 Ulsoon .... G 9
138 Ulva House .... D 2
135 Ulverston .... G 5
131 Ulzieside .... A 8
150 Umachan .... C 5
36 Umberleigh .... D 5
148 Unapool .... D 4
112 Uncleby .... A 6
132 Under Burnmouth .... E 3
42 Under River .... C 4
115 Underbarrow .... F 7
112 Undercliffe .... D 10
135 Underhills .... F 9
152 Underhoull .... A 8
96 Underwood .... E 2
57 Undy .... F 7
152 Unifirth .... D 6
147 Union Croft .... H 6
114 Union Mills .... H 2
96 Unstone .... C 1
96 Unstone Green .... C 1
132 Unthank, Cumb. .... H 2
115 Unthank, Cumb. .... A 8
115 Unthank, Cumb. .... B 7
137 Unthank, Northumb. .... E 12
115 Unthank End .... B 7
39 Up Cerne .... F 10
38 Up Exe .... F 3
57 Up Hatherley .... B 12
110 Up Holland .... G 4
41 Up Marden .... E 9
41 Up Nately .... A 8
40 Up Somborne .... C 5
39 Up Sydling .... F 9
40 Upavon .... A 3
43 Upchurch .... A 7
36 Upcott, Devon .... E 4
59 Upcott,
Heref. & Worc. .... G 8
38 Upcott, Somerset .... D 3
136 Uphall .... B 3
136 Uphall Station .... B 3
36 Upham, Devon .... E 7
41 Upham, Hants .... D 7
59 Uphampton,
Heref. & Worc. .... F 9
88 Uphampton,
Heref. & Worc. .... F 2
56 Uphill .... H 6
135 Uplawmoor .... D 9
57 Upleadon .... B 10
116 Upleatham .... C 6
43 Uplees .... B 8
39 Uploders .... G 8
38 Uplowman .... E 4
38 Uplyme .... G 6
86 Upminster .... E 6
38 Upottery .... E 5
71 Uppat .... B 7
59 Upper Affcot .... D 10
148 Upper Ardchronie .... G 6
88 Upper Arley .... D 1
85 Upper Arncott .... B 7
89 Upper Astrop .... H 8
148 Upper Badcall .... C 3
151 Upper Barvas .... B 5
85 Upper Basildon .... F 7
151 Upper Bayble .... D 6
42 Upper Beeding .... G 1
90 Upper Benefield .... F 1
88 Upper Bentley .... E 3
146 Upper Boddam .... E 4
89 Upper Boddington .... G 8
58 Upper Borth .... D 2
41 Upper Bourne .... B 9
146 Upper Boyndie .... A 6
88 Upper Brailes .... H 6
150 Upper Breakish .... F 6
59 Upper Breinton .... H 10
96 Upper Broughton .... H 4
84 Upper Bucklebury .... G 6
40 Upper Burgate .... D 3
147 Upper Burnhaugh .... H 6
91 Upper Caldecote .... L 3
40 Upper Canterton .... E 4
89 Upper Catesby .... F 8
58 Upper Chapel .... H 6
38 Upper Cheddon .... C 6
40 Upper Chicksgrove .... C 1
56 Upper Church Village .... F 4
40 Upper Chute .... A 4
40 Upper Clatford .... B 5
131 Upper Clifton .... F 10
60 Upper Clynnog .... F 4
151 Upper Coll .... C 5
130 Upper Craigenbay .... D 6
111 Upper Cumberworth .... F 10

56 Upper Cwmbran .... E 6
146 Upper Dallachy .... A 1
131 Upper Dalveen .... A 9
91 Upper Dean .... H 1
111 Upper Denby .... F 11
132 Upper Denton .... G 4
144 Upper Derraid .... F 6
142 Upper Diabaig .... D 2
42 Upper Dicker .... G 4
149 Upper Dournreay .... A 9
138 Upper Druimfin .... B 2
95 Upper Elkstone .... D 9
95 Upper End .... C 9
144 Upper Ethie .... C 3
57 Upper Framilode .... C 10
88 Upper Gornal .... C 3
91 Upper Gravenhurst .... L 2
84 Upper Green .... H 5
57 Upper Grove Com .... B 9
41 Upper Hale .... A 10
150 Upper Halistra .... B 2
85 Upper Halliford .... G 11
42 Upper Halling .... B 6
89 Upper Hambleton .... A 12
43 Upper Hardress
Court .... C 10
42 Upper Hartfield .... E 3
112 Upper Haugh .... G 2
59 Upper Heath .... D 11
92 Upper Hellesdon .... D 5
112 Upper Helmsley .... A 5
59 Upper Hergest .... G 8
89 Upper Heyford,
Northants .... F 10
84 Upper Heyford, Oxon .... B 6
59 Upper Hill .... G 10
132 Upper Hindhope .... B 6
111 Upper Hopton .... E 10
42 Upper Horsebridge .... G 5
95 Upper Hulme .... D 8
84 Upper Inglesham .... D 3
145 Upper Inverbrough .... G 4
141 Upper Kenley .... F 10
55 Upper Killay .... H 9
146 Upper Kinkell .... E 5
146 Upper Knaven .... C 6
144 Upper Knockando .... E 7
84 Upper Lambourn .... F 4
57 Upper Langford .... H 8
95 Upper Leigh .... F 8
147 Upper Lochton .... H 4
88 Upper Longdon .... A 4
149 Upper Lybster .... D 11
57 Upper Lydbrook .... C 9
59 Upper Lye .... F 9
150 Upper Milovaig .... C 1
84 Upper Minety .... E 1
111 Upper Moor Side .... D 11
57 Upper Morton .... E 9
146 Upper Mulben .... B 1
132 Upper Mumble .... E 2
137 Upper Nisbet .... G 9
85 Upper North Dean .... D 9
140 Upper Obney .... C 5
150 Upper Ollach .... E 4
88 Upper Penn .... C 3
112 Upper Poppleton .... B 3
145 Upper Port .... G 6
88 Upper Quinton .... G 5
40 Upper Ratley .... D 5
59 Upper Rochford .... F 11
130 Upper Rusko .... E 6
143 Upper Sandaig .... H 2
59 Upper Sapey .... F 12
134 Upper Scoulag .... C 6
84 Upper Seagry .... F 1
151 Upper Shader .... B 5
91 Upper Shelton .... L 1
92 Upper Sheringham .... A 4
136 Upper Side .... D 6
135 Upper Skelmorlie .... C 7
84 Upper Slaughter .... B 3
139 Upper Sonachan .... E 8
57 Upper Soudley .... C 10
57 Upper Stanton Drew .... H 9
91 Upper Stondon .... M 3
89 Upper Stowe .... F 10
40 Upper Street, Hants. .... D 3
92 Upper Street, Norf. .... D 7
88 Upper Strensham .... H 3
85 Upper Sundon .... A 11
84 Upper Swell .... B 3
92 Upper Tasburgh .... F 5
95 Upper Tean .... F 8
140 Upper Tillyrie .... F 6
150 Upper Tote .... B 4
57 Upper Town, Avon .... H 8
59 Upper Town,
Heref. & Worc. .... G 11
89 Upper Tysoe .... H 7

84 Upper Upham .... F 3
42 Upper Upnor .... A 6
89 Upper Wardington .... G 8
89 Upper Weald .... H 11
89 Upper Weedon .... F 9
41 Upper Wield .... B 7
85 Upper Winchendon .... C 8
40 Upper Woodford .... B 3
146 Upper Woodhead .... F 4
41 Upper Wootton .... A 7
88 Upper Wyche .... H 1
132 Upperby .... H 2
111 Uppermill .... G 8
146 Uppertack of
Gressiehill .... B 6
111 Upperthong .... F 10
147 Upperton, Grampian .... K 5
41 Upperton, W. Sussex .... D 11
152 Uppertown .... F 2
59 Uppington .... A 11
116 Upsall .... F 5
86 Upshire .... D 4
43 Upstreet .... B 11
85 Upton, Berks .... F 10
90 Upton, Cambs. .... E 2
91 Upton, Cambs. .... G 3
94 Upton, Cheshire .... C 3
36 Upton, Cornwall .... E 1
38 Upton, Devon .... F 4
40 Upton, Dorset .... G 1
39 Upton, Dorset .... H 11
40 Upton, Hants. .... D 5
96 Upton, Lincs. .... B 6
94 Upton, Merseyside .... A 1
92 Upton, Norfolk .... D 7
89 Upton, Northants .... F 10
96 Upton, Notts. .... C 5
96 Upton, Notts. .... E 4
40 Upton, Notts. .... A 5
84 Upton, Oxon .... E 6
38 Upton, Somerset .... C 3
39 Upton, Somerset .... D 8
88 Upton, War. .... F 5
112 Upton, W. Yorks. .... F 3
57 Upton Bishop .... B 9
57 Upton Cheyney .... G 10
59 Upton Cressett .... C 12
41 Upton Grey .... A 8
36 Upton Hellions .... F 7
40 Upton Lovel .... B 1
59 Upton Magna .... A 11
39 Upton Noble .... B 10
38 Upton Pyne .... F 3
57 Upton St. Leonards .... C 11
39 Upton Scudamore .... A 12
88 Upton Snodsbury .... G 3
88 Upton upon Severn .... H 2
88 Upton Warren .... E 3
41 Upwaltham .... E 10
91 Upware .... H 6
90 Upwell .... E 6
39 Upwey H10
91 Upwood .... G 4
152 Urafirth .... C 6
144 Urchal .... E 3
84 Urchfont .... H 2
152 Ure .... C 6
151 Urgha Beag .... G 3
116 Urlay Nook .... D 4
110 Urmston .... H 6
144 Urquhart, Grampian .... C 8
144 Urquhart, Highland .... D 1
116 Urra .... E 6
144 Urray .... D 1
116 Ushaw Moor .... A 3
57 Usk .... D 7
113 Usselby .... H 8
144 Ussie .... D 1
152 Ustaness .... D 7
133 Usworth .... G 11
111 Utley .... C 9
36 Uton .... F 7
113 Utterby .... H 10
95 Uttoxeter .... G 9
60 Uwchmynydd .... H 1
86 Uxbridge .... F 1
152 Uyeasound .... B 8
54 Uzmaston .... F 3
54 Vachelich .... D 1
60 Valley .... B 2
35 Valley Truckle .... A 8
150 Valtos, Skye .... B 4
151 Valtos, W. Isles .... C 2
58 Van .... D 5
87 Vange .... E 7
56 Varteg Hill .... D 6
150 Vatten .... D 2
56 Vaynor .... C 4
55 Velindre, Dyfed .... C 7
54 Velindre, Dyfed .... C 4

56 Velindre, Powys .... A 5
38 Vellow .... B 4
152 Vementry .... D 6
152 Veness .... B 3
38 Venn Ottery .... G 4
59 Vennington .... A 9
36 Venny Tedburn .... F 7
41 Ventnor .... H 7
84 Vernham Dean .... H 4
84 Vernham Street .... H 4
54 Verwig .... B 5
40 Verwood .... E 2
34 Veryan .... F 6
38 Vicarage .... G 5
114 Vickerstown .... H 4
35 Victoria, Corn. .... D 7
56 Victoria, Gwent .... D 5
152 Vidlin .... C 7
42 Vinehall Street .... F 6
42 Vine's Cross .... F 5
57 Viney Hill .... D 9
85 Virginia Water .... G 10
37 Virginstow .... G 3
39 Vobster .... A 10
152 Voe .... C 7
57 Vowchurch .... A 7
152 Voy .... C 1
116 Wackerfield .... C 2
92 Wacton .... F 5
88 Wadborough .... G 3
85 Waddesdon .... B 8
113 Waddingham .... G 7
110 Waddington Lancs. .... C 6
97 Waddington, Lincs. .... D 7
35 Wadebridge .... B 7
38 Wadeford .... E 6
91 Wadenhoe .... G 1
86 Wadesmill .... B 4
42 Wadhurst .... E 5
95 Wadshelf .... C 11
95 Wadsley .... A 11
96 Wadsley Bridge .... A 1
57 Wadswick .... G 11
112 Wadworth .... G 3
61 Waen .... D 10
61 Waen Fach .... H 11
97 Wainfleet All Saints .... D 12
97 Wainfleet Bank .... D 11
133 Wainfordrigg .... C 7
96 Waingroves .... E 1
34 Wainhouse Corner .... B 2
42 Wainscott .... A 6
111 Wainstalls .... D 9
115 Waitby .... D 10
111 Wakefield .... E 12
90 Wakerley .... F 1
87 Wakes Colne .... A 9
93 Walberswick .... H 8
41 Walberton .... E 11
133 Walbottle .... F 10
132 Walby .... G 3
90 Walcot, Lincs. .... B 2
97 Walcot, Lincs. .... E 8
59 Walcot, Salop .... A 11
59 Walcot, Salop .... D 9
88 Walcot, War. .... F 5
84 Walcot, Wilts. .... F 3
89 Walcote .... D 9
92 Walcott .... B 7
115 Walden Head .... G 12
112 Walden Stubbs .... E 3
42 Walderslade .... B 6
41 Walderton .... E 9
39 Walditch .... G 8
95 Waldley .... F 9
133 Waldridge .... H 10
93 Waldringfield .... L 6
42 Waldron .... F 4
96 Wales .... B 2
97 Walesby, Lincs. .... A 8
96 Walesby, Notts. .... C 4
57 Walford,
Heref. & Worc. .... B 9
59 Walford,
Heref. & Worc. .... E 9
94 Walford, Salop .... H 3
94 Walford Heath .... H 3
94 Walgherton .... E 5
89 Walgrave .... E 11
40 Walhampton .... F 5
111 Walk Mill .... D 7
110 Walkden .... G 6
133 Walker .... G 11
110 Walker Fold .... C 5
136 Walkerburn .... F 6
96 Walkeringham .... A 5
96 Walkerith .... A 5
86 Walkern .... A 3
59 Walker's Green .... H 10
141 Walkerton .... G 7

40 Walkford G 4
37 Walkhampton J 4
113 Walkington C 8
96 Walkley A 1
133 Wall, Northumb. F 7
88 Wall, Staffs. B 4
132 Wall Bowers G 4
59 Wall under Heywood C 10
131 Wallaceton C 9
130 Wallacetown A 4
94 Wallasey A 2
114 Wallend, Cumbria G 5
87 Wallend, Kent F 8
85 Wallingford E 7
41 Wallington, Hants. E 7
91 Wallington, Herts M 4
86 Wallington, London H 3
41 Walliswood B 12
152 Walls D 6
133 Wallsend F 11
114 Wallthwaite C 6
136 Wallyford B 6
43 Walmer C 12
110 Walmer Bridge E 3
111 Walmersley F 7
88 Walmley C 5
93 Walpole H 7
90 Walpole Crosskeys D 6
90 Walpole Highway D 6
90 Walpole Island D 6
90 Walpole St. Andrew D 6
90 Walpole St. Peter D 6
88 Walsall B 4
88 Wallsall Wood B 4
111 Walsden E 8
89 Walsgrave on Sowe D 7
93 Walsham le Willows H 3
110 Walshaw F 6
111 Walshford B 12
90 Walsoken D 6
136 Walston E 3
86 Walsworth A 2
85 Walter's Ash D 9
56 Walterston G 4
57 Walterstone B 7
43 Waltham, Kent C 9
113 Waltham, Humber. G 10
86 Waltham Abbey D 4
41 Waltham Chase E 7
86 Waltham Cross D 4
86 Waltham Forest E 4
96 Waltham on the Wolds H 2
85 Waltham St. Lawrence F 9
86 Walthamstow E 3
89 Walton, Bucks. H 12
90 Walton, Cambs E 3
132 Walton, Cumb. G 3
96 Walton, Derby C 1
89 Walton, Leics C 9
59 Walton, Powys F 8
94 Walton, Salop H 4
39 Walton, Som. C 8
93 Walton, Suffolk L 6
88 Walton, War. G 6
112 Walton, W. Yorks. B 2
111 Walton, W. Yorks. E 12
57 Walton Cardiff A 12
39 Walton Elm D 11
54 Walton East E 4
57 Walton-in-Gordano G 7
110 Walton-Le-Dale D 4
85 Walton-on-Thames G 12
110 Walton on the Hill, Merseyside H 3
95 Walton-on-the-Hill, Staffordshire H 8
42 Walton on the Hill, Surrey C 1
87 Walton on the Naze B 12
96 Walton on the Wolds H 3
57 Walton Park G 7
95 Walton upon Trent H 10
54 Walton West F 2
61 Walwen C 11
133 Walwick F 7
133 Walwick Grange F 7
116 Walworth C 3
54 Walwyn's Castle F 2
38 Wambrook E 6
131 Wamphraygate B 12
132 Wampool H 1
41 Wanborough, Surrey A 10
84 Wanborough, Wilts F 3
136 Wandel G 2
133 Wandon C 11
86 Wandsworth F 3
133 Wandylaw A 9
93 Wangford G 8
89 Wanlip A 9
136 Wanlockhead H 2
42 Wannock H 4
90 Wansford, Cambs. F 2
113 Wansford, Humber. B 8
86 Wanstead E 4
39 Wanstrow B 10
57 Wanswell D 10
84 Wantage E 5
57 Wapley F 10
89 Wappenbury E 7
89 Wappenham H 9
112 Warcop D 9
42 Warbleton F 5
41 Warblington E 8
85 Warborough E 7
91 Warboys G 4
110 Warbreck C 2
34 Warbstow B 2
94 Warburton A 5
93 Ward Green J 4
43 Warden A 9
89 Wardington G 8
136 Wardlaw, Borders H 5
135 Wardlaw, Strathclyde E 8
94 Wardle, Ches. E 5
111 Wardle, Lancs. E 8
89 Wardley B 11
95 Wardlow C 10
133 Wardon F 7
91 Wardy Hill G 6
86 Ware, Herts. C 4
43 Ware, Kent B 11
40 Wareham G 1
43 Warehorne E 8
133 Waren Mill C 12
133 Warenford C 12
133 Warenton C 12
86 Wareside B 4
91 Waresley, Cambs. K 3
88 Waresley, Heref. & Worc. E 2
85 Warfield G 9
37 Warfleet L 7
90 Wargate C 3
85 Wargrave F 9
92 Warham All Saints A 3
92 Warham St. Mary A 2
133 Wark, Northumb E 7
137 Wark, Northumb. E 11
36 Warkleigh D 5
89 Warkton D 12
89 Warkwork H 8
133 Warkworth B 10
116 Warlaby F 4
111 Warland E 8
35 Warleggan C 8
88 Warley C 3
42 Warlingham B 2
111 Warmfield E 12
94 Warmingham D 5
41 Warminghurst D 12
90 Warmington, Cambs. F 2
89 Warmington, War. G 7
39 Warminster B 11
43 Warmlake C 7
57 Warmley G 10
57 Warmley Tower G 10
112 Warmsworth G 3
39 Warmwell H 11
88 Warndon F 2
41 Warnford D 8
42 Warnham E 1
41 Warningcamp E 11
42 Warninglid E 1
95 Warren, Ches. C 7
54 Warren, Dyfed G 3
37 Warren House Inn H 5
85 Warren Row F 9
43 Warren Street C 8
89 Warrington, Bucks. G 12
94 Warrington, Ches. A 5
40 Warsash E 6
95 Warslow D 9
96 Warsop C 3
96 Warsop Vale C 3
112 Warter B 6
116 Warthermarske G 2
112 Warthill B 4
42 Wartling G 5
96 Wartnaby H 4
110 Warton, Lancs. D 3
115 Warton, Lancs. H 7
133 Warton, Northumb. C 8
88 Warton, War. B 6
132 Warwick, Cumb. G 3
88 Warwick, War. F 6
132 Warwick Bridge G 3
88 Warwickshire, Co. F 6
132 Warwicksland E 3
152 Wasbister B 2
114 Wasdale Head D 4
84 Wash Common H 5
35 Washaway C 7
37 Washbourne K 7
95 Washerwall E 8
38 Washfield E 3
116 Washfold E 1
38 Washford B 4
36 Washford Pyne E 7
97 Washingborough C 7
133 Washington, Tyne & Wear G 11
41 Washington, W. Sussex E 12
85 Wasing H 7
116 Waskerley A 1
88 Wasperton F 6
116 Wass G 6
38 Watchet B 4
84 Watchfield, Oxon E 3
39 Watchfield, Som. B 7
115 Watchgate E 8
131 Watchhill G 12
114 Watendlath D 5
37 Water, Devon H 6
111 Water, Lancs. E 7
86 Water End, Herts. C 2
112 Water End, Humber. C 6
90 Water Newton F 2
88 Water Orton C 5
85 Water Stratford A 7
56 Water Street F 1
114 Water Yeat F 5
91 Waterbeach J 6
132 Waterbeck E 1
92 Waterden B 2
85 Waterend C 11
95 Waterfall E 9
111 Waterfoot, Lancs. E 7
135 Waterfoot, Strathclyde D 10
40 Waterford, Hants. G 5
86 Waterford, Herts. B 3
114 Waterhead, Cumb. E 6
131 Waterhead, Dumf. & Gall. B 12
131 Waterhead, Dumf. & Gall. C 8
135 Waterford, Strathclyde H 10
147 Waterhead, Tayside K 2
136 Waterheads D 5
116 Waterhouses, Dur. A 5
95 Waterhouses, Staffs. E 9
97 Watering Dyke Houses B 7
42 Wateringbury C 6
152 Wateringhouse E 2
57 Waterlane D 12
96 Waterloo, Derby D 1
40 Waterloo, Dorset G 2
54 Waterloo, Dyfed G 3
110 Waterloo, Merseyside G 2
92 Waterloo, Norf. D 5
150 Waterloo, Skye F 6
136 Waterloo, Strathclyde D 1
140 Waterloo, Tayside C 5
38 Waterloo Cross E 4
41 Waterlooville E 8
136 Watermeetings H 2
85 Waterperry C 7
38 Waterrow D 4
94 Waters Upton H 5
41 Watersfield E 11
132 Waterside, Cumb. H 1
146 Waterside Grampian E 7
130 Waterside, Strathclyde A 5
135 Waterside Strathclyde E 9
135 Waterside, Strathclyde B 11
85 Waterstock D 7
54 Waterston F 3
86 Watford, Herts. D 1
89 Watford, Northants. E 9
116 Wath, N. Yorks. G 3
116 Wath, N. Yorks. H 2
114 Wath Brow D 3
112 Wath upon Dearne G 2
57 Watley's End F 9
90 Watlington, Norf. D 7
85 Watlington, Oxon E 8
96 Watnall Chaworth F 2
149 Watten B 11
93 Wattisfield H 3
93 Wattisham K 3
59 Wattlesborough Heath A 9
113 Watton, Humberside B 8
92 Watton, Norf. E 2
86 Watton-at-Stone B 3
135 Wattston B 12
56 Wattstown E 3
143 Wauchan L 3
58 Waun Fawr D 2
55 Waunarlwydd G 9
60 Waunfawr D 5
56 Waunlwyd D 5
89 Wavendon H 12
132 Waverbridge H 1
94 Waverton, Ches. D 3
132 Waverton, Cumb. H 1
113 Wawne C 8
92 Waxham C 7
113 Waxholme D 11
38 Way Village E 3
42 Wayfield B 6
39 Wayford F 7
39 Waytown F 8
38 Weacombe B 5
84 Weald D 4
86 Wealdstone E 2
111 Weardley C 11
39 Weare A 7
36 Weare Giffard D 3
115 Wearhead A 11
115 Weasdale E 9
92 Weasenham All Saints C 1
92 Weasenham St. Peter C 1
94 Weaverham C 5
117 Weaverthorpe H 9
88 Webheath E 4
57 Webton A 7
146 Wedderlairs D 6
137 Wedderlie D 9
89 Weddington C 7
84 Wedhampton H 2
39 Wedmore A 8
88 Wednesbury C 3
88 Wednesfield B 3
85 Weedon B 9
89 Weedon Bec F 9
89 Weedon Lois G 9
88 Weeford B 5
36 Week, Devon C 4
36 Week, Devon D 6
36 Week St. Mary F 1
40 Weeke C 6
89 Weekely D 12
113 Weel C 8
87 Weeley B 11
87 Weeley Heath B 11
140 Weem B 3
59 Weeping Cross, Shropshire A 10
95 Weeping Cross, Staffordshire H 8
93 Weeting G 1
110 Weeton, Lancs. D 3
111 Weeton, N. Yorks. B 11
137 Weetwoodhill F 12
111 Weir E 7
57 Weirend B 9
96 Welbeck Abbey C 3
92 Welborne E 4
97 Welbourn E 7
117 Welburn, N. Yorks. G 7
117 Welburn, N. Yorks H 7
116 Welbury E 4
97 Welby F 7
91 Welches Dam G 6
36 Welcombe D 1
89 Weldon C 12
84 Welford, Berks. G 5
89 Welford, Northants. D 9
88 Welford-on-Avon G 5
89 Welham C 11
86 Welham Green C 2
41 Well, Hants. A 9
97 Well, Lincs. C 11
116 Well, N. Yorks. G 3
39 Well Bottom E 12
85 Well End E 9
42 Well Hill B 4
38 Well Town E 3
88 Welland H 2
141 Wellbank C 9
131 Welldale E 12
88 Wellesbourne G 6
116 Wellfields A 4
147 Wellford L 2
86 Welling F 5
89 Wellingborough E 12
92 Wellingham C 2
97 Wellingore E 7
114 Wellington, Cumb. E 3
59 Wellington, Heref. & Worc. H 10
59 Wellington, Salop A 12
38 Wellington, Som. D 5
59 Wellington Heath H 12
59 Wellington Marsh H 10
57 Wellow, Avon H 10
40 Wellow, I.o.W. G 5
96 Wellow, Notts. D 4
39 Wells B 9
92 Wells-next-the-Sea A 2
146 Wells of Ytham D 4
89 Wellsborough B 7
37 Wellswood J 8
140 Wellwood H 6
90 Welney F 6
36 Welsford D 1
57 Welsh Bicknor C 9
94 Welsh Frankton G 2
54 Welsh Hook D 3
57 Welsh Newton B 8
56 Welsh St. Donats G 4
94 Welshampton G 3
59 Welshpool B 8
39 Welton, Avon A 10
114 Welton, VB. A 6
113 Welton, Humberside D 7
97 Welton, Lincs. B 7
89 Welton, Northants E 9
97 Welton le Marsh C 11
97 Welton le Wold B 10
113 Welwick E 11
86 Welwyn B 2
86 Welwyn Garden City C 2
94 Wem G 4
38 Wembdon C 6
86 Wembley E 2
37 Wembury L 4
36 Wembworthy E 5
135 Wemyss Bay B 7
91 Wendens Ambo L 6
84 Wendlebury B 6
92 Wendling D 2
85 Wendover C 9
34 Wendron G 4
93 Wendy K 4
93 Wenhaston H 7
91 Wennington, Cambs. G 3
115 Wennington, Lancs. H 8
86 Wennington, London F 5
95 Wensley, Derby. D 11
116 Wensley, N. Yorks. F 1
112 Wentbridge E 3
59 Wentor C 9
91 Wentworth, Cambs. G 6
111 Wentworth, S. Yorks G 12
56 Wenvoe G 4
59 Weobley G 9
59 Weobley Marsh G 9
90 Wereham E 8
88 Wergs B 2
56 Wern C 4
55 Wernffrwd H 8
57 Wernyrheolydd C 7
90 Werrington, Cambs. E 3
35 Werrington, Corn. A 10
95 Werrington, Suffolk E 8
94 Wervin C 3
110 Wesham D 3
96 Wessington D 1
145 West Aberchalder G 1
92 West Acre D 1
84 West Adderbury A 5
38 West Adsborough C 6
137 West Allerdean E 12
133 West Allotment F 11
37 West Alvington L 6
40 West Amesbury B 3
36 West Anstey C 7
36 West Ash D 2
97 West Ashby C 9
41 West Ashling E 9
39 West Ashton A 12
116 West Auckland C 2
117 West Ayton G 10
147 West Balhagarty K 5
38 West Bagborough C 5
97 West Barkwith B 8
117 West Barnby D 8
137 West Barns B 9
130 West Barr G 4
92 West Barsham B 2
39 West Bay G 8
92 West Beckham B 4
85 West Bedfont G 11
133 West Benridge D 10
87 West Bergholt A 9
39 West Bexington H 9
90 West Bilney D 8
137 West Blackadder D 11
42 West Blatchington G 2
136 West Bold F 6
133 West Boldon G 11
131 West Bowhill D 12
111 West Bowling D 10
92 West Bradenham E 2
110 West Bradford C 6
39 West Bradley C 9
111 West Bretton F
96 West Bridgford
88 West Bromwich
135 West Browncastle E
36 West Buckland, Devon
38 West Buckland, Som.
152 West Burrafirth
41 West Burton, W. Sussex E
115 West Burton, N. Yorks F
116 West Butsfield
112 West Butterwick
85 West Byfleet H
137 West Byres
92 West Caister
136 West Calder
39 West Camel
146 West Cannahars
112 West Carr
135 West Cauldcoats E
39 West Chaldon H
84 West Challow
39 West Chelborough
133 West Chevington C
41 West Chiltington D
41 West Chiltington Common D
39 West Chinnock
40 West Chisenbury
41 West Clandon A
43 West Cliffe D
149 West Clyne
149 West Clyth D
39 West Coker
39 West Compton, Dorset
39 West Compton, Som.
112 West Cowick
39 West Cranmore B
93 West Creeting Grn.
145 West Croftmore
55 West Cross
147 West Cullerley
132 West Curthwaite
134 West Darlochan
40 West Dean, Hants.
41 West Dean, Sus. E
90 West Deeping.
94 West Derby
90 West Dereham
133 West Ditchburn
36 West Down
86 West Drayton, London
96 West Drayton, Notts.
133 West Edington
113 West Ella
57 West End, Avon
85 West End, Berks.
60 West End, Gwynedd
40 West End, Hants.
86 West End, Herts
113 West End, Humber.
113 West End, Lincs. C
92 West End, Norf.
136 West End, Strathclyde
85 West End, Surrey H
40 West End, Wilts.
133 West Fallodon A
42 West Farleigh
94 West Felton
42 West Firle
84 West Ginge
55 West Glamorgan, Co. C
84 West Grafton
85 West Green
40 West Grimstead
42 West Grinstead
112 West Haddlesey
89 West Haddon
84 West Hagbourne
88 West Hagley
132 West Hall
96 West Hallam
113 West Halton
86 West Ham
84 West Hanney
87 West Hanningfield
112 West Hardwick
40 West Harnham
39 West Harptree
133 West Harrington H
116 West Hartlepool
38 West Hatch
57 West Hay
90 West Head
149 West Helmsdale
84 West Hendred
117 West Heslerton
57 West Hill, Avon
38 West Hill, Devon.

Northern Ireland map index